COMMERCE AND CULTURE

THE MARITIME COMMUNITIES

OF COLONIAL MASSACHUSETTS,

1690–1750

COMMERCE
AND
CULTURE

*The Maritime
Communities of
Colonial
Massachusetts
1690–1750*

Christine Leigh Heyrman

W · W · NORTON & COMPANY

NEW YORK · LONDON

The text of this book is composed in 10/11 pt Sabon, with display
type set in Garamond. Composition and manufacturing
by The Maple-Vail Book Manufacturing Group.
Book design by Margaret M. Wagner.

First Edition

Library of Congress Cataloging in Publication Data

Heyrman, Christine.
Commerce and culture.

Includes index.
1. Gloucester (Mass.)—Civilization. 2. Gloucester
(Mass.)—Commerce. 3. Marblehead (Mass.)—Civilization.
4. Marblehead (Mass.)—Commerce. 5. Massachusetts—
Social life and customs—Colonial period ca., 1600–1775—
Case studies. 6. Social classes—Massachusetts—History
—18th century. 7. Massachusetts—Church history—Case
studies. I. Title.
F74.G5H49   1984   974.4'5   83–8175

ISBN 0-393-01781-8

W. W. Norton & Company, Inc.
500 Fifth Avenue,
New York, N.Y. 10110
W. W. Norton & Company Ltd.
37 Great Russell Street,
London WC1B 3NU

1 2 3 4 5 6 7 8 9 0

For
CHARLES HEYRMAN,
and his son,
ROBERT

And for
MARGARET DILLON,
and her daughter,
VERONA MONFILS

Contents

Acknowledgments

"ONE DAY you will write about your own country," Sarah Orne Jewett told the young novelist Willa Cather. "In the meantime, get all you can," she continued, "for one must know the world so well before one can know the parish." Since this advice applies not only to the writers of local color fiction but also to historians who study individual communities, I would like to thank the people who have taught me about the world of history and ideas. I owe the greatest debt to Edmund Morgan, who challenged me to think and write and never betrayed the least doubt that I could do both. I became an historian because of his example and encouragement. I am also particularly grateful to the late Ernest Sandeen, who introduced me to American religious history and enabled me to continue my education in this field with other gifted scholars and teachers, Sydney Ahlstrom, Kai Erikson, Daniel Howe, Bruce Kuklick, and R. Stephen Warner.

I wish to express appreciation as well to the supportive and stimulating members of the History Department at the University of California, Irvine, for creating an ideal atmosphere for research and teaching. Jonathan Dewald, who interested me in the concerns of social history, read early drafts of this study with discerning care. John Patrick Diggins, who kept me thinking about the questions of intellectual history, has been a patient, perceptive, and persistent critic of my writing. Several other Irvine colleagues—Jon Jacobson, Patricia O'Brien, Karl Hufbauer, Theodore Koditschek, and Spencer Olin—have also sustained me with their kindness and clarified my thinking with their common sense and uncommon insight. I have been equally fortunate in the advice and encouragement that I have received from historians at other institutions. At a critical stage in my work, Philip Greven, David Hall, Robert Middlekauff, and John Murrin read the entire manuscript and offered many useful and illuminating comments. Joyce Appleby, Jonathan Chu, Edwin Gaustad, Joseph Ellis, James Henretta, and Anne Rose gave me solid criticisms of individual chapters, while my correspondence with Stephen Innes and Daniel Vickers enlightened me on numerous matters of mutual interest.

My research of "parish" life in early New England was made easier by the expertise and enthusiasm of many people. I spent much of 1979–1980 as an NEH fellow in residence at the American Antiquarian Society, where I benefited from the skill and cooperation of an excellent professional staff, especially Nancy Burkett, John Hench, William Joyce, and Kathleen Major. I am also grateful to Deborah Goodwin and William Presson of the Cape Ann Historical Society, Irene Norton and Ellen Mark of the Essex Institute, and John Merrow and Bette Hunt of the Marblehead Historical Society. These gracious and knowledgeable people not only gave me generous guidance in tracking down sources but also took a personal interest in my work. The officials and employees at various public archives made my long stints in these places both productive and pleasant. John Burke, the Clerk of Probate Records for Essex County and his co-worker, Gino Iannalfo; James Leary, the Clerk of the Essex County Court and his assistants, Margie Spencer and Tom Babineu; and the employees of the Gloucester and Salem City Clerk's Offices and the Abbot Town Hall in Marblehead all provided me with friendly assistance and space to work. Fred Smith, Richard Kaplan, and Jane Becker, the staff of the research room in the Massachusetts Archives, were also unfailingly cordial and helpful. George and Irma Sprague and Myrtle Severance, the historians of Marblehead's Old North Church and First Unitarian, respectively, arranged for my access to their early records and honored me with their hospitality, while Robert Howie of the Diocesan Library of the Episcopal Church in Boston shared with me his knowledge of St. Michael's, Marblehead. During the final months of my research, the librarians of the University of California, Irvine, did a first-rate job of locating several sources that I had overlooked while working on the east coast. Becky Baugh ingeniously pieced together the map of Gloucester that appears in this study, while Carol Roberts carefully typed several chapters. And for many months, James Mairs and Lee Strauss of W. W. Norton & Company have supplied me with excellent editorial assistance.

I owe a special debt to a number of other people. I will always be grateful to William Hamilton, who has accomplished the improbable by being both the best of critics and the best of friends. At every stage, my work has had the benefit of his perceptive scrutiny and I have had the pleasure of his understanding and affection. I would also like to thank my other good friends: Lynn Freedman and David Frankel; Rebecca Hyman, Kathleen Kook, Jean Lave, and Hilary Siebens; Tommy Carter, Kim Elliman, Bruce Mann, and Joey Parnes. They have never even hinted that anything might be more important than the history of New England seaports, but their company has helped me to remember that there is. Finally, I wish to acknowledge the contributions of my sister, Anne Heyrman, and of the four members of my family to whom this book is dedicated. It would be difficult to describe all of the ways in which they have made my work possible. But since they have always understood, even without words, I do not have to explain.

Introduction

A TYPICAL New England Puritan never existed. But if one had, it would have been the Reverend John Wise. John Wise spent most of his life in Chebacco Parish of Ipswich, a small rural community in northern Massachusetts that he served as pastor between 1683 and 1725. There he wrote sermons, ministered to his congregation, and tended his farm. Nevertheless, Wise's world was wider than his parish, for he was an active participant in some of the great controversies of his day. Throughout northern New England, he was known and respected as a shrewd and courageous politician and as a pamphleteer with a gift for satire. In 1689, Wise went to prison for his convictions after leading his Chebacco neighbors in a protest against the government of Sir Edmund Andros, who was attempting to tax the residents of Massachusetts without their consent. Later in his career, Wise wrote two celebrated treatises in support of the Bay colony's congregational system of church government. It is for these defenses of New England's political and ecclesiastical liberties that Wise is best known, but he was also an outspoken advocate of economic expansion and trade. "I say it is the Merchandize of any Country, Wisely and Vigorously Managed," he wrote, "this is the king of business for increasing the Wealth, the civil Strength, and the Temporal Glory of a People."[1]

Although Wise was a clergyman, he was no stranger to the world of commerce. In public life, he took part in the province debate over currency policy, proposing the establishment of a private land bank to insure the colony an adequate money supply. In managing his personal finances, he supplemented the income from his farm with the returns from his investments in two trading vessels. One of his sons, Joseph, set up as a shopkeeper in Boston, and another, Ammi Ruhammah, became a major merchant in Ipswich.[2] And while the members of Wise's Chebacco congregation engaged almost exclusively in subsistence agriculture, several surrounding coastal communities, towns founded as farming or fishing villages, were growing into important commercial centers. Over the course of Wise's lifetime, neighboring Gloucester, Marblehead, and Newbury in northern Massachusetts, as well as a few other towns in Maine and New Hampshire, developed maritime industries and an independent trade to the Caribbean and Europe. This economic transformation Wise greeted with enthusiasm. In 1721, he compared Gloucester, a flourishing center of the fishery, to the ancient seaport of Tyre, "that was but a Rock . . . Yet by Merchandize became the Queen of the Seas, the Metropolis of the World":

> That certainly if a great Rock spread out in the Sea may thus be cultivated, and brought to such perfection, by making it a Place for the World to meet at, and to Buy and Sell on; and a Rock which never Rolls; if in a few Ages may be over run with such a Moss as the Prophet clothes the Rock of Tyrus with. Then what a perfection may Cape-Ann or Gloucester, a Promontory

[1] John Wise, *A Word of Comfort to a Melancholy Country* (Boston, 1721), 180. On Wise's career, see Perry Miller, *The New England Mind: From Colony to Province* (Boston, 1953), 288–322; and George Allan Cook, *John Wise, Early American Democrat* (New York, 1966).

[2] Cook, *John Wise*, 165. Wise's contributions to the debate over colonial currency policy include *A Word of Comfort to a Melancholy Country* and *A Friendly Check, From a Kind Relation* (Boston, 1721). He wrote these two pamphlets under the pseudonym, "Amicus Patriae."

thrust so far into the Sea . . . be brought to, by Commerce and
Merchandize, in a few Ages more. . . .[3]

To Wise's mind, the growing trade and prosperity of port
towns was completely compatible with social stability and
solidarity and with a Puritan moral and religious order. In
the coming of commerce, he saw no challenge to the way of
life that he had known in New England.

The book that I have written is about the evolution that
John Wise witnessed. It describes how economic expansion
affected the lives of people in two provincial Massachusetts
port towns, Gloucester and Marblehead, and how the
inhabitants of the two communities responded to commercial development. My main concern is to explore the interplay between economic change and the contouring of colonial
New England's culture, that is, the beliefs and behavior,
relationships and institutions that formed the total pattern
of social experience in early seaports. The book belongs to
the large body of New England community studies that have
appeared since the 1960s, and it draws on the findings and
analytical techniques of this literature. But it departs from
most other town studies by emphasizing continuity rather
than change as the central characteristic of colonial New
England's history.

Many historians who have studied the trading towns of
John Wise's time do not share his assessment of commercial
development. The most influential interpretation of the evolution of colonial New England towns has been one that
posits a gradual "decline" or "breakdown" of community
over time. According to this model, demographic and economic changes wrought a major transformation in society
and culture over the later seventeenth and eighteenth centuries: the old Puritan communal order collapsed, and there
emerged in its place a more open society based on individualism. And in towns where significant commercial expansion
occurred, the breakdown of traditional values and patterns

---

[3] Wise, *A Word of Comfort to a Melancholy Country*, 180–81.

of communal life is said to have been most rapid and pro-nounced.[4]

With the coming of commerce, a number of important changes did take place in the material life of coastal and river port towns. The subsistence agricultural economy of the early seventeenth century gave way to one based on trade and the maritime industries. The conversion to a commercial economy also created marked inequalities; a sharper grada-tion between rich and poor replaced the rough equality of wealth that had existed in the first settlements. The occupa-tional structure of developing communities became more differentiated as well, as farmers turned to trade, the mari-time crafts, and fishing. At the same time, economic oppor-tunity fostered a more fluid social order: the fortunes of some families rose as a result of their entrepreneurial success, while the prestige and influence of others who failed to adapt to the new order declined. Mobility and diversity characterized port society in another sense, too. Unlike the insular, static communities established by the first New England settlers, the population of trading towns was shifting constantly. And while the earliest settlements had been able to restrict their membership to godly, industrious, like-minded English Puri-tans, employment and business opportunities drew into commercial centers a heterogeneous mixture of religious and ethnic groups.

According to the "communal breakdown" model, the consequence of these demographic and economic changes was the emergence of a materialistic, contentious, and secu-

---

[4]Town studies that relate the breakdown of community to the coming of trade include: Paul Boyer and Stephen Nissenbaum, *Salem Possessed: The Social Origins of Witchcraft* (Cambridge, Mass., 1974); Richard Bushman, *From Puritan to Yankee: Character and the Social Order in Connecticut* (Cambridge, Mass., 1968); Richard Gildrie, *Salem, Massachusetts, 1626–1683: A Covenant Community,* (Charlottesville, Va., 1975); Gary Nash, *The Urban Crucible: Social Change, Political Consciousness and the Origins of the American Revolution* (Cambridge, Mass., 1979); Darrett Rutman, *Winthrop's Boston: Portrait of a Puritan Town 1630 to 1649* (Chapel Hill, 1969); Patricia Tracy, *Jonathan Edwards, Pastor: Religion and Society in Eighteenth Century Northampton* (New York, 1980). Bernard Bailyn offers a similar explanation of the transformation of New England culture in *The New England Merchants in the Seventeenth Century* (Cambridge, Mass., 1955).

lar society in seaports. In their drive for profits and social advancement, townspeople forgot their responsibility to the public good, defied customary restraints, and violated the old religious ideals of brotherliness and asceticism. Ambition for gain drew port dwellers into risk-filled commercial ventures, sharp business practices, and the habit of resorting to the courts to collect their debts. This ruthless pursuit of self-interest, coupled with growing economic inequality, generated resentment among the lower orders of port society and strained relations between rich and poor. The intensifying conflict between social classes, as well as contests among different interest and occupational groups over land, debt, and currency policy, eroded civic consensus and weakened the authority of local leaders and established institutions. And while political factionalism undermined communal solidarity, mobility subverted the deferential social order: status became the reward of achievement in the marketplace rather than the badge of service to the community.

The result of commercial expansion, in this view, was not only social conflict but also cultural change. The inhabitants of trading towns are said to have accepted individualism and competition, dissent and diversity as the basis of the social order. By connecting coastal and river port towns to the wider market economy, the expansion of trade broke down their insularity and encouraged a more liberal and cosmopolitan outlook, especially among merchants. As traders developed ties to their counterparts in other towns, these bonds of interest lessened their attachment to their own communities. Involvement in business also blunted the force of religious fervor: worldliness rather than piety came to typify the outlook of the commercial classes. The spread of more secular attitudes, combined with the growth in seaports of dissenting sects such as the Quakers and the Anglicans, relaxed religious intolerance. In other words, the assumption of the "communal breakdown" model is that commercial capitalism and traditional Puritan culture were incompatible: the trading economy simply swept away the order established by an earlier generation.

When I started the book, it was with the expectation of tracing the process of communal "decline" in Gloucester and Marblehead as they became centers of the fishing industry

and trade. But what I discovered by the time I had finished
my research was the reason for John Wise's equanimity about
the growth of commerce. What I found—and the main argument of the chapters that follow—is that the conversion to
a trading economy did not precipitate a sweeping, uniform
set of changes in provincial seaports. Instead of confirming
the conventional view that the Puritan communal order collapsed under the pressure of economic expansion, the evolution of Gloucester and Marblehead illustrates the strength
and resilience of traditional patterns of association and
inherited beliefs and values. In Gloucester, the communitarian way of life established in the latter part of the seventeenth century as the town evolved from a fishing village into
a stable agricultural society persisted throughout its period
of commercial development after 1690. In Marblehead, which
for a century after its founding remained a disorderly fishing
camp, communal institutions, relationships, and attitudes
actually appeared for the first time as the town developed an
independent, direct trade during the 1730s.

Although both Gloucester and Marblehead grew larger,
their inhabitants more mobile and diverse, and their social
structures more stratified, these changes in material life did
not bring about corresponding shifts in the character of local
society and culture. By the middle of the eighteenth century,
the ethos prevailing in both towns, by that time important
seaports, was remarkably similar to that in the surrounding
agrarian villages of Essex County like Chebacco Parish. Most
people in Gloucester and Marblehead now relied for their
livelihoods on trade and the maritime industries, but the drive
for profit did not dominate social relationships or redefine
attitudes governing economic behavior. Forbearance toward
local debtors, a cautious approach to investment, limited
aspirations for expansion and innovation, and a concern for
communal welfare characterized the outlook of all participants in local commerce, even major merchants and
entrepreneurs. Tensions existed between different classes,
neighborhoods, and occupational groups, but these strains
did not threaten the stability of the social order or augur the
onset of a fundamental change in politics. Deference to an
acknowledged elite and an acceptance of the authority of
established local institutions were the basis of civic life and

social organization. Commerce created prosperity and afforded some families an improved standard of living, but the new affluence did not diminish the piety of port dwellers. Increasing church membership and enthusiastic participation in religious revivals attest to the centrality of spiritual concerns and ecclesiastical institutions among all social classes. Religious dissenters took up residence in both towns, but sectarian diversity did not dilute the prejudices of the Puritan majority. Orthodox seaport residents remained a remarkably intolerant group, unwilling to accord full acceptance to Quakers or Anglicans.

The "communal breakdown" model of early New England's evolution attributes to commercial development an inexorable dynamic: economic expansion prods colonial society along an undeviating course toward its inevitable rendezvous with individualism. But this one-sided view of the relationship between commerce and culture overlooks the ways in which older forms of belief and association shaped the process of economic change itself and modified the effects of expansion. In both Gloucester and Marblehead, the survival or resurgence of a communitarian culture limited the impact of commercial development. The profit motive did not dissolve the bonds of communal cohesion or the social strength of Puritanism; instead, personal ties, customary practices, and religious values shaped the conduct of commercial activity. Internal divisions among seaport inhabitants were offset by a sense of local loyalty; identification with the town community not only survived but was strengthened by awareness of and contact with the wider world. Reinforcing this localism for most residents of Gloucester and Marblehead was an increasingly intense commitment to Congregationalist orthodoxy that sustained communal particularism and solidarity. Rather than being at odds with the ideals of Puritanism or the ends of communitarianism, commercial capitalism coexisted with and was molded by the cultural patterns of the past.[5]

---

[5] There are now several studies of agrarian villages and smaller, rural towns in New England that emphasize the continuities between seventeenth- and eighteenth-century culture, and I have been influenced by the perspective that these works provide. See Robert A. Gross, *The Minutemen and Their World* (New York, 1976); James Henretta, "Farms and Families: Mentalité

Just as there is no such person as a typical New England Puritan, there is no such place as a representative New England town. If there were, it could not have eluded detection by the small army of historians who have written community studies over the last twenty years. So I do not want to make too many claims for the typicality of Gloucester and Marblehead. Besides, part of my intention in examining two communities is to draw attention to variations in the pattern of commercial expansion and to describe the different ways in which each port responded to economic growth. On the other hand, while Gloucester and Marblehead illustrate the uniqueness of trading towns, they were also in many basic ways similar to each other and to the dozens of coastal and river ports that played an increasingly prominent role in New England's economy after 1690. Although Boston, the largest and most intensively studied of New England's seaports, has served as the basis for many generalizations about the effects of trade on colonial society, it is in some respects the least characteristic of early commercial centers. Boston dominated New England's trade during the seventeenth century, but the town suffered from demographic stagnation and commercial decay over the eighteenth century. Yet as Boston declined, all of New England's other provincial ports, Gloucester and Marblehead among them, experienced an expansion of population and trade during the later colonial period. For this reason, these two communities, if not ideally typical, are at least a starting point for rethinking the relationship between commerce and culture.

in Pre-Industrial America," *WMQ,* 3rd ser., 35 (1978), 3–32; Christopher Jedrey, *The World of John Cleaveland: Family and Community in Eighteenth Century New England* (New York, 1979); and Michael Zuckerman, *Peaceable Kingdoms: New England Towns in the Eighteenth Century* (New York, 1970). The best theoretical critique of the communal decline model is Thomas Bender, *Community and Social Change in America* (New Brunswick, New Jersey, 1978). See also, James Henretta, "The Morphology of Early New England Society in the Colonial Period," *Journal of Interdisciplinary History,* 2 (1971), 279–98. A suggestive counterpoint to the assumption that trade transformed economic attitudes is J. E. Crowley, *This Sheba, Self: The Conceptualization of Economic Life in Eighteenth-Century America* (Baltimore, 1974).

Abbreviations

EIHC	*Essex Institute Historical Collections*
ENR	Essex County Notarial Records, 1697–1768, Office of the County Clerk, Superior Courthouse, Salem, Massachusetts
EPF	Essex County Probate Files, Registry of Probate, Essex County Courthouse, Salem, Massachusetts
Essex Ct. Recs	*Records and Files of the Quarterly Courts of Essex County, Massachusetts,* ed. George Francis Dow, 8 vols., (Salem, Massachusetts, 1911–21)
FCCP	Files of the Court of Common Pleas for Essex County, Superior Courthouse, Salem, Massachusetts
FGSP	Files of the General Sessions of the Peace for Essex County, Superior Courthouse, Salem, Massachusetts
GFCR	Records of the First Church of Gloucester, Cape Ann Historical Society, Gloucester, Massachusetts
GFPR	Records of the First Parish of Gloucester, Cape Ann Historical Society, Gloucester, Massachusetts
GTR	Gloucester Town Records, Office of the Town Clerk, City Hall, Gloucester, Massachusetts
MA	*Massachusetts Archives,* The Statehouse, Boston, Massachusetts
MFCR	Marblehead First Church Records, 1688–1800, Old North Church, Marblehead, Massachusetts
MGSP	Minutebooks of the General Sessions of the Peace for Essex County, Office of the County Clerk, Superior Courthouse, Salem, Massachusetts
MSCJ	Minutebooks of the Supreme Court of Judicature, Office of the Clerk of the Supreme Judicial Court for Suffolk County, Suffolk County Courthouse, Boston, Massachusetts
MTR	Marblehead Town Records, Office of the Town Clerk, Abbot Hall, Marblehead, Massachusetts
WMQ	*The William and Mary Quarterly*

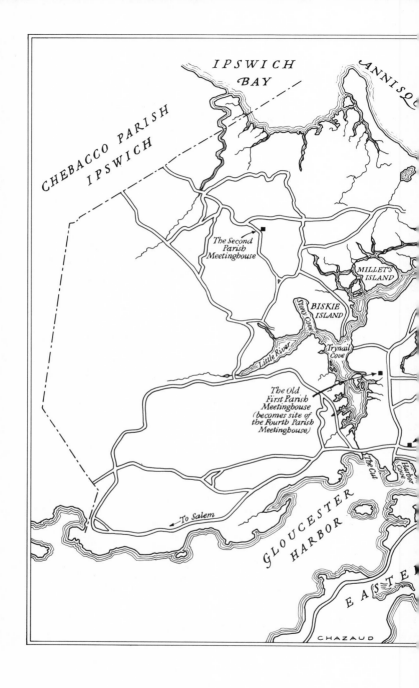

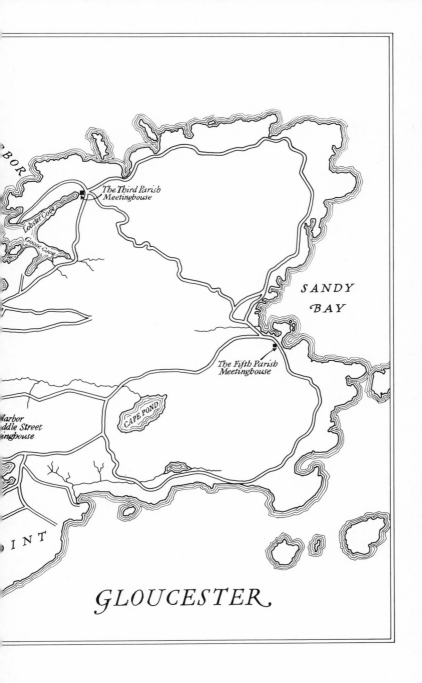

The Third Parish
Meetinghouse

Lobster Cove

Goose Cove

SANDY

BAY

The Fifth Parish
Meetinghouse

CAPE POND

Harbor
ddle Street
inghouse

INT

GLOUCESTER

PART I

View once more, from some lofty pro-
montory or Pisgah, those goodly tents
and tabernacles of Israel! Listen! Is
not God with them, and the shout of a
king amongst them? Are they not as
valleys spread forth, and as gardens
by the riverside, which the Lord hath
planted? And yet notwithstanding,
may we, must we . . . break up their
fences to give them another sort of
culture?

JOHN WISE
The Churches Quarrel Espoused
1710

GLOUCESTER

AT THE END of the seventeenth century, the town of Gloucester, Massachusetts, was a peaceable kingdom. No extremes of wealth or poverty, no strife between creditors and debtors, no resentments between old settlers and new-comers, no factional or family quarrels, no disputes between clergy and congregation marred the existence of this tiny, isolated village on the coast of Cape Ann. The celebration that took place on a spring day in 1700 when the congregation of the First Church raised their new meetinghouse captured the tone of local life. The selectmen, town fathers to whom inhabitants had entrusted their affairs year after year, supplied refreshments. The Reverend John Emerson, an aged and venerable orthodox minister in the thirty-sixth year of his untroubled pastorate at the First Church, provided some improving discourse for the occasion. The rest of the towns-people, mainly large families engaged in subsistence farm-ing, turned out for the merrymaking.

Over the first four decades of the eighteenth century, life in Gloucester gradually changed. The growth of maritime industries and a transatlantic trade transformed the town from a remote backwater into a bustling seaport, one of the centers of New England's production of and traffic in timber products and fish. Within the lifetime of a generation, most Gloucester inhabitants came to depend upon commerce with distant consumers for their livelihoods. As the economy expanded, local society grew steadily more diverse and com-plex. The growth of trade attracted to town families neither born in Gloucester nor bred to the Congregationalist faith. The flourishing commerce also created a class of people whose wealth and influence distinguished them from the rest of the community, a group that included merchants; "shoremen," the operators of large fishing businesses; and the most suc-cessful artisans in the maritime trades, blacksmiths and ship-builders.

In the wake of these shifts in Gloucester's economic and social life came a series of small disputes among townspeo-ple, and finally, starting in 1730, a severe and protracted conflict that seemed to signal the onset of fundamental changes in local culture. By 1738, the First Parish had acquired another new meetinghouse, but this time the event produced little communal conviviality. Instead, a quarrel over this new building had divided parishioners into irreconcilable camps that wrangled bitterly for more than a decade. The strife among townspeople subsided only in the 1740s, after many of Gloucester's inhabitants became caught up in the Great Awakening, a revival of evangelical religious piety. This long period of disruption in Gloucester was not unrelated to the changes wrought in town by commercial development. Almost all of the most economically successful families in town took the same side in the First Parish controversy and subsequently became deeply engaged in the revival. Their adversaries in the parish conflict were mainly families of farmers and fishermen, townspeople whose geographic location made their share in the profits of Gloucester's economic growth relatively smaller. This group responded less fervently to the revival.

In view of these alignments, what happened in Gloucester appears to fit a pattern of cultural transformation familiar to New England: the uneven rewards of commercial development produced a divergence of interests and values that tore apart the old corporate community. Gloucester's typicality may prove deceptive, but because the situation in its First Parish seems representative of the transition from a subsistence village to a commercial center, the town is a good place to begin reexamining some of our prevailing assumptions about the relationship between economic development and social and cultural change in eighteenth-century New England.

1

From Fishing Camp to Puritan Community

THE STABLE SOCIAL EXISTENCE enjoyed by Gloucester inhabitants in 1700 was not a legacy that they had inherited from the first generation of settlers but an achievement of the later decades of the seventeenth century. From the time of the first English settlement at Cape Ann in 1623 until the 1660s, Gloucester was caught in a crossfire of continuous conflict between groups with different backgrounds and competing economic ambitions. Not a likeminded band of Puritan covenanters but two rival fishing companies founded and fought over the first outpost on Cape Ann. After both companies abandoned the settlement, they were succeeded on the site by two other equally contentious groups of colonists from Wales and the West Country counties of England. The Welsh and West Country immigrants took an instant dislike to each other; tensions between them inhibited the development of both a coherent set of local institutions and a stable, acknowledged group of town leaders. Some settlers wanted as little contact as possible with either local government or the Congregational church, and many contested the legitimacy of both civil and religious authorities. The lack of cooperation among the early inhabitants complicated the problem of making a living at Cape Ann. The land was poor, even by New England standards, and the settlers were without the means for sustaining a fishery. As a result, few families stayed in town permanently. Finding neither a certain livelihood nor a settled social existence, most of the people who came to Gloucester prior to 1650 moved on after a few years.

Gloucester's turbulent beginnings seem out of character for an early New England community since the villages founded by the first generation are usually described as orderly, harmonious societies. After the initial settlement of these model communities by homogeneous groups of English Puritan families, there was little movement into or out of the new towns. The few late arrivals who sought admittance were carefully scrutinized by established settlers, who were slow to trust "strangers" and just as reluctant to pull up stakes themselves. The fixed and exclusive membership of these self-contained communities enabled their inhabitants to develop a strong sense of corporate identity as well as a consensus about how best to order local institutions. General agreement prevailed among them on policies governing the distribution of land and the conduct of town business. And the widely shared adherence to Congregationalist orthodoxy on the part of early settlers made for as little dissent in religious life as there was in politics and allowed for the rapid establishment of churches that included as full members the majority of adults in town. The organization of economic life also facilitated communal cohesion. A relatively even distribution of town lands afforded few opportunities for any individual or group to amass great wealth. Yet notwithstanding the rough economic equality of early settlers, society was still hierarchical, and the "pecking order" of each community was apparent to all its inhabitants. Villagers customarily deferred to the so-called "town fathers," men of middle age and older, whose piety, skills, education, and public service were rewarded by long terms in local office. But while the towns founded by the first generation are commonly portrayed as remarkably stable and unified, not all early New England villages conformed to this description. In Gloucester, for example, diversity in every sphere of life and dissension over fundamental issues dominated the early decades of settlement, and Puritan communitarianism did not take root until later in the seventeenth century.[1]

The history of Gloucester begins in 1623, the year in which the Dorchester Company established a small colony of fourteen fishermen on Cape Ann. The outpost was one of many fishing camps that dotted the New England coast from Marblehead to the Penobscot River, plantations financed by various companies and independent entrepreneurs of England's West Country throughout the 1620s and 1630s as western terminals of the transatlantic trade. Eager to enhance their competitive position in the European fish market, West Country merchants saw the advantage of permanent bases near the fishing grounds: such settlements would obviate the need for a costly and time-consuming annual voyage to the banks. Resident colonists could outfit their boats and begin fishing as soon as weather permitted, construct stages and saltworks for curing and drying the catch more efficiently, and sustain themselves in the interim months by planting, hunting, and trade with the Indians. Commending the plan of fishing plantations were not only the economic benefits of such outposts but also the social, political, and religious ends that these projects promised to promote. One founding member of the Dorchester Company, the Reverend John White, described the venture as motivated primarily by

---

[1] Probably most influential in establishing an image of early Massachusetts towns as peaceful, static societies was Kenneth Lockridge's study of Dedham, *A New England Town: The First Hundred Years* (New York, 1970), 3–77. But the Plymouth colony in the seventeenth century offers a striking contrast to Lockridge's portrayal of Dedham in terms of demographic development and social organization. See especially, Darrett Rutman, *Husbandmen of Plymouth: Farms and Villages in the Old Colony, 1620–1692* (New York, 1967), and John Demos, "Notes on Life in Plymouth Colony," *WMQ*, 3rd ser., 22 (1965), 264–86. The more recent work of several historians has shown that even the communities of Massachusetts Bay and Connecticut founded in the flush of first-generation utopianism were not always stable, unified places insulated from conflict and change. See David Grayson Allen, *In English Ways: The Movement of Societies and the Transferal of English Local Law and Custom to Massachusetts Bay in the Seventeenth Century* (Chapel Hill, 1981); Paul Lucas, *Valley of Discord: Church and Society Along the Connecticut River Valley, 1636–1725* (Hanover, N.H., 1976); and Stephen Innes, *To Labor in a New Land: Economy and Society in Seventeenth-Century Springfield* (Princeton, 1983). I am indebted to Professor Innes for sharing his study with me while it was still in manuscript.

"Compassion towards the Fishermen, and partly some expectation of gaine." He contended that

> although our New-found-land voyages prove more beneficial to the Merchants . . . these to New-England are found farre more profitable to poore Fishermen; so that by that time all reckonings are cast up, these voyages come not farre behind the other in advantage to the State.

White envisioned an industrious hive of pious fishermen-farmers flourishing in the salubrious atmosphere of Cape Ann, a settlement capable of provisioning the seasonal fishing fleet with food, salt, and shipping materials. He regarded such colonies as a means for relieving England's unemployment, for remedying the moral evils attending overcrowding and economic competition in the mother country, and for spreading Christianity to the Indians of the New World.[2]

Despite all these inducements to investors, the Dorchester Company in 1623 faced one difficulty: the Plymouth Company, another group of West Country adventurers, had also set their sights on Cape Ann's offshore fishery. The Plymouth Company did not plan to plant a permanent colony on the Cape, but intended to establish an outpost for prosecuting a seasonal fishery. The small, struggling Pilgrim settlement to the south founded by the company a few years earlier still needed food, and financial backers in England impatiently awaited some return on their investment. In the same year that the Dorchester adventurers settled their fishermen on the shores of Cape Ann, the Plymouth Company procured a patent to the region and in the spring of 1624 dispatched a fishing vessel, a saltmaker, and a ship's carpenter to the spot. When representatives of the two rival companies

[2] For an account of Gloucester's founding as a fishing camp, see John J. Babson, *History of the Town of Gloucester, Cape Ann, including the Town of Rockport* (Gloucester, 1860), 30–32. On other early seventeenth-century fishing settlements, see Charles Knowles Bolton, *The Real Founders of New England* (Boston, 1929); and Charles E. Clark, *The Eastern Frontier: The Settlement of Northern New England, 1610–1763* (New York, 1970), 14–15 and 21. For John White's promotion of fishing plantations, see *The Planters Plea* in *Massachusetts Historical Society Proceedings,* 62 (1929), 384, 386, and 414.

collided on Cape Ann, the result was neither commercial success nor the enhancement of Protestant piety and English patriotism.

For two years the Dorchester Company's poorly outfitted vessels miscalculated the sailing time to Cape Ann, arrived at the fishing grounds too late for a full loading, and failed to return a profit to its investors. The Plymouth adventurers were better equipped but no more prompt in their sailing; their ship arrived late in 1624 with a crew more interested in drinking than fishing and returned with only a small catch. Disappointment turned into disaster in 1625, when the Dorchester Company determined to make one final effort to improve their interest at Cape Ann. To supply the settlement with leadership, they recruited a governor and a minister, and to reduce the competition from Plymouth, the Dorchester men seized their rivals' fishing stage, a raised wooden shelter on the shore used for drying the catch. Captain Miles Standish and the Plymouth fleet arrived in the spring of 1625 to find that the Dorchester fishermen, barricaded behind hogsheads, refused to surrender the stage without a fight.[3]

Other tensions contributed to the intensity of economic competition at Cape Ann, for the Dorchester Company could not have selected a leadership less palatable to their Plymouth adversaries. Roger Conant, the Dorchester governor, was a former Plymouth "particular," a colonist not sponsored by the company who had paid his own passage to New England. Particulars received land in Plymouth but found themselves excluded from political privileges and the Indian trade. Disgruntled over his second-class status and the Pilgrims' "rigid principles of separation" from the Church of England, Conant had left Plymouth just a year before his recruitment by the Dorchester adventurers. The Dorchester Company's spiritual leader, the Reverend John Lyford, was a more recent and notorious outcast from Plymouth. Banished by Governor William Bradford early in 1625 for his outspoken support of "particular" grievances and for his

[3] Babson, *History,* 33–38; White, *The Planters Plea,* 415–18; George Langdon, Jr., *Pilgrim Colony: A History of New Plymouth, 1620–1691* (New Haven, 1966), 27–28; and William Bradford, *Of Plymouth Plantation, 1620–1647,* ed., Samuel Eliot Morison (New York, 1952), 145–47.

attack on separatism, Lyford, like Conant, had cast his lot with Plymouth's rivals for Cape Ann's riches.[4]

The keen competition between the two companies might have culminated in violence in the spring of 1625 if Standish and his Plymouth fishermen had not backed down from the confrontation and yielded the stage seized by the Dorchester mariners. Dismayed by their reception, the Plymouth adventurers terminated all connection with the northern fishery, and the company itself dissolved in 1627. Even for the victorious Dorchester men, it was the last fishing season at Cape Ann. Discouraged by three years of financial losses and the "ill-carriage" of their colonists, the Dorchester investors abandoned their design for a fishing plantation and broke up the Cape Ann settlement. Roger Conant and some of his men moved south to Salem, seeking a spot better suited to agriculture.[5]

For several years after 1625, as settlements developed to the north and south, Cape Ann remained virtually uninhabited, although during the 1630s encouragement from the governments of Massachusetts Bay and Plymouth revived a seasonal fishery by a handful of squatters on this section of the North Shore. But not until 1642 did the Cape attract a large enough number of permanent settlers to warrant incorporation as a town. They named the new community Gloucester because many of the inhabitants, a group of farmers, ship carpenters, and seafarers from Salem and other Essex County towns, had emigrated originally from that part of the West of England. Joining these settlers almost immediately upon the town's incorporation was a group from Wales, about twenty families led by the Reverend Richard Blynman, a native of Monmouthsire in the West of England.[6]

---

[4] Langdon, *Pilgrim Colony*, 19–20; Bradford, *Of Plymouth Plantation*, 147–69.

[5] Babson, *History*, 39.

[6] Babson, *History*, 50–52, 189–90; *Johnson's Wonderworking Providence*, ed., J. Franklin Jameson (New York, 1910), 205–6. Johnson estimated that about fifty families were settled on Cape Ann in 1642 and attributed the area's small population to its remote location. Of the twenty-one emigrants to Gloucester between 1620 and 1650 who appear in the lists compiled by Charles Banks, thirteen were from the West of England and eight from London and the eastern counties. (*The Planters of the Commonwealth*

Blynman and his band of followers had initially settled at the Plymouth Colony, but the pastor found separatism uncongenial, and his flock of ship's carpenters and other maritime entrepreneurs discovered little demand for their skills in that settlement. Bad luck in the fishery had soured interest in this enterprise among Plymouth inhabitants, most of whom were husbandmen without seafaring inclinations or skills; the colony as a whole, still saddled with a large debt, lacked the capital to build ships and sustain losses.[7] Once established in Gloucester, both the Welsh and the West Country settlers began building boats, erecting stages, and opening taverns, three indispensable appurtenances of the fishing industry. Blynman himself, the pastor of the First Church of Gloucester, gathered in 1642, oversaw construction of "the Cut," a canal that afforded families living along the Annisquam River more convenient access to Massachusetts Bay and a quicker route to the larger ports of Boston and Salem.[8]

But the common economic interests of the emigrants did not promote peace and unity in the new community, and a decade of turmoil ensued as two factions of newcomers again competed for control. Throughout the 1640s, Welsh and West Country leaders vied with each other for domination of the board of selectmen: twenty-four different men served an average of only two terms each during that decade.[9] Fac-

(Boston, 1930) and *A Topographical Dictionary of 2885 English Emigrants to New England, 1620–1650* (Philadelphia, 1937). For a full discussion of the conditions in the West of England that fostered migration to America, see James Horn, "Servant Migration to the Chesapeake in the Seventeenth Century," in *The Chesapeake in the Seventeenth Century: Essays on Anglo-American Society and Politics,* eds., Thad Tate and David Ammerman (Chapel Hill, 1979), 77–83; Mildred Campbell, "The Social Origins of Some Early Americans," in *Seventeenth Century America,* ed., James Smith (Chapel Hill, 1959), 78–88; and Allen, *In English Ways,* 87–89, passim.

[7] Langdon, *Pilgrim Colony,* 35–36.

[8] Babson, *History,* 7, 187–88. Babson's local history and his *Notes and Additions to the History of Gloucester,* 2nd ed. (Salem, 1891) contain a wealth of detailed information on seventeenth-century settlers, including their towns of origin, occupations, and places of residence in Gloucester, as well as genealogies and extracts from early town records.

[9] The first book of Gloucester's town records provides the names of officeholders up to 1694. (See "Gloucester Town Records, Book I, 1642 to 1694," Office of the Town Clerk, City Hall, Gloucester, Massachusetts. Cited here-

tional in-fighting focused on the ministry of Richard Blynman, whose spiritual leadership the West Country group refused to accept. They appeared regularly in county court for defaming the church, disturbing its meetings, libelling the character of its minister, and charging him with false interpretations of Scripture. In 1649, Blynman himself faced charges of tearing up a writ for debt that one of his parishioners had taken out against another. The pastor protested that he had intended no contempt for civil authority but had interposed to effect a private settlement of the difference; the contending parties in the debt suit, both West Countrymen from Essex County towns, were unwilling to accord Blynman that kind of authority. Blynman had to face not only antagonism to his leadership on the part of some townsmen but also apathy or antipathy toward religious matters by others. For example, in 1648, four local men appeared before the county court, charged with hunting raccoons instead of attending church services, and in the same year Richard Window paid a fine for swearing and saying "These are the brethren, the divill scald them."[10]

The disruptions in Gloucester during this decade were characteristic of other Massachusetts communities settled by immigrants from the institutionally diverse and religiously divided West of England. Emigrants from the western counties accounted for less than one-fifth of the early settlers of New England; more numerous among the first colonists were East Anglians from the counties of Suffolk, Essex, and Nor-

after as GTR.) Power on the board of selectmen during the 1640s was about evenly split between the Reverend Blynman's Welsh followers, who accounted for ten of the twenty-four selectmen during that decade, and emigrants from the West of England or from other Essex County towns, who made up nine of the twenty-four. The remaining five men had come from other Massachusetts towns that I could not identify.

[10] *Records and Files of the Quarterly Courts of Essex County, Massachusetts,* ed. George Francis Dow, 8 vols. (Salem, Mass., 1911–21), I, 69, 70, 134, 173, and 175. (Cited hereafter as *Essex Ct. Recs.*) The religious disengagement of some of Gloucester's early settlers bears out John J. Waters's observation that West Countrymen "took the new Puritan ethos lightly" and were on the whole less zealous than emigrants from other parts of England. ("Hingham, Massachusetts, 1631–1661: An East Anglian Oligarchy in the New World," *Journal of Social History,* I (1967–68), 353.) See also Banks, *The Planters of the Commonwealth,* 16–17.

folk. But despite their minority status, West Country settlers neither accepted the leadership of the larger East Anglian group nor developed solidarity among themselves. When West Countrymen—and women—were not tangling with the East Anglian-dominated civil and ecclesiastical establishments of the Bay, they were fighting with each other, and in Gloucester they could also contend against the Welsh. In New England's other West Country enclaves—Newbury, Marblehead, and Hingham in Massachusetts, and several Maine towns to the north—early seventeenth-century settlers engaged each other and their East Anglian neighbors in an endless succession of disputes over land, debt, religion, militia elections, and seating in the meetinghouse. Even the simplest cultural differences among inhabitants of these communities could occasion misunderstandings. Several Gloucester settlers, for example, took offense at the manners of one William Snelling, who declared upon "being toasted," "Ile pledge my friends for my foes a plague for their heeles and a pox of their toes." This "merry discourse" landed Snelling in the county court, where he insisted that he "intended only to declare the proverb of the West Country" but "acknowledged his weakness in saying it."[11]

The consequence of the constant strife in these West Country New England communities was an unusually high rate of out-migration. In 1651, about the same time that a substantial segment of settlers left Newbury for Woodbridge, New Jersey, Richard Blynman and his followers left Cape Ann to their adversaries and moved en masse to New London, Connecticut. Nor were disgruntled Plymouth emigrants the only people moving out of town. The majority of families who migrated to Gloucester between the late 1630s and 1660 passed in and out of town after only a few years

[11] *Essex Ct. Recs.*, I, 259. About 16 percent of all early New England settlers came from the West Country. The East Anglian counties of Suffolk, Essex, and Norfolk contributed nearly 25 percent of the emigrants. East Anglians tended to settle in Massachusetts Bay while West Country families gravitated toward Maine and New Hampshire. (Banks, *The Planters of the Commonwealth*, 13–15.) For descriptions of the Massachusetts communities founded by West Country emigrants, see Allen, *In English Ways*, especially 12 and 82–116; and Waters, "Hingham, Massachusetts, 1631–1661," *Journal of Social History*, I (1967–68), 351–70.

residence, a rate of out-migration exceeding considerably that of other early towns like Dedham or Hingham over the same period. Of the seventy-three householders who settled in Gloucester before 1650, over half had moved by 1660, the largest single group to New London, several families to Falmouth and other new Maine towns, and most of the rest to surrounding communities in Essex County. Mobility characterized later arrivals as well: of twenty-five families who came into Gloucester during the decade of the 1650s, eleven left after a couple of years.[12]

Compounding the difficulties of the diverse English backgrounds of the first settlers was Cape Ann's unpromising soil. The town's topography was irregular and uneven, its rugged, forested surface broken by rocky hills, granite ledges, and acres of boulders and separated into many small necks and headlands by marshes, swamps, and creeks. Even intense cultivation yielded land "fit for little else but pasturing and a great deal not even fit for that."[13] Towns elsewhere in Essex County offered better ground, and after 1658, when Massachusetts extended its jurisdiction to include Maine, settlements like Falmouth drew families farther north who might otherwise have ended their wanderings in Gloucester. Maritime pursuits afforded an equally uncertain livelihood. Abetted by the contacts and capital of London merchants, Boston, Salem, and Ipswich traders were developing the New England fishery. But these commercial beginnings were small,

[12] My computations are based upon data drawn from Babson's genealogies of early Gloucester settlers. He estimates that eighty-two families or individuals had arrived in Gloucester by 1650, and that of these, only one-third remained in town. But only seventy-three of the eighty-two persons that he lists as settlers appear to have intended to establish permanent residence in town. Nonetheless, his contention that the majority of early arrivals did not remain in town is correct. On out-migration from Newbury, see Allen, *In English Ways*, 93; for Dedham and Hingham, see Kenneth Lockridge, "The Population of Dedham, Massachusetts, 1636 to 1736," *Economic History Review*, 2nd ser., 19 (1966), 321–23; and Waters, "Hingham, Massachusetts, 1631–1661," *Journal of Social History*, I (1967–68), 365. In Dedham's early decades there was a 20 to 45 percent change in the town's population, and the rate of turnover in Hingham was even lower.

[13] Babson, *History*, 3; An Answer of the Town of Gloucester to the Petition of Nathaniel Coit, December 23, 1738, *Massachusetts Archives*, 11:531. (Cited hereafter as *MA*.)

markets remained limited, and the established fisheries of Marblehead and the Isles of Shoals supplied their needs. While outside investors were not attracted to the Cape Ann fishery, inhabitants lacked the financial resources and, apparently, the commercial connections to initiate trade on any significant scale. Edward Johnson, an early Bay colonist who chronicled the history of its first settlements, observed that Gloucester possessed the location and resources for a thriving fishery and shipbuilding industry but lacked "men of estates" to manage these enterprises. Sheer subsistence posed the most formidable obstacle: the settlement had to feed itself, and the local population was too small to sustain a combination of agriculture and an intensive fishery since both demanded the greatest investment of labor during the same seasons.[14]

After the departure of Blynman and his supporters, a small number of the town's remaining maritime entrepreneurs and laborers attempted to develop the fishery, but little came of their efforts. Their contribution to communal life was not the founding of a prosperous commerce but rather the creation of a disorderly subculture, comparable on a smaller scale to that of other seventeenth-century fishing villages like Marblehead. Fisherman John Jackson was representative of this group in Gloucester. Within the space of two years, he was presented to the county court for debt, for obscene language, and for the attempted rape of his servant maid; perhaps because neighbors suspected his wife of witchcraft, he sued two of them for slander. Throughout the fifties and early sixties, other shoremen and fishermen figured conspicuously in civil cases of debt and defamation and in criminal cases of assault, drunkenness, and husbands living apart from their wives.[15]

---

[14] Raymond MacFarland, *A History of the New England Fisheries* (Philadelphia, 1911), 68–76 and 81; George F. Dow, "Shipping and Trade in Early New England," *Massachusetts Historical Society Proceedings,* 64 (1931), 3–4 and 9–10; Bernard Bailyn, *New England Merchants in the Seventeenth Century* (Cambridge, Mass., 1955), 76–82; *Johnson's Wonderworking Providence,* ed. Jameson, 205; Babson, *History,* 40, 378–79.

[15] *Essex Ct. Recs.,* II, 235, 237–39, 256–58, and 318. These published court records indicate that between 1650 and 1669, five Gloucester inhabitants were defendants in cases involving assault or threats of physical violence,

Because of this combination of economic and social liabilities, Gloucester offered newcomers few of the comforts
and securities of a settled, corporate existence. Disenchanted, settlers moved on, compounding the problems of
establishing a coherent set of local institutions. Out-migration not only siphoned off ordinary settlers but also deprived
the town of any stable, ongoing leadership: thirteen of the
twenty-four selectmen serving in the 1640s left Gloucester
before 1652, and nearly half of the selectmen during the next
decade had departed by the early sixties.[16] The lack of continuity in leadership could hardly have enhanced the efficacy
of local government or the order of town life. Demographic
upheaval also reduced the ability of the town to provide for
a settled spiritual leadership. The exodus of Blynman and
his company in 1651 left Gloucester without either a clergyman or a population large enough to maintain one. To
offset their lack of a minister, inhabitants enlisted the services of two prominent laymen as teaching elders, but lacking the authoritative status of ordained clergymen, both faced
repeated challenges to their leadership. While members of
the maritime community brawled over women, fish, and stage
room, the families of "respectable society" splintered into
factions over the eldership. The first elder, William Perkins,
lasted in town only five years. Traduced by "scandalous
speeches" against his spiritual credentials, pestered with
civil suits alleging slander and financial improprieties, and
upbraided by one female member of his congregation who
found his preaching "soe dead" that he was "fitter to be a
lady's chamberman than to be in a pulpit," Perkins finally
fled to Topsfield. His successor, Thomas Millet, fared little
better. He was finally forced to sue the town for his salary

sixteen in cases of slander against neighbors, thirteen for reviling the minister or the church. Three Gloucester residents were presented for theft, two
for living away from their wives, two for swearing, two for absence from
public worship, one for drunkenness, and one for attempted rape and lewdness. Most of the defendants in these cases were identified in the court records as having maritime occupations. Gloucester inhabitants were defendants
in eight actions for debt in the 1650s and fourteen suits in the 1660s, and
again, most defaulters were identified as fishermen and mariners. See especially, *Essex Ct. Recs.,* II, 387–88 and 401.

[16] Most of these early civic leaders left with Blynman for New London.

and ended his ministry embroiled in a dispute with another inhabitant, Williams Stevens, who coveted the eldership for himself. He too contended with criticism from townsmen like William Brown who declared that "mr. Blinman was naught and P[erkins] was starke naught and Millet was worse than Perkins." After five years, Millet moved to Portsmouth.[17]

The intensity of religious strife took a personal toll upon members of the community, riddling social relations with tensions reflected in the county court presentments for this period. In 1657, Thomas Prince complained to the court that his wife had miscarried after William Brown had reproached her for defending Elder Millet and "called her one of Goodwife Jackson's imps . . . and that her time was but short and the deuece [devil] would fech her Away spedily. . . ." Brown's suggestion of malefic mischief stemmed from an earlier charge by Edmund Marshall that the wife of Elder Perkins and three of his supporters practiced witchcraft.[18] By 1656, one decidedly disenchanted townsman, John Rowe, was willing to consign all of Gloucester to Satan. Rowe announced that "if his wife was of his mind, he would set his house afire and run away by the light and the Devil should take the farm, and that he would live no longer among such a company of hell-hounds."[19] The county court fined Rowe, forced Marshall to recant publicly, and put Brown in prison for a week, but punishing the disaffected did nothing to retrieve the situation. While John Rowe stubbornly stayed on in town, most of his neighbors did not, and this constant overturning of membership in the community figured as both cause and effect of the chronic institutional instability that plagued Gloucester for two decades following its permanent settlement.

[17] For Perkins's difficulties, see *Essex Ct. Recs.*, I, 254, 256, 261, 275, 287, 302, and 306. On Millet's troubles, II, 38–40, 63–64, 161, and 216–17.

[18] *Essex Ct. Recs.*, II, 37, 38–40; I, 301. The incidence of slander and allegations of witchcraft, its most extreme form, was generally higher in colonial communities that were, like early Gloucester, isolated and lacking in established social leadership and strong religious authority. Cf., Clara Ann Bowler, "Carted Whores and White Shrouded Apologies: Slander in the County Courts of Seventeenth-Century Virginia," *Virginia Magazine of History and Biography*, 85 (1977), 420–21.

[19] *Ibid.*, I, 408.

The intervention of forces outside of town finally broke the cycle of upheaval and instability that characterized the first decades of Gloucester's existence. After the mid-1660s, local life started to assume a more stable cast as membership within the community consolidated, an acknowledged leadership coalesced, disorder abated, and the divisive influence of distinctive English backgrounds became more attenuated. The first of these external influences, the onset of military conflict with the Indians, laid the foundations for the kind of demographic development that was conducive to increasing consensus, cohesion, and continuity in institutional life. The possibility of an Indian attack on New England's frontier, which had materialized first in the mid-1660s, was realized in the summer of 1675 with the outbreak of King Philip's War, an offensive against English settlements by several tribes organized by Metacom, the sachem of the Wampanoags. Continuing Indian depredations along the Maine coast during the late 1670s discouraged both the removal of settled inhabitants from Gloucester and the migration of settlers from the south to northern New England.[20] As a result, the town's rate of inward and outward migration declined dramatically. In the thirty years between 1630 and 1660, about a hundred families had come to Gloucester, and most had moved on, but in the next thirty years after 1660, only thirty-seven new families arrived in town, mainly immigrants from other Essex County towns, and 80 percent of them stayed.[21]

[20] King Philip's War began in June of 1675 and lasted for two years. By the beginning of 1676, Essex County towns were building fortifications, and the attacks upon northern New England began in September of that year. Although the major attacks occurred north of Essex County at Casco Bay, Oyster River, Durham, Exeter, and York, an Indian raid on Andover claimed the lives of several inhabitants, and the residents of towns from Salem north felt threatened. (Douglas Edward Leach, *Arms for Empire: A Military History of the British Colonies in North America, 1607–1763* (New York, 1973), 61, 65; *Flintlock and Tomahawk: New England in King Philip's War* (New York, 1958); Thomas Franklin Waters, *Ipswich in the Massachusetts Bay Colony,* 2 vols. (Ipswich, Mass., 1905), I, 197, 206–7, 210, 214.

[21] Babson provides a list of settlers prior to 1650 and of those arriving in town between 1650 and 1700 in *History,* 52–54. The breakdown of inward and outward migration below, based upon his histories of the first settlers,

The rate of persistence among earlier arrivals improved as well: after 1660, few older settlers or their grown sons left town, and by the beginning of the 1690s over seventy percent of the adult males in Gloucester represented families who had come to town prior to 1660.[22] While the Indian raids of the 1670s contributed to a wave of reverse migration southward from Maine, only a few families fled to Gloucester, for the town lay too close to the embattled border and lacked the resources to relieve large numbers of refugees.

As Gloucester's population stabilized after 1660, the community's members also became more homogeneous. Among the second generation that came to maturity during the sixties and seventies, the peculiarities of regional English origins operated with less force than this heritage had for their immigrant fathers.[23] At the same time, the new arrivals were not Welsh migrants from Plymouth but mainly families from nearby New England communities. King Philip's War and the conflict with the Maine tribes fostered a feeling of "New English" identity among members of the second generation while also enhancing the unity of local residents by presenting them with a common enemy and a common peril.

reflects the improvement in the rate of persistence and the slackening of in-migration:

	Arrivals	Departures
	73 (by 1650)	7 (by 1650)
1650s	25	44
1660s	12	9
1670s	14	3
1680s	11	1

Among arrivals between 1660 and 1690 for whom I could identify a place of origin, twelve came from Ipswich, four from Maine, three of Newbury, two each from Salem, Beverly, Marblehead, and Weymouth, one each from Lynn, Manchester, and Roxbury, and two from Britain.

[22] All adult males in town in 1688 were listed in the town records when the first division of the common land was made in 1688. (Babson, *History*, 207–9). Out of the 140 sons of seventeenth-century settlers who stayed in town, it appears that only 22 left Gloucester.

[23] John Waters makes a similar point in "Hingham, Massachusetts, 1631–1661," *Journal of Social History*, I (1967–68), 369–70.

The town did not suffer Indian attack in the 1670s, but the threat was not remote. Indians decimated settlements just a few miles up the coast and inland, claiming among their victims and captives the relatives and former neighbors of Gloucester residents. Concern for the safety of their sons as well as the fear of invasion unified the town's inhabitants, for a quarter of Gloucester's adult males served as soldiers in the colony's forces during the war, and three were killed in the fighting. An indirect consequence of the hostilities that also contributed to the increasing commonality among inhabitants was the disappearance of Gloucester's distinct seafaring subculture. Discouraged by the fighting's disruption of their struggling fishery, most men employed exclusively in maritime pursuits drifted out of town after the mid-1660s, leaving the community to families involved mainly in farming.[24]

Over the same period that Gloucester unified to resist the threat of Indian incursions, the town succumbed to a more subtle kind of conquest by its important neighbor to the north, Ipswich. While the Indian wars helped to stabilize membership within Gloucester's population and fostered solidarity among its inhabitants, the influence of Ipswich on its institutional development also enhanced the cohesion of social life on Cape Ann. A populous commercial center in the seventeenth century, Ipswich exported to Gloucester not only the produce of its craftsmen but also, after 1650, some of its families and its pattern of political organization.[25] A prominent characteristic of early Ipswich was its East Anglican civic tradition of concentrating public leadership and

---

[24] Babson, *History*, 206; and Waters, *Ipswich*, I, 198–201. In addition to the conflicts with Indian tribes, the Anglo-Dutch wars of the 1660s disrupted New England's trade and probably encouraged the members of Gloucester's early maritime community to move to more established fisheries. (Bailyn, *New England Merchants,* 131.) The decline of maritime pursuits in town is also indicated by the occupation listed by fifty-five Gloucester men who took the oath of fidelity in 1677. Thirty-four described themselves as "husbandmen," seventeen as sailors or fishermen, and four as artisans. This list does not include all male inhabitants, and in fact excludes many of the town's mature male leaders, almost all of whom identified themselves as farmers in probate records and other public documents. (*Essex Ct. Recs.,* VI, 402.)

[25] On the preponderance of Ipswich immigrants, see note 21.

responsibility in the hands of a few wealthy and socially prominent men. The same influential families monopolized the most important local offices for years on end and directed the development of town life according to their discretion.[26] By the late 1660s, Gloucester was engrafting onto its own political culture these oligarchic practices. Between 1668 and 1690, an identifiable set of local leaders emerged in Gloucester: just eight men held eighty percent of all terms as selectmen, an office to which townsmen delegated increasing authority in managing local affairs.[27]

Although the resettlement of some Ipswich families in Gloucester may have fostered the spread of Ipswich's political traditions, it was probably the long pastorate of the Reverend John Emerson that played the most important role in disseminating the northern town's influence to Cape Ann. The Harvard-educated scion of a prominent Ipswich family and the son-in-law of former Bay deputy-governor Samuel Symonds, Emerson accepted the call to Gloucester's First Church in 1664 and remained in that pulpit for the next thirty-six years. His eminence quelled the divisions within his congregation, awed townsmen into building a new meetinghouse in the 1660s, and subsequently persuaded them to supplement his ministerial stipend with grants of land and the privilege of operating the town's principal mills. The successes of his untroubled pastorate included bringing most of the community's adult male leaders into the church as full members.[28] It seems likely that Emerson's leadership left its impress not only on ecclesiastical life but on other local institutions as well.

[26] Allen, *In English Ways,* 136–38.

[27] The first book of town records indicates that, in the twenty-one years after 1668, one hundred five total terms were served by twenty-one men on the board of selectmen, an average tenure of five years. Sixty percent of these terms were served by just four men, and eighty percent by eight men.

[28] Babson, *History,* 196–97 and 199. The lack of complete records for the First Church makes it impossible to determine precisely the number of church members, but a list of communicants in 1703 included fourteen of the twenty-eight selectmen between 1680 and 1700. Three other selectmen had owned the covenant, and five had neither full nor half-way membership; the remaining six died prior to 1703. ("Records of the First Church of Gloucester," MS, unpaginated, Cape Ann Historical Society, Gloucester, Mass. Cited hereafter as GFCR.)

The influence of Ipswich brought Gloucester more into the mainstream of the dominant culture of East Anglian Puritanism, but contact with its commercialized and highly stratified neighbor altered the town little in economic orientation or social structure. Ipswich from the outset of its settlement combined agriculture with trade and attracted a large number of merchants and a diverse assortment of craftsmen.[29] Perhaps some Ipswich entrepreneurs even considered expanding their interests by financing fishing ventures from Gloucester's two good harbors. But if they were tempted by Cape Ann's maritime potential, the prospects were never pursued. For their part, Gloucester residents, after the brief and unsuccessful attempts of early settlers to develop a commercial fishery and shipbuilding industry, were satisfied to scratch a subsistence from their stony soil. Undeterred by the town's natural agricultural disadvantages, virtually all of the villagers took up farming and displayed only a desultory interest in tapping the rich potential of the town's two chief resources, the timber of the common woodlands and the fish running off their shores. By 1690, Gloucester's selectmen had licensed a cornmill and a sawmill on both sides of the Annisquam River, but these mills supplied primarily local needs. Gloucester's farms yielded little grain or livestock for export, and marketable surpluses of fish and timber were also meager. The town had made only one division of the common forests by 1688, and local by-laws restricted individual access to wood on undivided land. Another indication that timber resources remained almost untouched and that the produce of fishing voyages fed families rather than distant consumers is the small number of vessels owned by townsmen. In 1693, only eight sloops of small tunnage and a handful of even smaller boats, shallops, and canoes belonged to the town.[30] These little craft regularly transported residents across the Annisquam River, occasionally engaged in offshore fishing, and infrequently made packet trips to Boston with small cargoes of cod and cordwood.

With its mixed economy of farming, fishing, and lumbering designed for subsistence and self-sufficiency, Gloucester

[29] Allen, *In English Ways*, 132–33; and Waters, *Ipswich*, I, 76.
[30] Babson, *History*, 202 and 214.

resembled the small settlements of Maine and New Hampshire more than its market-oriented neighbor, Ipswich. And the local attitude toward economic development distinguished Gloucester from Ipswich as well. While Ipswich cultivated the growth of commerce and local crafts, Gloucester was more oriented to economic restrictionism. Characteristic of local concerns was the town meeting's licensing of the Reverend John Emerson, John Fitch, and Thomas Riggs to operate a sawmill. The town made this privilege conditional upon their agreeing to sell cheaper to neighbors than to "strangers," to accept payment in kind, and to extend credit to any inhabitant for three months.[31] No doubt these restrictions, combined with those limiting access to the common woodlands, discouraged entrepreneurial activity. In 1682, for example, the town meeting granted Job Coit, Samuel Sargent, and Jeffrey Parsons, Sr., the privilege of running another sawmill, but the three men forfeited their license in 1693 without ever having set up operations.[32]

Gloucester's simple, subsistence economy, operating virtually in isolation from the wider market, nurtured a nearly model Puritan social structure in the town during the latter decades of the seventeenth century. No sharp gradations of wealth, no extremes of riches or poverty, but a rough economic homogeneity prevailed within its population. In Ipswich, the wealthiest decile of the population owned almost half of the town's wealth by the mid-seventeenth century, and its richest merchants amassed estates of several thousand pounds sterling. But in Gloucester, the top decile of inventoried decedents in the last decade of the seventeenth century held less than one-third of the total assets, and no one was worth over five hundred pounds sterling.[33] Along

[31] *Ibid.*, 202.

[32] *Ibid.*, 202n and 203n.

[33] The distribution of wealth in Gloucester, derived from twenty-one inventories between 1690 and 1699, is similar to that shown for the period between 1690 and 1715 in Table I (See appendix). The richest decile of decedents owned 32.7 percent of the total inventoried wealth, the middle 60 percent of decedents, 63 percent, and the bottom thirty percent of decedents, 4.3 percent (Source: Files, Registry of Probate, Essex County Courthouse, Salem, Mass.). The province assessment of 1693 bears out the conclusion of inventory data of a rough economic homogeneity prevailing in town at the end of the seventeenth century, for only a small discrepancy exists between the

with land ownership, age was the principal determinant of wealth in seventeenth-century Gloucester, as it was in adjacent Chebacco Parish, an agrarian community with a comparable economy. All of the men who ranked among the top quarter of Gloucester's ratepayers in 1693 were over forty years of age, save for a few sons who had recently inherited the estates of substantial fathers, while three-quarters of the bottom half of ratepayers were men under forty.[34]

Gloucester's more equitable distribution of wealth points up another important contrast with Ipswich. Besides its more extensive commercial development, differences in the policy of land distribution made Ipswich residents considerably wealthier than Gloucester's inhabitants. While Ipswich made substantial grants to townsmen shortly after its initial settlement, Gloucester pursued a more conservative course, and even by the end of the seventeenth century, large tracts of local acreage were still owned in common.[35] Another aspect of land policy in Gloucester inhibiting the concentration of wealth was its liberal allotment of acreage to newcomers. Later arrivals received admission to the proprietorship almost automatically, and when the town made its first division of the common woodlands in 1688, every householder and adult male over twenty-one acquired six acres. As a result, the date of a man's settlement in Gloucester bore little relationship to his economic standing: men who had arrived in town after 1660 were proportionately represented among the top quarter

average assessment of sixteen shillings and the median assessment of fourteen shillings and fourpence. (For a copy of this tax list, see Babson, *History*, 213–14.) For the distribution of wealth in Ipswich in the seventeenth century, see Allen, *In English Ways*, 134; for Essex County generally see William Davisson, "Essex County Wealth Trends: Wealth and Economic Growth in Seventeenth-Century Massachusetts," *EIHC*, 103 (1967), 291–342.

[34] Only three of the twenty-one men who ranked in the wealthiest quartile of taxpayers in 1693 were under forty, all members of the Parsons and Davis families who had recently come into their inheritances. Christopher Jedrey describes the same age-stratified distribution of wealth for eighteenth-century Chebacco Parish, Ipswich, a village adjacent to Cape Ann with a predominantly subsistence agrarian economy. (*World of John Cleaveland*, 63–64.)

[35] Babson, *History*, 233–34; on land distribution in Ipswich, see Allen, *In English Ways*, 121–31.

of ratepayers in 1693.[36] Because its limited material advantages attracted few newcomers to town before the 1690s, Gloucester could afford to open opportunities to later seventeenth-century arrivals, and this liberality, along with the relative equity of the distribution of wealth, contributed to the concord that came to prevail in town.

The growth of a settled, homogeneous population and the emergence of an effective civil and spiritual leadership both reflected and reinforced the strengthening of social bonds among townspeople by economic arrangements that insured all families a comfortable subsistence. After the 1660s, consensus replaced contention in local political and religious life, while the number of Gloucester presentments for debt and disorderly behavior dropped sharply, a decrease related to the departure of fishermen and sailors from town.[37] The most common criminal case that concerned Gloucester inhabitants in the later seventeenth-century involved violations of the Sabbath. In these prosecutions, townspeople usually appeared not as defendants but as witnesses against the godless mariners of Charlestown and Boston who had the temerity to set sail from Annisquam harbor on the Lord's Day. Any hapless shipmaster breaching this strict observance ended up in court with several outraged representatives of the respectable citizenry testifying against his offense.[38] The same oversight that snared seafaring Sabbath-breakers carried over into an equally intense watchfulness among neighbors. In his zealous scrutiny of John Pearce, Clement Coldom discovered that his neighbor was "accustomed to take the widow Stannard to his house at night and she was seen to go away in the morning." Coldom called Anthony Day and Deacon

---

[36] Babson, *History,* 207–8 and 233–34. About one-quarter (twenty-two of eighty-three) of the men who appeared on the Gloucester province tax list of 1693 had come to town after 1660. Ten of these twenty-two later arrivals ranked among the thirty-three men who were the richest 40 percent of ratepayers.

[37] This generalization is based upon the marked decline in criminal presentments of Gloucester inhabitants after the mid-1660s indicated in the published court records. By the 1670s, criminal activity was limited to three Sabbath violations, two cases of assault, one of drunkenness, and one of illegal retailing of liquor.

[38] *Essex Ct. Recs.,* IV, 45; V, 221 and 267–68; VII, 58.

James Stevens to the scene of the crime where they "saw enough" to warrant a complaint because Coldom in his eagerness to expose the evil-doers "heaved the door off the hinges."[39] Neighbors also noticed and complained about other domestic mischief: the delivery of a few young matrons too soon after marriage, Benjamin Jones's mistreatment of his young servant, and Thomas Prince's drunken abuse of his wife.[40] But these few, widely scattered instances of misconduct accounted for virtually all of the reported "crime" in late seventeenth-century Gloucester. Perhaps the most eloquent testimony to the stability of the town's social order by this time was the brief but intense dispute over Thomas Judkin's ordinary. For several years, Peter Duncan and Judkin had kept the town's two taverns, Duncan in Gloucester harbor and Judkin on the Annisquam River near the meetinghouse. But by 1674, with "Our Town . . . growing to a pritty fullnesse of younge people," some of the "town fathers" began to wonder about the wisdom of maintaining two retailers of spirits, especially Judkin's establishment since it was so near the meetinghouse. Here Gloucester's young men customarily gathered before Sabbath observances (and "some doe very much indispose themselves for the worship and servis of God") and before militia exercises, occasioning "disorders on trayning days." Over the protests of the young people, Gloucester's mature male leaders decided that by depriving Judkin of his license, "it will be wee doe conceive the easier to order" the rising generation. The county court complied with the town's request and shut down the tavern for several years.[41]

Following the troubled decades of its initial settlement, Gloucester attained an equilibrium in its economic, social, and political life. The early settlement encountered the divisions and difficulties characteristic of other West Country New English communities and coastal fishing camps. But beginning in the 1660s, Gloucester stabilized as a result of

---

[39] *Ibid.*, V. 231 and 259.

[40] *Ibid.*, IV, 440; VI, 116; VIII, 295. Prosecutions for fornication in Gloucester were relatively rare until the 1680s. Prior to that time, the published court records indicate only four prosecutions of inhabitants for that offense.

[41] *Ibid.*, V, 360–62.

the slowdown of migration into and out of town, the influence of Ipswich's East Anglian institutions and traditions, and the preference of local inhabitants for an isolated, self-sufficient village existence. The combined force of these influences converted Gloucester into a community indistinguishable from any other New England town where consciously utopian and corporatist commitments had shaped local life from the outset. When Gloucester began to develop commercially after 1690, it was not a raw, frontier settlement or a fishing camp with a floating population but a coherent community, most of whose members were natives. The bonds of a common past, a common set of institutions, and a common set of religious beliefs and values decisively influenced the way in which inhabitants responded to changes in the basic structure of local economic life that started at the end of the seventeenth century.

2

Commerce and
Community

GLOUCESTER was one of the several coastal and river
ports in New England that outgrew their subsistence-oriented
economies and developed commercially during the first half
of the eighteenth century. With populations that ranged
between only four to eight thousand by the 1770s, these towns
were not as large as the major provincial cities, and the total
volume of their trade was smaller and less diverse. Still, the
emergence of these secondary ports sustained the vitality of
New England's economy over the later colonial period as
Boston, the old center of its trade, suffered eclipse by New
York and Philadelphia. While the export of agricultural surpluses to the Caribbean dominated the trade of the southern
New England towns of Hartford, Middletown, New Haven,
New London, and Norwich in Connecticut, and Providence
and Newport in Rhode Island, the traffic in fish, timber, masts,
and ships to Europe and the West Indies fostered the growth
of northern New England ports like Newbury, Portsmouth,
Falmouth, and Gloucester.[1]

[1] Jacob Price, "Economic Function and the Growth of American Port Towns
in the Eighteenth Century," *Perspectives in American History*, 8 (1974),
140–151; Bruce C. Daniels, *The Connecticut Town: Growth and Development, 1635–1790*, (Middletown, Ct., 1979), 140–70; Bushman, *From
Puritan to Yankee*, 107–121; David VanDeventer, *The Emergence of Provincial New Hampshire, 1623–1741* (Baltimore, 1976), 85, passim; Clark,

The conversion from farming for family needs to the production for export wrought pronounced changes in population, economy, and social structure within these towns, transformations that Gloucester's development exemplifies. After 1690 Gloucester grew from a small backwater of about four hundred people to a large, prospering seaport supporting a population that approached three thousand by the middle of the eighteenth century.[2] As the growth of an intensive fishery and an extensive trade in its produce to distant markets supplanted the old, self-sufficient economy, private ownership and free enterprise displaced former arrangements based on collectivism and restrictionism. A more complex, differentiated economy evolved as men devoted more of their energies to fishing, trading, or manufacturing than to farming and as an increasing number of townspeople incurred debts to expand their businesses or to establish new ones. Finally, the thriving local trade concentrated wealth in the hands of an upper class of successful merchants and entrepreneurs. Although the precise timing, pace, and scale of these changes varied slightly from one town to another, most of New England's other secondary ports developed along essentially similar lines.

Can it be inferred from these shifts in patterns of demographic and economic development that other transformations were also taking place in Gloucester, changes in the

Eastern Frontier, 76–77, 90–119; and David Klingaman, "The Coastwise Trade of Colonial Massachusetts," *EIHC,* 108 (1972), 217–34.

[2] Babson estimates local population at 700 in 1704 and at 2745 in 1755. The 1765 census figure for Gloucester's population is 3772. (*History,* 237 and 349; and Evarts B. Greene and Virginia D. Harrington, *American Population Before the Federal Census of 1790* (New York, 1932), 21–25.) Babson's derivation of total population from number of households (or "families") is based upon a multiplier of 5, the conversion figure favored by more recent historians who have done demographic studies of eighteenth-century Essex County towns. (Jedrey, *World of John Cleaveland,* 193n and 194; and Philip Greven, *Four Generations: Population, Land, and the Family in Colonial Andover, Massachusetts* (Ithaca, New York, 1970), 104n.) Edward Cook, however, argues for using a multiplier of 4.5, while Greene and Harrington use a conversion figure of 4. (*Fathers of the Towns: Leadership and Community Structure in Eighteenth-Century New England* (Baltimore, 1976), 193.) Gloucester's tax list of 1693 with 85 ratepayers suggests a total population of between 383 and 420, based upon a multiplier of 4.5 or 5 respectively.

character of social relationships, values, and outlook? Did investment in various kinds of non-agrarian enterprise mark the emergence of a milieu dominated by risk-taking and the ruthless pursuit of profit and private advantage? Did greater social and economic diversity create tensions and divisions that undermined the old sense of corporate solidarity and local loyalty? The assumption that large-scale structural shifts in economic life produced such changes in society and culture has informed most studies of early seaports. But the history of provincial Gloucester presents a very different view of the relationship between commercial development and communal life. The town's experience suggests that the impact of the growth of trade upon society varied greatly from one place to another, according to the material and cultural circumstances attending a town's entry into the wider market economy.

The cause of Gloucester's commercial development was one common to other New England communities that experienced a similar transition from subsistence farming to trade during the eighteenth century: a finite supply of mediocre land could not support an increasing population. By the end of the seventeenth century, almost all of Gloucester's arable acreage was already under cultivation.[3] But besides the limitations imposed by the lack of good land, one other circumstance extrinsic to local conditions played a decisive role in reshaping the contours of material life in Gloucester: the military situation on the northern New England frontier and in the north Atlantic. In 1689, two important developments occurred. In Maine, the Eastern Indians renewed their attacks upon English frontier settlements, while in Europe a conflict, called King William's War in the colonies, broke out between England and France. After a brief break in the fighting between 1697 and 1702, hostilities resumed with both the Maine tribes and the Canadian French, the latter conflict coming to be known as Queen Anne's War. This situation necessitated the

[3] Babson, *History,* 184. One index of the increasing shortage of cultivable land is the town's changing practice with respect to the distribution of common rights. In 1700, the town meeting decided that newcomers buying houselots in town were no longer automatically entitled to a common right, and the market value of these rights increased steadily over the early eighteenth century. (*History,* 233,234; GTR, II, 79.)

intermittent mobilization of New England men through 1711. The Peace of Utrecht in 1713 formally concluded the war with the French, while the Indian threat to the frontier also subsided after the first decade of the eighteenth century. The sporadic raids that recurred briefly during the 1720s ended with a treaty between Massachusetts and the Maine Indians in 1725.[4]

These two decades of military crisis had important consequences for Gloucester's demographic and economic development. Natural increase accounted for most of Gloucester's population growth between 1690 and 1750, and native-born men and women predominated in the town. But immigration into Gloucester also picked up sharply during this period. In the forty years after 1690, about thirty new families came to Gloucester each decade, more than double the number for the years between 1660 and 1690. The 1730s witnessed even more intense in-migration, with nearly eighty new families entering town.[5] Men moved to Gloucester for many reasons, but military conditions probably provided the initial impetus for much of this movement. While some of the new settlers coming to Cape Ann during the late seventeenth and early eighteenth centuries were refugees fleeing the Maine frontier or men who migrated from overcrowded Ipswich, most came from the maritime communities of southern Essex County: Salem, Beverly, and Marblehead.[6]

[4] Leach, *Arms for Empire*, 88–151; Gerald S. Graham, *Empire of the North Atlantic: The Maritime Struggle for North America* (Toronto, 1950), 58–102; Waters, *Ipswich*, I, 301–9; II, 32–40; and MacFarland, *A History of the New England Fisheries*, 72–79. Although the peace ending Queen Anne's War was not formally declared until 1713, the fighting in North America ended in the summer of 1711 after a disastrous expedition against French Quebec.

[5] This estimate of in-migration per decade is based upon lists of arrivals to town between 1700 and 1750 compiled by Babson. (*History,* 208–9, 236–37, 259–61, and 298.) I estimated the decade of the arrivals' entry by comparing the appearance of surnames in town and church records against these lists.

[6] Because the same surname often appears in more than one town, it is difficult to trace the point of origin of many new arrivals, but I was able with some certainty to assign towns of origin to forty-six of the eighty-five immigrants to Gloucester between 1694 and 1720. Nineteen of the forty-six came from the Essex coastal communities of Salem, Marblehead, Beverly, Lynn, and Newbury; thirteen came from Ipswich and five from Maine

Many of these newcomers may have first glimpsed Gloucester's possibilities while enlisted or impressed into the service
of King William and Queen Anne or while serving in local
militia units dispatched north to secure the frontier. The large
expeditions organized against the French strongholds of
Quebec and Port Royal and the smaller campaigns against
Indian tribes broke men out of the isolation of their home
towns and brought them north, often through strategically
situated Cape Ann. Gloucester was still not the most militar-
ily secure spot on the New England coast, and during the
1690s fears of Indian attack or an invasion of Cape Ann by
French privateers mounted. But by the early eighteenth century, these anxieties had subsided, as the French threat
diminished and Indians confined their depredations to the
most remote reaches of English settlement.[7] With its safety
from enemy incursions more certain, Gloucester's attraction
to new arrivals increased.

Like the Indian wars of 1675–77, these later disruptions
on the frontier also contributed to population increase by
restricting the mobility of settled inhabitants. The vulnerability of Maine communities, the natural places for Gloucester's young men to migrate, made the alternative of moving
out of town unappealing. Even after the peace with the Eastern Indians in 1725 made Maine and New Hampshire more
secure, only a handful of Gloucester families overcame their
reluctance to resettle and moved north. Between 1727 and
1728, some twenty-five Gloucester men moved to Falmouth

towns. Among the remaining nine, four came from the coastal towns of
southern Plymouth County, three came from inland Essex towns, one from
Boston and one from the Isle of Jersey. To trace towns of origin, I relied
upon the index to the Essex County Probate Files to 1800 and several local
histories, including, Sidney Perley, *The History of Salem,* 3 vols. (Salem,
1924–1926), Alonzo Lewis and J. R. Newhall, *History of Lynn, Including
Lynnfield, Saugus, Swampscott, and Nahant,* 2 vols. (Boston, 1865); Joshua
Coffin, *A Sketch of the History of Newbury, Newburyport, and West New-
bury, from 1635 to 1845* (Boston, 1845); and Waters' history of Ipswich.
On migration from Ipswich to Gloucester, see also Jedrey, *The World of
John Cleaveland,* 61.

[7] On the fears of invasion in coastal towns, see Waters, *Ipswich,* I, 304 and
308; II, 34. For the relationship between mobilization and migration in
Dedham during King George's War, see Edward Cook, "Social Behavior
and Changing Values in Dedham," *WMQ,* 3rd ser., 27 (1970), 572.

(later Portland), a settlement from which some of their families had earlier fled. In 1739, the General Court granted another Maine township to Gloucester, but the threat of warfare kept New Gloucester (later Windham) small, and with the actual renewal of hostilities in 1744, the community broke up entirely and was resettled only after the peace of 1763.[8]

By encouraging the increase of Gloucester's population, the wars against the French and Indians exerted an indirect influence upon local economic development. Demographic growth created the potential for greater productivity while simultaneously, by putting pressure upon available land, it enhanced the attractions of maritime employments. The military situation also influenced local economic development directly by heightening demand, especially in Boston, for ships, building material, and fuel, commodities that Gloucester could now supply better than the embattled Maine frontier. Entry into the timber trade provided Gloucester inhabitants with their first regular involvement in a wider market. Timber resources opened up to individual development by a new division of the thickly forested common land among town proprietors in 1708 sustained the traffic. In 1711, for example, one local sawmill owner exported over five hundred cords of wood to the capital within the space of a few weeks. The growth of the timber economy also spurred the local shipbuilding industry. Throughout the 1690s and the first decade of the eighteenth century, a growing number of requests for masts and other building material from the common lands took up more and more time in selectmen's meetings.[9]

Even as the timber trade introduced the town to a larger economic network and encouraged maritime development,

[8] Babson, *History*, 296–98; 303–6.

[9] For commercial contacts with Boston in the timber trade, see GTR, II, 52, 137; MacFarland, *History of the New England Fisheries*, 81; Babson, *History*, 6, 380. For the growing number of requests for timber from the common for shipbuilding, see "Gloucester Selectmen's Records, 1699–1721," MS in the Office of the Town Clerk, City Hall, Gloucester, Mass., especially for the years between 1702 and 1711. On the town's small but steadily growing shipbuilding industry, see Bernard and Lotte Bailyn, *Massachusetts Shipping, 1697–1714: A Statistical Study* (Cambridge, Mass., 1959), 51 and 102–3.

the vestiges of earlier economic arrangements remained. Inhabitants abandoned restrictionism and the common ownership of land slowly, over a period of thirty years. Until the 1720s, town orders enacted a century earlier for controlling private access to the common timber resources remained in force, accompanied by stringent new provisions. The town continued to license millers, to set prices for sawing logs into boards, to stipulate the quantities of wood that could be sold out of town, and to regulate the amount and kind of wood that could be cut and gathered on the commons, where, when, and by whom. And in 1702 the town meeting stiffened these restrictions, forbidding the nonlocal sale of any shipbuilding material and requiring any inhabitant building a vessel with wood from the commons to post a bond ensuring that the ship would not be sold out of town for six years. The town also levied fines on anyone exceeding their quota of cordwood and empowered the treasurer to prosecute any violators of the timber laws.[10] Inhabitants appear to have abided by these regulations, while vigilant selectmen brought stray transgressors into line.[11] What finally obviated the need for restrictions were two final divisions of the common land, but the conversion to private ownership was not precipitate. After the initial division of 1688, the town meeting waited twenty years before voting a second division in 1708. They agreed to the third and last division in 1719, but did not actually set off the lots until two years later.[12]

The benefits of engaging in the timber traffic lasted only

[10] During the late seventeenth and early eighteenth centuries, discussions of laws and grants relating to timber dominated the business of nearly every town and selectmen's meeting. For the regulations of 1702, see GTR, II, 98–99; for regulations aimed particularly at promoting the use of wood for the benefit of inhabitants and protecting the forests from exploitation by nonlocals, see GTR, II, 45, 55, 56, 77–78, 101, 109, 123, and 136.

[11] In 1707, for example, the selectmen apprehended Ebenezer Elwell for illegally cutting wood and selling it out of town, but they suspended his fine "having taken into consideration . . . his being taken captive by the French and being with them a considerable time which was much to his damage." ("Gloucester Selectmen's Records, 1699–1721," 45.)

[12] GTR, II, 160, 166, 168; after 1713, the commoners met as a distinct body and made the subsequent divisions, the last in 1725. (See "Gloucester Proprietors' Records," in Office of the Town Clerk, City Hall, Gloucester, Mass.) For Babson's account see *History*, 233–34.

a few years, for Gloucester's woodlands were far less extensive than those of Newbury or the towns of New Hampshire and Maine, areas that became more reliable sources of supply in the 1720s as their military security increased.[13] But by establishing closer commercial connections with Boston, by stimulating the growth of local shipbuilding, by encouraging the conversion from joint to private land ownership, and by eliminating public constraints on private enterprise, the timber economy wrought fundamental changes in the structure of Gloucester's economic life. These changes prepared the town to make the most of another, even greater economic opportunity afforded to New Englanders by the British advantage at the end of Queen Anne's War.

The same British military success that ultimately reduced Gloucester's share of the timber trade by stabilizing the eastern frontier also secured the North Atlantic fishery for New England. Under the terms of the Peace of Utrecht in 1713, Britain's territorial gains and navigational privileges assured New Englanders' unmolested access to fishing grounds formerly dominated by the French and infested by enemy warships and privateers.[14] By eliminating the need for private entrepreneurs or individual towns to provide protection for their fishing fleets, the new British strength in the north Atlantic reduced both the costs and risks of the fishing industry that had previously discouraged the participation of smaller towns. At the same time, the quelling of privateering and piracy in the Caribbean and along Iberian trade routes enhanced the possibilities of trade to the West Indies, Spain, and Portugal. Population growth throughout the eighteenth century stimulated demand in all of these markets, as well as pushing up prices for fish.[15] Finally, towns like Gloucester

---

[13] Clark, *Eastern Frontier,* 97–101, 111–17; VanDeventer, *Emergence of Provincial New Hampshire,* 95–106, 159–78.

[14] The Peace of Utrecht gave England all of Nova Scotia, Newfoundland and its adjacent islands, and the Hudson Bay, and excluded the French from fishing on the Nova Scotia coast or within thirty leagues of it. The French retained Cape Breton Island and all of the islands in the Gulf of St. Lawrence, as well as the right to fish at Newfoundland. (MacFarland, *A History of the New England Fisheries,* 79–80.)

[15] Harold A. Innis, *The Codfisheries* (New Haven, 1940), 162–66. See also, Richard Pares, *Yankees and Creoles: The Trade Between North America*

with only limited capital resources benefited not only from the increased security but also the greater availability of money in the period after the cessation of hostilities. To replace the wartime emissions of currency being retired by taxation, the province of Massachusetts in 1721 and again in 1728 proportioned public bills of credit among the towns, which in turn lent sums to individual borrowers.[16]

The aegis of British superiority in the north Atlantic, the spur of rising demand, the encouragement of province loans, the growth of a larger and more skilled labor force, and the fleet of vessels developed from the timber traffic fostered the expansion of Gloucester's fishing industry. After the end of Queen Anne's War, the local fishery enjoyed uninterrupted expansion until the resumption of war in 1739. A growing number of vessels from the town ranged over a widening stretch of ocean. By 1716 Gloucester fishermen were working the waters off Cape Sable; in the 1720s several vessels regularly visited the Grand Banks; by 1741, the number had risen to seventy.[17] As the local fishery increased the size and

and the West Indies Before the American Revolution (Cambridge, Mass., 1956); and James G. Lydon, "The Massachusetts Fish Trade with Iberia, 1700–1773," *New England Quarterly,* 54 (1981), 547–50.

[16] An emission in 1716 was loaned to individuals through the counties of Massachusetts; for Gloucester borrowers, see Essex Deeds, vol. 34, Registry of Deeds, Essex County Courthouse, Salem, Mass. On the two emissions made directly to the towns, see GTR, II, 221 and 250. For a full discussion of currency and the public bills of credit, see Andrew M. Davis, *Currency and Banking in the Province of Massachusetts* (1900, repr. New York, 1970), I, 88–202.

[17] In the most recent study of the industry in colonial Essex County, Daniel Vickers estimates that Gloucester's fishery grew more dramatically over the later provincial period than that of either Marblehead or Salem, with the greatest gains taking place between 1720 and 1740, and 1760 and 1775. The expansion of productivity in the fishing industry throughout New England after 1675 was due in part to the conversion from an inshore shallop fishery to a bank fishery employing larger vessels such as ketches and schooners. While the fishery for most of the seventeenth century had been restricted to the northern New England shoreline and the Gulf of Maine, the use of larger boats during the later colonial period enabled fishermen to follow the cod from one ground to another and to stay at sea for longer periods, anywhere from ten days to a month at a time. (Vickers, "Maritime Labor in Colonial Massachusetts: A Case Study of the Essex County Cod Fishery and the Whaling Industry of Nantucket, 1630–1775" (Ph.D. diss., Princeton University, 1981), 195–97; and Douglas R. McManis, *Colonial*

scope of its operations, the town's share of shipping activity
to the markets for cod in the Caribbean, Spain, and Portugal
expanded as well. In 1717, only three Gloucester vessels of
small tunnage cleared the port of Salem-Marblehead, two
bound for the West Indies, one for Europe. Boston fish
exporters controlled the marketing of most of the produce
of Gloucester's infant fishery at this period, and the three
voyages made by locally owned vessels probably represented
the pooling of resources by several village entrepreneurs and
many smaller investors. After these beginnings, Gloucester's
independent trade increased dramatically during the subsequent decades. By the 1750s, the Salem-Marblehead cus-
tomhouse cleared annually about thirty of Gloucester's trading
vessels.[18] The average tunnage of these craft was still relatively small, and the extent of the town's involvement in the
direct trade to southern Europe remained limited. But the
growth of local shipping to the Caribbean was considerable,
and Gloucester's merchants had acquired the capital, commercial knowledge, and skilled craftsmen to pack, transport,
and market their fish without going through Boston. Instead
of relying upon the capital for these services, Gloucester was
benefiting from the relative decline of Boston as a center of
the codfishery over the middle decades of the eighteenth century. As early as the 1720s and 1730s, a combination of high
prices for foodstuffs, a glutted labor market, and two serious
smallpox epidemics began to drive fishermen and mariners
out of Boston to places like Gloucester and Marblehead.
Lower operating costs for other maritime industries like
shipbuilding also attracted artisans from the capital to these

New England: A Historical Geography (New York, 1975), 103–5.) On the
growth of Gloucester's fishery, see also, Innis, *The Codfisheries,* 160; and
MacFarland, *History of the New England Fisheries,* 85, 88, and 96. Other
secondary discussions of the colonial fishing industry that are helpful include
Andrew Hill Clark, *Acadia: The Geography of Early Nova Scotia to 1760*
(Madison, 1968), especially 227–29 and 303–23; and Lorenzo Sabine,
Report on the Principal Fisheries of the American Seas (Washington, D.C.,
1853).

[18] *Abstracts of English Shipping Records Relating to Massachusetts Ports.*
Copied from Original Records in the Public Records Office, London, 7 vols.
(Essex Institute, 1932), vol. II, part 1; and vol. III. See also Chapter X, note
3 below, and Bailyn and Bailyn, *Massachusetts Shipping,* 90–91 and 94–
97.

secondary ports. While the populations of these smaller towns expanded throughout the provincial period, Boston's stagnated; while the coastal trade of Massachusetts as a whole increased during the eighteenth century, the capital's fishery failed and its share of the province's shipping and shipbuilding activity declined. Although Boston merchants occasionally had an interest in shipments of fish from Gloucester, after mid-century local townsmen had gained control over all phases of the industry and trade.[19]

The history of the Parsons family illustrates the dramatic change in the local economy produced by the period of peace after the first decade of the eighteenth century. The family's first representative, Jeffrey Parsons, Sr., a farmer and carpenter, served frequently as selectman and at his death in 1689 left a good estate by local standards, consisting mainly of land and livestock but including two canoes for fishing. Several years later, his four sons James, Jeffrey Jr., John, and Nathaniel expanded family involvement in the fishery: they built a stage on one of the rocky beachheads of the Eastern Point and commissioned two local shipwrights to build several fishing vessels. By the time of John Parsons's death in 1714, the brothers owned three vessels, "flake room" on the shore for drying fish, and a sawmill, but commercial employments were not yet central to family economic activities. The most valuable items in John's inventory, as in his father's, were still farm land and animals. The fishing vessels in which he held a share were not much larger or worth more than Jeffrey Sr.'s canoes had been, and the outstanding debt of the estate was small and all of it due to local men. But when a second Parsons brother, Deacon Nathaniel, died in 1722, his inventory reflected a qualitative shift in family economic activity within less than a decade. Nathaniel himself owned three schooners and with his remaining brothers another two sloops, along with harbor property that now included a wharf, warehouse, and a separate building for housing fish; the gross earnings of the last voyage that

[19]Lydon, "The Massachusetts Fish Trade with Iberia, 1700–1775," *New England Quarterly*, 54 (1981), 556–61; Price, "Economic Function and the Growth of American Port Towns in the Eighteenth Century," *PAH*, 8: 143–49; Nash, *Urban Crucible*, 103–4 and 182–97; and Petition of the Town of Boston, February 20, 1756, MA: 55–66.

Nathaniel outfitted amounted to almost two hundred pounds sterling. In addition, he had developed a local retail trade in provisions for fishing voyages and maintained book accounts with large Boston fish exporters like James Bowdoin, who kept him supplied with salt, tobacco, rum, cloth, and other finished goods in return for consignments of cod. Even with his success in the fishery, Nathaniel had not entirely abandoned agrarian pursuits, and the produce of his farm could still supply family needs if maritime pursuits met with reversals. His investments in agriculture notwithstanding, Nathaniel had become mainly a shoreman, the operator of a large fishing business: waterfront property, a stock of shop goods, fishing vessels, and the returns of the fishing voyages together comprised the largest part of his inventoried assets. Valued at almost four hundred pounds sterling, the deacon's estate at his death made Nathaniel Parsons one of Gloucester's most substantial residents; but it was his only surviving son and sole male heir, William, who amassed the family's fortune between 1722 and 1755. William maintained and improved his father's interest in fishing, farming, and the retail trade but added to those activities a large coastwise commerce in fish to the Caribbean. In 1752, his vessels made four voyages to Virginia and the West Indies; three years later, William Parsons, "merchant," died with a net worth of over two thousand pounds sterling.[20]

The evolution of economic activity within the Parsons family encapsulates the timing and character of commercial development in Gloucester as a whole over the later colonial period. After the turn of the century, the town passed from the self-contained arrangements of the early settlers through an intermediate stage of producing timber. It was only following the first Anglo-French wars that the community embarked upon a full-fledged involvement in the commercial fishery and coastwise trade. The period of peace after 1713, however, promoted impressive commercial progress. By the middle of the eighteenth century, only Marblehead's fishing industry and trade surpassed Gloucester's in importance.

[20] Essex Probate Files, #20609, 20616, 20644, 20670. (Cited hereafter as EPF.)

The energies of men like the Parsonses were not incidental to the transformation of Gloucester from a farming village to a thriving seaport. But the interest of these early entrepreneurs in developing the fishery did not derive from a "dynamic" approach to "manipulating the natural setting" in order to satisfy "a rising set of aspirations."[21] Although local merchants and shoremen looked for a profit from their ventures, desires for personal gain and social mobility did not dominate their economic strategies. The Parsons brothers and their neighbors were living in a community like many others in New England where population was exceeding the extent and productive capacity of arable acreage. There was no place else to go, and even if there had been, it would have made little difference because the members of the Parsons family wanted to remain near the homestead of Jeffrey Sr., to live a life like his, and to approximate his respected position in local society. All that distinguished the Parsons brothers and their neighbors from the inhabitants of New England's interior farming towns was that Gloucester families had the option of subsisting from the sea once their land ran out and wore out. Necessity, not a restless passion for individual aggrandizement, turned townspeople toward industry and trade.

And while Parsonses and many others in Gloucester successfully adapted to maritime pursuits, their experiences gave them few illusions of having "conquered" their environment. Instead, at every turn the limitations and contingencies of the natural world continued to shape existence and awareness. It was the lack of cultivable acreage that had first dictated the conversion to maritime employments, and this seafaring livelihood was, as much as farming, subject to dislocation by natural forces. The consciousness of the control exerted by nature recurs as a constant theme in the diary entries of Eliezur Parsons. This third generation representative of the family in town chronicled the vicissitudes shaping local life: the violent storms and high tides that damaged vessels, marsh fences, and warehouses in Gloucester harbor in 1723 and again in 1727; the gale off Cape Sable that

[21] Richard D. Brown, "Modernization and the Modern Personality in Early America, 1600–1865," *Journal of Interdisciplinary History*, 2 (1972), 210.

claimed the lives of several fishermen from town; the hail-storm in the summer of 1728 and the severe winter of 1740 that spoiled crops and killed livestock; the series of earth-quakes that shook the entire coast between 1727 and 1730, swelling religious conversions. Eliezur Parsons was curious about these occurrences, and he had a penchant for precise observation, noting carefully the exact date and duration of the earthquakes' tremors and the value of salt consumed when warehouses were flooded with a tide "one foot higher than has been known in this age." But out of his interest in recording, calculating, and measuring the effects of natural forces emerges no confidence in his ability to dominate this environment.[22] The Parsonses and their neighbors responded to the necessities imposed and to the options created by the combined effects of geography, population growth, and mil-itary conditions in the north Atlantic. These circumstances turned Gloucester toward maritime and commercial employments as the best alternative forms of livelihood for an increasing number of inhabitants who could no longer support themselves solely through agriculture.

While the conversion to a maritime economy effected no major changes in assumptions about man's ability to manip-ulate the natural and social world, the process of commer-cialization did foster some significant shifts in the structure of local society. Wealth became more unequally distributed in town, more concentrated in the hands of merchants, shoremen, and the most successful artisans. While the rich-est decile of men in town between 1690 and 1715 had held about a third of the total wealth, between 1716 and 1735 their share jumped to over forty percent. Over the same period, the proportion of wealth held by the bottom sixty percent of

[22] "Diary of James Parsons, Gloucester," MS, Essex Institute, 116. The MS contains diary entries for James, Eliezur, and Moses Parsons. Eliezur Par-sons's interest in natural disasters could have grown out of his religious concerns rather than any scientific curiosity since many contemporary the-ologians and ministers, including the Reverend John White, related the beginning of the millennium to the occurrence of these catastrophes, espe-cially earthquakes. Both White and Cotton Mather contended that earth-quakes of increasing frequency and severity would precede the Second Coming of Jesus Christ. See John White, *New England's Lamentations* (Boston, 1734), 12; and Robert Middlekauff, *The Mathers: Three Generations of Puritan Intellectuals, 1596–1728* (New York, 1971), 340.

inhabitants shrank from just over a quarter to about seventeen percent. After the fishing industry took off in town, the rich became considerably richer too, and the range in estate value wider. In the last decade of the seventeenth century and the first decade of the eighteenth, the town's most affluent citizens were worth about 350 to 450 pounds sterling; in the 1720s and 1730s, estates within the top decile ranged from almost 600 to 1,000 pounds sterling. By mid-century, the tendency toward inequality had become even more pronounced, with the bottom sixty percent of society owning only twelve percent of the town's total wealth, the top decile, fifty-seven percent, and several merchants possessing assets in excess of three thousand pounds sterling. While the local social structure grew more unequal, a more differentiated occupational structure also evolved. Men with maritime or commercial occupations displaced farmers as the dominant group in the adult, male population, and the town slowly acquired a more diverse array of craftsmen.[23]

But despite the growth of relative inequality and occupational diversity, relations among the various orders of society in provincial Gloucester still bore the stamp of the latter seventeenth century. Underlying this basic continuity were the benefits that trade brought to ordinary townspeople. While commercial development made a few families richer, it also offered opportunity and economic security to most of the community's adult members, to the rising generation, and to a number of newcomers who immigrated to town every year for precisely that reason. Although in relative terms wealth did become more unequally distributed in the half-century after 1690, in absolute terms the prosperity produced by commerce improved the position of all of Gloucester's

[23] For changes in the distribution and range of wealth in Gloucester, see appendix, Tables I and II. The increasing importance of maritime and commercial pursuits is suggested by probate records between 1716 and 1745 identifying the occupation of the decedent: of sixty-two, only fourteen were identified as farmers, compared with fifteen as merchants or shoremen, thirteen artisans, eleven mariners, five fishermen, and two sawmill owners. (Essex Probate Files, Registry of Probate, Essex County Courthouse, Salem, Mass.) For a description of similar changes in wealth stratification and occupational structure in the neighboring North Shore port of Beverly, see Douglas Lamar Jones, *Village and Seaport: Migration and Society in Eighteenth Century Massachusetts* (Hanover, N.H., 1981), 13–15.

inhabitants. Median estate value rose steadily from eighty-one pounds sterling in the period between 1690–1715 to ninety-five pounds between 1716–1735 and had climbed to over one hundred pounds sterling by the middle of the eighteenth century.[24] In part the growth of median estate size and the continuing economic strength of Gloucester's "middling classes" was due to the investment opportunities offered by the growing fishery. Included in the administration of Deacon Nathaniel Parsons's estate is a list of people with an interest in his final fishing voyage, twenty-five names in all, most of them local residents venturing only a few pounds. Capital resources in town were not sufficiently concentrated to allow a handful of men to shoulder all of the risks and to monopolize all of the rewards of the industry.[25] But even more important to the economic security of the majority of ordinary townspeople were the employment opportunities created by the growth of the commercial and maritime sectors of the economy, a development that saved Gloucester from the economic stagnation overtaking inland New England villages during the eighteenth century. While men in Dedham, Andover, Concord, and Northampton faced the bleak choice between eking out a living on plots of diminishing size and fertility or leaving friends and family and emigrating to an uncertain future on the frontier, the growth of the fishery and the maritime trades offered a livelihood at home to Gloucester's inhabitants.[26] The demand for labor in town

[24] See appendix, Table I.

[25] EPF, #20644. James Henretta makes a similar point about late seventeenth-century Boston, where one-third of all adult males owned part of a vessel. According to Henretta, "The scarcity of capital in a relatively underdeveloped economic system . . . required that the savings of all members of society be tapped in the interest of economic expansion. . . . This widespread ownership of mercantile wealth resulted in the creation of a distinct economic 'middle class'. . . ." ("Economic Development and Social Structure in Colonial Boston," *WMQ*, 3rd ser., 22 (1965), 87–88.)

[26] Douglas Jones has argued that colonial seaports were able to accommodate population growth not only because of the greater job opportunities that they offered but also because of the higher mortality rates engendered by the maritime economy. (*Village and Seaport*, 3, 4, 15, 20–21, and 46.) On the decline of opportunity in agrarian towns, see especially Kenneth Lockridge, "Land, Population, and the Evolution of New England Society, 1630–1790," *Past and Present*, 39 (1968), 62–80.

also precluded the development of a large class of dependent poor: even by the mid-eighteenth century, Gloucester still provided for its handful of widows and disabled war veterans through a small budget covering the costs of out-relief, or cared for the needy in private homes.[27]

Because commerce improved the conditions of life for ordinary people, Gloucester escaped the tensions emerging among classes in larger urban centers like Boston or even a secondary port of roughly comparable size like Marblehead, where the growth of trade brought no overall increase in median estate value. Absent from Gloucester's social life were those symptoms of strain apparent in other eighteenth-century Essex ports. The underground networks for counterfeiting money and for pilfering and concealing stolen goods of masters, which sprang up sporadically within the servant and poor laboring communities of Salem and Marblehead, never appeared in Gloucester, where for sixty years after 1690 no resident was charged with theft and only two with assault.[28] Aside from the stable population of young people regularly accused of fornication, a tiny group of town "deviants" accounted for almost all of Gloucester's criminal activity during the first half of the eighteenth century.[29] The

[27] Gloucester built a "workhouse" in 1719, but in 1732 the building was leased for lack of occupants. (GTR, II, 211, 246.) Poor relief was handled on a case by case basis by the selectmen, who doubled as overseers of the poor throughout the first half of the eighteenth century. For examples, see GTR, II, 246 and 255; and Babson, *History,* 322 and 350.

[28] For Gloucester's two cases of assault, see Minutebooks of the Supreme Court of Judicature, Office of the Clerk of the Supreme Judicial Court for Suffolk County, Suffolk County Courthouse, Boston, Massachusetts, October 28, 1735 and July 10, 1753. (Cited hereafter as MSCJ.) For theft rings in Salem and Marblehead, see Minutebooks of the General Sessions of the Peace, September 26, 1704, July 8, 1710, and December, 1726, Office of the County Clerk, Superior Courthouse, Salem, Massachusetts. (Cited hereafter as MGSP.) See also MSCJ, November 26, 1700. On counterfeiting rings, see MSCJ, November 8, 1715, October 31, 1721, May 16, 1727, November 16, 1742, and October 16, 1753. See Suffolk Court File #47734 for a full description of the period's most extensive counterfeiting operation.

[29] Aside from the two assault cases and fifty-five cases of fornication, crime in Gloucester between 1696 and 1755 consisted of nine cases of absence from public worship, two of Sabbath violation, three of illegal retailing of liquor, and one each involving drunkenness, creating a public nuisance,

same few men turned up at the quarterly sessions of the peace, time and again, charged with the same petty offenses. Jethro Wheeler, for example, a mariner who shifted his residence back and forth between a lonely spot on Cape Ann and neighboring Rowley, appeared before the gentleman-justices for the first time in 1701, charged with illegally "occupying the trade of a tanner." In 1708, he stood accused of falsifying a seal on a writ and, five years later, of selling drink without a license. Another habitual offender was Richard Tarr, a farmer and occasional fisherman who also lived in the remotest reaches of the Cape and made intermittent sojourns to Marblehead. Tarr was prosecuted first for drunkenness and subsequently for defaulting on his debts and for absence from public worship.[30] Both Wheeler and Tarr were men whose mobility and distant residences reduced the efficacy of informal community pressures in controlling their behavior while heightening the level of public concern over their lapses. But the small number of local "deviants" and their relatively innocuous offenses underscore the ability of families and churches to regulate the behavior of most inhabitants without resorting to legal sanctions.

Additional evidence—and an underlying cause—of Gloucester's freedom from serious social friction was the remarkably low level of intratown civil litigation. As Gloucester's reliance upon fishing and commerce increased, its inhabitants did become involved in a larger total number of civil suits, almost all actions for debt. This rise in litigation at a rate outrunning population growth occurred throughout Massachusetts over the eighteenth century as a more interdependent, market-oriented economy evolved. But in Gloucester, as in most other New England communities,

entertaining strangers without notifying the selectmen, freeing a prisoner from the constable, and failing to support an illegitimate child. (Sources: MGSP and MSCJ.)

[30] MGSP, March 28, 1699, September 30, 1701, March 30, 1708, June 29, 1724. Stephanie Wolf has found the same general pattern characterizing criminal prosecutions in eighteenth-century Germantown, Pennsylvania. Here too the courts were used "as a final agent of social discipline" to handle (or harass) unpopular members of the community. (*Urban Village: Population, Community, and Family Structure in Germantown, Pennsylvania, 1683–1800* (Princeton, N.J., 1976), 184.)

it was the increase in intertown suits, actions involving parties from two different towns, that swelled the volume of debt litigation during the provincial period. To underwrite the enterprises of the new merchants, shoremen, and artisans of Cape Ann required capital, but the local economy during the early decades of the eighteenth century had not yet generated enough wealth to supply the necessary resources. Townsmen thus turned to increased borrowing and buying on credit from major fish exporters in Boston and from larger entrepreneurs in Salem and Marblehead. They also mortgaged their real property to the province government in return for public bills of credit. The result was a rise in the number of prosecutions for debt involving Gloucester residents and people from outside of town, usually suits that pitted nonlocal creditors against Gloucester defendants.[31] The defaulters in these debt cases involving nonlocal plaintiffs were typically not poorer fishermen and laborers but some of Gloucester's most substantial residents, who put off meeting their obligations to or disputed the claims of creditors who were not their neighbors.[32] And just as Gloucester men did not scruple to postpone repaying "outsiders," their creditors were far less willing to extend trust or indulgence to their debtors on Cape Ann than to members of their own com-

[31] See appendix, Table III. The volume of criminal activity and debt litigation that appears in the county court's minutebooks and files represents only those disputes that reached the full court. Individual justices of the peace handled some petty civil disputes and breaches of the peace, but it is impossible to tell how many because so few of their records survive. Nonetheless, the data from county court records, especially if several towns are compared over time, are a good general index of the level of social disorder and tension over economic matters. For a discussion of eighteenth-century legal institutions in Massachusetts, see John M. Murrin, "Anglicizing an American Colony: The Transformation of Provincial Massachusetts" (Ph.D. diss., Yale University, 1966), 149–94; and "Review Essay," *History and Theory*, 11 (1972), 250–51.

[32] For example, among the Gloucester defendants in the fifteen suits for debt brought by nonlocals in the year 1729, only two were identified as "fishermen" and none as "laborers." Two of the town's major entrepreneurs, Nathaniel Coit and Samuel Steven, Sr., were among the remaining defendants, a group that included four farmers, four artisans, and three "coasters," a term that designated a skilled mariner and petty trader. (See Files of the Court of Common Pleas for 1729, Essex Superior Courthouse, basement, Salem, Mass. Cited hereafter as FCCP.)

munities. Unless some kinship connection was involved, New Englanders drew the line between "stranger" and "brother" at their own town borders, and this mental division was an important source of the rising incidence of intertown debt prosecutions in Massachusetts over this period.

On the other hand, the same "in-group economic morality" that allowed for less charitable and circumspect treatment of "outsiders" in business dealings encouraged the private settlement of economic disputes among members of the same community.[33] Although more Gloucester residents appeared in court as parties to intertown suits during the first half of the eighteenth century, the period witnessed no corresponding increase in the number of civil actions in which both plaintiff and defendant were fellow townsmen. In the fifty years after 1700, Gloucester's intratown litigation amounted to only a few suits annually; the sums at stake were small and the parties concerned often agreed out of court before cases ever came to trial. This low volume of debt litigation within town suggests an intense aversion to the legal resolution of local economic disputes.[34] Communal

[33] For a more detailed discussion of the concept of "in-group economic morality" see Max Weber, "Religious Rejections of the World and Their Directions," in *From Max Weber: Essays in Sociology,* eds. H. H. Gerth and C. Wright Mills (New York, 1946), 329.

[34] On intratown litigation, see appendix, Table III. Charles Grant found similar patterns in his study of debt cases in Kent, Connecticut, between 1752 and 1786. According to Grant, "the vast majority of debt transactions [between Kent inhabitants] were settled without recourse to the law," an amicability that he attributes to "a tolerant or casual spirit among creditors." Of the debts that did end up in the courts, only one-quarter pitted fellow townsmen against each other, and in all cases, a high percentage of those being sued were prominent men, not humble farmers. (*Democracy in the Frontier Town of Kent* (New York, 1961), 69–74.) Grant's view is similar to that of Michael Zuckerman, who has been sharply criticized for arguing that "the men of Massachusetts had an aversion to lawsuits" because recourse to courts was costly and impeded the pursuit of consensus. (*Peaceable Kingdoms,* 88–90.) But the accuracy of Zuckerman's view depends on the kind of litigation that one looks at. In every county for which the volume of civil litigation has been studied, intratown litigation was declining or holding constant over the eighteenth century, while intertown suits were increasing. Both developments point to the persistence of a traditional economic morality, a willingness to favor fellow townspeople coupled with a strong mistrust of outsiders. New Englanders were litigious or accommodating depending on with whom they were dealing. Marblehead, which

distaste for creditors who used the law to harass defaulting neighbors, combined with the lack of effective enforcement agencies, made Gloucester inhabitants reluctant to sue each other. Those who relied upon the law to collect their debts quickly discovered its limitations, as merchant Epes Sargent's suit to recover a small sum from fisherman John Weston illustrates. When Weston was unable to post security for his appearance in court, Sargent demanded his imprisonment, but the constable refused to take Weston to the nearest jail in Ipswich until the following day and advised Sargent either to "entertain" his debtor himself or to hire his own guards. Other Gloucester inhabitants shared the constable's uncooperative attitude and probably facilitated Weston's "escape" from his temporary prison in the local tavern that evening. The tone of depositions describing the episode suggests that public sentiment was against Sargent, and that in resorting to such harsh measures against a fellow townsman, and a poor one at that, he had violated the canons of in-group economic morality and customary restraint.[35]

Few of Gloucester's other traders and shoremen were willing to risk popular disapproval by pressing their claims against less fortunate neighbors, and even economic equals preferred extralegal resolutions of their differences to encounters in court. When two of Annisquam harbor's most successful entrepreneurs, miller Jacob Davis and tanner Isaac Eveleth, fell out over a business deal, they turned to the church to adjudicate their dispute. The discipline of church mem-

represents a partial exception to this pattern of declining intratown litigation, departed from the norm because so many residents were not well-established in town. (For criticisms of the Zuckerman thesis, see David G. Allen, "The Zuckerman Thesis and the Process of Legal Rationalization in Provincial Massachusetts," *WMQ*, 3rd ser., 29 (1972), 456–58; and Zuckerman's reply, 463. On levels of litigation, see Murrin, "Review Essay," *History and Theory*, 11: 250–52; and William E. Nelson, *Dispute and Conflict Resolution in Plymouth County, Massachusetts, 1725–1825* (Chapel Hill, 1981), especially 45–46. For a thoughtful exploration of the relationship between legal rationalization and social development, see Bruce Mann, "Rationality, Legal Change, and Community in Connecticut, 1690–1760," *Law and Society Review*, 14 (1980), 187–218.)

[35] Sargent v. Weston, FCCP, 1718. On the constabulary, see Zuckerman, *Peaceable Kingdoms*, 85–88.

bers was severe, suggesting the strength of their disapproval of such breaches of Christian charity by two covenanting members. They suspended Eveleth from communion and demanded of Davis, who had initiated the complaint, a public confession that "in the management of my Lawful Affairs I am apt to be betrayed into rash and indiscreet expressions."[36]

Not only were individual Gloucester inhabitants averse to suing each other, but the town itself also tried to avoid initiating any actions against residents. The town meeting applied to the county courts as a last resort, only after private persuasion and public pressure had failed to produce a townsman's compliance with orders to clear waterways, open highways, or remove obstructions creating nuisance or inconvenience. The town also took steps to prevent situations that might result in townspeople pressing claims and publicizing grievances against each other in open court. In 1708, the town meeting's division of a portion of the common land created concern that "a great deale of trouble . . . may be likely to arise to the towne . . . which may occasion great expense at law if care be not taken for the timely preventing of same." To head off such an eventuality, the names of all commoners and their rights were entered in the town book, and the division proceeded smoothly. Only a handful of more than one hundred commoners challenged any of the land divisions made by the town during the early eighteenth century.[37]

In provincial Gloucester, communal sentiment opposed the legal resolution of economic disputes and public sympathy resided with debtors because most townspeople of all classes were more likely to be borrowing rather than lending. As a community of new traders and entrepreneurs, the

---

[36] GFCR, fall, 1713

[37] "Gloucester Selectmen's Records, 1699–1721," 70. The resolution came in response to a disagreement at the town meeting between members of the committee charged with implementing the division, who disputed some of the claims to common rights, and the majority of voters, who supported a liberal policy in recognizing such claims. Despite the disagreement, I could find only seven suits contesting the divisions in the Minutebooks of the Superior Court, all between 1719 and 1727. (See also, GTR, II, 169–72.)

town generally supported cheap money, easy credit, and inflationist currency proposals like the Land Bank of 1740.[38] Yet despite the popularity of fiscal measures to promote economic expansion, the approach of townspeople to commercial development was basically conservative and cautious. Even the biggest men resisted the temptation to overextend themselves by undertaking large financial risks. The same prudence that prevented the rapid division and exploitation of the common woodlands kept Gloucester's largest merchants and shoremen from succumbing to the bankruptcies that blighted the businesses of their more venturesome counterparts in other ports. Among the top quartile of Gloucester's inventoried decedents for whom estate administrations are available, there was not a single insolvency and only one instance in which debts against an estate exceeded more than half of the value of its assets in the forty years after 1715.[39] No large fishing business in town suffered a collapse until the 1760s, when the recession following the Seven Years' War bankrupted the partnership of Timothy Rogers and William Stevens.[40]

Gloucester, along with scores of other secondary ports in provincial New England, experienced certain uniform structural changes that typically accompany the transition from

[38] See appendix, Table III, for the contrast between the number of intertown suits involving Gloucester defendants and those involving Gloucester plaintiffs. For a history of the Land Bank of 1740 and a list of subscribers, see Davis, *Currency and Banking*, II, 130–218, 290–313. Nineteen Gloucester residents from every parish in town appear among the subscribers to the Land Bank.

[39] Of the eighty-two Gloucester decedents whose inventoried assets ranked them among the wealthiest quartile of decedents for the periods 1716–1735, 1736–1755, and 1756–1770, fifty-nine had administrations of their estates included in the probate file. Only four of these fifty-nine administrations indicate insolvency, all from the period between 1756 and 1770, a time of economic difficulty in the fishing industry generally. Just two of the fifty-nine administrations indicate that the decedent's outstanding debt exceeded more than half of the inventoried value of his assets. In other words, between 1716 and 1755, no major Gloucester entrepreneur for whom an administration exists died insolvent, and in only one case prior to 1756 did an estate's debt exceed more than half of its value. Cf. Chapter VII, note 16.

[40] EPF, #24074, 26449; Babson, *History*, 168, 357, and 372.

a subsistence to a market-oriented economy. Men invested in local industries and trade, social and occupational organization became more differentiated, wealth more concentrated, and credit structures more extended and complex. But as Gloucester's experience indicates, these developments did not always alter relations among classes or change the conduct of economic life. Although relative inequality became more pronounced, it did not strain relations between rich and poor. Although more opportunities for making money opened up, no headlong scramble to maximize profits ensued. Although trade created a greater reliance upon borrowing and buying on credit, no significant increase in intratown debt litigation took place. The basis of material life in Gloucester changed dramatically, but there is no evidence that local society became more individualistic and impersonal as a result.[41]

Several circumstances surrounding Gloucester's development fostered stability and continuity during the decades of the town's economic expansion. First was the community's comparative isolation from Massachusetts' larger commercial centers, a distance that left the determination of the direction and pace of economic development more to local discretion than to the demands of outside investors. Ipswich, the likeliest candidate among the bigger ports to dominate Gloucester's fishery, declined after the seventeenth century, and by the mid-eighteenth century the total volume of its trade and shipping was smaller than that of Cape Ann.[42] While the cause of Ipswich's decreasing commercial significance is not clear, the consequence for Gloucester was greater control over its home industry from the outset, for other major ports that might have attempted to convert Cape Ann into their "fishing plantation" did not. Farther north, the merchants of Portsmouth concentrated mainly on develop-

[41] Cf. Bushman, *From Puritan to Yankee*, 107–21, 135–43; Boyer and Nissenbaum, *Salem Possessed*, 87–88, 103–6; Gildrie, *Salem, Massachusetts, 1626–1683*, 156–60; VanDeventer, *Emergence of Provincial New Hampshire*, 181—200; Daniels, *The Connecticut Town*, 140–70.

[42] For example, in 1752–53, only five Ipswich-owned vessels cleared the port of Salem-Marblehead. (*Abstracts of English Shipping Records*, vol. 3.)

ing that region's timber trade and found their needs for fish satisfied by the produce of Kittery and the catches of other Maine towns.[43] To the south of Gloucester, the fishery of conveniently situated Marblehead became the chief supplier of Boston and Salem traders, their interests and investments making that town the central loading port for Essex County's fishery.[44]

Gloucester maintained close economic ties with the traders of Boston and, to a lesser extent, those of Salem, especially during the initial decades of the local fishery's development. Merchants from these larger ports supplied early Gloucester entrepreneurs like Deacon Nathaniel Parsons with the finished goods and some of the capital required to operate the fishing industry, and until the 1730s, they also acted as middlemen, marketing the catches of Cape Ann boats to the Caribbean and southern Europe. Nevertheless, nonlocal merchants played a far less prominent role in Gloucester's economic development than they did in Marblehead's, and their involvement spanned a much shorter time. Because of its subsidiary importance to Marblehead as a center of the regional fishery, Gloucester did not attract investors from larger ports intent on expanding the industry. Nor did factors from firms based in Boston or Salem take up residence in town and attempt to dominate the local economy. There were also fewer strangers of another sort in Gloucester— transient seafarers passing through town for the fishing season. English merchantmen anchored in and cleared from Marblehead and Salem harbors, and fishermen looking for seasonal employment were more likely to try their luck in these larger towns. Although more new families were settling permanently in Gloucester, comparatively few fishermen and sailors took up temporary quarters there. Even by the middle of the eighteenth century, nearly three-quarters of the town's fishing fleet consisted of native-born men.[45]

The ability of Gloucester inhabitants to control local development allowed for a more gradual rate of economic

[43] For Portsmouth's trade, see Clark, *Eastern Frontier*, 65, 73, and 76–77; VanDeventer, *Emergence of Provincial New Hampshire*, 88–93.

[44] On outside investors in the Marblehead fishery, see Chapters VI and VII.

[45] Vickers, "Maritime Labor in Colonial Massachusetts," 220.

expansion, one that minimized the potential for social disruption. But of equal importance in promoting internal stability was the fact that Gloucester entered its period of commercial expansion as a settled, institutionally coherent society. Neither a raw frontier outpost nor a turbulent fishing camp, Gloucester first encountered the pressures attendant on economic growth after almost two generations of stable social life. The majority of its inhabitants were descended from early settlers; families had become accustomed to living and working together. Both the local church and the town meeting had been functioning smoothly for nearly half a century. While fostering restraint in the conduct of economic life, this communal legacy also imbued most inhabitants with a commitment to maintaining traditional patterns in civic life, which tended to promote harmony and homogeneity. Since the later seventeenth century, a broad agreement had prevailed among Gloucester inhabitants about the importance of preserving consensus and corporatism as the basis of political order. Their behavior evinces a consistent concern for unanimity, attaining general agreement in matters affecting the entire town, avoiding open dissension, and resolving conflicts peaceably. Equally evident in local political life is the premium placed upon unity, the identification of all inhabitants with the town as a whole. This communitarian political culture not only survived the transition from farming to trade but also limited the centrifugal impact of commercialization upon local society well into the eighteenth century. For some forty years following the beginnings of Gloucester's economic growth in the 1690s, the civic tradition inherited from the seventeenth century continued to exert a vital influence upon local politics, and townspeople were able to resolve their differences within this established framework.

The persistence and resilience of consensual and corporatist patterns of thought and behavior are exemplified in the first partitioning of Gloucester into precincts or parishes. During the eighteenth century, many other New England communities subdivided in this manner as their outlying district swelled in population, split off from parent bodies, and established their own meetinghouses and schools as distinct parishes within the towns. Some of these parish separations occasioned heated debates between "town fathers" resisting the loss of taxpayers and "outlivers" seeking precinct status. As a result, separations have been seen as symptoms of a growing social diversity that diminished communal harmony, divided loyalties, and diffused authority at the local level.[46] But the story of the formation of Gloucester's Second Parish suggests that the diversity produced by demographic and economic expansion did not invariably engender fundamental conflict among different social groups. It indicates too that sectional contention could occur without critically weakening adherence to consensualism in political life, the controlling force of established institutions, or allegiance to the town as a whole.

The accident of its irregular topography made Gloucester unlike many early New England communities where all houselots were situated in close proximity to each other. Instead, rock formations and waterways had from the first fragmented Cape Ann's population into several small, widely spaced enclaves. Segments of local settlement clustered around the myriad of small coves, inlets, and creeks created by the Annisquam River and Ipswich Bay and within the capacious shelter of Gloucester harbor.[47] The increasing reliance upon agriculture over the latter half of the seventeenth century enhanced the need for physically separate neighborhoods, since the distances imposed by the lack of any extensive stretches of arable acreage precluded the creation of a

[46] Lockridge, *A New England Town,* 93–118; Cook, "Social Behavior and Changing Values in Dedham, Massachusetts," *WMQ,* 27: 549 and 558. The formation of the Second Parish in Gloucester was an instance of the general process of institutional differentiation that characterized other New England towns during the late seventeenth and eighteenth centuries. In seventeenth-century communities, the same group, comprised of virtually all adult male inhabitants, handled matters relating to land, other public business, and ecclesiastical administration, and often recorded their decisions in a single book. During the provincial period, however, the proprietors of the common land began meeting separately to determine land policy, while parishes or precincts took over much of the public business and matters relating to ecclesiastical affairs. In Gloucester, for example, the proprietors began meeting separately from the town in 1713, and the First Parish started handling its affairs in a session apart from the general town meeting in 1729.

[47] For Gloucester's geographic and topographical features, see Babson, *History,* 3, and especially his "Map of Gloucester, Cape Ann" (frontispiece) that shows the location of the residences of early settlers.

nucleated village. Each discrete neighborhood in Gloucester was situated adjacent to the fields tilled by the several families residing in that area. At the town's western border with Chebacco Parish lay the expanse of the best land in Gloucester, watered by a series of small streams flowing into Ipswich Bay. Adjacent to this area was a strip of settlement scattered along the western bank of the Annisquam River, clusters of homesteads lining the inlets of Little River, Stony Cove, Long Cove, and Walker's Creek. Directly across the Annisquam on the eastern side of Gloucester stretched another band of settlement from the southern terminus of the river at Trynall Cove northward to Lobster and Goose Coves. To the extent that Gloucester had any central point, it was this neighborhood along the eastern Annisquam, and here, near Trynall Cove, the meetinghouse was located. At the town's southern extremity in Gloucester harbor resided still another group of settlers whose farms lay within the Eastern Point, an extension of land that formed the southern harbor.

After 1690, the commercial development of the town fostered increasing economic diversity among its several neighborhoods. The eastern side of the Annisquam formed the hub of local entrepreneurial activity by the beginning of the eighteenth century, its commerce in timber and fish dominated by the Coit, Davis, Allen, Riggs, York, and Haraden families, whose homes and businesses dotted the bank of the river in a line running north from Trynall Cove. These local magnates had valuable landholdings and maintained family farms. Some still described themselves as "yeomen," but their inventories indicate that they were actually millers and shoremen, and a few general retail merchants and master mariners with substantial investments in mills, fishing and coasting vessels, waterfront housing, and shop goods. Together, the leading Annisquam harbor entrepreneurs comprised the wealthiest and most influential group in early eighteenth-century Gloucester. In the adjacent neighborhood around Gloucester harbor, the same kind of commercial activity that characterized Annisquam River was also sinking farming to subsidiary importance as leading southern harbor families like the Parsonses and Pooles, the Stevenses and Saywards, Sargents and Sanderses, Withams and Warners were also turning to shipbuilding, fishing, and trading. Collectively, southerners took second place to their eastern Annisquam neighbors in relative wealth and political influence, but both harbors were developing economically along the same lines.[48]

While most sections of Gloucester turned toward commercial and maritime pursuits after 1690, the western part of town retained a predominantly agrarian character, much like neighboring Chebacco Parish. From their situation on the western side of the Annisquam River and their northern border on Ipswich Bay, westerners could have entered the timber and fish traffic as easily as their fellow townsmen did, and a few families did augment the income of their farms with investments in sawmills and fishing vessels. But the comfortable living afforded by the better quality of the soil in their neighborhood put less pressure on westerners to abandon agriculture for maritime pursuits and limited their involvement in the wider market economy.[49] By 1710, natural increase and migration to this neighborhood from Ipswich made the population of the western part of town large enough to support a separate ministry. In that year, western-

[48] This characterization of economic activity in eastern Annisquam and Gloucester harbors is based upon an analysis of inventories between 1690 and 1735 similar to the reconstruction of the Parsons family businesses discussed above. For the economic preeminence of eastern Annisquam harbor entrepreneurs, see the chart in Chapter IV, note 10, which illustrates the breakdown by neighborhood of the top quartile of Gloucester decedents, 1716–1735. The political advantage of Annisquam residents of this period is reflected in their predominance within the ranks of important town officeholders. Between 1690 and 1720, eastern Annisquam residents held 52 percent of all terms on the board of selectmen and served fourteen of the twenty-eight terms as deputy to the General Court. John Newman, Gloucester's only justice of the peace between 1706 and 1729, also resided in the eastern Annisquam. (GTR, II, 1690–1720; William Whittemore, ed., *The Massachusetts Civil Lists for the Colonial and Provincial Periods* (Albany, New York, 1870), 132–33.)

[49] Because no valuation list survives for Gloucester during the provincial period, I have relied on more impressionistic evidence for characterizing the economy of the western part of town. Their more agrarian orientation is reflected in their inventories, fewer of which contain appurtenances of a commercial fishery (i.e., flakeyards, schooners, fish houses, etc.) or lumbering business than do the inventories of decedents from other parts of town after 1690. In court records, westerners were also more likely to identify themselves as "yeomen" than were the residents of other parts of town.

ers appealed for incorporation as a distinct parish within the town.

The problem of distance confronting western Annisquam farmers was severe enough in itself to account for their interest in a separation. They could reach the town's meetinghouse only by crossing the Annisquam, a hazardous and often impossible trip in the winter months when the river froze over, cutting them off from town meetings, public worship, and the local school.[50] Still, the differences among Gloucester's neighborhoods by the beginning of the eighteenth century make it tempting to see in the western bid for separation the "deeper grievances of diversity" as well. Did the politics of partitioning reflect the apprehension of western agrarians over the commercial character of eastern Annisquam and Gloucester harbors? Was the western interest in separation the measure of their alienation from the new economic order of mercantile capitalism emerging in town?[51]

Probably not. First, the alignments in Gloucester produced by the west's campaign for separation suggest that tensions between farmers and traders played no part in shaping sectional politics. While eastern Annisquam magnates opposed the partition, the western farmers found supporters from within the ranks of other shoremen, shopkeepers, and artisans in Gloucester harbor. These southern harbor dwellers experienced no inconvenience in travelling to the town meetinghouse, but many of their children were settling on the eastern portion of the Cape, a remote region known as Sandy Bay some four to six miles from the church.[52] Southern families could foresee that Sandy Bay would in the

---

[50] GTR, II, 176; Babson, *History*, 262–63. A total distance of about three to five miles separated westerners from the meetinghouse.

[51] For example, Kenneth Lockridge analyzes Dedham's conflicts over separations by emphasizing the "diversity" of outlying districts rather than their distance from local institutions, while Paul Boyer and Stephen Nissenbaum argue that the Salem witchcraft hysteria arose out of factionalism within Salem Village rooted in the ambivalence of western villagers toward the commercial development of the eastern part of the parish. (*A New England Town,* especially 100–103; and *Salem Possessed,* 80–109.)

[52] Babson, *History,* 332–40. Sandy Bay settlers included members of the Parsons, Witham, and Grover families from the southern part of town.

future require a separate meetinghouse and so supported the westerners in setting the precedent. The character of western leaders themselves also indicates that antipathy to commercialization did not underly the concern for sectional autonomy. The west's leading family, the Haskells, combined farming with interests in milling and commercial fishing, as did several other western supporters of the separation. But even families whose pursuits were purely agrarian had little basis for perceiving a threat to their way of life from the fact of their fellow townsmen selling wood and fish. If a few of the most successful shoremen and millers of the eastern Annisquam were worth twice as much as the most affluent western farmer, commercial fortunes were not yet so numerous as to exclude yeomen from the top of the local economic hierarchy. Nor was the growing importance of trade depriving rural leaders of political power in Gloucester, for westerners had steadily increased their representation on the board of selectmen in the twenty years after 1690.[53]

By 1710, Gloucester had become a community of more diverse and distinct neighborhoods and economic interests, but these new differences did not alienate western farmers from the merchants, craftsmen, and fishermen in other parts of town. The issue of forming a second parish aligned townspeople not along but across lines of class and economic interest. Rather than reflecting agrarian animosity toward commerce, the western bid for separation was simply a case of demography forcing a resolution of the difficulties created by geography. At issue for westerners was

[53] Besides the members of the Haskell family, a number of other westerners, like miller Jacob Davis and tanner Isaac Eveleth, also had significant commercial interests. (See EPF, #7257, 9164.) Other westerners supplemented farming with a trade and identified their occupations as "yeoman and weaver" or as "yeoman and tanner." Proportionate to their numbers within the total population, westerners were not underrepresented among the wealthiest decedents in town during this period or overrepresented among the poorest ones. (See the table in Chapter IV, note 12, for the years 1716 through 1735.) The continuing political influence of the west is equally evident. My estimate is that at the time of the Second Parish separation, westerners accounted for under one-fifth of Gloucester's population, but their strength on the board of selectmen increased from holding just 7 percent of all terms between 1700 and 1709 to over one-third of all terms between 1710 and 1729. (GTR, II, 1700–1729.)

distance, not an underlying sense of their differentness from other townspeople. For this reason, supporting the separation did not imply any weakening of commitment to wider town unity on the part of the Haskells and their neighbors. Quite the contrary, what is striking about the west's pursuit of a separate parish is their insistence upon attaining this aim within the established framework of consensus and unanimity. Westerners did not repeatedly importune the town with their demands: no protracted debate at town meetings, no adjournments by moderators representing factional interests, no acrimonious public exchanges, no flurry of petitions to the General Court accompanied efforts to establish their own institutions in a separate parish. There was instead a discreet silence surrounding the subject between 1710, when the westerners first presented their request to the town meeting, and 1716, when the meeting acceded to their separation. During the intervening years, however, the silence was accompanied by a shift in the composition of Gloucester's elected leadership, as westerners implemented a policy of persuasion.

Throughout the eighteenth century, Gloucester's political life retained the oligarchic and deferential patterns established during the latter half of the seventeenth century, and since that time the leaders of Annisquam harbor had dominated both the board of selectmen and the office of representative.[54] The decades of Annisquam's unchallenged political control ended abruptly with the western demand for separation. In 1709, two members of Gloucester harbor's Parsons family and another southerner took over three of the five seats on the board. Westerners did not have the votes within their own ranks to determine the outcome of local elections, but by joining forces with the inhabitants of Gloucester harbor, they gained that capability. The elections of the next year drew the pattern of local alignments even more clearly as a coalition of westerners and southerners swept four of the selectmen's seats, and John Parsons replaced Annisquam harbor leader John Davis as deputy to the General Court. Westerners then took their first formal step toward separation, a petition for their own meeetinghouse. By 1711,

[54] See note 47 above.

eastern Annisquam dwellers had rallied their forces but softened their opposition to the separation. In that year, they
recaptured three selectmen's slots by agreeing to a compromise drawn up by a committee of southerners and westerners to supply preaching to west Gloucester during the winter
months. But this concession failed to restore their political
control permanently because it did not go far enough in satisfying western demands. For the next three years, the south-
west coalition kept a majority of selectman's seats, supplied
the moderator for town meetings, and reelected John Parsons to the General Court. The only eastern Annisquam residents elected to the board had no previous political experience
and lived at some distance from the meetinghouse—an easily
controllable minority that would in the future seek separation on behalf of their own neighbors.[55]

At any time between 1710 and 1714, the southerners and
westerners who controlled the election of local leaders could
also have mustered a majority of voters in the town meeting
to approve the actual separation. Yet the meeting took no
steps to set off the west, and the Haskells and their supporters pressed no demands after presenting their petition. Mere
majoritarianism was unacceptable to townspeople. So instead
of overriding eastern Annisquam's objections by forcing a
vote through the town meeting, westerners awaited the
appearance of general agreement. It had come by March of
1715, when the composition of elected leadership suddenly
reverted to its earlier character: eastern Annisquam magnates reestablished their control over the board of selectmen
and the office of representative. The next year, westerners
received permission to form a separate parish as well as the
promise of a contribution from the town for the support of
their new minister.[56]

The experience of the western separation apparently
schooled the leaders of Annisquam harbor in the wisdom of
acceding gracefully to legitimate sectional demands. When
the inhabitants of the northern part of the Cape had become
numerous enough to support a separate ministry and
requested permission to form the Third Parish in 1728, the

[55] GTR, II, 130 and 190; and March and May elections for 1711 to 1714.
[56] GTR, II, 197–99, and 205.

town meeting readily granted approval. Gloucester inhabitants had come to pride themselves upon their ability to accommodate the needs of neighbors remote from the First Parish meetinghouse "without the least contention or difficulty." They saw in their peaceful partitions proof of public harmony and the broadly shared commitment to perpetuating institutions for preserving piety and order.[57]

Not every precinct division in Gloucester was to proceed as smoothly as those that formed the Second and Third parishes, and in many other New England towns, sectional strife was also a source of political contention.[58] But the Second Parish separation in Gloucester illustrates that "diversity" within provincial New England towns—even in the relatively complex societies of developing seaports—was often more apparent than real. Despite the appearance of distinct neighborhoods and different occupational groups in Gloucester, fundamental agreement still obtained about the ordering of communal life. The emergence of specific sectional interests did not necessitate a diminished commitment to the general welfare; neither did the development of neighborhood solidarities dictate a corresponding reduction in identification with the town as a whole. Westerners, their Gloucester harbor allies, and their Annisquam harbor opponents alike agreed about the importance of unanimity and unity among fellow townsmen and about the value of institutions inherited from the seventeenth century. By seeking a separation, the Haskells and their neighbors were not rejecting this structure of order and authority but were trying to

[57] Michael Zuckerman's depiction of provincial communities as "peaceable kingdoms" has been disputed by several historians. By focusing mainly on smaller towns and by relying on formal town records and the fragmentary data in the Massachusetts Archives, Zuckerman mutes the extent and underestimates the total volume of conflict in eighteenth-century towns. (See, especially, Murrin, "Review Essay," *History and Theory*, 11:245–57.) Still, Gloucester's history lends support to Zuckerman's view that town partitioning itself proves neither that a lack of peace nor that an abandonment of communal ideals characterized eighteenth-century communities. It also validates Zuckerman's emphasis on the tenacity of consensual ideals and the aversion to "mere majoritarianism" among New Englanders. (*Peaceable Kingdoms*, 85–153.)

[58] GTR, II, 242, 247, 250; Answer of the Town of Gloucester to the Petition of Nathaniel Coit, 1738, *MA*, 11: 531–531a.

promote social control within their own ranks by making local institutions more accessible. Once their petition was approved by the town, westerners immediately set about building a meetinghouse, arraying the neighborhood's pecking order in seating arrangements within the church, hiring a minister, and negotiating for the services of the local schoolmaster. The separation did not give greater scope to diversity by diminishing the control of traditional institutions but rather enhanced homogeneity by extending them to outlying districts. Not the presence but rather the absence of an interest among outliving families in forming separate parishes would point to real diversity and disengagement from inherited, established structures of social authority.

Gloucester's strong sense of local solidarity and identity survived not only the division of the town into distinct parishes but also the other major institutional change of the later colonial period, the increasing influence of the county and province governments over local life. As the experience of provincial Gloucester illustrates, the self-contained town was not the only entity making a vital impact upon the lives of inhabitants. The province's mobilization of men for campaigns against the French and Indians, its grants of land in Maine, its emissions of paper money and the inflationary spiral resulting from colonial currency policy all exerted a decisive effect upon individual localities. County government, too, was becoming important. The oversight of the peace in local communities by the justices of the General Sessions and the reliance upon the Courts of Common Pleas for adjudicating an increasing number of civil suits accorded new power to county institutions and officials. The greater control exercised by both county and province in the eighteenth century increasingly limited the actual autonomy and hedged the practical power of individual towns. But at the same time, the growing centralization of authority intensified particularistic pride and loyalties. A compensatory strengthening of localistic identification and an apotheosis of communal independence developed in response to the reality of receding local control.[59]

---

[59] For a fuller description of this process of political centralization, see Murrin, "Review Essay," *History and Theory,* 11: 257ff; Allen, "The Zucker-

The kinds of contacts that most Gloucester inhabitants had with colony and county authorities illuminate the logic of this reactionary localism. While the province government did provide townspeople with the military security and some of the capital required for expanding the commercial fishery, it extracted a price for these advantages: the service of Gloucester's husbands and sons in the military, higher wartime taxes, and runaway inflation. Townspeople's dealings with the county authorities were of an even more negative character. Writs issued against local debtors, meddlesome orders to hire a regular schoolmaster, and apportionments of county rates all came from the county courts. There is little evidence that Gloucester residents were actively hostile to the interference of central authorities, but whenever possible, townspeople tried to circumvent or minimize the influence of county and colony power on local life. In 1726, for example, the town meeting informed the General Court of their strong objections to a proposal for dividing Essex County. Inhabitants did not indicate the basis of their opposition, but a smaller administrative unit would have strengthened the efficiency of the county courts by reducing the number of communities that fell within their jurisdiction.[60] Military service was another area in which Gloucester residents at times attempted to evade the control of centralized authority. The province government's campaigns against the French and Indians generally received strong support from Gloucester inhabitants, who perceived their advantage in increasing English power in the north Atlantic. By the final years of Queen Anne's War, however, local men were exhausted by their earlier contributions to the fighting. Besides serving in expeditions against French Canada and mustering the militia to rout Indian tribes from Maine,

man Thesis," *WMQ*, 29: 443–60; and Daniels, *The Connecticut Town*, 176. Timothy Breen has traced the tradition of conservative reaction against challenges to local autonomy in both England and New England back to the seventeenth century in his essay, "Persistent Localism: English Social Change and the Shaping of New England Institutions," *WMQ*, 3rd ser., 32 (1975), 3–28. Thomas Bender also emphasizes the enduring importance of localism as a central cultural value in early America. (*Community and Social Change*, 61–68.)

[60] GTR, II, 24.

Gloucester men had twice in 1709 sailed north under the command of a fellow townsman, Captain Andrew Robinson, to conduct reprisals against the Indians and to capture a French privateer. So, in February of 1710, when the province ordered local men to pursue another French vessel off Cape Cod, Robinson was unable to raise a crew from the ranks of war-weary residents by enlistments, and when impressment was threatened, many men left town temporarily. Local leaders sympathized with the reluctance of their neighbors. Captain Robinson, the Reverend John White of First Church, all of Gloucester's militia captains, and its justice of the peace addressed exculpatory letters to the governor, pleading that hardship had prompted this defiance of the province's demands.[61]

Gloucester residents attempted to restrict the spread of centralized power not only in the sphere of politics but also in the realm of religious life. The preference for preserving local autonomy in religious matters was particularly apparent in their attitudes about the proper ecclesiastical polity. Like adjacent Chebacco Parish, the First and Third Parishes of Ipswich, and a number of other communities in Maine and eastern Connecticut, Gloucester was an eighteenth-century stronghold of support for lay-centered, congregational independence. Set forth by the first generation of Bay Puritans in the Cambridge Platform of 1648, this form of church organization accorded great power to the laity in matters of governance and discipline. It also guaranteed the autonomy of individual congregations in conducting their affairs by granting only an advisory role to ecclesiastical councils, ad hoc groups comprised of ministers and laymen from neighboring churches who might be called on to adjudicate disputes within another congregation.[62] Gloucester's strict

---

[61] Babson, *History*, 137–38.

[62] For the religious orientation of eastern Connecticut and Chebacco, see Jedrey, *World of John Cleaveland*, 11–12, 46–57. Some of the Massachusetts churches adhering to a conservative, congregational polity are indicated by a list of churches that subscribed to the conciliar decision against Samuel Fiske in 1734. Fiske became unpopular with some members of his church for a variety of reasons, but one charge particularly emphasized by his opponents was the parson's exercise of arbitrary authority and his aversion to ruling elders. Fiske's adversaries called an ecclesiastical council in

adherence to this older, more congregational form of polity was manifested in the process of selecting a successor to the Reverend John Emerson, who died late in 1700. After being disappointed in their initial choice of the Reverend Jabez Fitch, the First Church gave serious consideration to the candidacy of Joseph Coit, the New London cousin of a prosperous local miller and leading citizen, Nathaniel Coit.[63] But Joseph's impressive family connections could not overcome objections to his views on church government. He was one of a number of second and third generation New England ministers who were drawn to a more hierarchical, "presbyterianized" polity as a means of increasing clerical authority. He and they wished to form permanent, regional ministerial associations to advise neighboring churches on a broad range of issues and also to establish standing councils to adjudicate disputes in local churches.[64] As one who held such views, Joseph Coit could not completely conform his notions regarding ecclesiastical organization to the framework set forth in the Cambridge Platform. "In matters controversial [he] doth set up his own opinion in opposition to the Synod book," concluded the church at Norwich, Connecticut, where Coit had preached on probation before both candidate and congregation decided against proceeding to a permanent pastoral relation.[65] Conservative laymen at both Norwich

1734 comprised of ministers whose views on polity and doctrine were quite conservative. Among them were Nathaniel Rogers of First Ipswich, Samuel Wigglesworth of Third Ipswich, Jeremiah Wise of South Berwick, Maine, Samuel Moody of York, Maine, Richard Jaques of Second Gloucester, and John White of First Gloucester. (See *A Just and Impartial Narrative* (Boston, 1735) and *A Faithful Narrative* (Boston, 1735).)

[63] On Jabez Fitch, see GTR, II, 75, 82, 84–85, 86; "Diary of James Parsons," 15–18. For Joseph Coit, see John Langdon Sibley (vols. I–III) and Clifford K. Shipton (vols. IV–XVII), *Sibley's Harvard Graduates,* 17 vols. (Cambridge and Boston, 1873–1975), IV, 343–45. (Cited hereafter as *SHG.*)

[64] Many ministers who wished to modify the Cambridge Platform were interested in broadening church membership and in improving relations with other reformed Protestant denominations as well. For a full discussion, see David Hall, *The Faithful Shepherd: A History of the New England Ministry in the Seventeenth Century* (1972, repr. New York, 1974), 197–226; and J. William T. Youngs, *God's Messengers: The Religious Leadership in Colonial New England, 1700–1750* (Baltimore, 1976), 64–78.

[65] Cited in Frances Caulkins, *History of Norwich* (Hartford, 1866), 127–28.

and Gloucester regarded the Platform of 1648 as the bulwark of congregational independence, and they were not about to second guess the wisdom of the Cambridge synod because of the convictions of a young college graduate. The adoption of the halfway covenant and the decision to admit any townsman to the meetings in which the church deliberated the choice of a minister had exhausted the capacity of Gloucester's First Church members for innovation. And many feared that the ministry of Joseph Coit would move them even farther from the frame of ecclesiastical government formulated by the first generation. The result was Joseph Coit's withdrawal from consideration by First Goucester in the summer of 1702 after "finding us under some uncomfortable circumstances."[66]

Shortly after the First Church ended their negotiations with Coit, however, they discovered a candidate whose views on church government accorded completely with the local consensus upon the importance of congregational independence and lay power. The Reverend John White, a military chaplain to the fort in Saco, Maine, became the new pastor of First Gloucester at the beginning of 1703 after a delighted church committee pronounced him wholly acceptable in matters of doctrine and governance.[67] Gloucester's conservative laity felt secure in the soundness of their selection because of the man who engineered White's installation at

[66] John White's list of church members at the time of his installation in 1703 includes a number of halfway members, so First Church had adopted the halfway covenant during Emerson's pastorate. The church's decision in 1701 to allow townspeople who were nonmembers to attend deliberations over ministerial candidates by the brethren was a limited concession to the demand for a greater voice in selection than simply approving the choice of the church. ("Diary of James Parsons," 17.) For the negotiations with Coit, see GTR, II, 88, 90, and 100–101; "Diary of James Parsons," 17. Coit's theology may have been as uncongenial to Gloucester inhabitants as his view on church government. He was dismissed from his pulpit in Plainfield, Connecticut, after his ministry encountered violent opposition from New Lights in his congregation during the Great Awakening of the 1740s, a revival of evangelical piety that commanded strong support in Gloucester. (See *SHG*, IV, 345.)

[67] *SHG*, IV, 421–24; GFCR, October 9, 1702, January 6, 1703; GTR, II, 105–7; Babson, *History*, 226–28.

First Church, the Reverend John Wise of Chebacco Parish. White's friend and later his father-in-law, Wise was New England's principal spokesman for the congregational autonomy enshrined in the Cambridge Platform and most eloquent adversary of standing ecclesiastical councils and ministerial associations. A zealous proponent of the liberties of individual churches and the privileges of the lay brethren, he condemned any attempts to create a more centralized ecclesiastical polity in Massachusetts. To Wise's mind, plans for enlarging and consolidating ministerial authority portended the growth of a costly and ineffectual caste of privileged priestly bureaucrats, spiritual lords whose sway would extinguish the independence of local churches. In *The Churches Quarrel Espoused,* his classic defense of congregational autonomy, Wise lambasted one program for centralization, the *Proposals* of 1705, for "Something considerably of Prelacy in it . . . which Smells very Strong of the Infalliable Chair."[68] And several years before publishing *The Churches Quarrel* in 1710, Wise was politicking throughout northern New England to establish institutions within individual churches for preserving local autonomy and to settle clergymen who shared his convictions in as many pulpits as possible.[69]

[68] John Wise, *The Churches Quarrel Espoused* (1710, 2nd ed., Boston, 1715), 38–39. In lieu of calling in an ecclesiastical council, First Gloucester requested Wise and the Reverend Joseph Gerrish of Wenham to restore unity to the church following the withdrawal of Coit from consideration. ("Diary of James Parsons," 22–23.) The best description of Wise's views on church government is in Perry Miller, *The New England Mind: From Colony to Province* (Cambridge, Mass., 1953), 288–302.

[69] Historians have puzzled over why Wise waited several years after the appearance of the *Proposals* in 1705 before publishing his reply, *The Churches Quarrel Espoused,* in 1713. Miller intimates that the support of many powerful Boston clergymen for the *Proposals* may have made it difficult for Wise to find a publisher in the capital. But in addition, Wise's interest in promoting his own program for church reform within his immediate sphere of influence in northern New England may have taken precedence over an interest in engaging in a province-wide debate. Throughout the early years of the eighteenth century, Wise was actively lobbying for the institution of the ruling eldership in the Berwick, Maine, church of his son, Jeremiah, and at his son-in-law White's Gloucester pastorate. Wise also had a hand in settling clergymen who shared his conservative convictions over several

John White's settlement at First Gloucester was one of Wise's victories, for he shared his famous father-in-law's passionate aversion to ecclesiastical centralization. Both men strongly advocated revitalizing the institution of lay ruling elders, a church office provided for by the Cambridge Platform, as a strategy for strengthening the ability of local churches to regulate their own affairs. By monitoring the behavior of members, quelling minor disaffections within a congregation, and mediating between pastor and people, these ruling elders would minimize the number of controversies arising within individual churches. And fewer disputes would obviate the need for intervention by ecclesiastical councils of neighboring ministers and laymen.[70] The desire to reduce the interference of councils in local church life derived from the suspicion of both Wise and White that such bodies were bent upon arrogating to themselves greater permanence and power than the Cambridge Platform permitted. It was White who, along with another member of Wise's circle, the Reverend Samuel Moody of York, Maine, reissued *The Churches Quarrel* in 1715. And it was White who succeeded Wise as

churches in northern New England. (See John White, *The Gospel Treasure in Earthen Vessels* (Boston, 1725), 38; "Records of the First Church of Berwick, Maine," *New England Historical and Genealogical Register,* 82 (1928), 81; GFCR, 1707; and *SHG,* V, 549–53, 406–10, 544–45.

[70] On the eldership, see Wise, *The Churches Quarrel Espoused,* 14–22; White, *New England's Lamentations,* 34. Although the ruling eldership was an office that accorded greater influence to the brethren, many members of the laity were reluctant to adopt the office. Jeremiah Wise spent ten years persuading his Berwick congregation to institute an eldership, and the church finally filled the office by drawing lots. John White also admitted to encountering stiff lay opposition initially. Some laymen felt inadequate to the task of administering discipline; others were unsure that the Scripture warranted an eldership, despite the provision for the office in the Cambridge Platform; most probably opposed the office for the same reason that townsmen tried to avoid serving as constable—no one wanted to risk offending his neighbors. See "Records of the First Church, Berwick, Maine," *NEHGR,* 82: 81; and White, *New England's Lamentations,* 36. See also *Reasons for adhering to our Platform* (1734), an anonymous pamphlet appended to White's *Lamentations; A Letter to a Gentleman Relating to the Office of Ruling Elders in the Churches* (Boston, 1731); *Some Brief Remarks on a Letter to a Gentleman* (Boston, 1731); and *A Reply to Some Remarks on a Letter* (Boston, 1731).

the standard-bearer for the cause of congregational autonomy after he preached his father-in-law's funeral sermon in
1725.[71]

White's continuing success at First Gloucester underscores the persistence of localistic preferences among townspeople. Parishioners, like their pastor, wanted no part of
strong centralized bodies such as ministerial associations and
standing councils that could end up dictating policy to individual churches and encroaching on local independence and
lay power. Their approval of White's advocacy of ecclesiastical particularism kept the First Parish honest about adjust-
ing his annual salary to keep pace with inflation: in 1725,
Newbury minister John Tufts singled out the Gloucester
parson as the highest paid clergyman in Essex County.[72]
Members of the First Church's leading merchant families vied
for election to the office of ruling elder, and during the 1730s,
the congregation rallied in support of White when he attacked
Salem's Reverend Samuel Fiske for opposing that institution. And when the new congregations of Second and Third
Churches chose their new ministers, they selected clergymen
whose opinions on church government conformed to those
of John White.[73]

The extent to which localism dominated the outlook of
Gloucester townspeople is apparent not only in their public
conduct of political and ecclesiastical affairs but also in their
private records. One such personal document is the diary
containing entries by several members of the Parsons family.

[71] Wise, *The Churches Quarrel Espoused,* preface to 1715 edition.

[72] GTR, II, 189, 207, and 230; "Records of the First Parish of Gloucester,"
14, 33 (cited hereafter as GFPR); and John Tufts, *Anti-Ministerial Objections Considered* (Boston, 1725), 11.

[73] For Gloucester's role in the Fiske controversy, see White, *New England's
Lamentations,* 32; and GFCR, March 12, 1735. Richard Jaques of Second
Gloucester joined his senior colleague White in admonishing Fiske in 1734.
(See note 62 above.) Third Gloucester's Benjamin Bradstreet was a close
friend of White, with whom he sponsored the Awakening in Gloucester,
and of the Cleaveland brothers, evangelical clergymen who advocated a
conservative, Congregational polity. (*SHG,* VII, 457–60.) Ebenezer Cleaveland became the first minister of Gloucester's Fifth Parish in the 1750s, and
that church subsequently voted to institute ruling elders. (Babson, *History,*
340.)

James Parsons, one of Jeffrey Sr.'s sons, served as Gloucester's representative to the General Court for several years,
but he noted nothing in the diary about either his role in
provincial politics or the transactions of other deputies. Only
his accounts of the expenses that he incurred in travel and
and lodging indicate that James regularly spent time out of
town in Boston. But he left a detailed record of the births
and deaths in his family and of the process by which the
church and town had selected John White as the successor
to Emerson. James's son, Eliezur Parsons, whose entries begin
in the 1720s and who died in 1748, found only two nonlocal
events worthy of note: the deaths of Increase and Cotton
Mather, two of the colony's leading ministers. Damage suffered by the town through severe weather and natural disasters and the building of the new First Parish meetinghouse
made a much more profound impression upon Eliezur. As a
young ministerial candidate seeking a position, the Reverend
Moses Parsons, the third family diarist, moved about the
county more, preaching on probation and filling vacant pulpits. Yet travel did little to widen the scope of Moses Parsons's concerns. Accounts of the climate on Cape Ann and
of socializing with neighbors and relatives dominate his entries
as well, and the only nonlocal figure who drew his particular
notice was George Whitefield, a celebrated English evange-
list who preached throughout the American colonies. Parsons copied into the last leaf of the diary book a list of the
amounts that surrounding towns had contributed to Whitefield's Georgia orphanage in 1740 and reverently recorded
the great man's actual appearance in town in 1754. By the
mid-eighteenth century, the Parsonses and their neighbors
were aware—even uncomfortably conscious—of the world
outside of Gloucester: Moses's information about Whitefield's orphanage came from the *New England Weekly Journal*. But most occurrences beyond town borders held as little
interest for them as they had for James Parsons.[74]

After 1690, population growth, the conversion to a maritime economy, and Gloucester's entry into an interdependent commercial network transformed the material life of

[74] "Diary of James Parsons," including entries for Eliezur and Moses Parsons, 1, passim.

the town. But in terms of social behavior, values, and outlook, Gloucester residents still resembled the inhabitants of
a small, rural village. Isolated from the interference of larger
seaports, the town's industry and trade had slowly developed under exclusively local auspices, insulated from the
demands of outside investors and freed from the pressure of
accommodating a large laboring force of seafaring strangers.
This more gradual rate of economic growth, coupled with
the prosperity and opportunity shared by all levels of society, contributed to the continuity of the town's communitarian traditions and inherited values. These established patterns
of belief and behavior in turn acted as counterweights against
the molding of society by market forces. Conservative in theology, consensual in politics, indifferent or mistrustful of those
who lived beyond the borders of the community, townspeople maintained a sense of obligation to each other. Corporate loyalty survived both the diversity of occupations,
interests, and incomes introduced by economic development
and the division of the town into distinct parish neighborhoods dictated by demographic expansion. Over the first forty
years of commercial growth, Gloucester inhabitants succeeded in effecting private accommodations of their differences, avoiding protracted public controversies, and preserving
the peace.

On the other hand, because these important continuities
in local culture persisted despite major changes in material
life, Gloucester was not wholly immune from serious conflict. The town's deepest divisions did not arise from the
familiar effects of commercial development such as indebtedness, inequality, or occupational and sectional diversity.
Instead, fundamental conflict in Gloucester during the late
seventeenth and early eighteenth centuries grew out of the
same localistic concerns and allegiances that strengthened
social cohesion and facilitated harmony among the majority
of townspeople. The intensity of this localism created conditions that precluded the accommodation of one small
subgroup within the town and increasingly set them apart as
an unassimilatable element. This group, whose loyalties
assigned them a status outside of the local community, was
the Quakers.

3

Spectres
of Subversion,
Societies of Friends

ONE BASIC, irreconcilable antagonism existed in provincial Gloucester, but it was not one of rich against poor, fishermen against farmers, easterners against westerners, or congregations against clergymen. It was, instead, the opposition of the orthodox, Congregationalist majority to the town's tiny population of Quakers. The Quakers first appeared in Gloucester during the 1660s, and the sect enjoyed a period of expansion in town around the turn of the century. But most inhabitants of Gloucester became increasingly hostile to the Quakers within their midst, and by the 1730s the Society of Friends had few representatives left in town. Nor was Gloucester's experience with the Quakers exceptional. In surrounding Essex County communities, the division between orthodoxy and dissent also remained a basic element shaping local life and a continuing source of social friction well into the eighteenth century. Towns like Newbury and Salem, where the Friends had formerly shown some strength, saw a similar reduction in Quaker ranks. The sustained animosity to the Quakers in these towns is of particular significance because all three were seaports, places that supposedly accommodated religious diversity with greater ease because of their more cosmopolitan character. But the strongholds of Quakerism in provincial Massachusetts were not the larger commercial centers. They were rather a few small fishing and farming villages like Lynn and Amesbury in the north and Dartmouth and Tiverton in the south.

The persistence of anti-Quaker prejudice in many Essex County towns is surprising because of the contrasting impression of intersectarian relations that emerges from the laws and sermons concerning the Society of Friends in colonial Massachusetts. A clear progression from persecution and condemnation of Quaker dissenters during the mid-seventeenth century to an acceptance of the Friends by the beginning of the eighteenth century can be traced in the public pronouncements and actions of Massachusetts Bay's civil and clerical establishment. Following a period of severe repression between 1656 and 1665, colony leaders granted a grudging toleration to a somewhat less militant Quaker movement until the outbreak of King Philip's War in 1675. Sectarian hostilities rekindled during this conflict with the Indians, which the Friends regarded as divine retribution for New England's past persecutions and the Puritans interpreted as punishment for permitting the presence of heretics in their new Israel. The colony government reacted by passing stringent anti-Quaker legislation, while the Friends retaliated with displays of defiance and protests to the king. With the cessation of warfare, tensions between the Quakers and the Bay's civil and spiritual leaders abated again, and after 1691 the freedom of worship accorded all dissenters under the new Massachusetts charter promoted a progressive easing of discriminatory legislation. At the same time, the concern of the Congregationalist clergy over Anglican efforts to extend the influence of the Episcopal Church in New England enhanced their interest in a rapprochement with other dissenting sects like the Quakers. Leading Massachusetts ministers accordingly softened their strictures against the Friends in the later colonial era and publicly endorsed the official policy of toleration.[1]

Yet despite the evolution of formal, legal, religious toleration in Massachusetts, sectarian prejudice persisted at the

---

[1] The most recent study of Quakerism in colonial New England is Arthur Worrall, *Quakers in the Colonial Northeast* (Hanover, N.H., 1980). Earlier accounts include Rufus Jones, *The Quakers in the American Colonies* (London, 1911); and Frederick Tolles, *Quakers and the Atlantic Culture* (New York, 1960).

local level. Instead of following or forcing their leaders in the direction of greater religious liberalism, many orthodox lay people steadfastly resisted accommodating sectarian diversity. In Gloucester, relations between the Congregationalists and the Friends deteriorated steadily over the late seventeenth century, and the policy of liberty of conscience imposed on the Bay colony by England after 1691 actually augmented the apprehension and antagonism that most members of the Puritan laity felt toward dissenters. By the middle of the eighteenth century, sectarian prejudice had driven most of Cape Ann's dissenters either out of town or into the orthodox fold. The Congregational church retained its monopoly of religious life to the virtual exclusion of all competing sects as dissenting influence actually waned in town with the passing of time. Throughout the later colonial period in Gloucester as well as in other Essex County ports, religious differences aroused impassioned conflicts among people for whom sectarian distinctions were integral to social identity. This discrepancy between the growth of legal toleration and the actual resistance to religious diversity in many towns raises questions about the ways in which dissenting status affected social relationships within a community. It also requires an assessment of the sources that sustained sectarian prejudice among ordinary New Englanders into the eighteenth century.

Outside the vicinity of Lynn and Salem, the largest single concentration of Quakers in early seventeenth-century Essex County was probably in Gloucester. After 1660, traveling missionaries for the Society of Friends aggressively evangelized in the communities north of Salem that had been settled by emigrants from the West of England. The efforts of these itinerant Friends contributed to the spread of Quakerism in northern New England, but Gloucester's Quakers most likely contracted their heterodox sympathies in southern Bay settlements, where they had formerly resided or where family members still lived. A history of difficulties with Essex County magistrates drove Nathaniel Hadlock to Cape Ann after his indictment for declaring that "he profitted more by going to the Quakers' meeting" than he did by hearing Salem minister John Higginson. Gloucester's Elizabeth Kendall

Somes and several of her children, including a step-daughter, Mary Hammond, joined the Quakers after adopting the beliefs of their kin, the Kendalls of Cambridge, and Essex County's most outspoken dissenter, Thomas Maule of Salem. The Somes's influence also brought their neighbors in Gloucester, the Pearces, under conviction.[2]

While settlements to the north and south often dealt harshly with their dissenters, moderation marked Gloucester's initial response to the development of religious diversity in the seventeenth century. Orthodox inhabitants had little reason to feel threatened by local Friends: their numbers were small, a schism over the practice of male celibacy had deeply divided the Essex County sect, and the civil government of the Bay remained officially committed to the defense of the established Congregational churches. An even more important circumstance encouraging coexistence was that Gloucester's Quakers were content to occupy an obscure, circumscribed position on the outskirts of local society. Quite literally, the Friends resided on the fringes of late seventeenth-century settlement at Goose and Lobster Coves. A community apart, they never exercised any significant influence on local affairs or held important political offices. During the 1670s and 1680s, the town routinely reported their absences from public worship to the courts, but orthodox inhabitants resorted to reason rather than stringent repression to combat heresy. In 1678, for example, John Pearce, Jr., visited the Reverend John Emerson and invited him to a Quaker meeting that was to be held at the home of his father, the senior Pearce. The pastor "Labored to convince him of the evil of it and the breach of the Law of this Commonwealth," but the young Quaker was "very impudent and bold and sayd that they were neither afraid of the Laws nor the Magestrates nor any man." Emerson was dismayed that Pearce left "stiff and obstinate," but neither the minister nor any of his parishioners interfered with the young man as he went from "house

[2] On the strength of Quakerism in the West of England and the West Country origins of many Essex County Quakers, see Allen, *In English Ways*, 11. For Hadlock's legal difficulties, see *Essex Ct. Recs.*, IV, 74–75; V, 356; and VII, 367.

to house to invite mens children and servants the most part of that night."[3] Tithingman Thomas Day tried the same approach with Quakeress Mary Hammond that Emerson had attempted with her neighbor Pearce, but with just as little effect:

> I asked her the resen why she did hinder her dafter Mary from Coming to meting to which she said that when shee Came hom I tould her that she might goe to meting if shee wold but she should not have my consent to which I replyed you then wer as good say that shee should not goe: why Thomas said she you have Childeren would you be willing to let them goe to hell if you could help it to which I said noe I wold doe what I cold to hinder them and then said I why is goeing to meting the way to hell yea said she to goe to here your parson or prest or what you will Call him is the way to hell then said I it is not the way to hell to goe to John Pearces to her him and some time he ses nothing noe said she.[4]

Informal pressure of this kind rather than harsh persecution typified the response of the orthodox community to Gloucester's early Quakers. Perhaps for this reason, not all of Cape Ann's Friends were quite as "stiff and obstinate" as John Pearce, Jr. For example, Joseph Somes, one of the sons of local Quakeress Elizabeth Somes, joined other young townsmen in the fight against King Philip and gave his life to the cause. More militant Quakers, like Joseph's older brother, John, had to leave town to attain the satisfaction of suffering for their faith. He moved to Boston, where the magistrates obliged him with a whipping for publicly pro-

---

[3] The location of the residences of Quakers in Gloucester can be ascertained from Babson's "Map of Gloucester, Cape Ann," that appears on the frontispiece of his *History*. On Pearce, see *Essex Ct. Recs.,* VII, 150, 243, and 367. Jonathan Chu has also detected a restrained response to local Quakers among the orthodox Puritans of Kittery and Salem during the mid-seventeenth century; see his "The Social and Political Contexts of Heterodoxy: Quakerism in Seventeenth Century Kittery," *New England Quarterly,* 54 (1981), 365–84; and "The Social Context of Religious Heterodoxy: The Challenge of Seventeenth-Century Quakerism to Orthodoxy in Massachusetts" (forthcoming, *Essex Institute Historical Collections*).

[4] *Essex Ct. Recs.,* VII, 367.

claiming that King Philip's War was divine punishment for
New England's past persecutions.[5]

Yet for all the apparent willingness of townspeople to suffer the dissenters in their midst, an undercurrent of apprehension over the Quaker presence can be detected among
Gloucester's orthodox inhabitants during these years. Their
anxieties were reflected in a peculiar spate of criminal prosecutions that roughly coincided with the initial appearance
of Quakerism in town. Prior to 1670, crimes involving sexual misconduct were uncommon in Gloucester. Aside from
the charge of lewdness leveled against fisherman John Jackson, only one newlywed couple had been presented for fornication before this decade. But in 1673, John Pearce, Sr.
and his new wife were called into court to answer allegations
of premarital impropriety. In the same year, Christian
Marshman, a servant maid, claimed that she was pregnant
and accused as the father, John Stannard. During the next
year, Timothy Somes and his bride were prosecuted for fornication, and in 1682, newlyweds William and Naomi Sargent. This sudden outbreak of indictments for sexual
misconduct before marriage was not the result of declining
parental discipline: defendants John and Jane Pearce were a
middle-aged couple with grown children. What makes all of
the prosecutions comprehensible is rather the relationship of
all of the indicted couples to John Pearce, Sr. By his marriage
to the former widow Jane Stannard, the senior Pearce became
the stepfather of John Stannard and his two sisters, who subsequently married Timothy Somes and William Sargent. In
other words, all of the defendants in the fornication cases of
the 1670s and early 1680s were related by marriage to the
man whose household was the site of the Quakers' meetings
in Gloucester.[6]

There is no evidence to suggest that Jane Stannard Pearce
or any of her children contracted Quaker convictions from

[5] *Records of the Court of Assistants of the Massachusetts Bay Colony, 1630–
1692*, 3 vols. (Boston, 1901–1928), I, 12; and Babson, *History*, 162.

[6] *Essex Ct. Recs.,* V, 231, 250, 358, and 359; VII, 368. Aside from Quakers
and individuals with marital ties to the friends, only one other local couple
was presented for fornication between 1673 and 1682.

the Pearces, but Gloucester's orthodox inhabitants were watching closely and suspecting the worst about anyone in town connected with the small coterie of Quaker families clustered around Lobster and Goose Coves. The Congregationalist community encouraged local scandal over sexual misconduct as a way of discrediting the dissident sect and deployed criminal prosecutions as a way of disciplining people like the Stannards, who consented to alliances with Quakers. The logic behind their selecting the charge of fornication specifically derived from the longstanding association of all forms of religious antinomianism, including Quakerism, with licentiousness and sexual libertinism. Fornication was also an apt metaphor for conveying the Congregationalist perception of intersectarian unions as essentially illicit. Whether Jane Stannard Pearce or her children were actually guilty of breaching the boundaries of sexual propriety is uncertain, but what is unquestionable is that they had stepped outside the pale of sectarian exclusivity. The Quakerism of John Pearce made less than legitimate in the eyes of local Congregationalists not only his union with Jane Stannard but also the marriages between his stepchildren and the sons and daughters of orthodox families. The Puritans were consistent in their belief that religious affinities ran in families. Just as the assumption underlying the halfway covenant was that one generation of "visible saints" would transmit their virtuosity to another, informing the community's suspicion of the Pearce-Stannard marriages was the conviction that the contagion of heresy spread in the same way.[7] Like Quakeress Mary Hammond, John Pearce would try to stop the members of his family from going to hell along with the Congregationalists.

As the prosecutions of the Stannards and their partners suggest, Congregationalist suspicions fastened not only on the Quakers themselves but also on those people whose social ties to the Friends raised questions about their own religious loyalties. This uneasiness over the merging of orthodox and dissenting families was perhaps the cause of Clement Col-

---

[7] Edmund S. Morgan, *The Puritan Family: Religion and Domestic Relations in Seventeenth Century New England* (1944, repr., New York, 1966), 173–86.

dom's troubles in the 1660s. Coldom was a farmer in Goose Cove, an officer in Gloucester's militia, and unlike many of his near neighbors, a Congregationalist. In 1666, Coldom's militia company, "upon some difference . . . or dislike among some of them," suddenly stripped him of his rank as ensign. Townsmen gave no reason for their decision, but Coldom's fall from grace could have been brought about by his new son-in-law, Francis Norwood, Sr. Norwood had come to New England after the restoration of the Stuart monarchy made England an inhospitable environment for someone with his radical religious and political convictions. He first kept a tavern in Lynn, a center of early Baptist and Quaker enthusiasm, but after a few years, he settled in Gloucester at Goose Cove amidst the Quaker Pearces and Hammonds and the Congregationalist Coldoms. In 1663, he married Clement Coldom's daughter.[8] Whether this marriage was actually the cause of Coldom's loss of his military rank is uncertain, but his subsequent behavior suggests some connection. As if atoning for his daughter's "defection," Coldom began personally policing the border between the orthodox and dissenting communities. It was Coldom who tore John Pearce, Sr.'s door from its hinges to expose the illicit intimacies attending his neighbor's wooing of the widow Stannard. It was also Coldom who testified in court against John Stannard, alleging that "he saw John Stainwood [Stannard] and Christian Marshman together outdoors . . . and he was kissing her." Undeterred by the testimony of local midwives that Christian had never been pregnant, Coldom appeared in court the following year as a witness against Timothy Somes and

[8] Babson, *History,* 118. Francis Norwood, Jr.'s name appears in the Salem Monthly Meeting Records, but I could find no direct evidence confirming his father's Quakerism. Nevertheless, everything about Francis Sr.'s career points to this conclusion: the family tradition that he emigrated to New England because of his radical opinions; his choices of residence in Lynn and Gloucester's Quaker enclave; his failure to join the First Church; his purchase of land from John Pearce, Jr. when the latter left town in 1682. The lack of Quaker records for much of the seventeenth century makes criminal prosecutions the best source for identifying members of the Society of Friends. In Gloucester, however, older members of the Quaker community tended to be more circumspect about confronting the Congregational establishment than younger people. This makes it more difficult to identify the mature, adult members of the local Quaker community.

his wife.[9] But if Coldom managed to acquit himself of guilt by association through his vigilance in exposing the evildoing of dissenters, he was unable to arrest the spread of heresy within his own family: Francis Norwood, Jr. fulfilled his grandfather's worst fears by inheriting the Quaker convictions of his father and namesake.

Gloucester's orthodox opposition to Quaker dissenters living in their midst was muted for most of the seventeenth century, expressed mainly in indirect modes bespeaking an underlying uneasiness. But in the closing years of that century intersectarian tensions in town increased in intensity. While the sources of this greater animosity toward the Friends are complex, its manifestations are unmistakable, for they figured in a familiar and intensively studied episode in early American history, the witchcraft hysteria that swept through several Essex County towns during the year 1692.

Although the witchcraft outbreak started in Salem Village in the winter of 1692, discrete outcroppings of mass panic occurred in at least two other towns, Gloucester and neighboring Andover. In Andover, where the hysteria over witchcraft began in the summer of 1692, the first flurry of allegations resulted in a round-up of all the usual suspects: Martha Carrier, the acid-tongued wife of a Welshman whom everyone in town had regarded as a witch for years; Mary Parker, a crazed, impoverished widow who had lost a son in King Philip's War; and Samuel Wardwell, the village fortuneteller who read palms and "mayd sport" of his misdeed. But following these eccentrics and outcasts to prison were nearly forty other Andoverians who were all solid and respectable members of the community. This group of suspected witches included the wife of Deacon John Frye, the wife of militia captain John Osgood, two of the Reverend Francis Dane's daughters, his daughter-in-law, several of his grandchildren, and the wife of Dudley Bradstreet, the town's representative to the General Court. These defendants provided the judges of the Court of Oyer and Terminer with full

[9] *Essex Ct. Recs.*, III, 338; V, 231, 250, and 358–359. On Coldom's role in the witchcraft trials in 1692, see Paul Boyer and Stephen Nissenbaum, eds., *The Salem Witchcraft Papers*, 3 vols. (New York, 1977), II, 457. (Cited hereafter as *Witchcraft Papers*.)

confessions of conversations with feline "familiars," trips by broomstick to Salem Village for coven gatherings, and rebaptisms by Satan himself (who preferred full immersion to sprinkling) in the Shawshin River.[10] Almost immediately after the Andover outbreak, the hysteria spread to Gloucester, triggered there by claims on the part of a number of inhabitants to have sighted Frenchmen and Indians in the remote reaches of Cape Ann. Failure to find these invaders led locals like the Reverend John Emerson to the conclusion that "Gloucester was not alarumed . . . by real French and Indians, but that the devil and his agents were the cause of all the molestation which . . . befell the town." The search for the source of these disturbing apparitions eventuated in the arrest of an assortment of village scolds, misfits, and poor widows during September of 1692.[11]

As Emerson's observation suggests, the susceptibility to hysteria that instigated these two outbreaks of witchcraft in

[10] Sarah Loring Bailey, *Historical Sketches of Andover* (Boston, 1880), 194–237.

[11] Gloucester's "invasion" by French and Indians is described in Babson, *History,* 212; David T. Konig, *Law and Society in Puritan Massachusetts: Essex County, 1629–1692* (Chapel Hill, 1979), 167. Emerson's account of the town's spectral enemies is in Cotton Mather, *Magnalia Christi Americana* (Hartford, 1855), 621–23. The most detailed narrative of the involvement of Gloucester inhabitants in the witchcraft trials of 1692 is Marshall W. S. Swan, "The Bedevilment of Cape Ann," *Essex Institute Historical Collections,* 117 (1981), 153–77. Eleven women connected with Gloucester were arrested for witchcraft in that year. The first two suspected witches, Abigail Somes and Anne Doliber, had formerly resided in town but were living in Salem at the time of their arrests and were accused by Salem Village's "afflicted girls." Somes was an invalid, and Doliber, the daughter of Salem's Reverend John Higginson, was a poor, deranged woman who, after being deserted by her husband, a Gloucester mariner, returned to Salem and depended upon her family for support. (*Witchcraft Papers,* III, 733–37; and Babson, *History,* 81.) Among the six Gloucester women arrested in September, probably in connection with the "spectral invasion," Elizabeth Dicer was the wife of a Boston seaman who had drifted into Gloucester; widow Margaret Prince, whose daughter Mary and in-law Phebe Day were also accused, was notorious among her neighbors for her history of loud, violent domestic quarrels; widow Joan Penney was too poor to be rated in 1693; and another widow, Rachel Vinson, belonged to a family implicated in an earlier witchcraft case. (*Witchcraft Papers,* II, 651–53, 641–42; Babson, *Notes and Additions to the History of Gloucester,* 72; *Essex Ct. Recs.,* I, 301; IV, 440; VI, 116.)

northern Essex County was fostered in part by popular fears of vulnerability to attack by the French and Indians. Most locals could remember the Indian raid upon Andover in 1676 that had killed several inhabitants; now the onset of King William's War exposed both towns to the same perils again. This climate of dread and apprehension, coupled with the contagion emanating from Salem Village, caused panic in Gloucester and Andover to coalesce into accusations of witchcraft, an alchemy that Cotton Mather captured in *Wonders of the Invisible World,* written a few months after the outbreak of the delusion in northern Essex County. Deftly conflating fears over earthly armies with those of Satanic legions, Mather conjectured that "there is a sort of Arbitrary, even Military Government among the Devils. . . . Think on, Vast Regiments, of cruel and bloody, French Dragoons, with an Intendant over them, overrunning a pillaged Neighborhood."[12]

That anxieties over military attack contributed to the climate producing the witchcraft panic in northern Essex County is also suggested by the character of the delusion in Andover. Accusations not only reached into the top of the local social structure with surprising speed, but in addition, many townspeople admitted freely to covenanting with Satan or charged members of their own families. Those who at first denied diabolical dealings were easily persuaded of their mistake by close friends and relatives. Many Andoverians probably confessed to save themselves, but the town's unique pattern of recriminations against relatives and community leaders and of frequent self-incriminations also constituted a kind of collective purgation. Seventeenth-century New Englanders commonly construed catastrophes like epidemics or wars as "afflictions" sent by God to punish an entire community, either for collective backsliding or for failure to chasten individual sinners in their midst.[13] So in response to the renewal of warfare, Andoverians sought to preserve

[12] Cotton Mather, *Wonders of the Invisible World* (Boston, 1693), 232. The Indian attack on Andover is described in Bailey, *Historical Sketches of Andover,* 173.

[13] Edmund S. Morgan, *The Puritan Dilemma: The Story of John Winthrop* (Boston, 1958), esp. 69–83.

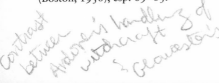

themselves from another scourging by the rod of divine wrath by a frenzied searching out of secret sin within individual souls, family circles, and high places, followed by mass admissions of wrongdoing.

Meanwhile Gloucester's townspeople also sought to stave off suffering at the hands of external enemies by rooting out internal subversives and hidden sin within their community. But the hysteria here assumed a configuration different from Andover's course because the source of divine displeasure with Gloucester was more apparent to its inhabitants. While uncertainty over how they had transgressed spiraled Andoverians into widening circles of suspicion, the panic among Gloucester's people did not spawn mass confession but came to focus upon a single case of sorcery that points to a distinctive source of communal anxiety, the possession of Mary Stevens.

Even before her alleged bewitchment in the fall of 1692, Mary Stevens had probably become an object of local concern because of her courtship by Francis Norwood, Jr., the Quaker grandson of Clement Coldom. The marriage of Mary to Francis would not have been the first merging of orthodox and dissenting families in Gloucester, but it was a union of tremendous social significance. For Mary was not a servant maid or the daughter of an ordinary local farmer up in Goose Cove, but the child of Deacon James Stevens of the First Church, one of Gloucester's most prominent citizens; and Francis was not the stepson of an obscure Quaker farmer, but an avowed Friend from a fairly affluent family. Francis's suit of Mary Stevens thus marked the first movement of the Friends in Gloucester out of their circumscribed position on the periphery of local society and the neighborhood of the remote northern Cape and into the mainstream. Their betrothal persuaded Lieutenant William Stevens, Mary's older brother and a major local merchant, that only demonic influences could have prevailed upon his sister to accept the attentions of a Quaker. As alarmed by the discovery of dissenting affinities among his own kin as Clement Coldom had been earlier, William Stevens acted to defend his family's integrity and to dissuade his sister from a disastrous alliance by declaring that she was bewitched. Stevens also sent for four of Salem Village's "afflicted girls," the instigators of the witchcraft trials held earlier in 1692, who claimed the power to discern who troubled the victims of malefic magic.[14] But when William Stevens sought assistance from Salem Village, he and his neighbors already suspected who had bewitched his sister: her prospective father-in-law, Francis Norwood, Sr., whom everyone in Gloucester had long believed to be a wizard. In 1679, when the Newbury household of William Morse became the haunt of evil spirits that made strange noises and sent objects flying about the room and down the chimney, Morse's suspicions fastened upon Caleb Powell, a seaman whose apprenticeship had been served under Gloucester's sorcerer. "He was brought up under [Francis] Norwood," the Reverend John Emerson told the county court, "and it was judged by the people there [in Gloucester] that Norwood studied the black art."[15]

John Emerson and his parishioners were willing to believe that their neighbor Norwood was a wizard because seventeenth-century Puritans linked religious heresy not only with sexual license but also with witchcraft. While all of the contending religious groups of this era commonly claimed that their competitors were in league with the devil, the Friends were especially subject to charges of either being possessed or practicing witchcraft because of their emphasis upon "the Light Within" and the bodily convulsions manifested by believers at Quaker meetings.[16] Allegations of witchcraft were made against the English founder of Quakerism, George Fox, and New England Puritan leaders quickly appropriated this slur in their attacks on his followers who crossed the Atlantic. In 1656, Massachusetts magistrates ordered midwives to search for "witches marks" on the bodies of Ann Austin and Mary Fisher, two of the first Quaker missionaries to arrive in the Bay colony, and early in the 1660s Governor John

[14] Babson, *History*, 211–212; Waters, *Ipswich*, I, 298; Mather, *Wonders of the Invisible World*, 232.

[15] *Essex Ct. Recs.*, VII, 355–60. Although Caleb Powell was the focus of Morse's suspicions, the testimony of their neighbors resulted in the conviction of Morse's wife for witchcraft in 1679. She was later reprieved by the Court of Assistants in 1681. (*Records of the Court of Assistants*, I, 159, 190.)

[16] Keith Thomas, *Religion and the Decline of Magic* (New York, 1971), 477, 487.

Endecott alleged that three other Quakeresses imprisoned at Boston were witches.[17] First generation ministers took a similar view of their sectarian competitors. Alarmed by the Friends' conversions within his own Salem congregation, the Reverend John Higginson characterized the "Quakers Light" as "the Devil's Sacrifice" and "a stinking Vapor from Hell." In Barnstable, Massachusetts, where local Quakers had their property seized after refusing to pay the minister's rate, the pastor there alleged that the Friends had bewitched his daughter to death as retribution.[18] Ordinary New Englanders shared the suspicions of their civil and clerical leaders. At Portsmouth, when Quakeress Mary Thompkins disrupted the sermon of Thomas Millet, Gloucester's former elder, "some of his unruly Hearers" threw her down a flight of stairs, "which might reasonably have broke her Neck, and which they themselves confessed, had she not been a witch (as they said of her. . . .)." Shortly thereafter at Newbury, Mary was disputing with the Reverend Thomas Parker: John Pike heard her stomach growl and concluded that "She has a Devil in her."[19] Widespread belief that the Quakers, and particularly female heretics, practiced witchcraft continued even after the most vigorous attempts to suppress the sect had ended in the mid-1660s. In 1669, Nathaniel Morton ascribed the miscarriages of both Anne Hutchinson and Quakeress Mary Dyer to their pacts with Satan.[20] During the 1680s, the connection between Quakerism and diabolism received renewed emphasis in the writings of Increase Mather, the pastor of Boston's Second Church and a leading member of the second generation of New England clergymen. Like his Puritan predecessors and contemporaries, Increase believed that the Quakers were prone both to demonic possession and to the practice of malefic magic. In *Illustrious Providences,* he linked the Friends to a group of Ranters on Long Island suspected of bewitching their neigh-

[17] George Bishop, *New England Judged by the Spirit of the Lord* (London, 1703), Part I, 12; Part II, 21, and 404–5.

[18] Bishop, *New England Judged*, Part II, 394, and 492–93.

[19] Bishop, *New England Judged*, Part I, 223; Part II, 394 and 400.

[20] Nathaniel Morton, *New England's Memorial* (Cambridge, Mass., 1669), 106–10.

bors and recounted the havoc that poltergeists created in the home of a Portsmouth Quaker.[21]

But the most forceful assertion of the traditional association between Quakerism and diabolism appeared in the years between 1689 and 1691 as a response to the open evangelism of George Keith in New England. A onetime Quaker schoolmaster turned itinerant preacher, Keith arrived in Boston in June of 1688 and promptly posted "in the most public place" a paper calling upon the Puritans to repent of their "degeneracy" and challenging four local ministers, Cotton Mather, John Allin, Joshua Moodey and Samuel Willard, to an open debate. Keith failed to draw Boston's clergymen into a confrontation, but upon his return to Philadelphia a few months later, he published an attack on the doctrine, polity, and ministry of New England's Congregational churches and a refutation of Increase Mather's earlier imputations against the Quakers.[22] This outspoken tract prodded Boston's ministers into a heated pamphlet exchange with their persistent critic. In 1689, Cotton Mather defended his father Increase's view that "Diabolical Possession was the thing which did dispose and encline men unto Quakerism" by bringing out a long account of the bewitchment of the four children of John Goodwin, one of whom had resided for a time in Cotton's household. The latter, an adolescent girl at the time of her "affliction," was able to read "a Quaker or Popish book" but not the Bible or any other edifying orthodox literature; her brother's bewitchment took the form of "torment" at being taken to the Congregational meetinghouse that subsided only when his father spoke of going to other assemblies, "particularly the Quakers." According to Cotton, what finally reclaimed the Goodwin children from

[21] Increase Mather, *An Essay for the Recording of Illustrious Providences* (Boston, 1684), 160, 188, and 341–46. Increase also described the haunting of the Morse house in 1679, although he did not make any connection between this case and the Quakers. Possibly it was Francis Norwood, Sr. to whom Increase was alluding when he reported that some in Newbury "were apt to think that a seaman suspected . . . to be a Conjurer, set the Devil on work thus to Disquiet Morse's family." (156)

[22] George Keith, *The Presbyterian and Independent Visible Churches in New England* (Philadelphia, 1689), esp. 198–228; *The Diary of Samuel Sewall*, ed. M. Halsey Smith, 2 vols. (New York, 1973), I, 172.

"the strange liberty which the Devils gave unto them to enjoy
the Writings and Meetings of the Quakers" were the prayers
of those same Boston clergymen so maligned by George
Keith.[23] Throughout the next year, 1690, Mather and his
colleagues kept up their attacks, producing two passionate
denunciations of the Friends that reiterated the affinity
between Quakerism and demonic forces. Keith retaliated in
kind later that year by alleging that the efforts of Boston's
ministers to relieve the young Goodwins' suffering were
nothing less than "a conjuring of the Devil." This charge
aroused a last retort from Cotton Mather in 1691: after
accusing Keith of blasphemy, he reminded his readers of the
resemblance between "quaking" and diabolical possession
and of an early Quakeress who had appeared naked in Puritan assemblies "like a Devil."[24]

   With this kind of anti-Quaker polemic as prologue—and
particularly the repeated linkage of the Friends with the devil's legions that poured from Boston's presses and pulpits in
the years immediately prior to 1692—it is not surprising that
William Stevens perceived his sister's acceptance of a Quaker
suitor as evidence of demonic possession. What is more
unexpected is that the seduction of the deacon's daughter by
the spells of a Quaker wizard did not set the stage for a
wholesale purging of dissenters from Gloucester through a
campaign cloaked in accusations of witchcraft. Stangely
enough, after the "afflicted girls" of Salem Village told William Stevens of seeing three people "sitting on his sister until
she died," they charged not the Norwoods but three local
women, all relatives of accused witches. Stranger still, although

[23] Cotton Mather, *Memorable Providences, Relating to Witchcrafts and
Possessions* (Boston, 1689), 1–47; appendix, 1, 6–7.

[24] John Allin, Joshua Moodey, and Samuel Willard, *The Principles of the
Protestant Religion Maintained and the Churches of New England Defended*
(Boston, 1690), preface; Cotton Mather, *The Serviceable Man* (Boston, 1690),
34–36; George Keith, *A Refutation of Three Opposers of the Truth* (Philadelphia, 1690), 71 and *The Pretended Antidote Proved Poyson* (Philadelphia, 1690); and Cotton Mather, *Little Flocks Guarded Against Grievous
Wolves* (Boston, 1691). Keith had the last word in this exchange, issuing
two tracts rebutting Mather in 1692. But in that year Keith was becoming
embroiled in another theological controversy, this time with his own brethren in Pennsylvania. Their differences resulted in the Keithian schism and
his formation of the Christian Quakers.

everyone in Gloucester suspected that the sorcery of Francis Norwood was the source of Mary Steven's possession, William and his neighbors accepted the guilt of the "witches" named by the girls.[25]

What endows the story of Mary Stevens with some importance for understanding the history of heterodoxy in Massachusetts is that this case was not singular. In fact, the same fears of heresy infecting orthodox families through intermarriage or other ties to dissenters that stirred William Stevens underlay many of the other witchcraft prosecutions in Essex County during 1692. The center of the hysteria that had peaked earlier in that year was Salem, the town with the largest single concentration of Quakers in the county. As in Gloucester, the connection in Salem between actual prosecutions for witchcraft and religious heterodoxy was indirect: few Quakers were accused of the crime and none of Essex County's most prominent Friends. The situation in Salem differed from the Stevens possession in Gloucester in only one way: here it was the "witches" rather than the bewitched who had ties of blood, marriage, affection or friendship to the Quakers. But many of the Salem trials, like the Stevens case, reflect the same anxieties over the merging of the orthodox and dissenting communities.

A substantial number of the witches accused by Salem Village's "afflicted girls" came from families or households that included Quaker members. A case in point is the apparently puzzling prosecution of Rebecca Nurse. The pattern of indictments in Salem conformed to that of Andover and Gloucester insofar as those initially accused were all social outcasts in some sense—poor or shrewish women prone to violent or unseemly behavior, and usually reputed for practicing malefic magic against their neighbors.[26] The sole

---

[25] The three women implicated in Mary Stevens's affliction all had family ties to other suspected witches: Abigail Row was Margaret Prince's granddaughter; Rebecca Dyke was Anne Doliber's sister-in-law, and Esther Elwell was the daughter of Grace Dutch who had been charged with witchcraft earlier in the seventeenth century. (*Witchcraft Papers*, I, 305–6; Babson, *History*, 81; *Essex Ct. Recs.*, I, 301.)

[26] The four women indicted before Rebecca Nurse in 1692, Sara Good, Sara Osborne, Martha Corey, and Tituba, a Negro slave, all conform to this description. See Boyer and Nissenbaum, *Salem Possessed*, 203–4, 193–94, and 146–47; and Konig, *Law and Society*, 184, and 146–47.

exception was Rebecca Nurse, a paragon of matronly piety, a pillar of respectability, a church member, and the wife of a substantial Village farmer, Francis. There was only one reason that her neighbors had for disliking Rebecca Nurse: in 1677, young Samuel Southwick, the orphaned son of a local Quaker farmer, John Southwick, chose the Nurses as his guardians and they took the boy into their home.[27] Rebecca and Francis were not Quakers, but their ward was.

Among those accused of witchcraft later in the trial proceedings were a large number of people who shared with Rebecca Nurse the same kind of indirect Quaker affinities, connections of kinship and friendship with religious dissidents. There was the Proctor family, for example, of which five members—John, his wife Elizabeth, and three of their children—were charged with witchcraft. What made the Proctors suspect in the eyes of their neighbors was less that John ran a tavern on the Ipswich Road than that his wife's family, the Bassets of Lynn, included a large number of Quakers. Joining the Proctors in prison were two members of the Basset family, along with four members of Lynn's Hawkes, Farrar, and Hart families, all of whom had Quaker connections.[28] The same was true of Andover residents Samuel Wardwell, his wife and two daughters, all relatives of the Quakeress Lydia Wardwell who in 1663 had appeared naked in the Newbury meetinghouse to protest persecution by the Puritans.[29] Another accused witch, Job Tookey of Beverly,

---

[27] *Essex Ct. Recs.*, VI, 294.

[28] On the Proctor family, see *Witchcraft Papers*, II, 655–95; Charles Upham, *Salem Witchcraft*, 2 vols. (Boston, 1867), II, 307. Accused witches Elizabeth Proctor and Mary DeRich were the daughters of Lynn Quaker William Basset, Sr.; accused witch Mary Basset was his daughter-in-law and the wife of William Basset, Jr., another Lynn Quaker. Mary Basset's maiden name was Hood, which connected her to another Lynn Quaker family. Thomas Farrar, Sr., charged with being a wizard, was the father of Lynn Quaker Thomas Farrar, Jr. Accused witches Sarah and Margaret Hawkes also had Quaker connections, but I have been unable to trace their precise family relationship to Quakers in the Hawkes family. This reconstruction of Quaker connections is based upon names culled from the "Records of the Salem Monthly Meeting," Microfilm Reel #1, Rhode Island Historical Society, Providence, Rhode Island; and from Alonzo Lewis and J. R. Newall, *History of Lynn*, I, 295, 298, and 305.

[29] Bailey, *Historical Sketches of Andover*, 212; *Essex Ct. Recs.*, III, 64.

had for years denied the gossip that his father, an English clergyman, was "an anabaptistical quaking rogue that for his maintenance went up and down England to delude souls for the Devil."[30] And in at least one instance, an accusation of witchcraft figured as a way for one of the "afflicted girls" of Salem Village to disassociate herself from the Quaker community. Ann Putnam, Jr.,described to the Court of Oyer and Terminer "an old gray head man" whom "people used to call father pharoah" who tormented her by insisting that he was her grandfather. The old man whom Ann Putnam, Jr., publicly denied as a blood relative was Thomas Farrar Sr., the father of a leading Lynn Quaker.[31] Shortly after the trials, one of Salem's chief Friends, Thomas Maule, hinted that some linkage existed between dissenting affinities and the witchcraft prosecutions, comparing the trials to the Quakers' sufferings and expressing relief that none of his "relations" had been charged.[32]

As well as bonds of blood and marriage, geographic propinquity to the Quaker community figured in the cases of many of the accused witches of Salem Village. Since most of the accused witches from Salem Village lived in its more prosperous eastern part, situated adjacent to Salem Town, and the majority of the accusers came from the more remote and economically stagnant western side of the village, it has been suggested that western farmers both envied and resented the east's easier access to the affluent, cosmopolitan seaport. But western Villagers may have been less disturbed by the proximity of their eastern neighbors to commercial Salem Town than they were by the even shorter physical distance separating the residences of the accused from Salem's Quaker enclave. The largest number of Salem's Friends lived just south of the eastern part of Salem Village in the area lying between the Ipswich Road and the bridge leading into Salem Town. In many cases, the homes and farms of Quaker families bordered on those of accused witches like the Proctors, George

---

[30] *Essex Ct. Recs.*, VIII, 330–38.

[31] Lewis and Newhall, *History of Lynn*, I, 295.

[32] Thomas Maule, *Truth Held Forth and Maintained* (New York, 1695), 206–7.

Jacobs, Sr., and Giles Corey. And if eastern Salem Villagers had greater contact with Salem Town than westerners did, they would also have had frequent contact with the Quaker families whose homes were situated along the major access routes to the town.[33] In any case, this close geographic connection appears to have encouraged some eastern Villagers to take on some of the characteristics of their Quaker neighbors, forms of behavior that blurred sectarian boundaries in the same way that close social ties to dissenters did. The justices examining suspected wizard George Jacobs, Sr., for example, asked, "Are you not the man that made disturbance at a Lecture at Salem?" "No great disturbance," Jacobs replied.[34] John Proctor's appeal to Boston ministers to take the trials out of Salem echoed the language of earlier Quaker denunciations of Puritan persecutions as "very like the Popish cruelties. . . . They have already undone us in our Estates, and that will not serve their turns, without our Innocent Bloods." Anticipating Thomas Maule's charges, Proctor contended that the supporters of the trials were "inraged and incensed against us by the Delusion of the Devil."[35] Testimony on behalf of John and Elizabeth Proctor signed by several of their Quaker neighbors probably helped to seal their fate. And when the condemned witch Sarah Good stood on the scaffold, she threatened Salem's assistant minister Nicholas Noyes, ". . . if you take away my life, God will give you blood to drink." In these words, Noyes found his vindication, for thirty years earlier, Marmaduke Stevenson and William Robinson had addressed the same sanguinary

[33] The best source on the location of residences in Salem during this period is Sidney Perley's series in the *Essex Antiquarian*, "Parts of Salem in 1700," 2 (1898) through 13 (1909), and his article "Brooksby, Salem in 1700," *EIHC*, 50 (1914), 357–65. For identifying Quaker families, Perley's essays are an excellent source; see also, "Records of the Salem Monthly Meeting" and Chu, "The Social Context of Religious Heterodoxy" (forthcoming, *Essex Institute Historical Collections.*) The residences of accused witches in Salem Village can be reconstructed from the "Map of Salem Village, 1692," with an accompanying key, in Upham, *Salem Witchcraft*, I, following p. xvii.

[34] *Witchcraft Papers,* II, 476.

[35] "Petition of John Proctor to the Ministers of Boston," July 23, 1692, in *Witchcraft Papers*, II, 476.

prophecy to Boston magistrates just before the two Quakers were hanged.[36]

Even among the accused who had no familial or geographic affinities with the Friends, the sort of behavior most likely to invite suspicion, to attract unfavorable notice, or to incur the censure of the presiding magistrates was distinctly Quakerlike. During the examination of Boston mariner John Alden, "all were ordered to go down into the street where a ring was made; and the same accuser cried out, there stands Aldin, a bold fellow, with his hat on before the judges. . . ."[37] Alice Parker of Salem Town first incriminated herself by foretelling the fates of men at sea, her claim to prophetic powers evoking an association with Quakerism.[38] And the general characteristics displayed by or ascribed to many of the accused—the cavilling questioning of authority, the refusal to confess error in spiritual loyalties and, among women, publicly dominant, assertive behavior in dealing with men— were all traits familiar to Essex County residents and magistrates in the context of their experience with Quakerism.

In a few cases tried in 1692 and even earlier, the relationship between Quakerism as well as other forms of religious heterodoxy and witchcraft accusations was direct and unmistakable. Philip English and his wife, who fled Salem Town to New York after being indicted in 1692, were both vocal supporters of the Church of England; George Burroughs, the former minister of Salem Village who was executed as a wizard, held Baptist convictions; Abigail Somes, the invalid daughter of Gloucester Quakeress Elizabeth Somes, lived in the household of Samuel Gaskill, one of Salem Village's leading Friends, until her imprisonment for witchcraft. Even before the Salem hysteria, deviance from orthodoxy could invite indictment for malefic magic: Goody Glover, the old woman charged with bewitching the Goodwin children in 1689, was an Irish Catholic.[39] But more typ-

---

[36] Cited in Boyer and Nissenbaum, *Salem Possessed,* 7–8; compare with the "Letter of Marmaduke Stevenson and William Robinson from the Boston Jail," August, 1659, in Bishop, *New England Judged,* Part I, 237.

[37] Mather, *Wonders of the Invisible World,* 211.

[38] *Witchcraft Papers,* II, 623.

[39] On Phillip English, a Jerseyman who was an outsider ethnically as well as religiously, see Henry W. Belknap, "Philip English, Commerce Builder,"

ically the accused witches were not themselves members of dissenting sects, and their connections with heterodoxy consisted in more tangential ties to dissenters among blood relatives, in-laws, household members, or neighbors and friends. Even in the case of Abigail Somes, accusations passed over Samuel Gaskill, for decades a central figure in the Salem Meeting, and focused instead on his ward, the child of an orthodox father and an heretical mother. Her background and those of many other accused witches suggest that the focus of anxiety was less upon dissenters themselves than those individuals who because of their relations or residences fell under suspicion of harboring if not heterodox sympathies then at least sympathy for the heterodox. Like the bewitched Mary Stevens, the alleged witches of Salem had ambiguous social affinities. Their ties of family and friendship to dissenters cast doubt on their religious loyalties, making such figures even more threatening to the maintenance of orthodoxy than known dissenters.[40]

The widespread anxiety over religious allegiances reflected in the witchcraft hysteria had been building for almost a

Proceedings of the American Antiquarian Society, new series, 41 (1931), 17–24, and Konig, *Law and Society,* 184. Mary Warren, a servant in the Proctor household, was the first to accuse Abigail Somes, who admitted during her examination that she was the sister of John Somes, the Quaker cooper earlier punished by Boston authorities. No verdict survives in the Somes case, but Abigail was not executed, possibly because she alleged to the court that she was herself afflicted by "many persons [that I have seen] at my mother's camp at Gloucester." (*Witchcraft Papers,* III, 733–37. I am grateful to John Murrin for bringing to my attention that George Burroughs had refused to have his younger children baptized, something that came up during his examination by the justices. (See Upham, *Salem Witchcraft,* II, 157–63.) On Goody Glover, see Mather, *Memorable Providences,* 7 and 9. The correspondence between ties to dissenters and suspicions of witchcraft may have figured in earlier prosecutions as well. For example, John Godfrey, a herdsman indicted for witchcraft several times during the 1650s and 1660s, was originally a servant of John Spencer, a follower of Anne Hutchinson. In a detailed study of Godfrey, John Demos describes the alleged wizard's tendency to "startle," "confuse," and "deliberately provoke" his neighbors, assertive traits often associated with the Quakers and other Antinomian dissidents. ("John Godfrey and His Neighbors: Witchcraft and the Social Web of Massachusetts," *William and Mary Quarterly,* 3rd ser., 33 (1976), 244–45.)

[40] David Konig makes a similar argument respecting the significance of accusations against women married to non-English men. (*Law and Society,* 184.)

decade before it burst into panic at Salem and Gloucester in
1692. At its source were changes forced upon Massachusetts
Bay by England that challenged the hegemony of Congregationalist orthodoxy. For more than fifty years, the government established by the charter of 1629 had supported the
public worship of God in the Congregational way and had
protected the colony's churches from dissent. But in the 1680s
imperial policy "destroyed the accustomed order of things
by which the Puritans had maintained supremacy and supposedly advanced God's kingdom."[41] The ambition of the
Stuart kings to centralize the administration of their empire
throughout North America resulted in the confiscation of
the old Massachusetts charter in 1684 and in the consolida-
tion of all of the New England colonies into a single entity,
the Dominion. The Dominion radically altered the government that Massachusetts Puritans had established under their
former charter by abolishing the colony's elected assembly,
restricting town meetings, and according all powers of taxation and legislation to a royally appointed governor and his
council. The abrasive Sir Edmund Andros, a military officer
and the governor of New York, was named to head the
Dominion in 1686, and he pursued a course still more
alarming to Bay colonists. Andros not only threatened their
livelihoods by calling land titles into question and by strictly
enforcing the Navigation Acts, but he also implemented policies aimed at undermining the close relationship that had
existed between the Congregational churches and the state.
He remodelled the procedure for jury selection to reduce the
influence of church members and insisted upon swearing on
the Bible in the courts, a practice repugnant to the Puritans.
He ousted church members from important positions in the
militia and replaced them with Anglican officers. And finally,
Andros imposed liberty of conscience upon Massachusetts
Bay.

The extension of toleration to all dissenters in the Dominion afforded the Friends complete freedom of worship and
gave Quaker missionary George Keith license to preach freely
in the streets of Boston. At the same time, the Bay's small

[41] David S. Lovejoy, *The Glorious Revolution in America* (New York, 1972),
180.

Anglican minority, formerly forced to attend Puritan worship services and compelled to contribute to the support of
Congregationalist ministers, now enjoyed the particular favor
of the new Episcopal governor. To the Puritan majority's
dismay, after the Bishop of London assigned the Reverend
Robert Ratcliffe to Boston as the Bay's first resident Episcopal priest, Andros seized part of a public burial ground as
the site for an Anglican church, King's Chapel. And while its
construction was being completed, he commandeered the
Congregationalists' Old South meetinghouse for Episcopal
services. These developments, combined with Andros's revo-
cation of tax support for the salaries of orthodox clergymen,
led many Congregationalists to fear that the Dominion's policy
would pass from protecting liberty of conscience to perse-
cuting the Puritans and attempting to establish Episcopalianism as the state religion.[42]

The successful rebellion of Massachusetts inhabitants
against Andros in April of 1689—an event that followed in
the wake of the Glorious Revolution in England—did little
to restore order to the troubled colony. But the aftermath of
the rebellion did reveal the depth of anxieties occasioned by
the Dominion's challenges to Puritan preeminence. While Bay
colonials waited for the new king, William III, to determine
their future, Massachusetts endured three years of chaos under
a temporary government unequal to coping with the disarray in the colony's judicial system and military defenses, a
serious trade recession, and the continuing threat of French
and Indians on the frontier. Uncertainty over the fate of the
colony and internal difficulties notwithstanding, the interim
government immediately began making inroads upon
Andros's imposed toleration by reinstating tax support for
ministerial maintenance and by turning a deaf ear to dissidents' complaints of mistreatment. At the same time, the
orthodox clergy campaigned to reclaim any souls that they
had lost to competing sects during the period when liberty
of conscience had prevailed. Boston Anglicans, whose new
chapel had been vandalized and threatened with total
destruction during the upheaval, came under virulent attack

[42] *Ibid.*, 179–95.

for their alleged complicity in a "Catholic conspiracy" to deliver all of England's colonies to the Pope.[43]

Yet the chief concern of Congregationalist leaders was not the Anglicans, who had in any case been badly discredited by their close ties to the hated Dominion regime. It was instead the Quakers that Cotton Mather singled out in his election sermon of 1690 as the Bay colony's "most Malicious as well as most Pernicious Enemies," who "by Writing, Railing, and the Arts peculiar to themselves . . . are Labouring to Unchurch all the Lord's People here."[44] In June of 1689, just two months after the overthrow of Andros, Mather and other members of the Boston clergy initiated their counteroffensive against George Keith, "to furnish the Churches in this Land with an Antidote against the contagion of Quakerism." Besides calling up the old associations of Quakerism with witchcraft, the flurry of treatises and sermons published by Mather and his colleagues between 1689 and 1691 advised Massachusetts laymen on how to confute Quaker proselytizers, providing specific responses to all controverted theological points. Although Mather and his brethren believed that "our Churches have yet had very little Impression from any [Quaker] Seducers hitherto," the frequency with which they administered these "Antidotes" belies their expressed confidence in the immunity of their congregations to the infection of heresy.[45]

Almost a decade of confusion in all spheres of the colony's life and of concern over the maintenance of social order and authority came to an end in the fall of 1691 when William III finally gave Massachusetts Bay a new charter that provided for rule by a royally appointed governor and an elected assembly. But other items included in the new charter only aggravated the apprehensions aroused by the Dominion's attack upon the Congregationalist establishment. The new constitution precluded the possibility of religious discrimination in voting rights by replacing, as the basis of the franchise, church membership with a property qualification;

[43] *Ibid.*, 238–45, 281–88, 324–25, and 350–53.

[44] Mather, *The Serviceable Man*, 34–35.

[45] Allin, et al., *The Principles of the Protestant Religion Maintained*, preface.

it also guaranteed liberty of conscience to all Christians except Catholics. While the king allowed the Bay government to continue the policy of supporting the Congregationalist clergy by taxes on all inhabitants, orthodox and dissenters alike, the charter imposed once and for all a real liberalization of religious life upon Massachusetts.[46]

The progress of legal toleration was an unwelcome and unsettling development for most Massachusetts colonials, who still regarded themselves as a people in covenant with God to uphold orthodoxy. On the other hand, the developments of the intercharter period had placed the Bay's civil and clerical leaders in a delicate position, presenting them with political exigencies that dictated their lending lip service, at least, to liberty of conscience. Andros's aggressive pro-Anglican policies had demonstrated that toleration might be a principle worth upholding for the protection of Puritan orthodoxy itself. During the years between 1689 and 1691, when the Bay colony's agents were negotiating for a new charter with the king and his ministers, several Massachusetts spokesmen had proclaimed their adherence to religious liberty, hoping by this strategy to limit royal interference in ecclesiastical affairs. And after 1691, the Bay's leadership continued to support publicly the official policy of toleration as the price for preserving the other privileges restored to the colony under the new charter.[47]

The situation that had evolved in Massachusetts between 1684 and 1691 thus made it impolitic and impossible to renew civil repression aimed directly at religious dissenters. But over the same period, intersectarian tensions were stretched to the breaking point: hysteria over rumored Papist conspiracies, attacks upon King's Chapel and its adherents and, especially, the impassioned invective against the Quakers expressed the extreme excitability over religious differences that gripped the orthodox laity. They had long held that to profane the holy commonwealth by granting religious equality to dis-

[46] Lovejoy, *The Glorious Revolution in America,* 347–48; and Timothy Breen, *The Character of the Good Ruler* (New Haven, 1970), 183–84.

[47] Worrall, *Quakers,* 49–50; see also, Increase Mather, *A Vindication of New England* (Boston, 1690), passim; and Cotton Mather, *The Serviceable Man,* 35.

senters was to invite divine retribution in the form of Indian wars, epidemics, or natural disasters. And by 1691 the prospect of a genuinely pluralistic religious culture supplanting orthodox purity and distinctiveness seemed a real and ominous possibility. Not only had the new charter compromised the Bay's original spiritual mission by outlawing the civil suppression of heresy and by according political rights to propertied dissenters, but the accommodation to heterodoxy had also started to manifest itself at the level of social relationships. The amalgamation of orthodoxy and dissent exemplified in the courtship of Mary Stevens and in the merging of Congregationalist and Quaker families in the neighborhood networks of Lynn and Salem augured the emergence of a new order that profoundly threatened the majority of pious Puritans.

This background of popular resistance to religious liberalization provides one context for understanding the Essex County witchcraft panic of 1692. Although political exigencies ruled out the persecution of known dissenters by the state, they did not prevent an alarmed laity from trying to reclaim "marginal" members of orthodox society, those whose religious loyalties social ties to the dissenting community had rendered ambiguous. If the civil government could no longer stamp out heresy at its source, other measures might at least contain its contagion by arresting the spread of dissenting influence through families and neighborhoods. The closing of ranks among the Congregationalists in Essex County was expressed in allegations of diabolical possession and accusations of witchcraft made against people linked to the Quakers. William Stevens could not attack the Norwoods themselves, but he could try to intimidate his sister into rejecting a Quaker suitor by insisting that she was possessed by the devil. Neither could Salem Villagers strike directly at the Friends in their midst, but they could demand that their neighbors with Quaker ties confess to being in league with Satan's legions and publicly repudiate the connection.

Irreducible to any single source of social strain, the witchcraft hysteria of 1692 reflected a wide array of antagonisms and uncertainties. Many accusations within Salem Village grew out of longstanding factional rivalries. Other allegations figured as a collective retaliation against village scolds or women long suspected of using malefic magic against their neighbors. Still others spilled over from disputes between near neighbors over land and livestock or from tensions generated by the renewed anxieties over military attack, as the Andover outbreak illustrates. Many of these simmering local antagonisms boiled over in charges of witchcraft because of disruptions in the judicial system during the intercharter period: the creation of the powerful court of Oyer and Terminer in 1692, commissioned to adjudicate only witchcraft cases, encouraged Essex County residents to cast all of their complaints in supernatural terms.[48] But yet another skein of the tangled threads that wove the witchcraft delusion were spun by popular fears over the spread of religious dissent. Although sectarian tensions cannot account for all of the prosecutions, they figured in enough cases to indicate that religious differences played a significant role in shaping the witchcraft outbreak, and that the episode constituted in part a counteroffensive against the Quaker heresy under the conditions imposed by the new Massachusetts charter.

As several historians have pointed out, the entire intercharter period displayed the vulnerability of many of the "boundaries" established by the old colonial order in Massachusetts Bay.[49] Political upheaval created uncertainties over land titles, the powers and jurisdictions of the judicial system, and the authority of a succession of colony governments. Military crisis simultaneously raised fears over preserving the security of Massachusetts' physical borders from attack by the French and Indians. The witchcraft delusion came as a response to the stress and insecurity created by these confusions of social, legal, and territorial boundaries. But the hysteria also registered the strain resulting from the blurring of boundaries in the realm of religious life, the diffusion of sectarian divisions portended by the policy of

---

[48] Among the recent historians of the witchcraft hysteria, Paul Boyer and Stephen Nissenbaum emphasize the village antagonism, while Kai Erikson and David Konig place the delusion within a wider context of cultural disorientation and institutional disruption occasioned by the intercharter period. (*Wayward Puritans: A Study in the Sociology of Deviance* (New York, 1966), 137–59; *Law and Society*, 158–68.)

[49] See Kai Erikson and David Konig on this point, and also Lovejoy, *The Glorious Revolution in America*, 353 and 373–74.

official toleration. Cotton Mather's account of the witch-craft hysteria expressed aptly both the collective anxieties induced by the anticipated obliteration of older distinctions under the new charter and the strategy of New England's counterattack: ". . . such is the Descent of the Devil at this day upon ourselves, that I may Truly tell you, the Walls of the Whole World are broken down! The usual walls of Defense about Mankind have such a Gap made in them that the very Devils are broke in upon us. . . ." Mather placed witchcraft within the succession of other afflictions that had befallen New England, the "sorcery" of hostile Indians, the loss of the old charter, the onset of King William's War, and the heresies of "Seducing Spirits," the Quakers and other heterodox sects. His advice was unity among the faithful: "Let us not be a Troubled House, altho' we are so much haunted by Devils." To insure that no one missed his mean-ing, Mather included an account of "a sort of daemon" who "stirred up Strife" among the inhabitants of a ninth-century German village. "He uttered Prophecies, he detected Villan-ies, he branded People with all kinds of Infamies. . . . Let us be aware lest such Daemons do, Come hither also!"[50] "Dae-mons" of this description had a great deal in common with Quakers who were also given to prophecies and to strictures against the orthodox majority. Lieutenant William Stevens did not want his sister to marry one.

But neither the Court of Oyer and Terminer nor the admonitions of Cotton Mather could remedy the difficulties in the "Troubled House" of William Stevens: those accused of afflicting Mary Stevens were set free as the hysteria sub-sided in 1693, the same year that she wed Francis Norwood, Jr. The prosecutions also failed to drive the devils out of the "Troubled House" of New England: the trials at Salem backfired badly as a device for shoring up orthodox loyal-ties, and revulsion at the complicity of local clergymen like Samuel Parris and Nicholas Noyes in the discredited prose-cutions produced a wave of Quaker conversions in the area

---

[50] Mather, *Wonders of the Invisible World,* 42, 48, and 60–61. Mather endorsed legal toleration, but he remained a stringent critic of Quakerism until the last years of his life. See especially, Middlekauff, *The Mathers,* 316–17.

around Lynn and Salem.[51] In Gloucester inhabitants also experienced compunction over their participation in the panic, and for a brief period the suspicion of dissenters receded. In 1694, enough voters were willing to overlook the Quakerism of John Pearce, Sr., to elect his son-in-law Timothy Somes to a term on the board of selectmen. When Samuel Bownas, a traveling English Quaker missionary, stopped in town in 1706, some curious Congregationalists deserted the Sabbath services at the First Church to attend his two meetings, "It being a New Thing." Even the Reverend John White came to the second of Bownas's meetings and attempted to reduce the Quaker from his erroneous beliefs about water baptism, perfectionism, and election. Over the same period, some additional Quaker families arrived in town: shipwrights, mariners, and blacksmiths attracted by Gloucester's growing maritime economy.[52]

Although popular hysteria over the spread of heterodoxy subsided briefly in the years after the Salem trials, the anxieties that the Quakers aroused within the Congregationalist camp did not die out with the witchcraft delusion. On the contrary, the lull in sectarian hostilities did not even outlast the first decade of the eighteenth century. Despite his "quiet and civil" reception at Cape Ann, Samuel Bownas admitted nevertheless to encountering "great opposition" at Gloucester in 1706.[53] Antipathy to dissenters was again rising in town: the orthodox had resumed closing their ranks, and this time, reprisals against local Friends assumed a more direct and effective form. Throughout the opening decades of the eighteenth century, the Congregationalist majority in Gloucester advertised their aversion to dissenters by deploying economic tactics that discouraged the Friends from staying on in town. The career of Gloucester's most prominent

[51] Worrall, *Quakers,* 49–50.

[52] Babson, *History,* 585; Samuel Bownas, *An Account of the Life of Samuel Bownas* (Philadelphia, 1759), 127–29. During the first decade of the eighteenth century, Quaker shipwrights Thomas and Nathaniel Sanders, Scituate blacksmith Jonathan Springer, and Lynn mariner Joseph Goodrich settled in Gloucester. There may have been others as well, but the lack of complete records of membership in the Society of Friends for this period makes a precise count impossible.

[53] Bownas, *An Account,* 127.

Quaker during this period reveals both the strength and the efficacy of local exclusivism.

Blacksmith Jonathan Springer came to Gloucester from Scituate in 1704 and set up as a general retail merchant, selling provisions for fishing voyages, running a packet trade to Boston, and peddling locally produced commodities along the Atlantic coast. Springer's commercial investments and connections were impressive compared to the scale of other local operations at the time: he held partial interest in four small sloops and a valuable stock in trade with two Quaker partners, John Maule of Salem and Walter Newberry of Boston, and he dealt directly with major fish exporters in the capital.[54] But despite the advantages of financial backing by nonlocal coreligionists, opposition from within town thwarted Springer's schemes for seizing the opportunity offered by Gloucester's infant fishery. Springer's suit for debt against John Vittum in 1712 reveals the extent to which religious intolerance limited business success. Springer had hired Vittum, a mariner, to pilot a sloop to Boston where a cargo of bullets, tar, and bread awaited. Vittum loaded part of the goods waiting on the Boston wharf but sailed off before the Negro porter who was transporting the commodities from a warehouse to the dock had completed the loading. Questioned later about why he had left half of Springer's merchandise behind, Vittum replied that he "did not care what became of the rest of the goods but the bullets . . . but the Quaker dog shall never have one of them again for a negro is noe evidence in court and it is as good going a privateering as taking anything from him [Springer] as from a french man for I doe account him noe better."[55] Vittum's attitude toward doing business with Springer specifically and with the Friends generally was typical of other men in and around Gloucester. A year later, when Springer went to court again, this time suing Adam Cogswell, a member of a prominent landed family in Ipswich, the defendant related the history of Springer's hard dealings with him. Cogswell took particular

[54] EPF #26043. For a full discussion of the ways that religious fellowship benefited the businesses of Philadelphia Quakers, see Frederick Tolles, *Meetinghouse and Countinghouse: The Quaker Merchants of Colonial Philadelphia, 1682–1763* (1948, repr. New York, 1963), 68, and 89–90.

[55] Springer v. Vittum, 1712, FCCP.

exception to one of Springer's demands for repayment of a debt in "a Railing, Reviling Letter after the Manner of the Quakers."[56]

These cases represent only a small proportion of the abundant legal difficulties that blighted Springer's business career in Gloucester. Until his early death in 1714, he appeared constantly before the court, both as a plaintiff charging malfeasance on the part of his pilots and as a defendant in suits brought by farmers who alleged that he embezzled the profits of produce on consignment. Even after Springer died, litigation involving his affairs continued to crop up on court dockets as Maule and Newberry attempted to recover debts due his estate.[57] Springer's Quakerism did not dissuade all orthodox local residents from doing business with him, and he did not always have to resort to the courts to collect his obligations. But considering his capital, his influential connections in other ports, the growing local demand for his stock of provisions and the limited availability of all these resources in Gloucester around 1710, Springer's inability to attract a larger clientele is surprising. Only a handful of inhabitants had book debts or bonds due to his estate in 1714, and for credit he remained almost totally reliant upon outsiders, especially the more affluent Friends of Lynn, Salem, and Boston. His venture into the Gloucester fishery a failure, he died insolvent.[58]

Springer's distant origins and the periodic military crises of the first decade of the eighteenth century may have hampered his chances for success, but among his orthodox contemporaries were other recent immigrants engaged in similar enterprises who managed to make money in Gloucester. The

[56] Springer v. Cogswell, 1713, FCCP.

[57] Springer v. Elwell, 1714; Putnam v. Springer, 1712; Estate of Springer v. Tarr, 1719, v. Babson, 1719, v. Bennet, 1719, v. Elwell, 1719, FCCP. Estate of Springer v. Sanders, November, 1717 and May 20, 1718, MSCJ. Springer's legal problems in Gloucester are an instance of the more general phenomenon that William Nelson found in the towns of Plymouth County for the same period: that the presence of Quakers significantly raised levels of intratown debt litigation, even in otherwise nonlitigious communities. (*Dispute and Conflict Resolution in Plymouth County, Massachusetts, 1725–1825*, 58, 59, and 61.)

[58] EPF #26043; "Petition for the Sale of Real Property," November 8, 1715, MSCJ.

real source of Springer's troubles in establishing a local trade
was his status as a dissenter: the resentment and mistrust
resulting from his religious nonconformity both limited the
willingness of inhabitants to deal with him and provided those
orthodox farmers and mariners who did with a pretext for
exploiting him economically.[59] Intolerance trapped Springer
in a vicious circle: the orthodox perception of Quakers as
unscrupulous, litigious sharpsters discouraged the fair treatment of dissenters in business dealings; Springer's recourse
to the courts to collect his debts simply reinforced the prevailing stereotype.

The in-group economic morality that operated in
Gloucester, not only within defined geographic limits but also
within a narrow cultural compass, impaired not only Jonathan Springer's business career but those of other Gloucester
Quakers as well. Exemplifying even more pointedly the difference that religious orthodoxy made in determining commercial success are the disparate careers of the Sanders
brothers, who came to Gloucester from Plymouth at about
the same time as Jonathan Springer and set up a shipyard in
the southern harbor. Nathaniel Sanders held Quaker sympathies, and it is likely that his brother Thomas did as well—
at least when he first arrived in town. Both brothers did business with Jonathan Springer, making joint investments in
fishing and trading vessels. But Thomas subsequently became
a pillar of the First Church, claimed the title of "Captain"
for commanding a government sloop during the Indian wars
of the 1720s, and amassed one of the largest estates in town
by the mid-eighteenth century. Nathaniel retained his Quaker
connection and drifted out of town sometime in the 1730s
without ever sharing his brother's success.[60] Difficulties like

---

[59] Max Weber, "Religious Rejections of the World and Their Directions,"
and "The Protestant Sects and the Spirit of Capitalism," in *Essays from
Max Weber,* eds. Gerth and Mills, 302–22, and 329. On the Quaker reputation for slyness and dishonesty in business dealings and its currency
throughout the Anglo-American world during the seventeenth and eighteenth centuries, see Tolles, *Meetinghouse and Countinghouse,* 47–48 and
60–61.

[60] Babson, *History,* 241. At the time of his death, Thomas Sanders's estate
was worth 632 pounds sterling. (EPF #24778.) For a certificate of ownership of a vessel with Springer, see *MA,* vol. 7, dated November, 1707. See
also MGSP, July 17, 1728.

those of Nathaniel Sanders and Jonathan Springer were not unusual among the Friends in other North Shore ports at this time. Many other Essex County Quakers with commercial ambitions moved to more congenial communities, either to the north in Maine and New Hampshire or to the south in Rhode Island and Pennsylvania. In Salem, for example, neither John Maule nor any of his fellow Friends succeeded his father, Thomas Maule, among the ranks of that town's major traders.[61]

While professed Quakers like Jonathan Springer and Nathaniel Sanders, because of their involvement in trade, became the most visible and vulnerable targets for popular religious animosity, intense suspicion also continued to surround individuals in Gloucester of more obscure status whose ties to the Friends were only through the affiliation of family members. An example is the career of James Dyke, who appeared more frequently in court than any other Gloucester inhabitant between the 1720s and 1740s. Dyke's first offense in 1720 was bringing into town a child judged likely to become a public burden; four years later he allegedly introduced another "chargeable" child to Gloucester, a bastard that he fathered but refused to support. During the same decade, Dyke also brought suit against the town proprietors, protesting that they had deprived him of his rightful share in the division of the commons. Throughout the 1730s and 1740s, Dyke's legal difficulties continued: in 1735, he was imprisoned for assaulting his neighbor Nathaniel Rust, and compounded his offense by breaking jail with a fellow prisoner convicted of rape; a few years later, the town took him to court for enclosing part of a common highway. James Dyke did not conform to the pattern of Gloucester's other

[61] On the Salem province tax list of 1700, four Quakers ranked among the top decile of ratepayers, a group that included trader Thomas Maule and two members of the Buffum family who also had commercial interests. But in the province tax list of 1748, only two Quakers, both farmers, ranked within the top decile and no Quakers appeared among the town's major merchants. (Tax and Valuation Lists for Massachusetts Towns, comp. Ruth Crandall, Harvard University Microfilm Edition, Reel #8.) As Frederick Tolles points out, the use of economic weapons for religious persecution of the Quakers has a long history, dating back to the sect's origin in seventeenth-century England. (*Meetinghouse and Countinghouse*, 36.)

petty criminals. A long-established resident of Second Parish, a steady farmer, a full church member, he seems an unlikely habitual offender. Still, something did set Dyke apart from his fellow townsmen—his two sisters were Quakers.[62] As Thomas Sanders's successes suggest, it was possible for some former religious dissenters or for those with heterodox family connections to ingratiate themselves with local society. But James Dyke was not like Sanders, a military hero, and for him, acceptance never came.

What explains the persistence of anti-Quaker prejudice in provincial Essex County? Why were local Friends widely regarded with suspicion, mistrusted as businessmen, disdained as marital partners, and discouraged from settling in town? In part, the continuing prejudice against the Quakers reflects the preservation of the past in the long memory of local society. One orthodox generation recounted to another the peculiarities of Quakerism's prophetic period in the mid-seventeenth century, repeated to them the traditional association of heresy with witchcraft, and reminded them that religious distinctiveness should not be lost to the encroachments of diversity. But the cast of mind capable of equating Quakers with Frenchmen and dogs and intent upon eliminating dissenters from local life seems less like the residue of an inherited antagonism than the product of a present provocation. What makes the animus against the Quakers seem still more unaccountable is that it coincided with the period in the early eighteenth century when Quaker doctrine and practice was coming increasingly to resemble Congregationalism, and when the Friends themselves were underplaying their sectarian peculiarities.[63]

Doctrinal differences continued to divide Puritans from Friends in provincial New England, but popular interest in these theological discrepancies peaked in intensity early in the eighteenth century and afterwards subsided. In 1702, for example, the apostate George Keith's debate at Lynn with English "Public Friend" John Richardson drew a large audi-

---

[62] Babson, *History,* 81; MGSP, June 28, 1720, January 1, 1726; MSCJ, October 28, 1735 and October, 1724; and "Records of the Salem Monthly Meeting," 1728, and 1731.

[63] Worrall, *Quakers,* 43–80.

ence from throughout Essex County. Keith, whose local notoriety dated from his former career as a Quaker evange-list, had now defected to the Episcopal Church and had become a missionary for the Society for the Propagation of the Gospel. With all the zeal of a new convert, he "had boasted much of what he would prove against the Friends," and so "in great Expectation to hear the Quakers run down . . . a great many People gathered together of Several Professions and Qualities . . . coming from every Quarter to see and hear How matters would go."[64] Similarly, in 1706, when Samuel Bownas preached at Newbury to a skeptical and unruly crowd of Congregationalists, "there were many Bibles then appeared," as his auditors tested against revelation the truth of the missionary's message.[65] Yet after the first decade of the eighteenth century, theological differences began to pale in importance as a point of division between the Friends and the orthodox. Missionaries like Bownas and even ardent Foxian laymen like Thomas Maule attempted to minimize their sect's doctrinal divergences from orthodoxy, and their efforts told in the comment of one Congregationalist cler-gyman, who confided to Bownas in the 1730s that the Friends' theology had become "more refined" than their earlier doc-trine.[66]

Over the same period that Quaker doctrine was becom-ing more acceptable, the sect's ecclesiastical practices were conforming more to the Congregationalist model. Supplant-ing the self-appointed or popularly acclaimed spiritual lead-ers of the seventeenth century were ministers chosen by the Friends' business meetings after a formal examination. Sit-ting on raised "facing benches," Quaker ministers and elders presided over worship services which had by the early eigh-teenth century become more restrained gatherings than their enthusiastic antecedents.[67] Even as their own polity assumed a less lay-centered character, Quakers kept up their objec-tions to Congregationalism's "hireling" clergy, to whose

[64] John Richardson, *An Account of the Life of John Richardson* (Philadel-phia, 1759), 95 and 106.
[65] Bownas, *An Account,* 123.
[66] Bownas, *An Account,* 177.
[67] Worrall, *Quakers,* 91.

support the Friends were compelled to contribute until 1728.[68] Yet this Quaker critique of the establishment actually enhanced the sect's appeal to some orthodox laymen, who believed that maintenance by taxation compromised the clergy's stance as "otherworldly prophets." The appearance of Samuel Bownas in Gloucester emboldened one member of John White's church to declare that "Religion could never prosper, so long as it was made a Trade to get Bread by."[69]

The discipline of members and the arbitration of personal and economic differences was another area in which Quakers created a set of institutions similar in character to those of the orthodox community. The Congregational system for regulating the behavior of members involved the pastor, the saints, and, in some congregations, lay ruling elders, who heard testimony concerning the transgressions of backsliders or the quarrels between individuals and then punished the guilty or adjudicated the controversy. Private conferences outside of the church with the parties involved were often a preliminary to public proceedings. The Quakers undertook a similar oversight of their members' behavior: the "Discipline" set forth in 1708 codified rules for conduct essentially similar to orthodox standards. In the same year that the "Discipline" was adopted, the Salem Meeting also started a system in which two-man committees regularly visited all families of Friends in the area, an institution similar to the visitations conducted by Congregationalist pastors and elders.[70] A related means of regulating the behavior of members were travel certificates, the Quaker counterpart to the pastoral letter of dismission used to acquaint the Congregational churches of other communities with the piety and good character of migrating members. Quaker certificates improved upon the orthodox system by including not only members who moved permanently, but also those who traveled on business or as missionaries. James Goodrich, for example, "being bound to sea," received a letter from the Salem Meeting attesting to his good conduct and to his status as a single man; John Maule acquired a similar recommendation before

[68] Worrall, *Quakers,* 122–23.
[69] Bownas, *An Account,* 129.
[70] "Records of the Salem Monthly Meeting," 1708; Worrall, *Quakers,* 70.

moving to Philadelphia. Certificates served a religious, social, and economic function for traveling sectarians, establishing their integrity with distant meetings as well as with prospective marital partners and business associates. At the same time, by insuring them a welcome, such letters of introduction helped to confine the contacts of members on the move to Quaker circles. Meetings did not grant such recommendations as a matter of course and often withheld certification from members as a means of discipline. In 1717, the Salem Friends strengthened their restrictions on mobility even more by voting against admitting to their Monthly Meeting "any stranger" without a certificate.[71]

Although in many ways Quakerism was coming to resemble Congregationalism in this period, there was one distinctive practice retained by the Friends that continued to raise the hackles of orthodox laymen—preaching by women. While Congregationalists generally accorded a hearing to traveling male missionaries, attempts by female Friends to pray aloud or to testify publicly disrupted any gathering with a large orthodox attendance. Samuel Bownas recounted his meeting at Newbury in 1706 where Quakeress Lydia Norton "having a very strong Manly Voice extended it very loud but to no purpose, for the People were as loud as she, calling for a Dram and sporting themselves in their Folly." John Richardson attended a meeting a few years earlier in Boston, where, "when one of the . . . worthy Women was declaring Excellently . . . as the Manner of Inhabitants of Boston had been for many Years to Encourage, or at least suffer a rude Mob to bawl and make a Noise, they did so now." The basis of orthodox objections was St. Paul's proscription of female preaching: "We hold it Unlawful," a Newbury justice of the peace informed Bownas, "therefore we think it not proper to give them a hearing."[72] But in addition, the assertiveness of female preachers and the greater equality accorded all women within the Quaker community was tinged in the

[71] "Records of the Salem Monthly Meeting," 1689, 1707, and 1717.

[72] Bownas, *An Account,* 121; and Richardson, *An Account,* 71. Thomas Maule defended the role of women in "prophecy," but he explicitly denied them any place in church government, for in participating in these matters, "she comes to Usurp Government over the Man." (*Truth Held Forth and Maintained,* 124.)

orthodox imagination with a suggestion of sexual libertinism. George Keith created a considerable stir in Lynn with
his charge that the Quakers "used many Ceremonies, as taking one another by the Hand, and Men saluting one another,
and Women doing so to one another, and he said that Women
did salute Men; yea, they had done it to him." Keith afterwards retracted this "foul Reflection" to the relief of local
Quakeresses, "especially before their zealous Neighbors the
Presbyterians who . . . fell hard upon our Women Friends
about their Saluting Men . . . as was generally understood in the Plural . . . [and] probably might have twitted
them."[73] This merging of fears over women publicly assum-
ing priestly roles with anxieties over the exhibition of aggressive female sexuality surfaced again in New England during
the Great Awakening of the 1740s. Then the targets of
attack were "New Light" Congregationalists—female lay exhorters and women who carried religious emotionalism to
extremes.[74]

But aside from the Friends' sustained support of "Wom-
en's Preaching," there was little in Quaker practice by the
early eighteenth century that affronted orthodox sensibili-
ties. The Friends themselves had forsworn ritualized displays
of defiance: no more did naked Quaker women march down
the aisles of meetinghouses, nor did Quaker prophets stri-
dently publicize in the streets the errors of the Congregationalist establishment. With its prophetic period past, the sect
settled down to strengthening its institutional structure,
developing a hierarchy of monthly, quarterly, and yearly
meetings, promulgating a "Discipline," and evolving measures for its implementation. This interest in enhancing
internal organization was particularly strong in the Salem
Meeting, as local Friends attempted to capitalize on the conversions that occurred after the witchcraft trials. Like the
Congregationalist clergy of Massachusetts—but more successfully—the Friends' ecclesiastical leaders sought to consolidate their control over membership, to maintain uniformity

[73] Richardson, *An Account,* 98 and 103–4.
[74] For an example, see Ebenezer Turrell, *Mr. Turrell's Directions* (Boston, 1742).

in doctrine and practice, and to establish clear lines of authority.[75]

This institutional reorganization was precisely what sustained the suspicions of Congregationalists against the Friends during the later colonial period. By the eighteenth century, the Quakers of Essex County were no longer a real "counterculture." Unlike the sect of the seventeenth century, Quakerism of this period did not represent a striking alternative to orthodox values, ideals, and models of behavior. Except for a few variations, the standards of personal conduct and religious practice that the Friends urged on their members were similar to those held by the Congregationalists. The differences between the two groups were less sharply defined than they had been in the past and far less dramatic than those that separated Anglicans and Congregationalists in New England or Anglicans and evangelical church members in the eighteenth-century South.[76] But while provincial Quakers did not constitute a counterculture, by the eighteenth century the Friends had developed a "countercommunity," a network of institutions for ordering the lives of their members separate from but closely parallel to those within individual New England towns. As a result, what lay behind the antipathy to Quakers in places like provincial Gloucester was less an objection to the Friends' religious convictions and conduct than uncertainties about their public loyalties.

The source of this concern over Quaker allegiances was the sect's discipline itself, one that encouraged solidarity and separateness. The Friends sought to strengthen social bonds within their fellowship by proscribing activities that increased the orthodox majority's contact with and control over individual Quakers. A case in point is the treatment of Friends who married outside the fellowship. While the Congrega-

[75] Worrall, *Quakers*, 67–80. Among Congregationalists, the *Proposals* of 1705, the Saybrook Platform, and the formation of ministerial associations were intended to effect the same kinds of centralizing reforms. See Youngs, *God's Messengers*, 64–76.

[76] Rhys Isaac, "Evangelical Revolt: The Nature of the Baptists' Challenge to the Traditional Order in Virginia, 1765 to 1775," *William and Mary Quarterly*, 3rd ser., 31 (1975), 345–68.

tionalists frowned on mixed marriages and employed informal pressures to prevent them, they stopped short of using
church discipline to discourage such alliances. Among the
Quakers, much stronger institutional sanctions operated. In
1706, for example, the Salem Meeting sent Samuel Collins
to speak with Edward Webb about "his Marrying outside
the Unity of the Friends." The Society also objected to members marrying "contrary to the Good Order of Truth," that
is, in a service conducted by a clergyman or a civil magis-
trate. Quaker marriage customs prescribed that a couple first
declare their intentions, give proof of being single, and then
gain the consent of the entire meeting. The wedding ceremony itself took place without the presence of clergy. After
Nathaniel Wood violated these procedures in 1706, the Salem
Meeting insisted that he write "a public paper of self-
condemnation," the usual penalty for "outgoing."[77] Quakers perceived an equally potent threat to the integrity of their
fellowship in an array of offenses surrounding the participation of their members in the sociability of neighborhood
taverns. Throughout the opening decades of the eighteenth
century, the Salem Meeting frequently chastised members for
"disorderly behavior" in such places, for keeping "bad company," and for retailing liquor illegally, the last offense being
the subject of an explicit stricture in 1730.[78] Congregationalists also discouraged excessive drinking, but their discipline of members for this offense was more occasional, and
the churches left the punishment of illegal retailers entirely
to the courts. The source of more intense concern among the
Quakers over conviviality and the illicit sale of spirits was
twofold. First, the regular contact of individual Friends with
their orthodox neighbors at local inns or private stills increased
the likelihood of their integration into the wider network of
the neighborhood community. At the same time, Friends
involved in the illegal sale of alcohol afforded secular magistrates a legitimate pretext for exercising their authority over
dissenters.

[77] "Records of the Salem Monthly Meeting," November 11 and 14, 1706.
See also Kenneth Carroll, *Quakerism on the Eastern Shore* (Baltimore, 1970),
71–78.
[78] "Records of the Salem Monthly Meeting," February 11, 1713, February
14, 1722, and March 12, 1730.

A similar interest in keeping at arm's length the ortho-dox-dominated civil government is evident in the Salem Meeting's opposition to members suing each other in the Court of Common Pleas. In 1689, after Lynn mariner Jacob Allen and Salem merchant Thomas Maule had quarrelled over a vessel, the Friends deputed two arbitrators to treat with Allen about settling the dispute privately, "so that the difference may be disposed of without going to law." At the same meeting, James Goodrich also complained that Allen had slandered him "to the world's people," probably a ref-erence to another civil suit.[79] Congregationalist clergymen deplored the litigiousness of their parishioners from the pul-pit and attempted to resolve disputes arising over bad debts and business deals privately, but the churches did not penal-ize members for recourse to the courts. Not so the Quakers: when Allen proved obdurate and resisted private arbitration of his differences with Maule and Goodrich, the Friends denied him a certificate of travel. To his coreligionists, Allen's deci-sion to redress his grievances against fellow Friends outside of the Salem Meeting and in the civil courts controlled by Congregationalists constituted a betrayal.

The Friends attempted to curtail their members' contact with and dependence upon the Congregationalist commu-nity not only by strong sanctions against intermarriage, tavern-haunting, and recourse to the courts but also by providing certain benefits. Essex County Quakers maintained a private fund for relieving their own poor and sick, and in 1716, the Salem Meeting proposed that "friends have Schooles Amongst themselves and not Suffer our Children to be brought up in the Corrupt Customes and Fashions of Our Enemys."[80] To further the religious education of adults, members circulated among themselves the writings of George Fox and other books supplied by the London Meeting. Quakers even had a cem-etery in Salem separate from the burial places of the Congre-gationalists.[81] Informally, Friends favored each other in their

[79] "Records of the Salem Monthly Meeting," July 18, 1689; cf. Tolles, *Meetinghouse and Countinghouse,* 58–59, 73–74, and 75–76.
[80] "Records of the Salem Monthly Meeting," 1712, August 11, 1716, May 13, 1731, and September 11, 1744.
[81] "Records of the Salem Monthly Meeting," 1713 and 1720. The Quaker cemetery was situated on land in Salem donated by Thomas Maule.

economic activities, as Jonathan Springer's reliance upon his fellow Quakers in Boston and Salem indicates. So close was the connection between sectarian membership and daily subsistence for some men that the sundering of ties to the Quaker community meant a loss of livelihood. Ostracized by the fellowship for failure to attend meetings regularly, Richard Oakes of Marblehead protested that "the Friends had denied him for Nothing, and that they have Ruined him and his family."[82] The Salem Meeting's ability to supply members' needs for relief, education, employment, and credit served to reduce the influence of both civil government and orthodox society over the lives of dissenters.

In some ways, the growth of the Quaker counter-community gave the Congregationalists just what they wanted—as little as possible to do with religious dissidents. But on another level, the development of Quakerism from an antiauthoritarian aberration into an effective, authoritative, institutional church was what made the Friends so threatening. For what the Quakers had created was not just an alternative to the Congregational church but also to the local community itself. Although Essex County Quakers established specific institutions that replicated the functions served by those of the orthodox churches and civil society, there was one singular element in the Friends' social organization: it was translocal. The Salem Meeting stands out on the social landscape as one of the few voluntary organizations that cut across the borders of individual towns and involved the inhabitants of several distinct geographic areas. Its membership included not only families from Salem but also residents of Boston, Lynn, Marblehead, and Gloucester, as well as visitors from more distant places. Until the founding of St. Michael's Episcopal Church at Marblehead in 1714, the only other religious fellowship in the county that supposedly commanded such strong translocal loyalties was the "witch coven"—centered, like the Quaker Meeting, at Salem—that the Andover defendants of 1692 confessed to attending. In addition, through their Quarterly and Yearly Meetings and their far-flung business contacts and marital networks, Essex County Quakers maintained close and reg-

[82] "Records of the Salem Monthly Meeting," January 15, 1717.

ular connection with their co-religionists elsewhere in New England and in New Jersey, Long Island, and Pennsylvania. When Boston Quakers had become numerous enough to establish their own meeting, the Friends in Essex County contributed to a fund for building their new place of worship; when Salem Quakers suffered from epidemics, they received relief funds from the Philadelphia Meeting.[83] Because the Friends identified themselves as members of a religious fellowship that transcended geographic boundaries rather than as inhabitants of a particular town, their first loyalty was to fellow sectarians irrespective of where they resided.

By contrast, among the orthodox, purely localistic identification based upon residence in a particular town was considerably more intense, and intercourse among Congregationalists from different geographically defined communities was far less frequent, particularly in northern Essex County with its strong tradition of congregational autonomy. Unlike the Salem Meeting, whose membership came from several surrounding communities, orthodox congregations were comprised of families who all lived in the same town, and membership within the church enhanced the sense of belonging to that town. Occasions that brought together the representatives of different churches from separate towns—ordinations, meetings of ministerial associations, and ecclesiastical councils—aroused suspicion among a large segment of the laity and the clergy alike, who feared that such gatherings infringed upon the independence of individual congregations and encroached upon the integrity of local life.[84] The same exclusivistic ethos characterized the rituals of civil society at the local level, many of which aimed at defining the community and preserving it from contamination by external influences. Annual "perambulations" of town borders delineated the physical boundaries that separated Gloucester from adjacent communities. Town selectmen regularly "warned out" families not admitted as inhabitants. Effecting any public improvement entailing cooperation between two towns required infinite patience on the part of

[83]"Records of the Salem Monthly Meeting," 1709; Tolles, *Meetinghouse and Countinghouse,* 69–70 and 89.
[84]Youngs, *God's Messengers,* 92–98.

county officials, who had to cope with the inevitable clash of particularistic concerns. The simple process of building a bridge between Ipswich and Gloucester took years because of intertown haggling.

The inhabitants of colonial New England's communities prized their autonomy, and nowhere was this local identity more intensely and uniformly felt than in northern Essex County, where native son John Wise made independence from centralized control as much an object of folk adoration as were ancestors.[85] Only the Friends withheld their homage from this icon. The Quaker fellowship was not just indifferent to geographic boundaries—its essential ethos was anti-localistic. The Salem Meeting not only limited and discouraged its members' engagement in the town community but also fostered actively their antagonism to local society itself by the ritualized accounting and recounting of "sufferings." Obligations like paying the minister's rate, contributing to the meetinghouse fund, and participating in militia training that the orthodox accounted as identifying badges of membership within the community the Quakers styled as "sufferings" extracted from dissenters. The Salem Meeting's leading laymen made regular "inspections" of these losses and entered "what friends suffered, when and at whose hands" in a ledger that it "may not be forgotten but that it may stand upon record for generations yet unborn, to see how faithful friends took Joyfully the Spoyling of their goods for the answer of a good Conscience towards God."[86] It was this antilocalistic animus of provincial Quakerism that constituted the link between social experience and religious prejudice among the orthodox during the eighteenth century. The Friends' real heresy lay less in their challenging of religious loyalties than in their subversion of proper social loyalties by eroding the claim of individual towns upon the allegiance of inhabitants.

[85] See, especially, John Wise, *The Churches Quarrel Espoused;* and *Vindication of the Government of New England Churches* (Boston, 1717).

[86] The records of the Salem Monthly Meeting contain several "Accompts of Sufferings" interspersed throughout the minutes. In 1712, the Salem Meeting ordered published the "sufferings" of two Quakers forced to serve in the Port Royal expedition, and in 1716 the Meeting reminded members to keep a precise record of their financial losses in goods distrained to pay the minister's rate.

As the Friends enhanced their denominational cohesion in the early eighteenth century, they developed an increasingly ambiguous relationship to the localities where they resided; Quakers were in the community but not of it. Membership in a translocal religious organization claiming their primary allegiance made the Friends' civic status suspect, a situation similar to that of American Catholics up until quite recently. Or to draw a parallel closer in time: just as ambiguous sectarian loyalties made people vulnerable to accusations of witchcraft in 1692, ambiguous social and political loyalties sustained discrimination against dissenters into the eighteenth century. As objections to Quaker doctrine and practice diminished after 1690, this new source of friction sustained an old antagonism.

In 1726, Samuel Bownas returned to northern New England and passed through Essex County. The state of his sect at Newbury was dismal: the growing port held "only a very few Friends . . . not above nine or ten in all." An equally dispiriting reception awaited him in the vicinity of Lynn and Salem. Here the Friends retained some numerical strength, but the promising growth of the earlier part of the eighteenth century had not continued. Quaker ranks consisted chiefly of the descendants of believers, while the absence of any significant traders and the propensity of Salem Friends to "constant Cavil or Dispute" attenuated their influence.[87] Bownas did not even bother to stop at Cape Ann. There the evolution of informal mechanisms for restricting membership in the community to the orthodox had effectively suppressed all sectarian competition. Perhaps by 1730 Gloucester's orthodox majority had come to regard the Friends as "a benign if heretical sect."[88] If so, inhabitants had little occasion to express this enlightened outlook, for the town had spent the last forty years excluding Quaker families from their community.

[87] Bownas, *An Account*, 175 and 178.
[88] Worrall, *Quakers*, 43. Besides the sisters of James Dyke, no names of Gloucester inhabitants appear in the records of the Salem Monthly Meeting after 1730; probate records also identify no inhabitants as Quakers. Four people were fined for absence from public worship in Gloucester after 1730, and two of these may have had Quaker sympathies, since they were members of the Hadlock family.

The growth of a closed religious community constituted another element that enhanced the town's stability during the eighteenth century. Elsewhere in Essex County, the focus of orthodox animosities and anxieties shifted during the provincial period from the Society of Friends to the Episcopal Church's Society for the Propagation of the Gospel. But Gloucester proved even more immune to threats from that quarter. The only inhabitant of town even suspected of harboring Episcopal sympathies was Daniel Gibbs, a prosperous shopkeeper who wisely attended and ostentatiously supported the First Congregational Church.[89] This continuing orthodox monopoly of local sectarian loyalties attests not only to Gloucester's likemindedness in religious matters but also to the absence of serious divisions in other aspects of social relations. While the town's staunch theological conservatism created an inhospitable climate for individual dissenters, the essential harmony of local life during the early decades of the eighteenth century left no factional antagonisms for Anglicans or Quakers to exploit to their advantage.[90] But if religious dissenters had not all but given up on establishing themselves in Gloucester by the 1730s, they might have enjoyed greater success in converting conflicts within the Congregationalist camp into sectarian gains. For it was during this decade that a severe controversy rent the orthodox community itself.

[89] Babson, *History,* 229; and EPF, #10807 and 10812.

[90] On sectional strife in Dedham being exploited by S.P.G. missionaries, see Cook, "Social Behavior and Changing Values in Dedham," *WMQ,* 27: 564–65. Cook argues that the multiplication of Congregational churches and religious dissenters in Dedham during the eighteenth century forced the town to accept religious diversity. Whether Dedham's handful of liberal Calvinists, ten nominally Anglican families (mainly Congregationalist tax evaders), and single family of Baptists amounts to real religious "diversity" is questionable, but the more important point is that the appearance of religious dissent cannot be equated with the acceptance of diversity or the approval of pluralism.

4

Status and the Social Order in a Provincial Seaport

OVER the life span of a generation, a great deal changed in Gloucester, but much more remained the same. Nearly half a century of demographic growth and commerical development after 1690 had produced no basic dislocation of local life. Townspeople managed with a minimum of difficulty to allocate their common lands, to expand their trade in fish and timber, to collect their debts from each other, to form new parishes, and to conduct town and church business. Until the 1730s, the only source of sustained tension in town was the animosity between the Congregationalist majority and the Quaker minority. Four decades of economic growth had also done little to alter Gloucester's essentially conservative, communitarian ethos. Despite commercial development, the character of social relations remained remarkably constant, and townspeople retained the outlook, inclinations, and prejudices of an earlier era. Gloucester's definitive cultural characteristics remained localism, insularity, intolerance toward outsiders, an aversion to risk, and an attachment to tradition. It was, ironically, the vitality of this widely shared set of values and attitudes that not only made for decades of friction with local Quakers but also lay behind a more divisive conflict that shook the community during the 1730s and early 1740s.

While local culture changed little during Gloucester's early decades of economic growth, other aspects of life in town were less impervious to the impact of trade. By the 1720s, commercial expansion and prosperity had started to reshape the structure of Gloucester society. Some families that had formerly dominated the town were experiencing a reduction of their economic power, social prestige, and political influence, while a few new families, most relative newcomers to town, were acquiring impressive estates. These developments posed a problem for Gloucester's inhabitants. The set of beliefs about the ideal social order that they had inherited from the seventeenth century posited a static social structure, an unchanging system in which status was inherited rather than achieved. While this conception of society as a fixed hierarchy of ascribed positions was once roughly congruent with the actual character of Gloucester's social order, it was increasingly challenged by the kind of economic mobility that was coming to characterize the town's commercial neighborhoods, particularly the First Parish.

By the early 1730s, this contradiction between social reality and ideals was becoming acute, and the result was a bitter conflict, the First Parish controversy. This dispute was the only serious breach of harmony within Gloucester's orthodox community during the century after the 1660s, the single instance in which townspeople departed from the consensual and corporatist patterns that usually prevailed in political life. What triggered the controversy was an ostensibly trivial occurrence: the members of the First Parish disagreed over where to locate their new meetinghouse and over how to arrange the seating within the church. Squabbles of this sort were common in eighteenth-century New England towns and usually signified little more than Yankee cantankerousness. But the duration and intensity of the troubles in Gloucester indicate that something fundamental was at stake for both sides in this contest, and that more than sheer stubbornness sustained the dispute for more than a decade. What underlay the First Parish controversy was the challenge that economic development posed to the old order. A reflection of the tensions occasioned in town by the decaying fortunes of some families and the greater economic success of others, Gloucester's meetinghouse dispute dramatizes how provincial New Englanders responded to the reshaping of local society by the impact of economic expansion. Specifically, the First Parish controversy casts light on the way that economic opportunity and mobility affected attitudes toward status and perceptions of the social order in developing seaports.

At the beginning of the year 1729, all members of the First Parish were in accord about the importance of constructing a new meetinghouse. By now, the parish meetinghouse raised in 1700 was a weatherbeaten, badly overcrowded building in dangerous disrepair. Replacing the old edifice was well within the means of the First Parish, for it was the most populous and prosperous part of town. But the general agreement about the need for a new meetinghouse did not last long. When the inhabitants of Gloucester harbor, the southern part of First Parish, made known their interest in relocating the new meetinghouse in their own neighborhood, Annisquam harbor dwellers in the northern part of First Parish immediately withdrew their support for a new structure. In the spring of 1729, Nathaniel Coit, one of the north's leading men, drew the lines of battle at a town meeting. As the moderator of the meeting, Coit steered discussion toward ways of making the old church more "accommodable" and designated a committee, comprised chiefly of his fellow Annisquam harbor residents, to enlarge that edifice.[1] Southerners nonetheless remained committed to moving the parish's public worship to a new site in Gloucester harbor.

Members of the First Parish attempted to deal with their differences over the new meetinghouse in the same way that townspeople had handled their earlier division over the Second Parish separation: they relied on the passage of time to foster a consensus. After the initial disagreement between the two parts of the parish in 1729, the inhabitants of Gloucester harbor allowed two years to elapse before raising the issue again in the spring of 1731. At that time, several southern leaders petitioned the General Court for permission "to remove our meetinghouse" to a site in Gloucester harbor. After another hiatus of two more years, the First

[1] GFPR, 1; GTR, II, 257.

Parish voted to construct a new building in the southern harbor. But a substantial minority of fifty northerners dissented from this decision, and by 1734, they had mustered enough votes to defeat a proposal for financing the new construction.[2] By now five years had passed since the parish first considered the meetinghouse question. At this point, southerners could have rallied their supporters and rammed a measure for raising rates through the parish meeting, but northern resistance made them reluctant. Instead, the parish voted to put off doing anything more about the new meetinghouse. There matters remained until the fall of 1737, when, on their own initiative, eight of the southern harbor's principal entrepreneurs erected a spacious meetinghouse on Middle Street in Gloucester harbor. The builders of the new church personally defrayed the construction costs of several hundred pounds sterling. The new structure was raised in a matter of days, but the builders did not offer the Middle Street meetinghouse to the First Parish for a full year, in the fall of 1738. At that time, a parish majority voted to relocate public worship in the new building.[3] In all, the First Parish had awaited general agreement on the meetinghouse issue for almost a decade; but the old formula had failed. Immediately after the majority's acceptance of the Middle Street meetinghouse, the defeated northern minority, led by Nathaniel Coit and Captain Joseph Allen, demanded a separation from the First Parish.[4]

Naturally northerners were piqued by the removal of the meetinghouse from a site just a few yards away from most of their homes to its new location in Gloucester harbor. They complained to the General Court of their "great discouragement and inconveniences" in traveling the longer distance to Middle Street. This protest notwithstanding, distance could

[2] Petition of Samuel Stevens, Sr., et al., April 2, 1731, *Journal of the House of Representatives* (Boston, 1929), 10:55; GFPR, 6 and 11.

[3] Eliezur Parsons's account of the building of the Middle Street meetinghouse is among his entries bound in the "Diary of James Parsons," MS, 45–46.

[4] Petition of Nathaniel Coit, et al., November 29, 1938, MA, 11: 507–509a. (Cited hereafter as Coit's petition / 1738.)

not have been the chief reason for the northerners' opposition to the new church and their support for separation. Unlike the farmers living on the western side of the Annisquam, the inhabitants of the northern part of First Parish faced no real difficulties attending public worship. The new Middle Street meetinghouse was just a mile and a half from the residences of a majority of northern families. Almost half of the other members of First Parish had to travel that far on the Sabbath, and some living in the remote eastern part of the Cape had between four and six miles to cover. The town meeting promptly dismissed the northerners' issue as a red herring, pointing out to the General Court that the First Parish had allowed separations in the past when the problem of access to public worship had been legitimate. Coit continued nevertheless to protest on behalf of his adherents, "Many of them seafaring men and have no conveniences for going to meeting but on foot; which is very uncomfortable for elderly people, women, and children."[5]

What bothered northern dissidents more than their physical distance from the new meetinghouse was the rearrangement of social distance within the Middle Street structure. First of all, they objected, "the bigger part" of the new Harbor church was "Built into pews, to the number of eighty or ninety." Gloucester's earliest meetinghouse had rows of benches but no pews; after 1700, the town's parishes had only occasionally granted to certain of their prominent families the "privilege" of building a pew in vacant space on the floor of the meetinghouses.[6] In a second departure from pre-

[5] *Ibid.*, An Answer of the Town of Gloucester to the Petition of Nathanial Coit, December 23, 1738, *MA*, 11: 531–531a; Names of Northerners with Assessments and Distances from the Old Meetinghouse, October, 1740, *MA*, 243: 55. The Cape Ann Historical Society has a map prepared at the time of the parish controversy by John Batchelder showing the location of the residences of northern dissidents.

[6] Coit's Petition / 1738. It is difficult to determine whether Gloucester's parishes freely "granted" or actually sold pew space. By the late 1720s, the Second and Third Parishes were selling both pews and pew space to their members, but earlier, actual sales had occasioned some controversy in the Second Parish. In 1718, the seating committee there sold space to the Haskells, the most prominent family in the parish. But following this transac-

vious practice, almost all of the seats in the Middle Street meetinghouse—all of the pews and some of the gallery seats—came at a cost. Really choice spots commanded unprecedented prices, but all seating, northerners claimed, was beyond their means.[7] The builders of the new meetinghouse planned to cover the expenses incurred in construction by the sale of seating, so while they deeded the new building itself to the First Parish, they reserved all property in pews and gallery space to themselves. And along with the property in seating, the builders and a committee composed entirely of other southerners retained the right of determining placement by valuating and selling all seating. This prerogative marked a major break with the traditional procedure of the entire parish electing the seating committee and approving all of its assignments.[8]

The matter of seating provoked intense controversy within the First Parish because social status was at stake. Since placement in the meetinghouse reflected the order of society in the world outside, "dooming the seats" was, as the phrase suggests, a deadly serious business. The location and quality of seats occupied by families represented their social posi-

tion, a parish majority abruptly voted to terminate such sales, even though they continued to approve grants to certain families. ("Church Record Book of the Second Parish," MS, unpaginated, Cape Ann Historical Society; see meetings between 1717 and 1733 for indications of practice respecting seating.)

[7] Coit's Petition / 1738. In the Second Parish during the 1730s and 1740s, pew space sold for under one pound sterling; at the Third Parish, Joseph York, that church's wealthiest member, owned an unspecified number of "pew privileges" valued at fourteen pounds sterling. By contrast, the builders of the Harbor meetinghouse offered Captain Joseph Allen a single pew worth about seventeen pounds sterling.

[8] GFPR, 22–24. A file labelled "Miscellaneous Church Documents" at the Cape Ann Historical Society contains a copy of the deed to the Harbor meetinghouse dated September 27, 1738. This document lists the builders of the Middle Street structure as Epes Sargent, Thomas Sanders, Andrew Robinson, Nathaniel and William Ellery, William Parsons, Joseph Allen, Jr., and Philemon Warner, Jr. Along with Samuel Stevens, Sr., John Corney, and Daniel Witham, these builders were the principal spokesmen for the southern part of the First Parish, except for William Ellery, who joined the dissidents, and Joseph Allen, Jr., who died in 1739. For previous placement practice, see GTR, I, 337; II, 185.

tion within the community.[9] In other New England churches, the removal of a congregation to a new meetinghouse was usually accompanied by some rearranging of the seating order. But the system of placement at Middle Street promised more than just the reshuffling of a few families: seating by the sale of pews and other space constituted an alteration of the procedure for allocating status in town. At the new meetinghouse, status seemed to rest squarely upon economic standing without any of the traditional allowances for age, service to the community, family dignity, or other noneconomic considerations.

Underlying the apprehensions of individual northerners over the new in placement arrangements was a shift in the relative importance of Gloucester's two harbor neighborhoods, a change that the relocation of public worship to the south reflected. As the coastwise and transatlantic trade became more central to the local economy, the greater natural advantages of wide, deep, well-protected Gloucester harbor in the southern part of the parish accorded an advantage to men who conducted their businesses from that part of town. Annisquam harbor was shallower, and its narrow opening onto Ipswich Bay was obstructed by sand bars. Although suitable for the smaller boats of the fishing fleet, Annisquam harbor was unable to accommodate larger trading vessels and fishing schooners, and less accessible from Boston and Salem. As the fish trade assumed increasing importance, this geographic difference became decisive in determining the course of local development. During the 1720s, Gloucester's economic center of gravity began moving gradually from Annisquam to Gloucester harbor, from the northern to the southern part of First Parish. In that decade, as many vessels were fitted out at Gloucester harbor as at Annisquam, and by the 1730s, the south decisively sur-

---

[9] Just how serious a matter seating was is indicated by the procedure followed in the First Parish for adjudicating disputes over placement. Each party to the dispute appointed an "agent" who, together with a representative appointed by the parish, generally one of the deacons, resolved the issue. (GFPR, 2); see also Ola Winslow, *Meetinghouse Hill* (New York, 1952), 118–49; and Robert J. Dinkin, "Seating the Meetinghouse in Early Massachusetts," *New England Quarterly*, 43 (1970), 450–64.

passed the north as a commercial center.[10] As the accidents of
geography shaped the maritime potential of Gloucester's different neighborhoods, according an edge to the southern
harbor, they also influenced the opportunities available to individual families. And after the 1720s, the advantage clearly
belonged to the merchants, shoremen, and tradesmen of
Gloucester harbor rather than to those of the Annisquam. The
result was northern resentment over and sensitivity to the
declining importance of their neighborhood and its leading
families. Tensions building between the northern and southern
parts of the First Parish since the 1720s coalesced in the
controversy over placement at Middle Street in the 1730s.

The fortunes of one of the north's most prominent families, the Davises, exemplify the impact of diminishing commercial opportunity upon men operating out of the
Annisquam. In 1735, Elias Davis left an estate of almost one
thousand pounds sterling, the largest amassed in town up to
that time. The seventeenth-century representatives of the Davis
family had been among the most substantial farmers in town,
and Elias's father, Lieutenant James Davis, and Elias's uncle,
Jacob, were among the first to engage in the fish and timber
trade. By successfully capitalizing on his inherited advantages, Elias became the owner of four schooners, a wharf, a
warehouse, a flakeyard, a dry goods business, and a blacksmith shop. All of these profitable enterprises he conducted
from Annisquam River during the early decades of the eighteenth century, when that harbor could still compete for trade
with the south. But Elias Davis was the last major merchant

[10] Babson, *History*, 2, 381. The table below is a breakdown of the top quartile of Gloucester's inventoried decedents according to their place of residence in town to illustrate the shift in the distribution of wealth in Gloucester:

1716–1735 Decile Group	Annisquam Harbor	Gloucester Harbor	Second
Richest 91–100	4	1	1
76–90	5	3	1
1736–1755 Decile Group			
Richest 91–100	3	8	3
76–90	9	8	3

SOURCE: Probate Files, Registry of Probate, Essex County Courthouse, Salem, Mass.

to operate out of the northern part of First Parish. The less favorable location of Annisquam harbor steadily eroded the opportunities available to the surviving members of the Davis family. Elias's sons Mark and Job inherited their father's businesses, but both died with estates that were considerably smaller than his, and their administrators had to sell substantial portions of the brothers' real property to cover outstanding debts. Nor were Elias's brothers able to equal or even to approach his success.[11]

The same disadvantages that decayed the Davises' commercial interests restricted the prospects for expansion and development among other northern families as well. The problem was not that Annisquam harbor after 1730 was becoming a pocket of poverty while the southern part of the parish surged ahead. The representation of Annisquam residents within the both wealthiest quartile and the poorest half of inventoried decedents between 1736 and 1755 was proportionate to their numbers within the town's total population. But the stature of Annisquam dwellers was declining after 1730 from what it had been at the beginning of the eighteenth century, when they constituted half of Gloucester's population and 60 percent of its wealthiest quartile of townsmen.[12] After 1730, leading northern entrepreneurs were

[11] The net worth of Elias Davis's estate was 908 pounds sterling; his son Job left an estate worth 392 pounds sterling, and his son Mark, 96. Lieutenant James Davis, who survived his son Elias, left 492 pounds sterling. (EPF #7265, 7277, and 7313) The petitions for the sale of the Davises' real property appear in the MSCJ, October 15, 1751.

[12] The table below illustrates the distribution of the wealthiest quartile and the poorest half of Gluoucester's inventoried decedents by neighborhood between 1716 and 1735, and 1736 and 1755:

1716–1735	*% Total Decedents*	*% Poorest Half*	*% Richest Quarter*
Annisquam Harbor	5 1	43	60
Gloucester Harbor	37	46	27
Second Parish	1 2	1 1	1 3
1736–1755			
Annisquam Harbor	3 5	3 0	3 5
Gloucester Harbor	5 0	5 5	47
Second Parish	1 5	1 5	1 8

SOURCE: Probate Files, Registry of Probate, Essex County Courthouse, Salem, Mass.

not falling fast or far, but they were slipping out of their positions at the top of Gloucester society into a substantial middling group. Still more affluent than the average inhabitant, northerners continued to reap solid gains from their skills as shoremen and millers. The difference was that northern families were now no longer preeminent in Gloucester. They had no share in the large profits that accrued from actually marketing catches of fish to distant consumers and from retailing fishing provisions and finished goods at home. By the time of the First Parish controversy, most northerners had returned to supporting themselves by farming or by selling the catches of their small fishing craft to bigger men in Gloucester harbor or by serving as members of a schooner's crew in return for part of the profits of the voyage. The wealthiest northerners, men like Nathaniel Coit, had made their money earlier, when Annisquam harbor was at its peak, but by the 1730s, they had relinquished their commercial interests almost entirely and gone back to farming.[13]

Accompanying the shift of business activity and wealth out of the northern part of First Parish was a gradual diminution of that neighborhood's political importance. Until the 1720s, the northerners of Annisquam harbor had dominated the board of selectmen and had usually supplied Gloucester's representatives to the General Court. But during the 1720s, selectmen's terms were apportioned almost equally among the three sections of town, with Annisquam harbor residents holding only a slim edge on the board of selectmen

[13] At its height, the northern cause had the support of from eighty to one hundred adult males. About two-thirds of these men came from fourteen family groups whose names appear repeatedly among the subscribers of northern petitions. (Proceeding of Parish Meetings, 1732/33 and 1733/44, MA, 243: 43; Petition of Nathaniel Coit, et al., 1739, MA, 243: 50; Coit's Petition/1738; Names of Northerners, etc., MA, 243: 55. I was able to locate inventories for thirty-one northerners who died between 1736 and 1755. Usually these men are described as farmers or fishermen. The median value of their estates is 110 pounds sterling, roughly the same as for the town overall, but only two northern leaders, Nathaniel Coit and Captain Joseph Allen, ranked within the richest decile of inventoried decedents with estates valued at 1141 and 3755 pounds sterling, respectively. Allen, who represents a special case, lived at Annisquam harbor but actually operated out of Gloucester harbor. Coit's inventory contains no indication of commercial involvement. (See EPF, #5875.)

and southerners repeatedly filling the office of representative. And by the 1730s, Gloucester harbor dwellers were able to match the north's strength on the board of selectmen and to send southerners to the General Court for six out of the ten years between 1730 and 1739.[14] Underlying the gravitation of political power away from the Annisquam was the growing concentration of population in other parts of town, a trend reflected in the settlement pattern of immigrants to town. In the two decades after 1710, the proportion of newcomers to Gloucester who established their homes in the northern part of First Parish declined precipitously, while an increasing number made their homes in the southern harbor and in the new Third Parish on the northern end of Cape Ann. By the 1730s, a decade during which the rate of inmigration almost tripled, over half of the new arrivals settled in the southern harbor and another quarter in the Third Parish. What few immigrants the north did attract during the 1730s were typically men of little stature or substance, fishermen and sailors employed by the shoremen of Annisquam harbor.[15]

Both a symptom and a contributing cause of the changes taking place within the First Parish that underlay the alienation of northerners and southerners was the closing of "the Cut." The Cut was a canal between the terminus of the Annisquam River and Gloucester harbor that accommodated shallops and other small boats, a local landmark that, like the meetinghouse, had once been a point of contact between the two parts of the First Parish. By linking Ipswich

[14] Selectmen's Terms, 1720–1739:

	Annisquam Harbor	Gloucester Harbor	Second Parish
1720–29	18	16	16
1730–39	20	20	10

[15] Parish Settlement Patterns of New Immigrants to Gloucester, 1701–1740:

	1st North	1st South	2nd	3rd	Unknown
1701–10	9	10	8	5	4
1711–20	7	12	8	5	4
1721–30	1	13	10	5	4
1731–40	18	41	6	13	0

Bay with Massachusetts Bay, this narrow channel afforded Annisquam boats access to Gloucester harbor and saved packet vessels bound for Boston and other southern ports a time-consuming and sometimes hazardous journey around Cape Ann. As Gloucester's traffic in timber developed at the end of the seventeenth century, the Cut became increasingly important to Annisquam River residents engaged in the trade to Boston. Its use was so regular that the town meeting voted to levy fines upon boatmen who neglected to turn down the bridge over the Cut after they had passed through.[16] But, although the town regulated its traffic, the canal itself was privately owned, and at the beginning of the eighteenth century the proprietor of the Cut was Nathaniel Coit.

This prosperous miller, landowner, and trader was one of Gloucester's principal men and the leader of the northern dissidents. Nathaniel was the grandson of John Coit, Sr., a shipwright from Marblehead who had been one of Gloucester's most prominent seventeenth-century settlers. Discouraged by the early difficulties of developing the town's maritime potential, the senior Coit had left for New London in the 1660s. His son John Jr., who remained in Gloucester, died shortly thereafter, leaving an orphaned son, Nathaniel, to be raised by Henry Walker, a substantial local farmer and prominent political leader. Although Nathaniel was no kin to Walker, he quickly became the favorite of his guardian, and on the strength of that recommendation, married into the Davis family. The Davises had chosen wisely, for when Walker died in 1693, he passed over his own relatives and left virtually his entire estate to his ward. Political recognition and success in the timber trade followed Nathaniel's windfall inheritance and advantageous alliance with the Davises, and he subsequently acquired the Cut through his second marriage to Widow Abigail Stevens.[17]

Coit's satisfaction with Abigail's inheritance soured somewhat in 1704 when a storm choked the canal with sand and gravel, and the town ordered him to clear the passage. Coit at first refused, insisting that the town was responsible

---

[16] Babson, *History,* 8–9; GTR, II, 120, 422

[17] Babson, *History,* 71–72; for the disposition of Henry Walker's estate, see EPF, #28778.

for maintaining the Cut. But public pressure from all parts of town, especially from his northern neighbors, and an order from the General Court in 1706, finally compelled Coit to open the channel at his own expense.[18] In 1723, the Cut resurfaced as the subject of local debate after high tides from another storm closed the canal again. By this time, legal ownership had passed to Coit's stepson, Samuel Stevens, Jr., who had inherited his mother's property after her death. Stevens was no more willing than Coit to assume the cost of repairs, and his resistance to the selectmen's orders stirred up another round of demands and refusals between 1723 and 1728. But while in the earlier dispute over the Cut townsmen from every neighborhood in Gloucester had pressed Coit to defray the costs, in the 1720s, it was southerners who sustained the campaign against Stevens. Over a period of five years, four town-appointed agents, all residents of Gloucester harbor, first tried to persuade Stevens privately of his duty and finally took him to court. When Essex County justices refused to adjudicate and turned the matter back to the town, it was a meeting dominated by southerners that "after much debate" voted against reopening the channel at public charge and declared that . . . "the Towne (so fare as they are consarned) give leave to anyone to clear the Cut."[19] Although their insistence upon Stevens's responsibility for maintaining the Cut conformed to the town meeting's consistent stance on the question, southerners were clearly exploiting the issue to garner electoral support. A month after the town's final refusal to use public funds for clearing the canal, Gloucester harbor inhabitants swept three of the five selectmen's seats, giving them a majority on the board for the first time since the agitation over the Second Parish separation. The Cut never reopened. Access to Gloucester harbor was important for northerners, but sectional spite and private pique among them proved stronger than economic interest. Neither Stevens nor Coit nor any other Annisquam harbor resident stepped forward to clear the canal, their refusal contributing to the economic stagnation of the northern part of the parish.

[18] GTR, II, 124 and 134–35.
[19] GTR, II, 227–28, 232, 239, 243 and 247–49.

The decision of northerners to keep the Cut closed amounted to a self-imposed isolation from the south and from the society of men like Captain Andrew Robinson, one of the builders of the Middle Street meetinghouse. The Robinson family appeared in Gloucester at about the same time in the seventeenth century as the Coits arrived, and they too attained some local prominence. Especially successful was widow Mary Robinson, who married Henry Walker and raised her grandson Andrew in his household. When young Andrew entered the Walker home, Nathaniel Coit was in his twenties, already secure in his guardian's favor: Henry Walker bequeathed Andrew only twenty pounds. Where Andrew first went after Nathaniel Coit succeeded to the Walker estate is uncertain, but he ended up living "in a great house" surrounded by 184 acres of land on the Eastern Point overlooking his wharf and a fleet of vessels in Gloucester harbor. The profits from his voyages to the Grand Banks and from his shipyards, the produce of one farm worked by three Negro slaves, and the income of another that he rented made Andrew Robinson a wealthy man. Military services performed on behalf of the provincial government—protection of the fishing fleet off Cape Sable from hostile Indians, the capture of a French privateer, and the construction of a fort in Maine—also brought Robinson financial reward, along with a military title and a local reputation for daring and bravery.[20]

While none of Captain Robinson's neighbors in Gloucester harbor enjoyed such lucrative government contracts, like him they were thriving through the luck of their location. One index of the prosperity of the southern part of town was that an increasing number of Gloucester's inhabitants now made their homes in that neighborhood. Earlier in the eighteenth century, southerners had comprised only about one-third of the town's total population, but after 1730 they made up about half. Increasingly, too, the richest families were residing in Gloucester harbor. Southern representation among the wealthiest quartile of townsmen rose from just over one-third at the beginning of the eighteenth century to nearly one-half after 1730. Proportionate to their numbers within the total population, southerners were still not over-

[20]Babson, *History,* 134–43; for Robinson's estate, see EPF, #23869.

represented within either the top quarter or the upper half of Gloucester's economic hierarchy. And because of the heavier flow of immigrants and transient fishermen into their part of town, the south still had relatively more people who numbered among the poorer half of Gloucester's inhabitants. But considered in absolute terms, the success of leading southerners was impressive. In that part of the parish resided more men who ranked among the top decile of inventoried decedents in the twenty years after 1735 than in all of the other sections of town combined.[21] Virtually all of Gloucester's major merchants and tradesmen made their homes and conducted their enterprises in the southern harbor. The leaders of the southern part of the First Parish who built the Middle Street meetinghouse and persuaded others to accept it included five of the town's major merchants and shoremen, its two principal shipbuilders, two prosperous tanners, a rich blacksmith, and a master mariner. All of them left estates of considerably larger value than those left by most northern leaders and enjoyed a style of life more luxurious than that of their opponents. These southern leaders were also the most politically preeminent group in town after the 1720s.[22]

The divergence between the relative prosperity, political success, and future prospects of Annisquam and Gloucester harbors precipitated the First Parish controversy. North-

[21] See notes 10 and 12 above.

[22] Inventories exist for nine of the eleven leaders of Gloucester harbor who built the new meetinghouse and persuaded the parish to accept it. Seven of the nine ranked within the richest decile of mid-eighteenth century decedents, with estates in excess of 600 pounds sterling, and two others ranked close to the top decile with inventoried assets worth between 400 and 5499 pounds sterling. The inventories of personal property for these southerners include items that appear in none of the northern inventories except that of Captain Joseph Allen: large amounts of household furniture, silver plate, chaises, slaves, etc. (EPF, #465 [Allen], 8680 [Ellery], 6361 [Corney], 23869 [Robinson], 20594 [Parsons], 26426 [Stevens], 28972 [Warner], 24610 [Sargent], and 24778 [Sanders].) Between 1720 and 1750, southerners filled 37 percent of all selectmen's terms, northerners, 23 percent; southerners served as deputies to the General Court in twenty of those thirty years, northerners, only nine years. Southerners were always elected clerk and treasurer of the First Parish between 1729 and 1742, and they served as moderators of parish meetings a total of twenty-six times compared to three for northerners. (For officeholders, see GTR,II and GFPR.)

erners resented the relocation of public worship in the southern harbor and the rearrangement of seating at the Middle
Street meetinghouse because both changes underscored the
relative decline of Annisquam harbor families. They forced
once prominent inhabitants to acknowledge the loss of their
supremacy in town. Commercial development had reshaped
local patterns of population density, wealth distribution, and
the concentration of political power, giving greater influence
to Gloucester harbor because of its natural advantages for
conducting trade. But did the troubles over the meetinghouse signify something more than simply the climaxing of
the rivalry between the town's two harbor neighborhoods?
Did deeper differences fuel the enmity between northerners
and southerners?

Innovations in placement practices like those introduced
at the Middle Street meetinghouse have often been adduced
as evidence that a basic change in attitudes concerning status
was occurring in New England, particularly among the successful merchants and entrepreneurs of provincial trading
towns. Instead of adhering to the traditional Puritan ideals
of a fixed social order, successful traders are said to have
adopted more modern values that validated individual social
mobility. The purchasing of pews is particularly construed
as a sign of growing materialism among the commercial classes
and of their acceptance of wealth as the sole determinant of
social prestige.[23] It could be argued, then, that the controversy over the Middle Street meetinghouse in Gloucester grew
out of a fundamental divergence of values concerning status
allocation, a basic difference between the two parts of the
parish over the qualities that society should acknowledge and
reward. Southerners, in this view, were seeking to translate
their commercial success into social prestige in the form of a
high-priced pew. They were willing to allow the market to
determine the allocation of honor because they looked for
legitimacy as an elite by calibrating social status according
to economic standing. Northerners, accordingly, resisted the
new seating arrangements, regarding the change as a betrayal

---

[23] Dinkin, "Seating the Meetinghouse," *New England Quarterly*, 43:455;
Tracy, *Jonathan Edwards, Pastor*, 125–29; and Bailyn. *New England Merchants*, 139.

of an older set of values governing the distribution of honor. By upholding this traditional view of the social order—one in which the noneconomic attributes of age, public service, education and family dignity determined rank—northerners were defending their own status interests as well as rejecting the materialistic values advanced by their adversaries. This interpretation of the meetinghouse controversy rests on two assumptions: first, that commercial expansion imbued its beneficiaries with more modern conceptions of the social order, and second, that the emergence of these new attitudes toward status can be accurately inferred from institutional innovations like the sale of pews. But a closer inspection of the families of Gloucester harbor and the church that they built casts doubt on the validity of this view of social change.

The commercially successful Gloucester harbor families who built the new meetinghouse and persuaded the First Parish to accept it were newcomers neither to the town nor to the top of local society. Like the Robinson family, the ancestors of the eighteenth-century Parsonses, Sargents, Ellerys, Withams, and Corneys had settled in the southern part of the First Parish at the same time that those of leading northern families like the Coits and the Davises had arrived at the Annisquam River. The founding members of these southern harbor families had engaged in the same kind of economic activity as northerners, and several had enjoyed election to important local offices. Although Annisquam harbor dwellers had held sway in town during the late seventeenth century and the opening decades of the eighteenth century, the south's several established families still prospered and held prominent positions of public trust.[24] In other

[24] Among the fourteen principal northern families, twelve had settled in town before 1680, and only one had arrived in town after 1700. The provincial tax list of 1693 shows eleven Annisquam harbor residents among the top quartile of twenty-one taxpayers. Of the other ten taxpayers who ranked in the top quartile, five resided in Gloucester harbor, and five in the western part of town. Among the twenty-one men who served as selectmen between 1668 and 1690, ten came from Annisquam harbor, nine from Gloucester harbor, and two from the western part of town. Nine of the fourteen principal dissident families had ancestors who served as selectmen. (For the 1693 tax list, see Babson, *History,* 213–14; lists of officeholders were compiled from GTR, I.)

The families of nine of the eleven southern leaders had settled in Gloucester

words, the opposing sides in the First Parish controversy were not an old, deeply rooted northern elite and an aggressive set of upstarts to the south, but two factions within the established town leadership. Because southerners possessed all of the traditional noneconomic attributes of an acknowledged local leadership, they did not have to rely on their wealth for recognition. As part of Gloucester's entrenched ruling group, southern families did not need to redefine the basis of status allocation in order to attain high standing in town. For this reason, the support for the new seating arrangements among the leaders of Gloucester harbor must be read as signifying something other than an acceptance of a modern, materialistic conception of the prestige order. But if southerners were not trying to purchase social honor, what accounts for their insistence on instituting family pews and the other new placement practices at the Middle Street meetinghouse?

To comprehend the motivations of the leading southern families involved in the First Parish controversy requires an understanding of the way that they experienced and responded to Cape Ann's commercial expansion. Like almost all social groups in Gloucester, the southern elite had witnessed transformations of unprecedented magnitude in their old way of life within the span of a generation. As a result of economic growth and diversification, material change of significant dimensions had taken place, and more than any other group in town after 1730, the principal families of Gloucester harbor reaped the rewards of the town's maritime development. But although southerners became the chief beneficiaries of commerce, the experience of change was no less deeply disturbing to them than to economically declining northern families. On the contrary, far from being insulated from uncertainty and anxiety by their success and prosperity, southerners in some ways bore the brunt of the new developments that were making life in Gloucester less secure and

during the seventeenth century, and seven of these nine heads of seventeenth-century families served as selectman or as representative. Information on the economic standing of the fathers of the eleven southern leaders was available in seven cases, and in six out of seven fathers ranked among the wealthiest quartile of Gloucester decedents inventoried during the same decade or within the richest quartile of ratepayers in 1693.

self-contained. The strain registered in the conservative reaction of elite Gloucester harbor families to the ways in which commerce was reshaping social life in their neighborhood. Their keen interest in instituting family pews at the Middle Street meetinghouse was only one part of this larger pattern of defenses adopted by southern families to minimize the disruption of the town's traditional order by demographic and economic expansion.

Part of the problem facing southerners was the very source of their neighborhood's prosperity. Because of its superior harbor, the south had become the point of contact between Gloucester and the wider world, the place where local life intersected with external influences, often with unsettling consequences. First, Gloucester harbor had to assimilate not only the bulk of new families that established themselves permanently in town, but also a number of transient fishermen and mariners. In the 1720s and 1730s, Gloucester's contingent of seafaring strangers was not as large as Marblehead's, but this floating population still constituted a presence that established southern families found troubling. Captain Andrew Robinson complained to the General Court that the transients paid nothing in taxes or ministerial support but "Sail with every Wind and Will Cast Anchor in any Harbour that will best Suit them. . . ." In a telling oversight, Robinson neglected to mention to the Court that the largest number of these nonnative sailors and fishermen took up their temporary residences in Gloucester harbor. Instead, he left the Court with the impression that they predominated in the northern part of the First Parish.[25] That Robinson and his neighbors dealt with their discomfort at discovering maritime transients in their midst by mentally shunting them into another part of town reveals the depth of southern resistance to even acknowledging change.

Second, as the center of the fish traffic in town, the place where the local catch was collected, stored, and finally shipped, the southern harbor was also the most vulnerable to all of the risks inherent in colonial commerce. While

[25] Andrew Robinson, et al., Answer of the First Parish to the Petition of Nathaniel Coit, December 1, 1738, *MA*, 11: 510–512a. See also, note 15 above.

southern families enjoyed greater affluence than any other group in Gloucester from their participation in this trade, their profits came at the cost of accepting an economy riddled with contingency. Storms at sea, small, easily glutted markets, continuing currency depreciation, price inflation, and the threat of renewed warfare between England and her European rivals were all potential threats to southern economic security.[26] An added source of uncertainty for southerners especially was the increasingly interdependent character of the town's commercial life. More people in all of Gloucester's neighborhoods now relied for their livelihoods on distant sources of supply and remote markets. But Gloucester harbor's principal families were those most intimately tied to external markets and most closely connected by business to men who were not neighbors. The inhabitants of other parts of town were usually involved in economic transactions only with other local men; they sold fish and bought finished goods from traders in the southern harbor. But the southerners' circle of commercial contacts typically included major merchants in the fish trade in Salem, Marblehead, and particularly Boston. They counted on this network of "outsiders" for large consignments of manufactured goods and provisions as well as for advances of credit.[27]

Southern entrepreneurs were uncomfortable with the newly hazardous and interdependent character of local economic life. That insolvencies and bankruptcies were unheard of among Gloucester's major merchants attests to their determination to guard against overextension. Similarly,

[26] The best descriptions of the range of contingencies hampering colonial commerce and maritime activity appear in the notarized protests of sea captains, explanations of the conditions responsible for delays in sailing or damages to vessels and cargo intended to protect the ship's captain from civil prosecution. See "Essex County Notarial Records, 1697–1768," MS, Office of the County Clerk, Superior Courthouse, Salem, Mass. See also Stuart Bruchey, *The Roots of American Economic Growth, 1607–1861* (New York, 1965), 48–54; and Thomas Baxter, *The House of Hancock: Business in Boston, 1724–1775* (Cambridge, Mass., 1945).

[27] A survey of all of the available administrations of estates for Gloucester decedents between 1690 and 1770 indicates that, after 1730, only major Gloucester entrepreneurs ranking in the top decile of inventoried decedents had extensive dealings with nonlocal men. Any of the probate files cited in note 22 above will illustrate this connection.

Gloucester's incidence of intertown litigation, although rising over the first half of the eighteenth century, was still
insignificant in comparison to that of other Essex County
ports. This, too, suggests that local entrepreneurs carefully
avoided overcommitment in financial dealings, especially when
doing business with strangers. Finally, the investment of many
local inhabitants in trading and fishing voyages, a practice
necessitated in part by the scarcity of capital, also served to
spread the risk of such ventures among multiple sharehold-
ers. When the First Parish controversy began to unfold in
the 1730s, Gloucester had not yet suffered from any acute
economic dislocations. Military conflict had not imperiled
local prosperity by interrupting trade and upsetting the
interlocking commercial system of which the town was now
a part. But Gloucester harbor's merchants, shoremen, and
tradesmen were clearly intent on reducing the risks that
attended colonial commerce, even in periods of peace.

Cape Ann's increasing integration into the wider market
economy imposed on Gloucester harbor the burden of
absorbing the most sweeping material changes that took place
in town during the early eighteenth century—the largest
number of mobile, maritime laborers, the greatest economic
risks, and the necessity of doing business with men who were
not neighbors. In response, southern leaders either averted
their eyes to change or, more often, devised strategies for
coping with potential threats to their economic security and
for insuring the future of their families in Gloucester. But
there were still other consequences of the conversion to commerce in the southern part of First Parish: for Gloucester
harbor's established families, more than any other group in
town, the expansion of economic horizons also widened the
scope of social awareness. This new consciousness of the world
outside of town created its own kind of anxieties that, like
the apprehensions surrounding economic life, called forth a
conservative reaction from southerners. Seen in the light of
these social insecurities, the basis of southern support for the
novel placement practices at the Middle Street meetinghouse
becomes clearer.

Through their close business contacts with the traders of
other ports, the southern elite was introduced to the life of
larger commercial centers in Massachusetts, particularly that

of Boston, where a "codfish aristocracy" had amassed enormous fortunes by Cape Ann's standards.[28] In Gloucester during the 1730s and up until the War for Independence, an estate ranging anywhere from several hundred to a few thousand pounds sterling represented real money. And while men possessed of this much wealth were mainly merchants, a substantial minority of artisans in the maritime trades, shoremen, and even farmers were also able to acquire estates of this size. But by comparison with some merchant princes of Boston's upper class, men worth tens of thousands of pounds sterling, the fortunes of Gloucester harbor faded considerably in magnificence. And occupational credentials for entry into the upper echelons of the capital's economic hierarchy excluded all but merchants and a few royal officials.[29] While the larger scale of economic success in the capital confirmed for elite southern harbor families that they were big fish only in the small pool of Cape Ann, even more intimidating to the established leaders of Gloucester harbor was the fluidity of the social order in these larger ponds. Not only was Boston wealthier, but its social structure was characterized by a kind of instability that the members of the First Parish were just beginning to find out about. Men in the capital rose and fell rapidly on the social ladder; old families declined and new ones appeared to take their places.[30]

That Gloucester's leading families found deeply unsettling their exposure to the society of larger urban centers is indicated by their singular lack of interest in succeeding in the world outside of town. Contact with bigger ports did not infuse Gloucester harbor magnates with a restless ambition to compete on a grander scale in these greater theaters, and surprisingly few of them made use of the standard avenues

[28] The accounts of administration for the estates of successful southerners point to their especially close connection with Boston traders. Among the records of debts owed by estates, Boston merchants James Bowdoin, Ebenezer Storer, and Isaac Smith appear with the greatest frequency. Salem and Marblehead merchants appear more occasionally.

[29] For comparative estate values, cf. Nash, *Urban Crucible,* appendix, Tables 5 and 7 with the figures for Gloucester in my appendix, Table II.

[30] G. B. Warden, "Inequality and Instability in Eighteenth-Century Boston: A Reappraisal," *Journal of Interdisciplinary History,* 6 (1976), 585–620; Perry Miller, *The New England Mind: From Colony to Province,* 40–52.

to advancement in provincial society. Although the costs of a college education for their children were well within their means, only a few southern families sent sons to Harvard. And for the handful of Gloucester boys who went to Cambridge, the college figured not as a stepping stone to more glittering social and commercial contacts but only as a place for training in the ministry or medicine.[31] The scions of southern families for the most part went instead to sea, apparently preferring their chances of surviving an apprenticeship in the Atlantic to navigating the unknown depths of Cambridge. Nor did southern families attempt to advance by forming marital alliances with the principal merchant families of other ports, but rather contented themselves with partners from other leading local clans.[32]

Although Gloucester's traders were not in a league with some of the merchant princes of Boston and Salem, opportunities to attain greater gains and glory outside of town were within their reach, as the exceptional career of Epes Sargent indicates. The owner of a commercial fishing business and a general retail store, Sargent married his son and namesake to a Boston heiress, Katherine Osborne, and as his own second wife he selected Katherine Browne, the widow of Salem's most prominent merchant. Upon his remarriage, Epes moved into the Browne mansion in Salem, where he hobnobbed with other Essex County notables over madeira at meetings of the exclusive Monday Night Club. But aspiring men like Epes Sargent were few and far between in Gloucester. His own sons were content to remain in Gloucester and reluctant to parlay their father's influential connections into bigger and better things for themselves. Even

[31] Two of the eleven southern leaders had themselves attended Harvard College: Epes Sargent did not graduate, but Daniel Witham did, and became the town physician. Only two of the eleven southern leaders sent their sons to Harvard, and both became ministers. (*SHG*, V, 288; X, 52–59; and XVII, 78–82.)

[32] Out of a sample of forty-two marriages of the children of leading southern entrepreneurs, exactly half were to other Gloucester harbor residents of equal status, eight were to less prominent southerners, five to less prominent families in other town parishes, and eight to partners out of town. In these out-of-town marriages, only one involved an alliance with an important commercial family from a larger port. (Sample drawn from Babson's genealogies in *History* and *Notes and Additions*.)

Epes insisted on being buried back in Gloucester.[33] Perhaps to the local imagination the brief but instructive career of John Coit rather than the accomplishments of Epes Sargent seemed more typical of what the world outside Gloucester offered. At the time when his own commercial star was still ascending, Nathaniel Coit had intended great things for his son: John graduated in the Harvard class of 1712 and taught school in Marblehead until a relative's legacy enabled him to set up as a merchant in that town. But John and his Boston partner, Jonathan Sewall, made several bad business deals that resulted in a flood of suits for debt from disappointed creditors. John tried his luck again in Boston but again failed dismally. Finally he went to the West Indies, probably in flight from his creditors, where he died almost immediately. So much for the attractions of venturing into the greater world outside of Gloucester.[34]

The fortunes of Epes Sargent and John Coit embodied the opportunities and risks afforded by the more mobile society of larger seaports. What was most troubling about this social fluidity to the southern harbor elite was not that it was new or unknown to local experience, but that it was, in fact, ominously familiar. For examples closer to home of the corrosive effects of commercial development on the standing of established families, southerners had only to look north. And for examples of the way that a trading economy allowed for the ascent of new men, southerners had only to look around them. By the 1730s, the successful entrepreneurs of Gloucester harbor included not just members of established southern families but also a number of men whose wealth was recently acquired in commerce. These newly affluent men were not the descendants of early seventeenth-century

[33] Babson, *History,* 150–51; *SHG,* V, 645–46.

[34] Babson, *History,* 71–72; and Reed v. Coit and Sewall, 1719, FCCP. My conclusion that John Coit's career made more of an impression than that of Epes Sargent is based on a random sample of the careers of the male children of leading families in Gloucester harbor at the time of the First Parish controversy. Of the thirty-five sons from thirteen families, only four moved out of town, one to Boston, one to Byfield where he was called as a minister, and two others to Falmouth and New Gloucester, Maine, where other former Gloucester inhabitants had migrated. (Sample drawn from Babson's genealogies in *History* and *Notes and Additions.*)

Gloucester settlers or the scions of privileged families from neighboring ports. They were instead the sons of "middling" mariners and tradesmen who, upon coming of age, had moved to Gloucester, set up as sea captains, shoremen, shop-keepers, blacksmiths, and shipbuilders, and turned energy and skill into financial success. Neighboring Essex County towns supplied the largest single group of these emigrant entrepreneurs: Jabez Baker and Edmund Grover came from Beverly, Peter Doliber from Marblehead, Nymphas Stacey and Benjamin Perkins from Ipswich, James Littlehale from Haverhill. A few, like John Poole, had moved down from Maine, and one, innkeeper James Broome, had emigrated from England. At the time of the First Parish controversy, all of these new men probably ranked in the top quartile of the town's wealthiest residents.[35]

What is most remarkable about these nonnative entrepreneurs is not their economic success but the tangential position that they occupied in local society despite their material achievement. The incompleteness of their integration into the local elite points up the ambivalent attitude of established southern harbor families toward such self-made men. Through cooperation in business enterprises with settlers of long standing, some of these newcomers were able to amass estates that often equalled the fortunes of Gloucester harbor's established families. Nevertheless, the social and political stature of economically successful emigrants remained carefully circumscribed. The configuration of the town's politi-

[35] There were eight men who arrived in Gloucester between 1700 and 1730 who ranked among the wealthiest quartile of the First Parish's inventoried decedents between 1736 and 1770. (See EPF for Jabez Baker [#1433]; Edmund Groever [#11947]; Peter Doliber [#8122]; Daniel Gibbs [#10812]; Benjamin Perkins [#21273]; John Poole [#22268]; Philemon Warner [#28972]; and Ezekiel Woodward [#30639]. Three other post-1700 arrivals for whom no probate files exist, James Broome, Nymphas Stacey, and James Littlehale, appear to have been equally wealthy because they were often called on to assess large estates, a function that the probate court usually assigned to the economic peers of the deceased. Of these new arrivals, only Philemon Warner, a blacksmith whose family had lived on the border between Ipswich and Gloucester since the seventeenth century, took an active role in the First Parish controversy on the side of the south. The kind of opportunity for economic advancement that Gloucester offered migrants was typical of other eighteenth-century Essex County ports. See Jones, *Village and Seaport*, 60–65.

cal power structure reflects the limitations imposed on the influence of newcomers. Only three men (or their sons) who emigrated to Gloucester after the end of the seventeenth century ever held the office of selectman between 1700 and 1755, and the whole group of nonnative selectmen served a total of only five terms in fifty-five years.[36] Old southern families continued to dominate political life: members of the same established families held the same important posts year after year, and upon retirement, they were often succeeded by their brothers, sons, sons-in-law, or nephews.[37] In other words, the growth of trade in Gloucester rewarded ability and luck by enriching the most successful entrepreneurs, regardless of the length of time that they had lived in town or their former family dignity. But the wealth won in commerce did not translate into access to positions of public trust and importance for men who lacked the noneconomic credentials that conferred prestige.

Confronted with significant alterations in many of the basic conditions of local life, leading Gloucester harbor families attempted to preserve as much of the old order in town as possible. Aversion to change recurs as the constant theme in their responses to the growth of a transient maritime population, the town's integration into an interdependent trading economy, their contact with larger seaports, and the economic success of nonnative entrepreneurs. All of these developments evoked among the south's established elite a closing of their ranks and a determination to protect the local stand-

[36] Edmund Grover served three terms as selectman; Jabez Baker and Philemon Warner each served a single term. (GTR, II.)

[37] The political careers of the eight southern leaders in the First Parish controversy who served as selectmen illustrate the concern for family continuity in public life. The fathers of six of these men had served as selectmen, and, in the cases of the two men without selectman-fathers, one represented the first generation of the family in town and the other was raised as the ward of a town selectman. In addition, all eight southern leaders who served as selectmen except one were succeeded in that position by their sons. The average terms served on the board by southern leaders were also quite long, unless they were elected or appointed to more prestigious political posts. Four of the eight southern leaders served as selectman for seven years or longer; those serving under seven years gave up their positions on the board only to accept positions on the General Court or judicial or military commissions.

ing of their families from the inroads of change. Caution in business investments and trading ventures, endogamous marital alliances that consolidated the resources of the major trading clans, limited exposure of young people to influences that might draw them out of town, efforts to insure continuity in important public offices—these were all elements in the southerners' strategy to perpetuate the position of their families in Gloucester. In the manner of elites in all traditional societies, Gloucester harbor's merchants, shoremen, and tradesmen maintained their monopoly of "ideal and material opportunities."[38] And the seating arrangements in the new church at Middle Street constituted just one other dimension of the southern establishment's defensive reaction to the changes attending Gloucester's entry into the Atlantic trading network.

Participation in commercial development had not fostered among elite southern families a more "modern," materialistic view of prestige as the prize of successful competition, but just the opposite. Their introduction to the life of larger, fluid, seaport societies and their witnessing the decline of Annisquam harbor magnates made southerners acutely aware of the potential precariousness of their own position. And their growing consciousness of the economic gains of emigrant entrepreneurs in Gloucester harbor itself added even greater intensity to the attachment of established southern leaders to a traditional social order based on ascribed, inherited status. The newly affluent, nonnative men seem like precisely the sort of social group that would be anxious to translate their recently acquired wealth into social honor by purchasing pews in the new meetinghouse. But how ardently these new men coveted such acknowledgment is uncertain, because they played almost no part in the First Parish controversy. Their presence in the First Parish did, however, provide the established southern elite with an incentive for closing off entry to the top of local society by "freezing" the local status order in the configuration that it had assumed by the 1730s. This was the main motive of

[38] Max Weber, "Class, Status, and Party," in *Essays from Max Weber,* eds. Gerth and Mills, 190–91.

southern leaders in instituting the new seating arrangements at the Middle Street meetinghouse.

The introduction of pews at Middle Street reflected the determination of established southerners to preserve and consolidate the social position of their families by exerting greater control over the conferral of prestige. What is significant about the arrangements at the new meetinghouse is not that seating was bought and sold, but that pews thus acquired became permanent family property. Gloucester harbor's elite leaders did not need to purchase prestige, for they already possessed all of the noneconomic credentials that commanded honor and deference. What they did want and need were institutions that insured the transmission of family status from one generation to another and that hedged the status order against the contingencies of commerce. The old meetinghouse did not offer this kind of future security to established families. First of all, the space for building pews was limited from the start, and most of it had been taken up by 1712, when the town ordered that no more "pew privileges" could be granted without the express consent of the town meeting.[39] With space at a premium, parents could not provide their children and their children's families with accommodations reflecting family prominence. In addition, at the old meetinghouse parents could not pass pews on to their children because seating was not treated as private property. Not a single will or inventory drawn up prior to the First Parish controversy includes a pew among the possessions of the deceased. Only after the Middle Street meetinghouse was built do pews begin to appear prominently in the probate records of prosperous First Parish members.[40] One index of the importance attached to the family pew is that seating is one of the few items singled out in wills for specific conveyance to surviving children. Pews were also precisely valued in estate inventories and were usually listed under the category of real property along with the deceased's

[39] GTR, II, 184.

[40] Only one inventory of a Gloucester decedent before 1740 includes a "pew privilege," but after that date, pews appear frequently. The inventories of prominent First Parish members listed in note 22 above all include pews among the decedents' real property, and usually more than one.

pastures, marshes, and woodlots. Just as the ownership of real property and the transmission of land insured the economic continuity of the family, the title to pews secured the continuity of the lineal family's social position. Like the endogamous pattern of marriages among Gloucester harbor's elite and the efforts to preserve family continuity in public offices, the institution of pews points to the concern for consolidating and perpetuating local standing.[41]

The new seating arrangements at the Middle Street meetinghouse operated in another way to protect the position of established southern families. The sale of seating was not a free market competition with the best berths going to the highest bidders, but a transaction in which the leading southerners who built the church and ran the seating committee offered everyone else a chance to invest at a certain level. Successful nonnative men were allowed to purchase whatever quality pew or gallery seat established families deemed appropriate to the condition of the newcomers. For example, although his estate of over 1500 pounds sterling made Captain Jabez Baker one of the wealthiest men in Gloucester, the placement committee awarded this newcomer from Beverly only half a pew in the Middle Street meetinghouse, a seat worth just six pounds sterling. Similarly, when Epes Sargent discovered that he had purchased more pews than he had produced family members to fill them, he allowed James Littlehale, a new arrival from Haverhill, the privilege of "improving" his third-best pew until there

---

[41] For an example of the careful assignment of pews in wills, see EPF, #24610. For a more general argument concerning the role of family continuity in shaping social values, see James Henretta, "Farms and Families: Mentalité in Pre-Industrial America," *WMQ*, 3rd ser., 35 (1978), 3–32. In her study of Northampton, Massachusetts, Patricia Tracy explores the introduction of family pews into Jonathan Edwards's church and relates their adoption to "the desire of the rich to assert the importance of the family group," because "especially for the rich, family was the determinant of wealth and occupation." (*Jonathan Edwards, Pastor,* 126.) While Tracy is correct in emphasizing the importance of family considerations in changing placement practices, she confuses the significance of this relationship. Pews became preferred seating arrangements because, as a result of commercialization—or land scarcity, in the case of Northampton—fathers could no longer insure that sons would inherit their economic status and social position. In Gloucester, even among the affluent, family was no longer the sole determinant of wealth, as the decline of the Davis family indicates.

were sufficient Sargents to seat in it.[42] Rather than representing an acceptance of upward mobility and a democratization of the system of status allocation, the new seating arrangements actually enhanced the ability of the southern elite to restrict entry to the top of society.

The defensive strategy that shaped the response of leading southern families to the changes taking place in Gloucester suggests that the controversy over the Middle Street meetinghouse did not result from a divergence of values and views of the social order within the First Parish. Instead, the conflict grew out of a common experience of change that caused both northerners and southerners to attach extreme importance to the preservation of local status. For northerners, that meant staying out of the new meetinghouse; for southerners, it meant getting into it. For Captain Joseph Allen, it meant doing both. His indecision reveals most clearly the conservative concerns motivating both factions in the dispute, for at different times, and for the same reason, he sided with each.

At the time of the First Parish controversy, Joseph Allen was probably the richest and most successful merchant in Gloucester, the descendant of an old and prominent family, and the head of a thriving commercial clan. He first appeared as a spokesman for the north in 1731, arguing before the General Court against the southern leaders' initial effort to relocate parish worship in Gloucester harbor. But sometime in 1734 Allen began to waver in his allegiances. At a parish meeting of that year, in which the proposal to grant money for building the new meetinghouse was defeated in a close vote, the captain, heretofore conspicuously present, was suspiciously absent. Shortly thereafter, he turned up granting "free liberty" to the builders of the new meetinghouse, among them his son Joseph, Jr., to "cutt timber on his land" for that purpose.[43] Then suddenly, in 1738, Allen's sympathies changed again: he returned to the northern camp, bringing

[42] For example, the southern seating committee "offered" Captain Joseph Allen a specific pew valued at one hundred pounds, New England money. See Answer of the First Parish to the Petition of Nathaniel Coit, December 1, 1738, *MA*, 11: 510–512a; EPF, #1433, 24610.

[43] GFPR, 3, 11; Answer of the First Parish to the Petition of Nathaniel Coit, December 1, 1738, *MA*, 11: 510–512a.

with him a number of other prominent merchants, including his brother Thomas, his son William, and his son-in-law Captain William Ellery.[44] For the duration of the controversy, Captain Allen remained one of the bulwarks of the northern cause.

In part, conflicting loyalties created by his business and family connections produced Allen's pattern of shifting allegiances. While he resided in the northern part of the First Parish, Allen's life style was comparable to—if not grander than—that of successful southerners. The captain could afford the luxury of a fine home and a carriage because he and the other members of his family actually conducted their fishing business and many of their other enterprises from the southern harbor.[45] And while Joseph Allen himself had married the daughter of his northern neighbor, Nathaniel Coit, many of his own children had married into prominent southern commercial families, the Sargents, the Stevenses, and the Ellerys.[46] Finally, while Allen based his business in Gloucester harbor, strong bonds of economic interdependence still tied him and the members of his family to northerners. Many of the small fishermen who repeatedly turn up as subscribers to northern petitions were employed aboard Allen-owned schooners and supplied with fishing equipment, provisions, rum, and liberal credit from Thomas Allen's store. For other northerners, the Allen family acted as middlemen, buying up and marketing their small catches of cod and stocks of timber.[47]

Although both parts of the First Parish had a claim on Allen's loyalties, in the end the captain identified himself as

[44] Coit's Petition/1738. Thomas and William Allen immediately followed Joseph into northern ranks. William Ellery's name does not begin to appear on northern petitions until 1740. Since Ellery at first joined his brother Nathaniel as one of the builders of the Harbor meetinghouse, he too was torn by conflicting loyalties.

[45] Joseph's inventory of personal property included eight slaves, a large quantity of silver plate, expensive apparel and household furnishings, a chaise, and three pews at the Fourth Parish. (EPF, #465)

[46] Joseph's daughters were married to William and John Stevens, sons of southern leader Samuel Stevens, Sr.; his son Nathaniel to Sara Sargent, the daughter of Epes Sargent. (Babson, *History,* 56–57.)

[47] Babson, *History,* 307–8; Thomas Allen, "Account Book," MS Cape Ann Historical Society.

a northerner. What finally made allegiance to his immediate neighbors paramount for Allen was intimated by Andrew Robinson in his recollection of an encounter between the captain and several other southern leaders at the site of the newly completed Middle Street meetinghouse in 1738. "With a great deal of seeming good humor and pleasant discourse," Allen had asked the builders what they "would give him for his timber," Robinson recalled. When they responded, "a pew for fifty-five pounds that was worth an hundred . . . he bought one and seemed well pleased." "However," Robinson concluded, "he seems to have altered his mind since." The southerners tried to lure Allen back into their camp by offering him a position on the seating committee of the new meetinghouse, but by that time the captain had retreated north for good. He frostily declined their offer "on account of his lameness," aggravated no doubt by his distance from Gloucester harbor.[48]

Perhaps Captain Allen prized his timber at more than a hundred-pound pew. But more likely, his exchange with Robinson and the rest alerted him to avoid a situation in which other elite leaders could offhandedly assign him a pew before it crossed their minds that a man of Allen's eminence belonged on the seating committee. After the northern dissidents separated from the First Parish and formed the new Fourth Parish, the Allens did not have to deal with such slights, and no one dared to put them in their place. The family ran the new parish like a private fief, with Joseph or Thomas Allen moderating all meetings, William Allen serving as treasurer, and the three of them joining Captain William

[48] Answer of the First Parish to the Petition of Nathaniel Coit, December 1, 1738, *MA*, 11: 510–512a; GFPR, 24. The presence of the commercial successful Allen clan within the northern camp also helps to delineate the specific character of Annisquam harbor's resentments. While northern farmers and fishermen opposed wealthy southern entrepreneurs, their hostility apparently did not extend to all commercially successful men, even those like Joseph Allen who had close connections to the southern harbor. In the First Parish, neighborhood allegiances and attachments still limited the development of antagonisms based on economic differences, allowing northerners' to accept the Allens' leadership. The same loyalties ultimately prevailed with the Allen family as well, dictating their decision to make common cause with their neighbors rather than seeking solidarity with southerners of their own class.

Ellery, their in-law, on all other important committees. And as one of its first actions, the Fourth Parish granted liberty to build pews to two members of the Allen family and to Captain Ellery.[49]

Despite his commercial success, Captain Joseph Allen was not actually such an anomaly among northerners; despite his ultimate support for the dissidents, his concerns were not so different from those of leading southerners. What kept Joseph Allen changing sides was the same consideration that made other men more consistent, the preoccupation with preserving and perpetuating family status. Although he was drawn to the prospect of owning a family pew at Middle Street, Allen realized after reflection that an even more secure berth awaited him and his family at the Fourth Parish, up in the north, away from all competition.

The desire to preserve the social order of the past motivated all parties during the dispute over the Middle Street meetinghouse and, paradoxically, it was this intensely conservative aim that led both northerners and southerners to make changes in local institutions. Maintaining continuity in one sphere of life came at the cost of accepting innovation in another. To retard the development of a fluid, competitive status order and to protect the standing of established elite families, southerners altered the First Parish's traditional placement practices, lobbying for some eight years to move the site of the meetinghouse and to institute family pews. And by 1738, northerners too were willing to initiate changes in local institutions in order to maintain the position of their families. To hold on to their old way of life, symbolized by the old meetinghouse at the former center of town and the seating arrangements within, northerners were willing to separate from the First Parish to establish a new precinct, the Fourth Parish.

But while the efforts of both parts of the First Parish to preserve the traditional social order in town entailed changing local institutions, neither northerners nor southerners were able to accept innovation on any significant scale. And it was

[49] "The New or Fourth Parish Book of Records," MS, unpaginated, Office of the Town Clerk, City Hall, Gloucester, Mass. For grants of pew privileges, see the meetings of March, 1745 and August, 1750.

this limited tolerance for alterations in the organization of local life that set in motion the cycle of strife within the community, a pattern of recurrent conflict that persisted after the removal of public worship to Gloucester harbor in 1738. Just as the south's campaign for the new meetinghouse had aroused the resistance of northern families, the north's insistence on dismembering the First Parish community now triggered the opposition of leading southerners. Like the northerners who had rejected the novel placement practices at Middle Street, southerners now opposed the parish separation as too radical a departure from the arrangements of the past. Because the northern bid for separation was not based on distance, as the parish partitions of the past had been, southerners were entrenched in their opposition. As a result, the conflict between Gloucester and Annisquam harbors continued for another four years.

To restore to the community as much of its former unity as possible, southerners mounted a vigorous opposition to the separation while at the same time devising ways of forcing the most deeply disaffected northerners out of the First Parish. This strategy first took the form of offering northern families the option of joining Third Parish. If the dissidents simply faded out of the First Parish and into the Third, the controversy would leave no lasting traces, and old divisions might die out more quickly. The Third Parish, still a small, struggling precinct, supported the annexation, for the addition of northerners would mean an increase in ratepayers; the town meeting also applauded the proposal as a "public-spirited" suggestion. The prospect of joining the Third Parish even found favor among some rank-and-file northern families worn out by the wrangling. But when the issue came to a vote at a First Parish meeting in 1738, some of the northern "principals" created such a "disturbance" that the meeting was adjourned. Southerners tried the same ploy in another meeting a few weeks later, but by that time northern leaders had persuaded the wavering within their ranks to settle for nothing but a separate parish, and again the vote was "interrupted."[50]

[50] GFPR, 25–26; Petition of the Third Parish, December 23, 1738, *MA,* 11: 530; An Answer of the Town of Gloucester to the Petition of Nathaniel

Rather than fostering reconciliation, the south's resistance to the separation only spilled the conflict over parish borders and extended the lines of battle throughout the town. From the fall of 1738 to the summer of 1741, northerners refused to move out of the old meetinghouse and constantly renewed their demand to be "set off." Drawn into the fray on the side of the south, Second and Third parishioners scolded the dissidents for their stubbornness. By now the province government too had become more closely involved in the controversy, sending a special investigating committee to Gloucester to study the situation and suggest a solution. As a result, in July of 1741, the General Court ordered the First Parish to continue carrying on public worship in both meetinghouses and to call an assistant to the Reverend John White to preach at the old church. The Court further ordered that if, after a year had elapsed, north and south were not reconciled and no second minister was settled, northerners would become a separate parish.[51]

Although the General Court's action made the formation of the Fourth Parish almost inevitable, southern leaders stubbornly refused to accept defeat. They still hoped to avert the separation by pushing their most determined opponents out of the First Parish and into the Third. To this end, they fashioned from the Court's order to retain an assistant minister a strategy for making the old meetinghouse as unacceptable to the northern dissidents as the new church. The candidate that the southern majority of the First Parish called to preach "in a probationary way" at the old meetinghouse was Moses Parsons, the son of a prosperous tanner in Gloucester harbor who was one of the most outspoken opponents of the separation. Northerners naturally resisted this scheme to settle over them the son of an archenemy, and at the end of the year allotted by the Court they renewed their demand for a separation. Again the south protested,

Coit, December 23, 1738, *MA,* 11: 531–531a; Answer to the Petition of Nathaniel Coit by the First Parish, 1739/40, *MA,* 243: 44–46; and Petition of Epes Sargent, et al., 1742, *MA,* 243: 70.

[51] *Acts and Resolves, Public and Private, of the Province of Massachusetts Bay, 1692–1780,* ed. Abner C. Goodell, et al. (Boston, 1869–1922), 13: 21.

claiming that the First Parish had, after all, attempted to comply with the Court's order.[52]

At this stage in the separation controversy, both parts of the parish seemed poised for yet another round of debate. Instead, in the fall of 1742, southerners abruptly acceded to northern wishes and offered their adversaries leave "to be sett off into a Distinct and Separate Parish." This decision, southerners told the Court, "was come into purely for the sake of peace." The truth was less flattering: southerners suddenly jumped to allow the separation because they were about to be pushed. Just weeks before the First Parish finally approved the separation, the Court had learned of the plan to settle Moses Parsons on the dissidents from a group of thirty-three First Parish members led by Captain Jabez Baker. The petition of Baker and his neighbors represented the entry of yet another part of Gloucester into the dispute—the inhabitants of the far eastern end of Cape Ann. Situated in a remote part of the First Parish, this neighborhood had sided with the south in the earlier controversy over the meetinghouse. But Cape-dwellers, whose homes lay at some distance from the more densely settled parts of town, foresaw that population growth would someday make possible their own separation from the First Parish. An increasing number of families on the Cape would allow their neighborhood to build its own meetinghouse at a more convenient location. This consideration made the Cape's residents averse in principle to opposing any separations.[53] Perhaps too, Captain Baker, an economically successful shoreman who had moved to Cape Ann from Beverly, was not entirely satisfied with the seating allotted to his family in the Middle Street meetinghouse.

The formation of the Fourth Parish at the beginning of 1743 rid the southerners of the troubling and troublesome presence of their old rivals in Annisquam harbor. Yet the response in Gloucester harbor to the departure of northerners was not relief but regret. The commitment to protecting

---

[52] GFPR, 42–44; GFCR, July 8 and July 28, 1742; Petition of the Northerly Part of First Parish, 1742, MA, 243: 63; and Petition of Epes Sargent, et al., 1742, MA, 243: 65.

[53] GFPR, 44; Petition of Epes Sargent, et al., 1742, MA, 243: 70; and Petition of Jabez Baker, et al., September 22, 1742, MA, 243: 71.

family status that animated both northerners and southerners had brought about not only innovations in local institutions but also repeated departures from customary practice
and preference for resolving internal disputes. The northerners' opposition to the new seating arrangements had forced
the First Parish to abandon the quest for consensus and, with
the approval of a mere majority, to move public worship to
the Middle Street meetinghouse. The intensity of the controversy had also exhausted local resources for reconciliation.
The conflict had spilled over Gloucester's borders as both
parties applied to an external authority, the General Court,
for redress of their grievances. The unity and unanimity that
townspeople had successfully sustained during disputes earlier in the eighteenth century had, at least temporarily, become
elusive goals, objectives sacrificed to the stronger desire to
preserve another part of the old order, the position of the
First Parish's established elite families.

But more than a decade of contention in the parish had
done little to foster among Gloucester harbor's leaders an
acceptance of open factionalism and dissent in political life.
On the contrary, they expressed considerable uneasiness over
their inability to resolve differences within the old framework of consensus and corporatism. And the stigma of
involvement in a parish separation was a source of particular shame and discomfort. Even after the Fourth Parish was
an accomplished fact, southerners still sent agents to Boston
to lecture the General Court on the desirability of annexing
northerners to the Third Parish. They were concerned above
all to vindicate Gloucester harbor by insuring that the blame
for the dismemberment of the old community fell publicly
and squarely on the shoulders of their adversaries. In all of
their statements to the Court, southerners portrayed northerners as a crew of malcontents who preferred their particular interests to the common good of the town. It was the
northerners who had created "disturbances" at parish meetings, obstructed the Court's plan for reconciliation, "Used
all Art to dissuade others from it," and fomented discord
that would "Confound, Ruin, and Destroy the Whole." In
the same petitions, southerners styled themselves as peace-
loving, public-spirited guardians of the common good of the

town, eager to maintain public worship, true religion, and an orthodox ministry at the Third Parish.[54]

Did southern leaders really believe in these communal ideals that they espoused—or did they only believe that they were supposed to believe in them? In a sense, it does not matter. For whatever the state of their "sincerity," the southerners' appropriation of these values decisively influenced their behavior and the duration of the intraparish conflict. A weaker commitment to communal considerations on their part would actually have reduced the level of strife within the community and shortened the span of the dispute. What gave the separation controversy a long and bitter life was, ironically, southerners' insistence on the primacy of the common good and the importance of preserving continuity with the order of the past.[55] In the contest over the formation of the Fourth Parish, as in the dispute over the Middle Street meeting-house, attempts to inhibit change only accelerated it; consequences confounded intentions. Instead of retrieving whatever unity was possible among First Parish members, the southern resistance to the separation deepened the alienation of northerners while it spread conflict to other parts of the town.

On the other hand, knowing how sincerely Gloucester harbor's elite adhered to communitarian values is important for assessing the influence of commercial development on social character. Had the coming of trade turned southern entrepreneurs into self-aggrandizing "Yankees" for whom the venerable shibboleths of the corporate community were so much hollow rhetoric? The answer is not easy. Because the principal promoters of change are often those who most loudly proclaim their devotion to the past, true conservatives can be difficult to identify. But while it is possible that southern leaders belong within the ranks of these historical

[54] See especially An Answer of the Town of Gloucester to Nathaniel Coit, December 23, 1738, *MA,* 11: 531–531a; An Answer to the Petition of Nathaniel Coit by the First Parish, 1739/40, *MA,* 243: 44–46; and Petition of Epes Sargent, et al., 1742, *MA,* 243: 65, 70.

[55] Quentin Skinner makes a similar point about the role of ideas. He argues that prevailing ideologies and values are not simply rationalizations for a predetermined course of action, but rather they set limits on available behavior and thus define the contours of historical controversies. See especially his essay, "The Principles and Practice of Opposition: The Case of Bolingbroke vs Walpole," *Historical Perspectives,* ed. Neil McKendrick (London, 1974).

"double agents" who conceal their abandonment of older
ideals by appearing to embrace them, it is more likely that
they do not. Sometimes people mean just what they say. And
in the case of the southern elite, what enhances the credibility of their profession of communal ideals is the lack of modern, liberal traits in the broader pattern of their behavior.
Among these established, elite families, the ties of neighborhood and membership in the community still limited the
rationalization of their economic relationships with fellow
townsmen, while religious intolerance restricted with whom
they would do business. Within their ranks too, lineal family
values took precedence over accumulation in allocating status, and localistic concerns loomed larger than the lure of
the wider world. To a world-view comprised of these elements, a genuine longing for the restoration of the consensual community would not be an anomalous addition.

The process of commercial expansion in Gloucester sub-
jected certain communal bonds to strain and produced a
conflict that civic traditions could not resolve. It created the
conditions that finally forced all members of the First Parish
to choose between two aspects of their former way of life:
preserving the position of established families and maintaining the integrity and traditional institutions of the parish.[56]
Both northerners and southerners made the same choice.
Unsettled by the uncertainties introduced by economic growth,
southerners could perpetuate the standing of their families
only at the cost of altering older placement practices.
Threatened by the erosion of their former eminence, northerners could retrieve their slipping status only at the expense
of dividing the parish. But although both parties to the parish dispute altered old institutions to accommodate new exigencies, these innovations did not signal the emergence of
more modern attitudes toward the social order. For rather
than reflecting the rise of new values, the First Parish controversy marked only a reluctant reordering of older ones.

[56] Edmund Morgan argues that the same preference for family over the religious community—in this case, a pure church—led to the adoption of the
halfway covenant. (*The Puritan Family*, 173–86.)

5

Revivalism and the Wars of Religion

DURING the final years of the 1730s and for several thereafter, many New England communities became caught up in a revival of piety known as the First Great Awakening. This religious revitalization movement began in Northampton, Massachusetts, and the surrounding towns along the Connecticut River Valley; after 1739 the enthusiasm spread throughout New England, sustained by itinerant preachers like George Whitefield and Gilbert Tennent and by scores of settled clergymen.[1] Descriptions of the Awakening abound in metaphors drawn from natural cataclysms to convey the impact of the revival upon society. A "psychological earthquake," a "torrent" of pietistic fervor, a "firestorm" of religious zeal "rocked," "flooded," or "burned" one town after another as enthusiasm spread like a "contagion." While these expressions capture the force of feeling generated by the Awakening, they mislead by implying that the revival everywhere represented a dramatic rupture with the past. Many communities that embraced the "New Light" did not experience the Awakening as a discontinuous or disruptive epi-

[1] The best general account of the Awakening in New England is Edwin S. Gaustad, *The Great Awakening in New England* (New York, 1957). See also C. C. Goen, *Revivalism and Separatism in New England, 1740–1800* (New Haven, 1962).

sode in local life, and Gloucester was one such place.[2] There, the enthusiasm of the 1740s simply intensified the deeply religious outlook and pietistic sensibility that had always characterized local culture. And rather than unsettling the basic structure of society and setting the stage for fundamental change, the Awakening in Gloucester instead restored equilibrium to the town by reaffirming the attachment of inhabitants to a common ethos and outlook.

Like the revivals in many other New England towns, Gloucester's religious renewal began among the community's young people. In January of 1742, Moses Parsons, the master of a school in Gloucester harbor, noticed signs of heightened spiritual concern among his students. Parsons's "religious exercises" fostered their fervor, and the excitement quickly passed to adults. Parents of the youngsters started turning up at the schoolhouse, praying alongside of their children, and attending to Parsons's preaching. Elated by these developments, the Reverend John White took steps to nurture the new zeal. He invited "New Light" pastor Nathaniel Rogers of Ipswich to a day of prayer and fasting at the Middle Street meetinghouse and also solicited the assistance of Third Parish's sympathetic minister, Benjamin Bradstreet. This meeting at Middle Street affected "especially the young," according to White, but the enthusiasm also gathered momentum among the adults of his congregation, converting the formalists and "refreshening" the saints. "Old and young, male and female, bond and free" organized nine separate religious societies for private devotions.[3] With the revival underway in the southern part of town, the Reverend Bradstreet, fresh from his triumphal lectures in Gloucester harbor, carried the New Light to the Third Parish. That neighborhood's young people, formerly "too much addicted to quarreling, swearing, and drinking," now "wonderfully reformed" and joined religious societies.[4] The mature members of the congregation also became caught up in the

[2] Jedrey, *The World of John Cleaveland,* 46–57.
[3] John White to Thomas Prince, *Christian History,* 2 vols. (Boston, 1744–45), II, 44–45.
[4] Benjamin Bradstreet to Thomas Prince, *Christian History,* I, 187–89.

excitement and swelled attendance at Bradstreet's weekly lectures.[5]

Gloucester's clergymen played an important role in promoting the revival in town, particularly John White, the community's most senior spiritual leader and a prototypical Calvinist evangelical. Well before the Awakening revitalized Reformed orthodoxy and popularized a direct, emotional style of preaching, White was delivering sermons that mixed equal doses of rigidly orthodox Calvinism with warm denunciations of "the decay of the power of godliness." "Legal Convictions without Evangelical Ones will end in Presumption or Despair," White told his congregation in 1725, "but when Evangelical Convictions are added to Legal, they end in Conversion."[6] On the subject of worldliness, White's models were the Mathers' jeremiads, sermons calling for repentance, moral reform, and rededication to the ascetic ideals of Puritanism. The cadences of Cotton's treatises especially echo through White's criticisms of people "overheated and deeply engaged in their Affections, toward the Profits, Pleasures, and Preferments of the World." Like his more brilliant and eloquent partner in evangelical endeavor, the Reverend Jonathan Edwards of Northampton, White was also persuaded that New England was pervaded by Arminianism, a more liberal theological outlook that accorded greater scope to man's free will than did Reformed orthodoxy. For both ministers, the antidote to both materialism and Arminian "will-worship" was the spiritual rebirth that resulted from man's recognition of his utter dependence upon divine grace for salvation. And, although White lacked his Northampton colleague's refined talent for psychological terrorism, he too appreciated and exploited the value of fear as an instrument for converting sinners and smug liberals alike.[7] His study of Scripture had convinced White of the imminence of "the Conflagration," the end of the world in fire before the Last

[5] Ibid.

[6] John White, The Gospel Treasure in Earthen Vessels, 1 and 2. For the similar theological and evangelical affinities of Benjamin Bradstreet and Moses Parsons, see SHG, VII, 457–60; and Moses Parsons, "Sermons, 1734–1788," MS Essex Institute.

[7] John White, New England's Lamentations, 2–14, 20–29.

Judgment, and he impressed the horror of this prospect upon his congregation. White's sermons were remarkable neither for literary imagery nor intellectual content. But his plain, blunt style of address and his discourses sprinkled with homely metaphors and spiced with hellfire satisfied Gloucester, where "our people . . . came in to the church one after another" even before the Awakening and "in troops or clusters" during the revival of 1742.[8]

White's belief in God's sovereignty and man's impotence saved him from suspecting that he had "worked up" Gloucester's Awakening. Nevertheless, his evangelical orientation had surely helped him "pray down" the revival that took place in town. White's awareness of the mass conversions of the 1730s in Jonathan Edwards's Northampton church imbued the pastor with "sincere, sensible, and fervent Desires, that the God of all Grace would visit us [in Gloucester] with the like Plentiful Effusions." He even began to voice his hopes from the pulpit in the Middle Street meetinghouse, "in publick Addresses to ask for the Gift of Gifts, the Holy Spirit."[9] It was shortly thereafter that his prayers were answered in the schoolroom of Moses Parsons in the southern harbor. But important as White's ministry was in generating religious enthusiasm in town, other circumstances also shaped local susceptibility to the Awakening. Townspeople had been sitting under White's preaching for forty years, but it was only in 1742 that they suddenly started entering the First Church "in troops or clusters." A closer look at the character of the revival itself supplies some clues about what conditions were particularly influential in heightening religious concern in town at that time.

The striking feature of Gloucester's Awakening was its strength in two parts of town. Although all of Gloucester's churches were receptive to the New Light, the revival's impact

[8] White to Prince, *Christian History*, II, 41. White told Prince in 1742 that were 260 full church members at First Gloucester, 80 men and 180 women. Babson's estimate of the First Parish's population in 1755 is 275 families. (*History*, 349.) If all male church members were heads of households, this would suggest that between one-third to one-half of the adult males in the First Gloucester congregation were full church members at the time of the revival.

[9] White to Prince, *Christian History*, II, 42.

was most intense in Gloucester harbor and the Third Parish. The appeal of the Awakening in these two neighborhoods suggests a connection between vulnerability to religious fervor and tension over troubles in First Parish. By the beginning of 1742, the First Parish separation was a foregone conclusion. Southern harbor dwellers, who had insisted on relocating the meetinghouse and on rearranging the seating, and Third Parish members, who had actively supported the south and stood to benefit the most from the First Parish's troubles, now confronted the bitter outcome of their actions. The strain registered in the intense response of these neighborhoods to the revival. Less affected by the fervor were the northern part of First Parish, whose inhabitants felt little remorse at the prospect of parting from their neighbors, and agrarian Second Parish, whose members had stayed farthest from the fray. The Reverend John White himself seems to have sensed that the evangelical excitement in Gloucester harbor was related to the difficulties within his congregation. He may even have harbored a slim hope that the religious renewal would avert the impending split and repair his relations with the northern dissidents. In a revealing assurance to his colleague in Boston, Thomas Prince, White remarked that the Awakening in Gloucester had produced "no separations" over religious doctrine and practice, and that "Little had been said about New Light . . . and as little about opposers."[10] In fact, White could take comfort from the apparently unanimous acceptance of evangelicalism among Gloucester's orthodox. Still, if the revival bred no additional dissension in town, neither did it forestall the separation.

The relatively greater receptivity to the New Light in the southern harbor and at the Third Parish also points to a link

[10] Letter of John White to the residents of the northern part of First Parish, July 30, 1742, *MA*, 243: 68; and White to Prince, *Christian History*, II, 44. In general, Gloucester's Awakening was a restrained affair. In both parishes, the revival enhanced religious engagement, but the fervor apparently produced neither emotional excesses nor democratic demands for social levelling, nor a conservative, "Old Light" criticism of the new evangelicalism. White's strictures against "outcries" and "trances" discouraged the enthusiastic extremes that characterized the final phase of the Awakening in some of the churches of Boston, Salem, and Marblehead. See chapter XI.

between evangelical enthusiasm and commercial development, for these two neighborhoods were the focal points of
maritime activity in town. Gloucester harbor was the hub of
the coastwise and transatlantic trade, while the Third Parish
was quickly becoming a second center of the local fishing
industry.[11] Not only did the revival exhibit the greatest
strength in the commercialized parts of Gloucester, but it
also appealed most powerfully, at least at first, to the most
successful families of these neighborhoods. Although the
enthusiasm for the Awakening became "general," the revival
started at the top of society in the southern harbor before
spreading to other groups.

While gaps in the First Church records make it impossible
to reconstruct a profile of the revival's new converts, John
White's account of the Awakening indicates that the renewal
of piety originated among his more prominent parishioners.
The excitement began among children and parents at a school
in the southern part of town where Moses Parsons was
employed "by a number of gentlemen to train up their children." And according to White, the "most visible and powerful effusions of the Spirit" occurred during his preaching
"in two religious societies in the Harbor," the district where
the most affluent southerners made their homes. A more
ambiguous piece of evidence for the revival's appeal to the
best Gloucester harbor families is the large number of their
Afro-American "servants" who joined in the excitement.
White took particular notice of "one religious society of
Negroes,

> who in their meetings behave very seriously and decently. . . .
> one of them gave a very satisfying account of his experiences,

[11]Both demographic and economic data reflect the quick growth of the
Third Parish. By 1755, the parish was the third largest neighborhood in
town with 415 inhabitants, just slightly smaller than Second Parish, which
had been founded ten years earlier. Third Parish's representation at the top
of Gloucester's economic hierarchy also increased rapidly: only one inventoried decedent in the wealthiest quartile of townsmen between 1736 and
1745 was a resident of Third Parish, but during the next decade, three
Third Parish members ranked within the top quartile and one in the top
decile of inventoried decedents. (Source: Essex Probate Files, Registry of
Probate, Essex County Courthouse, Salem, Mass.)

and was taken into church fellowship; most of them entered the covenant, and they were baptized themselves and also their issue.[12]

Possibly evangelical enthusiasm developed independently among Gloucester harbor's blacks: the opportunity for fellowship in the "society of Negroes" offered a real incentive for religious zeal. On the other hand, Afro-American participation in the Awakening could also reflect the atmosphere prevailing in Gloucester harbor households affluent enough to include slaves or the pressure of pious masters newly anxious about the souls of their property.

In general, then, Gloucester's Awakening made the most profound impression upon the town's predominantly commercial and maritime neighborhoods, parts of the community that also remained deeply disturbed over the strife occasioned by the First Parish controversy. And in Gloucester harbor and the Third Parish, it was younger people and the most economically successful families who were, at least initially, the most responsive to the religious fervor. These correspondences suggest that the causes of the revival in Gloucester could be similar to the conditions that may also have fostered the Awakening in the towns of eastern Connecticut. Like Gloucester, the Connecticut communities caught up in the revivals of the 1740s had become increasingly involved in the market economy during the decades after 1690. Accompanying their commercial expansion and growing prosperity, it is argued, was intense social conflict. Acquisitive individuals pursued profit at the expense of communal unity and welfare and in defiance of traditional authorities. But the worldly success of these new Yankee entrepreneurs came at a great psychic cost. Guilt over their desire to accumulate "hollowed out" their lives; their opposition to the traditional, Puritan order generated unbearable anxiety. In this view, the stress induced by economic com-

[12] White to Prince, *Christian History*, II, 43–44. A profile of revival converts would not in any case indicate the impact of the Awakening upon inhabitants who were already church members, and in Gloucester their numbers were considerable even before the revival. For the appeal of the Awakening to blacks throughout the American colonies, see Albert J. Raboteau, *Slave Religion: The "Invisible Institution" in the Antebellum South* (New York, 1978), 128–30.

petition and social conflict prepared the way for the Awakening: participation in the revivals and the catharsis of conversion afforded eastern Connecticut's entrepreneurs an outlet for their inner tension.[13]

The notion that the wages of wealth is the burden of a bad conscience is not unappealing, and within Puritan culture in particular worldly success was regarded with considerable ambivalence. Even so, applying this conception of the relationship between commercial development and evangelical enthusiasm to Gloucester raises some difficulties. Men had been amassing large estates from trade in town for half a century before the revival, and the Reverend John White had probably not allowed many Sabbaths to pass without denouncing "the Profits, Pleasures, and Preferments of the World." If these strictures had awakened the mass religious excitement of 1742, why had they had so little effect during the preceding decades of economic expansion? Perhaps remorse over their role in the First Parish controversy suddenly aroused the consciences of the prosperous merchants, shoremen, and tradesmen in White's congregation. But these entrepreneurs had little reason for feeling that it was their "covetousness" that had caused the rupture within the community. Although the rivalry between Annisquam and Gloucester harbors had arisen from commercial expansion, the unrestrained pursuit of profit did not characterize local economic life. Gloucester harbor prospered more than the Annisquam because of the south's better location and geographic advantages, not because of the greater ruthlessness of its businessmen. Neither did the First Parish controversy pit acquisitive individualists against "traditional authorities" among the town's political and religious leaders: the contest involved two different factions within the established local elite.

If guilt over entrepreneurial activity is an unlikely source of the Awakening in Gloucester, the strength of the revival in the southern harbor and the Third Parish nonetheless indicates that receptivity to religious enthusiasm was in some way related to the town's transformation from village to seaport. What the connection between commercial develop-

[13] Bushman, *From Puritan to Yankee*, 187–92.

ment and cultural response might be is suggested by the configuration of influences affecting local life in the years just prior to and during the Awakening. By the end of the 1730s, the same remote forces of empire that had helped to engineer Gloucester's economic growth after 1690 now threatened the town's undoing. In 1739, the rivalry among European powers for trading rights in the Caribbean and Central America triggered an armed conflict between England and Spain, the War of Jenkins' Ear. Since the first theater of the hostilities was in the Western Hemisphere, Massachusetts men were immediately mobilized for military duty. A thousand soldiers from the North Shore were among the force of thirty five hundred colonial troops launched by the British in 1740 against the Spanish town of Cartagena on the Colombian coast. Casualties from the fighting, combined with the toll taken by a yellow fever epidemic, made for a staggering loss of lives among the American forces: only six hundred colonial soldiers survived the expedition. And after the disastrous Cartagena campaign, the Caribbean remained a battleground. Spain's privateers patrolled the basin while the British continued their recruitment of colonials to defend imperial interests. England made peace with Spain in 1742, bringing about a brief lull in the fighting in the Western Hemisphere, but anticipation of a French challenge to Britain's imperial objectives kept colonials apprehensive. Although England did not declare war on France until 1744, New England men were mobilized as early as 1742 in order to secure the northeastern American frontier against attack.[14]

[14] In 1740, England's war with Spain widened into a general European conflict, the War of the Austrian Succession (1740–1748). The fighting with France, which began in 1744, was known in the colonies as King George's War (1744–1748). The best general accounts of the Spanish and French wars are Leach, *Arms for Empire*, 206–61 and Graham, *Empire of the North Atlantic*, 103–42. For discussions of New England's role in the fighting against Spain, see Nash, *Urban Crucible*, 169, and W. T. Baxter, *The House of Hancock: Business in Boston, 1724–1775* (Cambridge, Mass., 1945), 78, 82, and 92.

No information survives concerning the number and names of Gloucester men who served in the Cartagena expedition or the subsequent campaigns against the French and Spanish. Gloucester's Captain Charles Byles commanded a company of forty-one men at the siege of Louisbourg in the summer of 1745, and presumably most were locals. Captain Thomas Sanders, another Gloucester resident, commanded a government sloop during

Gloucester's economy suffered heavily from the hostilities with Spain and France. By 1740, townspeople claimed that because of the drain of local manpower resulting from military demands, there were "not half so many fishermen fitted out as used to be." A year later, the situation was even worse. The Reverend John White reported to the General Court that "of above Seventy fishing vessels, there are few, if any above ten in that business. . . . Our people are scattered abroad to get their bread: many serving as volunteers in his Majesty's service; many pressed. . . ." And the future looked more ominous still, for the entry of France into the conflict appeared imminent, a prospect that imperiled the security of the entire north Atlantic fishery. White's remarks to the General Court convey the feelings of powerlessness and confusion that pervaded Gloucester in the early years of the 1740s as the fighting wreaked havoc on the local economy:

> Almost our whole dependence, under God, is upon our Navigation and Fishery. . . . and that has so farr failed by reason of the war with Spain and the fears of warr with France, as also by reason of the smallness of the price of fish and the dearness of salt, bread, and craft. . . . and the cry of the many for necessaries is very affecting. And we have had three contributions for the relief of the poor in the last year in our congregation, and other Families are very pressing for relief.[15]

Depression and unemployment in the fishing industry, high prices for provisions, military mobilization uprooting young men, families suddenly impoverished by the loss of jobs and wage-earners—these were the effects of war. And to this litany of local difficulties, White could have added the failure of the Land Bank of 1740. Men from every parish in Gloucester had invested in this scheme for emitting paper

the French war and probably drew most of his crew members from local fishermen and mariners. (Babson, *History,* 320.) In earlier military campaigns against French Canada, Gloucester had contributed heavily to the province's military manpower. According to Francis Parkman, two-thirds of all able-bodied Gloucester men served in Phips's expedition against Quebec in 1690. (*Count Frontenac and New France under Louis XIV* [Boston, 1880], 246.) On recruitment in seaports generally, see Nash, Urban Crucible, 57–58.

[15] White's report is cited in Babson, *History,* 381.

currency backed by land security, and now they had to pay for the redemption of the bank's bills.[16] These economic dislocations augmented the town's dismay at the prospect of the First Parish separation, which augured an added financial burden of supporting another minister.

The military and economic crises of the 1740s did not permanently disrupt local society. The return of war imposed temporary hardships upon Gloucester's inhabitants by producing a short-run recession and by interrupting the fishing industry and trade. Nevertheless, the conflict with Spain and even the entry of France into the fighting in 1744 did not deal the same kind of crippling blow to Cape Ann's economy as the one that hastened Boston's decline during this period. The war caused setbacks but did not create a large, permanent underclass of dependent widows, orphans, and disabled soldiers. Even at the end of the fighting in 1748, Gloucester was relieving only seven individuals at an annual cost to the town of about twenty-five pounds sterling. Nor did levels of crime and debt within the community rise during the decade of military crisis. Essentially sound at the start of the wars, the local economy recovered, fishing and commerce resumed, and prosperity returned with the restoration of peace. Population continued to increase and median income to rise as Gloucester benefited from the flow of families and businesses escaping Boston's high taxes and prices.[17]

But while the wars with Spain and France inflicted neither irreparable losses on Gloucester's economy nor long-term social dislocation, the years of fighting created a climate of instability and uncertainty. Moreover, the onset of the military crisis coincided with the culmination of more than a decade of internal disunity in town—the controversy within the First Parish—and the confluence of these events augmented the psychological burden on townspeople. What the war revealed was the extent to which commercial develop-

[16] A list of subscribers to the Land Bank, including nineteen Gloucester men, appears in Davis, *Currency and Banking*, II, 290–313.

[17] On the difficulties of Boston during the war years, see G. B. Warden, *Boston, 1689–1776* (Boston, 1970), 126–38, and Nash, *Urban Crucible*, 182–97. For median estate value in Gloucester during the 1740s and 1750s, see appendix, table I. On population increase and poor relief, see Babson, *History*, 322, 349, 407, and 542.

ment had made the town vulnerable to changes of a far more sweeping and ominous character than those experienced by inhabitants over the last fifty years. For a more established center of the fishery like Marblehead, where people had relied on maritime pursuits exclusively since the beginning of settlement, the years of fighting after 1739 were unwelcome. Still, these wars with Spain and France were only the most recent in a series of disruptions that Marblehead had weathered in succession, starting with the Anglo-Dutch wars of the mid-seventeenth century. For Gloucester, however, because of its later development as a center of the commercial fishery, the hostilities after 1739 represented the first real experience of the effects of war on the local economy. The earlier spate of Anglo-French conflicts over the years between 1690 and 1710 had actually enhanced Gloucester's economy by enlarging demand in Boston for timber and ships. This enterprise had entailed risk neither in tapping raw materials nor in dispatching local produce to market. After 1710, as the town turned more to fishing and trading with distant markets, inhabitants enjoyed more than a quarter century of prosperity from maritime pursuits, except for the brief interruption caused by the war with the Maine Indian tribes between 1723 and 1725. It was only in the years after 1739 that England's clashes with her imperial competitors made real trouble for Gloucester. The Atlantic filled with privateers, endangering local fishing and trading vessels; the hostilities impeded both production and trade, threw people out of work, and raised prices. Unlike Marbleheaders, Gloucester residents were not accustomed to economic dislocation on this scale. It was a novel phenomenon, one that defied local control. That Cape Ann came through the military crisis without suffering permanent economic and social decline was not a consolation available to its inhabitants in the early 1740s.

It is not at all surprising that these dislocations of local life first evoked a response from the young people of Gloucester's maritime neighborhoods. Since the tasks of fishing and fighting fell chiefly to the young, they were most sensitive to the uncertainties occasioned by the lack of work and to apprehensions over military mobilization. By casting a pall over their future prospects and by threatening their lives and livelihoods, the military crisis played an important role in heightening youthful susceptibility to spiritual influences. Although the anxieties of Gloucester's adolescents and young adults were manifested mainly through religious enthusiasm, an increased interest in the supernatural in all of its forms characterized the behavior of some of them. In 1745, for example, several young Gloucester soldiers paid a visit to "Peg" Wesson just before they joined the expedition against the French fortress at Louisbourg on Cape Breton Island. Peg was a poor, old woman who had succeeded Francis Norwood, Sr. as the town witch, still a position of some significance in the mid-eighteenth century. What the young soldiers probably wanted from Peg was some prediction of their fates or a charm for warding off French fire. But the meeting ended badly, and what they got from the witch were threats of a terrible end awaiting them at Louisbourg.[18]

For both Peg Wesson's visitors and John White's converts, the early 1740s were times of anxiety and uncertainty. In New England's inland towns, the premature deaths of adolescents were often followed by sudden outpourings of religious piety among young people; in Gloucester, the dangers of suffering from injury or disease during military service focused young minds upon the fate of their eternal souls in the same way.[19] In addition, by threatening the security of the north Atlantic, the wars cast into doubt the expectations of sons to succeed their fathers in commercial and maritime employments at home. If the Spanish shut off the Caribbean and Iberian trade or if the French repossessed the fishing grounds, the children of Gloucester's merchants, shoremen, tradesmen, and fishermen would face a future of being "scattered abroad in the world to get their bread." The fighting and the economic troubles that it created thus confronted Gloucester's adolescents and young adults with contingency and discontinuity: religious conversion pro-

---

[18] Babson, *History*, 321.

[19] For an example of premature deaths as a catalyst of religious concern among adolescents, see Jonathan Edwards's account of the deaths of a young man and a young married woman prior to the "frontier revivals" of 1734–1735 in the Connecticut River Valley in *A Faithful Narrative of the Surprising Work of God*, repr. in *The Works of President Edwards*, ed. S. B. Dwight, 10 vols. (New York, 1829–1830), IV, 19–30.

vided consolation and reassurance. In this respect, the Awakening in Gloucester closely resembles the revival in the inland, agrarian towns of New England. In these communities, too, the evangelical message initially appealed most powerfully to younger people, and a plausible source of their enthusiasm was a similar uncertainty over the future. The pressing problem for adolescents and young adults in farming villages was less the prospect of military mobilization than an increasingly severe shortage of land. But, like Gloucester's young people, the children of farmers were facing serious obstacles to perpetuating in their own lives—and preferably within their own hometowns—the pattern of existence established by preceding generations.[20]

The intense disruption of economic and social life in Gloucester after 1739 by the impersonal forces of empire supplies a context for understanding the relationship between social change and religious experience. It was not the consciousness of their complicity in the transformation of their town that afflicted Gloucester inhabitants on the eve of the Awakening. It was neither remorse over promoting commercial development nor ambivalence over making money nor even compunction over the impending First Parish separation that paved the way for the revival. Not a guilty sense of their responsibility for fostering change, but quite the opposite, a growing conviction of their impotence to resist its inroads was what made people in Gloucester receptive to the New Light. The military crises after 1739 and the ominous economic difficulties of the 1740s, combined with the decade of discord over seating and separation, impressed on townspeople their powerlessness to control the course of local life. Young people, the most dependent and vulnerable members of the community, experienced these feelings of helplessness with particular acuity. But their elders, especially those who had come to rely on commerce and maritime employments for their livelihoods, were gripped by the same apprehensions. In the morphology of Puritan conversion, this acknowledgment of utter dependency and the recognition of

[20] Greven, *Four Generations*, 276–79; John Bumsted, "Religion, Finance and Democracy in Massachusetts: The Town of Norton as a Case Study," *Journal of American History*, 57 (1971), 828–31; and Tracy, *Jonathan Edwards, Pastor*, 91–108.

human inability is identified with the final stage of despair that precedes the first stirring of spiritual assurance in the soul of a sinner.[21] It was this state of mind that made Gloucester harbor and the Third Parish so susceptible to the revival's appeal for their total surrender to the divine sovereign. The experience of all townspeople in the years before the Awakening, but especially that of the inhabitants of maritime neighborhoods, gave the old tenets of orthodoxy a new resonance. The evangelicals' reassertion of the Calvinist doctrines of divine omnipotence and man's dependence assumed a compelling relevance in the early 1740s as a framework for comprehending and coping with the dislocation of local life.

There was, of course, another side to strict Calvinist orthodoxy, one that emphasized man's importance rather than his inability. Revivalists were intensely concerned with personal salvation, which they believed could be obtained through faith alone; outward moral behavior and formal religious observances were by themselves insufficient to a Christian life. And once men and women had received some assurance of their salvation, converts were responsible only to God and the dictates of their own consciences. This religious individualism implicit in the evangelical message, it has been suggested, paved the way for the emergence of a more liberal social order in New England during the middle of the eighteenth century. In this view, as New Light theology took hold in the churches, ideas about the conduct of business and politics also became more individualistic. Revival converts became "new men, with new attitudes toward themselves, their religion, their neighbors, and their rulers in church and state." They perceived the old "Puritan" culture as "alien to their identity," an authoritarian anachronism that threatened their peace of mind. By devaluing older forms of authority, evangelicalism legitimated resistance to the traditional order; the revival's legacy of individualism tacitly sanctioned self-interest in economic life, contention in civic

---

[21] Edmund S. Morgan, *Visible Saints: The History of a Puritan Idea* (Ithaca, New York, 1963), 66–78.

life, and "other departures from the approved pattern of community."[22]

While a heightened concern for personal salvation did characterize the evangelical movement of the 1740s, Gloucester's experience of the revival does not support the idea that its message of religious individualism either widened the scope of personal liberty or released those awakened from the authority of the past. On the contrary, the concern of Gloucester's converts was to strengthen the hold of the old order over the lives of individuals, especially those who deviated from the norms of orthodox belief and behavior. The force of this conservative consensus is reflected in both the First Church's strict discipline of backsliding members and the submission of some of the southern harbor's most prominent citizens to the closer oversight of their morals. In 1745, for example, Ensign John Rowe complained to the First Church about Colonel Epes Sargent for "his abusing s[ai]d Rowe by giving him many blows." Sargent's wealth and rank were no proof against the indignation of other church members, who condemned "the evil and uncharitableness" of his actions. After the First Church voted "pretty unanimously that their said brother Coll. Sargent had thereby given offense," he appeared before them immediately and admitted his guilt. A few years later, the brethren called on John Poole, a wealthy shoreman, to answer charges of adultery; unsatisfied by his responses to their inquiry, the church suspended Poole for a year and a half before accepting his repentance and restoring him to fellowship.[23]

Not only did the Awakening fire Gloucester's inhabitants with a militant zeal to effect reform within their own ranks, but it also prompted them to search out sinful deviations from true religion outside of their community. By 1744, they had found such a menace in, of all places, Bradford, Massachusetts, a sleepy farming village about thirty miles to the northwest. The source of their concern was the pastor of Bradford's Second Church, the Reverend William Balch, an Arminian and a strident "Old Light" critic of the Awaken-

[22]Bushman, *From Puritan to Yankee,* 187, and 194–95.
[23]GFCR, April 17, 1745 and August 30, 1753.

ing. Despite his theological liberalism, Balch was popular with the farmers in his congregation, save for a single family of self-proclaimed New Lights. After ending up on the losing side of an ecclesiastical council's decision that vindicated Balch, Bradford's New Light critics were suspended from the Second Church. They retaliated by calling on First Gloucester for support in sustaining opposition to the Bradford parson's heresy. Despite having dubious grounds for intervening in Bradford's ecclesiastical affairs, Gloucester rose to arrest the decay of orthodoxy abroad. The Reverend John White went to Bradford, where he planned to confute Balch on the steps of the Second Church; his deacons and ruling elders accompanied their pastor on his mission to witness the spectacle. But Balch spoiled the drama, simply by refusing to appear, and after standing alone on the meetinghouse steps for some time, White retreated to his Gloucester parsonage. A well-publicized exchange of salvos between First Gloucester and Second Bradford followed, with White denouncing Balch as "corrupt in his principles." In White's view, Second Bradford was an alarming example of "an Inclination in Ministers and Churches to forsake the Sound Principles of the Reformation; the Principles of the good old Puritans, as well as the Principles of the First Planters of this Wilderness."[24]

Merely a nostalgic attachment to a residue of traditional values might have induced many men to praise "the good old Puritans." But it would not have compelled their submission to the discipline of the brethren or have sent them into the wilds of Bradford to flush out the village Arminian. Nor are these the actions of men who regarded the old order as "alien to their identity." Instead, conformity to that order and its imperatives was fundamental to the identity of Gloucester inhabitants. And as locals became more conscious of the larger world lying outside of Gloucester, adherence to the Puritan tradition became increasingly important to their self-esteem. The way in which militant evangelicalism developed out of the insecurities spawned by this wider

---

[24] For Balch's career, see *SHG*, VII, 296–303; on the controversy with First Gloucester, see *Letters from the First Church in Gloucester to the Second in Bradford* (Boston, 1744), 5–6 and 11–12.

social awareness is illustrated by a discourse that Benjamin Bradstreet delivered in 1742 at the Middle Street meeting-house. "There are many Things which I believe I may venture to stile offensive to God," Bradford declared to the congregation,

> which among many may pass muster under the Notion of being fashionable, and among others, of being genteel. . . . in the free Use of the sacred name of God, by some, in their Table and common Talk; and in the genteel and fashionable way of drinking by others who write themselves Gentlemen and Men of Quality. And in the liberty some take to ridicule the Mysteries of the Gospel, and every point of Faith which depraved Reason can't see into. . . . In a word, Live by Faith and not by Sense, amidst the Flouts, Jeers, and Scoffs of an Infidel World, depending on a Promise of Things unseen, amidst 10,000 Discouragements and Temptations to Infidelity.[25]

The tone of embattled defensiveness in Bradstreet's sermon reflects what many of his hearers must have felt at discovering the comparative rudeness and simplicity of their way of life when set against the society of larger seaports with which townspeople were increasingly coming into contact. For all of their prosperity, Gloucester residents were still living in the universe of Samuel Sewall, the pious Bostonian who a generation earlier had fretted over Anglican royal officials "chittering about" with their wheelbarrows on the Sabbath and clattering through town in their carriages after a night of drinking and carousing.[26] Perhaps Epes Sargent, who succumbed to the lure of the Browne mansion in Salem, squirmed in his seat at hearing Bradstreet's strictures. But most of the congregation at the Middle Street meetinghouse could construe the sermon as a criticism of corruption located in the outside world and as an implicit confirmation of the moral superiority of local life. They liked Bradstreet's remarks so well that they paid to have the sermon published.

Besides suggesting the psychological appeal of zealous evangelicalism, Bradstreet's discourse provides additional

[25] Benjamin Bradstreet, *Godly Sorrow Described* (Boston, 1742), 11.
[26] *The Diary of Samuel Sewall,* ed. M. Halsey Smith, 2 vols. (New York, 1973), I, 121; II, 779.

insight into the logic of Gloucester's alarm over Arminianism. While orthodox townspeople mistrusted liberal theology in part because its emphasis on human ability ran counter
to the primary lesson of local experience, they also associated the Arminian reliance on "depraved Reason" with the
"genteel and fashionable" society of larger towns. In these
cosmopolitan centers, parvenus presided, upstarts who styled
themselves "Gentlemen and Men of Quality" but flouted the
canons of conventional, orthodox morality. Because religious liberalism and urban decadence were joined in the minds
of John White's parishioners, they believed that a crusade
against Arminianism would also arrest the encroachment on
Cape Ann of other cultural innovations of "the Infidel World."
The campaign against liberalism would affirm the superiority of local culture at a time when cosmopolites were ridi-
culing its values with "Flouts, Jeers and Scoffs." If it seems
somewhat odd that Cape Ann's conservatives targeted Bradford for their first offensive, American evangelicals have ever
since pursued a similar course. Bradford was no provincial
metropolis, and William Balch stood in no danger of being
taken for the urbane, Old Light liberal, Charles Chauncy of
Boston's First Church. But that the corruption of Arminianism had spread even to this remote backwater made it all
that more alarming—and gave Gloucester's saints a safe place
to fire the first shot in their holy war.

The battle to save Bradford from Arminianism was in some
respects a rehearsal for another crusade of the mid-1740s,
the campaign to secure the north Atlantic from the scourge
of an even more menacing presence, the Catholic French.
Despite the uncertainties created by military conflict, Britain's declaration of war against its chief imperial competitor
in 1744 was a popular cause among New Englanders, particularly in those coastal towns which stood to benefit most
directly from an English victory.[27] Patriotism and the opportunity to become local heroes led many of Gloucester's young
men to enlist in the fight against the French, while the desire
to drive their rivals from the fishing grounds engaged the

[27] Thomas Hutchinson, *The History of the Province and Colony of Massachusetts Bay,* ed. Lawrence Shaw Mayo, 3 vols. Cambridge, Mass, 1936),
II, 313; and Leach, *Arms for Empire,* 227.

support of all townspeople. But conjoined with the pride of empire and the economic interests that promoted participation in the military effort was also the perception of King George's War against the "Papist" French as a religious crusade. While anxieties over impending mobilization for military service promoted revivalistic fervor in Gloucester, the Manichean ethos of evangelicalism in turn fostered military zeal. Not coincidentally, some of the most committed evangelical preachers in northern New England were also the most outspoken advocates of the fight against the French. Among them was the Reverend John White, who urged his congregation just before the beginning of the Louisbourg expedition that

> Some have not unfitly called Cape Breton a hornet's nest. . . . We have already, ever since the war commenced, been great sufferers by them. They harbor our enemies that come to lay waste our infant eastern settlements; they molest and break in upon our fisheries, and break them to pieces; they lie near the roadway of our European merchandise, and they can sally out and take our corn vessels. . . . We must remove these enemies, or they will destroy us. There is a plain necessity of it and woe to us if it be not reduced.[28]

Identifying Britian's imperial objectives with the holy wars of the New Israel, Gloucester inhabitants set out to secure not only their own neighborhood of northern Essex County, but all of the north Atlantic for reformed Protestant orthodoxy.

The result of the Awakening in Gloucester and of the subsequent campaigns against external enemies was the resto-

---

[28] This extract from White's sermon was reprinted in Babson, *History*, 318–19. The full text of the sermon has disappeared. George Whitefield, who preached at the Boston dockside before the departure of the Louisbourg expedition, is often cited as the exemplar of the enlistment of evangelicals into the service of military mobilization, but Whitefield actually opposed the expedition and delivered the sermon only at the insistence of the commander of the troops, Sir William Pepperell. (Clark, *Eastern Frontier*, 288–89.) The careers of White, his colleague and relative by marriage, Samuel Moodey, John Cleaveland, and even the more moderate New Light John Barnard more aptly illustrate the affinity between militancy against the French and evangelicalism. (See *SHG*, IV, 356–64; Jedrey, *World of John Cleaveland*, 123–28; and chapter XI.)

ration of harmony to communal life on Cape Ann. Hunting out Arminian heretics in the backcountry and mobilizing against the Catholic menace became the consuming local concerns.[29] These crusades to secure the "Infidel World" for Congregationalist orthodoxy unified townspeople behind a common cause and drew attention away from the divisions of the past decade. By 1744, signs of an accommodation between the First and Fourth parishes were already apparent. Gloucester and Annisquam harbor residents stopped haggling over the boundaries between their two precincts. And at the beginning of that year, the Fourth Church invited John White to join Benjamin Bradstreet and Second Church's pastor, Richard Jaques, in ordaining their first minister, the Reverend John Rogers. The new parson of Fourth Church was as ardent a New Light as White and Bradstreet—and as receptive to purging Arminians from the pulpits of northern Essex County. Rogers was a choice ideally suited to remind townspeople of everything that they could still agree upon. For that reason, Rogers was also to be the only settled minister of the Fourth Parish. By the early 1750s, the First and Fourth parishes had started to reconcile, and as a result, Rogers's congregation was melting away. There was no disaffection with the pastor himself, who remained at the Fourth Parish until his death in the 1780s. But many members of Rogers's congregation renewed their ties to the First Church and returned to worship with their brethren at the Middle Street meetinghouse in Gloucester harbor.[30] Thus concluded the most serious internal conflict that occurred in Gloucester during the later colonial period.

Social change was not always the solvent of a Puritan world-view, but sometimes its validation. For this reason, the Awakening in Gloucester did not bring about the birth of a new social character but instead perpetuated an older one. Situations that defied human comprehension and local control—the troubles in the First Parish and the social and economic dislocations of the war years—provided townspeople with an experiential basis for reaffirming their com-

[29] *Letters from the First Church in Gloucester,* 7–9. Balch shrewdly perceived in Gloucester's campaign for conformity abroad a device for redressing divisions at home.

[30] *SHG,* X, 401–3; Babson, *History,* 312–16.

mitment to a Calvinist outlook. The outpouring of religious feeling in 1742 expressed their collective recognition of a meaningful correspondence between present experience and the beliefs and forms of the past. And once persuaded of their powerlessness to effect anything through their own efforts, the inhabitants of Gloucester embarked on campaigns to transform everything, from reforming their Arminian neighbors in Bradford to routing the remote French in Canada. This paradoxical response to the conviction of human impotence is a recurrent pattern in the psychology of Calvinist converts. Belief in a world stripped of free will but structured by providential design robs men of autonomy but assures them that all events and actions assume some significance in the greater predestinarian scheme. Reconfirmed in this certainty by the revival of 1742, the townspeople of Gloucester set about reclaiming the community of their fathers.

EIGHTEENTH-CENTURY New Englanders are often depicted as a people escaping the cultural chrysalis of Puritanism. Anxious to abandon the outmoded ideal of a static, hierarchical society, the unattainable goal of communal unity, and the embarrassing zeal of previous generations, they sought release from the old order. But a search among Gloucester's inhabitants for these stereotypical "Yankees" of boundless initiative and ambition, restive under the restraints of established institutions and inherited values, turns up instead Puritan traditionalists. Well into the eighteenth century, the townspeople of Cape Ann were mistrustful of change, uncomfortable with civic conflict and social mobility, wary of economic competition and innovation, and intolerant of religious dissent. This kind of cultural conservatism characterized not just the farmers of the Second Parish and the declining magnates of Annisquam harbor, but even the most successful entrepreneurs of the southern harbor.

The course of Gloucester's evolution over the first century of its settlement also fails to conform to the familiar pattern of communal "decline." If Gloucester by the middle of the eighteenth century was not quite the "peaceable kingdom" of 1700, neither was it the chronically disrupted village of the early seventeenth century. The bitterness of the First Parish controversy notwithstanding, this provincial seaport was still more remarkable for the extent of its stability and essential social consensus than the community founded by the first generation had been. Even after the decades of commercial expansion had transformed an agrarian village into an important seaport, the communitarian way of life established in Gloucester during the latter seventeenth century persisted essentially unchanged. Provincial Gloucester remained committed to corporatism despite its controversies, to a hierarchical social order despite its opportunities for economic advancement, and to localism and conservative Calvinist orthodoxy despite its connections with more cosmopolitan and secular places. In a sense, it was because of their experience of economic interdependence, social diversity, and political contention that Gloucester inhabitants held so tenaciously to older ways of believing and behaving. Instead of producing a decisive shift in social relationships and values, the changes accompanying commercial development reinforced even as they challenged the order and outlook inherited from the past.

PART II

The Greatest Distaste a Person has to
this Place is the Stench of the Fish;
the whole Air seems tainted with it.
It may in Short be Said its a Dirty,
Irregular, Stincking Place.

—*Journal of*
Captain Francis Goelet,
a visitor to Marblehead in
1750

MARBLEHEAD

S O U T H of Cape Ann, some twenty miles down the Atlantic coast, a smaller neck of land juts into Massachusetts Bay. Situated on this elevated, rocky peninsula that forms one side of Salem Bay is the town of Marblehead. Like Gloucester, Marblehead was settled as a fishing village in the first half of the seventeenth century, and by the middle of the eighteenth century, it too had become a prosperous seaport. But during the intervening decades, these two towns made up such entirely different worlds that they might be taken as exemplars of the diversity of colonial maritime communities.

While Gloucester's transition from a farming village to a trading center probably typified the pattern of development in a dozen other provincial seaports, Marblehead's evolution made it more singular among New England communities. Throughout the seventeenth century, and for much of the eighteenth century, Marblehead's population was as mobile and diverse as the membership of most Massachusetts towns was stable and homogeneous. Sheltering a sizeable constituency of seafaring transients placed an additional strain on a town that lacked the strong local institutions established elsewhere in New England. While most towns began as or quickly became independent, corporate entities, Marblehead was first settled as part of the Salem grant in 1629, belatedly attained autonomous status in 1649, and long afterward remained a satellite of its parent community. Local government in Marblehead for much of the colonial period entailed the haphazard, occasional, and contentious conducting of public business. Strong doses of outside interference in local life alternately supported and strained the maintenance of public order. A Congregational church formed fifty years after the first settlement of the town played a minimal role in the lives of inhabitants, who were either disengaged from religious concerns entirely or else attracted to Episcopalianism. Other institutional cornerstones of most New England communities, such as strong, patriarchal families and a stable, acknowledged elite, also appeared in Marblehead only in attenuated form. And added to all of these difficulties was the chronic poverty and indebtedness of many inhabitants and a comparatively high incidence of crime and disorder. Not surprisingly, social divisions and conflicts were deeper and more fundamental in Marblehead than in most other New England towns. Neighbors in Gloucester spilled ink and spent words over which faction of the town's traditional leadership would occupy what space in the meetinghouse. Down in Marblehead, inhabitants contested the legitimacy of the elite itself and came to violent confrontations over whether the Sabbath should be spent at the meetinghouse or the Episcopal church.

If the old communal order actually was dying out elsewhere in New England by the end of the seventeenth century, in Marblehead the mourning of its passing was delayed for lack of a corpse. Marbleheaders had nothing to lament over because they had so little of the New England way to lose—at least until the opening decades of the eighteenth century. For then, life in Marblehead gradually began to change. In fact, the town's response to commercial development, especially after the 1720s, recalls the experience of Gloucester in many respects. And by the middle of the eighteenth century, the former "fishing plantation" of Marblehead had become remarkably like the community on Cape Ann.

6

A Fishing
Plantation

EIGHTEENTH-CENTURY OBSERVERS described Marblehead as "a whole town built upon a rock, high and steep to the water." The entire village covered an area "not much bigger than a large farm," its limited acreage and irregular surface containing little good pasture or planting ground. These conditions discouraged agriculture from the outset, and inhabitants were "forc't to get their living from the sea." Geography itself fostered Marblehead's reliance upon maritime pursuits. The "Great Neck," a small peninsula connected to the mainland by a narrow isthmus, extended out into the Atlantic for a mile, forming an excellent natural harbor.[1] By the mid-seventeenth century, the village's natural advantages and convenient location had already induced merchants from Salem and Boston to develop the local fishing industry. Backed initially by London fish exporters, these New England traders began outfitting vessels, hiring crews, and financing voyages out of Marblehead harbor, as well as from several other small coastal villages. The catches of cod they marketed with increasing success in the West Indies, the

[1] "Extracts from Captain Francis Goelet's Journal, 1746–1750," *New England Historical and Genealogical Register*, 24 (1870), 58. See also, Samuel Roads, *History and Traditions of Marblehead* (Boston, 1881), 1; and William Hammond Bowden, "The Commerce of Marblehead, 1665–1765," *EIHC*, 68 (1932), 133.

Wine Islands, and southern Europe. By the latter decades of
the seventeenth century, the profit of these enterprises allowed
Boston and Salem traders to dispense with their English
partners and to gain complete control over this transatlantic
traffic. And, as their interest in the fish trade increased, so
too did the efforts of Boston and Salem merchants to improve
the fishery at Marblehead.

The development of the fishing industry was the most significant force molding life in seventeenth-century Marblehead. Like farming in rural New England villages, fishing in
coastal towns followed regular, seasonal cycles that shaped
daily existence and work routines. The spring and summer
months were the times of most intense activity in maritime
communities. Fishing vessels made three "fares" between the
end of February and mid-September, and sometimes a final
voyage during the late fall or early winter. Throughout the
same months, large transatlantic merchantmen owned in
Boston, Salem, or the ports of Great Britain arrived with salt
for curing the catches and departed laden with fish for foreign markets. In the late fall and early winter, "coasters" in
their smaller craft took the poorer quality or "refuse" fish to
the middle and southern colonies and the West Indies. After
winter set in and the harbor froze over, business virtually
ceased until the thaw began, the first shipments of salt and
rigging material arrived, and the shoremen and fishermen
once again readied their boats.[2]

2 For the growth of the New England fishery, see Bailyn, *New England Merchants,* 76–82. The first fishing fare began in late February or early March
when the fleet sailed to Sable Island. The spring fare was at Brown's Bank
and other banks near Cape Sable, the summer fare at George's Bank, and
the last fare at Sable Island. A fare lasted about two months. (Innis, *The
Codfisheries,* 5, 9; MacFarland, *History of the New England Fisheries,* 96.)
The best recent description of the organization of the Essex County fishery
in the seventeenth century and of the conditions shaping maritime life is
Vickers, "Maritime Labor in Colonial Massachusetts," 74–103.

The pattern of the seasonal trade to the southern coast, the Caribbean,
and the Mediterranean during the colonial period can be traced in the
Abstracts of English Shipping Records, vol. II, part I. The trade to the Mediterranean was dominated by British and Bostonian shippers for a century
after 1630. Their merchantmen arrived in Marblehead harbor with salt in
April, May, and June, with a few coming in late summer. During July,
August, and the early fall, the largest number of these vessels engaged in
the European trade left port, followed in late fall and early winter by vessels

As this seasonal pattern of economic activity emerged in Marblehead during the seventeenth century, the social and occupational structure that was to characterize the town throughout most of the colonial period also took shape. Local society consisted of essentially two groups, the men who managed the fishing industry and those who performed the labor at sea. Shoremen, members of the first group, were the operators of fishing businesses, some managing their affairs from home port, and others stationing themselves in major north Atlantic harbors like Canso, Nova Scotia, or St. John's, Newfoundland, while they awaited the return of men and vessels that they had dispatched to the fishing grounds.[3] They shipped and provisioned crews, hired and repaired vessels, oversaw the final curing and temporary storage of the catch, kept accounts of voyages, and negotiated the final sale of the fish to merchants. Most owned fishing vessels and harbor property in wharves, warehouses, and flakeyards; a few retailed rum, tobacco, and other small items from shops or taverns in town or from makeshift stores in Newfoundland and Nova Scotia during the spring and summer. Toward the end of the seventeenth century, the wealthiest of these Marblehead entrepreneurs, the "gentlemen-shoremen," began styling themselves "merchants." Along with the local agents and family representatives of large fish exporting firms in Boston and Salem, these early Marblehead merchants specialized in consigning the catches of local fishermen to transatlantic traders in the capital and the county seat. In return they received stocks of rum, bread, tobacco, clothing, cordage, canvas, codhooks, and duck, provisions essential to

of smaller tunnage owned principally by Salem merchants and bound for the southern colonies and the Caribbean.

[3] A typical probate file illustrating the range of a shoreman's economic functions is that of Ambrose Boden, EPF, #2820. MacFarland puts the crew size of a fishing vessel during the mid-eighteenth century at seven and estimates that the average schooner size was fifty tons. My research suggests that fishing schooners were slightly smaller and that crews ranged from three to seven men during the late seventeenth and early eighteenth century. A suit for debt brought by merchant Benjamin Marston against his captain includes a number of documents that provide detailed information about the organization of labor on a fishing schooner and the wages paid each crew member. (See Marston v. Holmes, 1709, FCCP; "John Palmer's Account Book, 1748–1749," MS, American Antiquarian Society.)

fishing voyages that they sold in large lots to shoremen and retailed in smaller quantities to fishermen. Just as shoremen were intermediaries within the fishing industry, Marblehead merchants were the middlemen of the fish trade, the suppliers of fish to bigger dealers in larger ports who also acted as the brokers for British firms.

While merchants and the most successful shoremen dominated the town's economic life, fishermen, the second group in local society, made up the largest segment of Marblehead's population. The fishing community was not an undifferentiated mass of unskilled laborers, but rather a hierarchy in which skill, age, experience, and resources determined an individual's position and his share of the voyage's profits. Expertise in navigation, knowledge of methods for curing the catch, skill in constructing small boats, and familiarity with the fishing grounds and the migratory patterns of the cod accorded higher pay to pilots, ship carpenters, older hands, and "boat-shoremen" conversant with the "art or mystery" of salting fish. Boys, servants, and less seasoned men hired to fill out a crew commanded commensurately smaller shares. A few successful fishermen owned their own small vessels and staffed each voyage requisitioned by shoremen with the same crew, usually a collection of male family members, in-laws, and neighbors.

Local economic activity was in some respects less specialized than this sketch of occupational categories suggests. Despite the importance of shoremen as the managers and middlemen of the industry, merchants also maintained vessels and outfitted fishing voyages, and sold wholesale as well as retail. Shoremen set up sidelines in innkeeping, shoemaking, brewing, and practicing medicine. Fishermen of all levels of skill and experience doubled as sailors on coasting vessels making winter trading voyages or worked as day laborers and small craftsmen. At the same time, Marblehead's small contingent of artisans and farmers invested in fishing vessels and voyages, sidelined as shoremen, and spent some seasons fishing.

Steadily improved by Salem and Boston investors, the fishing industry in Marblehead grew throughout the seventeenth century. But the sustained exploitation of the local fishery kept the town from developing the more stable social life that Gloucester established after 1660. First of all, Marblehead's commitment to a fishing economy swelled the ranks of early settlers with a steady stream of seafaring immigrants. While the village in 1650 was, with roughly one hundred inhabitants, about the size of Gloucester, by 1680 Marblehead's population was approximately six hundred, twice the size of its northern neighbor. Marblehead owed its larger population to a surge of in-migration that continued long after movement into Gloucester had slackened and membership in that community had stabilized. By the 1670s, Marblehead's original forty-four householders had grown to just over one hundred. An equal number of adult males, mainly young, single fishermen who were neither householders nor the sons of householding families, also resided in town. But only about one-third of this group of nonhouseholders remained in town permanently; the rest eventually moved on. In addition, the seasonal demands of industry and trade brought a large number of men to town for even shorter periods. Some of these transients were young men from surrounding Essex County towns who shipped out on occasional fishing voyages, while others were crewmen of English merchant vessels that took on cargoes in Marblehead harbor. Over this floating population of nonhouseholders and seasonal laborers, the town had little control. Because of its interest in developing the commerce in cod, the Massachusetts Bay government gave Marblehead no power to exclude anyone "who Came on a fishing account," a restriction troubling to inhabitants. In the 1660s, townspeople complained to the General Court that "many . . . persons undesirable, and of noe estates butt rather Indebtted . . . have been burthensum to the place."[4]

---

[4] *Essex Ct. Recs.*, V, 373. A figure of about six hundred for Marblehead's population at 1680 is a conservative estimate. In 1674, there were 114 householders in town. (Roads, *History*, 28.) If these householders were all heads of families, the total population of all householding families was between 513 and 570. But in 1677, 103 men took the oath of fidelity in Marblehead who were neither householders nor male members of householding families. (*Essex Ct. Recs.*, VI, 398–401.) If all of the 103 nonhouseholders were single, which some were not, the total local population was between 616 and 673 in 1677. I traced persistence in town over this period by following the surnames of the nonhouseholders through town

Marblehead's population during this early period was as diverse as it was mobile. The people who first settled in town and sustained its growth were a volatile mixture of emigrants from the ports of Wales and Ireland; England's West Country counties; Jersey, one of the Channel Islands; and Newfoundland, another center of the British colonial fishery. As Gloucester's experience indicates, the diversity of West Countrymen complicated their accommodation to communal life in New England; Marblehead's shows that the assimilation of Jersey immigrants was more difficult still. Although nominally a part of the British Isles, the Channel Islands were geographically, linguistically, and culturally closer to France. The Newfoundlanders presented problems too: a conglomeration of Welsh, Jersey, Irish, and West Country fishermen, they usually fled to Marblehead to escape the demands of their creditors or the discipline of fishing masters or ship captains. All of these different ethnic groups coexisted uneasily in early Marblehead, the tensions among them often surfacing in personal disputes. Richard Rowland sued for defamation after Captain James Smith called him "a thievish Welsh rogue," and when John Brock fell out with John Waldron over a debt, the latter labelled his adversary, "knave, Jearse cheater, and French dog". Solidarity among members of the same ethnic group also made for mistrust within the wider community. For example, Mary Tucker agreed to arbitrate her differences with Abraham Kuitvil and any third party "except a Jerseyman," who would favor his countryman.[5] As Gloucester's population grew more homogeneous and the friction produced earlier by diverse English backgrounds subsided after 1660, the continuing ethnic variety of Marblehead inhabitants sustained divisions in that

and court records. On in-migration, see also Innis, *The Codfisheries,* 99–103.

[5] The ethnic groups that made up early Marblehead are discussed in Philip Chadwick Foster Smith, ed., *The Journals of Ashley Bowen, Publications of the Colonial Society of Massachusetts* (vols. 44 and 45, Boston, 1973), 44: 1; and Roads, *History,* 7. Banks's list of early emigrants who settled in Marblehead suggests an especially strong West Country influence. Nine of the thirteen Marbleheaders listed came from the western counties of Dorset, Devon, and Somerset. On tensions growing out of ethnic diversity, see *Essex Ct. Recs.,* IV, 108; V, 90–92; VIII, 194.

town. Jersey merchant Phillip English, who settled in Salem in the 1670s, financed the transportation of many of his countrymen to Essex County as indentured servants. By the late seventeenth century, Jersey families formed a distinct community on the southern side of Salem Neck, and several settled in Marblehead. Jersey women worked as domestic laborers in Salem households and men as Marblehead fishermen. In addition, smaller numbers of another French-speaking group, the Huguenots, also came to Marblehead during the late 1680s.[6]

Not only the mobility and diversity of Marblehead's population but also its preponderance of men caused considerable tension within the town during the seventeenth century. The county court encouraged the establishment of more families by prosecuting seafarers who settled in Marblehead but failed to send for their wives. But the slim resources of many fishermen, as well as the reluctance of some spouses to join their husbands, often thwarted these efforts.[7] The continuing imbalance of the sex ratio created intense competition for the companionship of the community's women. The level of domestic disruption and tension between the sexes was higher in Marblehead than in Gloucester and other towns in New England, where the numbers of men and women were more equal. While reported cases of rape were rare, misconduct of a more serious nature than fornication by young, engaged couples occurred in town with some frequency. A number of Marblehead prosecutions involved men who "offered abuse" to local women and adolescent girls. Mrs. Mary Gibbs and several other young Marblehead matrons charged that Vinson Stilson, Jr., had tempted them with money "to play the rogue with me," and some of Stilson's fellow townsmen faced allegations of other untoward advances.[8]

[6] David Konig, "A New Look at the Essex 'French': Ethnic Frictions and Community Tensions in Seventeenth Century Essex County," *EIHC,* 110 (1974), 167–180; Konig, *Law and Society,* 69–74.

[7] The *Essex Ct. Recs.* show twenty-seven cases of Marblehead men prosecuted for living away from their wives between 1650 and 1680, compared with only two Gloucester men during the 1650s. On the difficulties of reuniting fishing families, see *Essex Ct. Recs.,* V, 65–67.

[8] *Essex Ct. Recs.,* II, 236; VI, 67, 149–50, and 169; VIII, 344–45.

Some fishermen apparently dealt with the dearth of women by sharing their wives with less fortunate men. For example, Joseph Gatchell sired two children by his brother Samuel's wife after the couple had separated, while another brother, Jonathan, also appeared in court for fathering a child by the wife of another man. As the Gatchells' careers indicate, marriage in Marblehead did not always mean monogamy. After allotting his own wife to brother Joseph, Samuel Gatchell addressed his attentions to his landlady, the wife of Robert Laverance. Robert's objections to this dalliance produced a brawl among the occupants of his household, as Gatchell, Laverance's wife, and another promiscuous couple assaulted the prudish husband. When the constable asked Mrs. Laverance why she "entertained such company in her house," she retorted that "she would do it in spite of him or any man or in spite of the devil." The same scarcity of women underlay the domestic difficulties of William and Martha Beale. Martha had obtained an annulment of her first marriage to wed Beale, a man of some means. But gossip about the legality of their marriage brought the Beales into court several times to sue their neighbors for slander, and one night two outraged residents armed with clubs besieged their house, taunting William, "come out, you cuckolly cur: we are come to beat thee: thou livest in adultery." To make matters worse, William suspected—justifiably—that the wife he had won at this cost was carrying on with his servant.[9]

The surplus of men in Marblehead not only gave women a greater choice of partners but also fostered assertiveness in their dealings with men. Alexander Megilligan was one of several husbands who complained of being beaten by his wife, while many others alleged verbal abuse. One night, in the midst of a downpour, the embattled William Beale appeared with his mattress at the door of his neighbor's dwelling because "he could not live in quiet in his own house on account of his wife who 'Did upbraide him that his father was in hell.' " Nor was Beale was the only beleaguered Marblehead husband trucking his bed about town. After Rich-

[9] *Essex Ct. Recs.*, I, 17; II, 59; IV, 269, 280–82, and 286–87; V, 245, VII, 146–47; VIII, 101—02, and 219. Another factor contributing to Beale's difficulties in a predominantly West Country community was his East Anglian origin; see Bolton, *The Real Founders of New England*, 145.

ard Rowland's wife came home drunk, beat him, and turned him out of the house, he retreated to a neighbor's and "prayed him to let him leave his bed there for the devil was at home." Robert Laverance left the field to his rival too after his wife called him "a bald pated old rogue and struck him with her fist."[10] In dealings with men outside of their own families, Marblehead women displayed equal aggressiveness, a trait that the frequent absence of husbands on fishing voyages also encouraged. When the town clerk attempted to impound the property of fisherman Peter Harling for his neglect of military training, Harling's wife thrust the clerk out of the house and threatened "to knock his brains out." After Leonard Bellringer insulted tavern-mistress Mary Tucker, she "took him by the hair of his head and pulled him to the ground upon the stones that paved the yeard, beating his head upon the stones." A servant maid finally intervened, reminding Mary that "she was not acting like a Christian to pull a man's hair off" and bidding Bellringer's companion to take the victim away "before her dame killed him."[11]

The preponderance of males within the local population gave Mrs. Laverance an opportunity to exchange an old, bald spouse for a more desirable partner and allowed Martha Beale the chance to improve her social position by a second marriage. But the fact that they were relatively few in number did not appreciably enhance the status of women within the community.[12] Marblehead women occupied a position roughly similar to that of indentured servants in seventeenth-century Virginia: scarcity made both groups sought-after but not greatly esteemed. Wives and daughters complained frequently of verbal and physical abuse by male relatives and neighbors who resented the assertiveness of local women and the necessity of competing for their favors. For example, one young fisherman sued Hester James for slander after she told his friends that he ran after a girl "like a

[10] *Essex Ct. Recs.*, II, 344, 431; IV, 108, and 280–82; VII, 238; VIII, 101–02.

[11] *Essex Ct. Recs.*, VII, 42; VIII, 226–27.

[12] For a discussion of the position and status of women in other preponderantly male-populated settlements, see especially Lorena S. Walsh and Lois Green Carr, "The Planter's Wife: The Experience of White Women in Seventeenth-Century Maryland," *WMQ*, 3rd ser., 4 (1977), 520–41.

dog." As early as 1645, John Bartoll confessed to "defaming certain of his women neighbors . . . calling some captains, some lieutenants, etc." Thirty years later, Vinson Stilson's defense against charges of lewdness evoked the same image of a tyranny of fishwives. "It is very well known unto most of Marblehead," Stilson told the justices, "that this woman Mary Gibbs is an abusive woman as any is in Marblehead."[13]

Domestic disruptions were only part of Marblehead's difficulties during the seventeenth century. While the reported incidence of assault and drunkenness, swearing and slander dropped sharply in Gloucester after the mid-1660s, in Marblehead the level of disorder remained high. Indicative of Marblehead's deeper social difficulties was not only the larger volume but also the character of criminal activity. The clandestine trysts of John Pearce and the Widow Stannard sufficed to scandalise Gloucester's vigilant inhabitants. But Marbleheaders countenanced the revels of Mrs. Laverance and her boarders until the decibel level of domestic discord kept neighbors up nights. And while Gloucester's sober residents protested renewing the license of Thomas Judkins's inn, one of two in town, taverns and other private "tipling houses" proliferated in Marblehead. By 1678, Marblehead selectmen faced such a severe problem that they asked the courts to license no retailer without their approval:

> where as Theare are much Disorder in the towne and the sin of drunkenness much Increased by Reson of the manifold ordinaries ore Rather private Litienced Houses that are in the Towne . . . whether neither Constable, grandjurryman, nor Tithingman can Com Nere them to prevent them. . . .[14]

[13] Examples of the physical and verbal abuse of women by Marblehead men appear in *Essex Ct. Recs.*, I, 81; II, 443–44; III, 182; IV, 43; VI, 398; VII, 118–19, 242; VIII, 344–45, 104. For violence involving only women, see I, 208 and 244; IV, 413, 419–420, and 443.

[14] *Essex Ct. Recs.*, VI, 227; VII, 70–71. During the 1670s court records indicate that six Marblehead inhabitants were prosecuted for assault or breach of the peace, ten for slander, another nine for affronts to civil authority, eleven for drunkenness, ten for living away from their wives, thirteen for illegally retailing liquor, five for swearing, and three each for attempted rape and lewdness, theft, and Sabbath violations. For the contrast with Gloucester, see Chapter I, note 37.

And because of many Marbleheaders' contempt for civil authority, recorded breaches of the peace probably represented only a small proportion of the total number of offenses actually committed in town. While the mere sight of the constable's black staff quickly quelled mischief in Gloucester, matters were different in Marblehead. A typical exchange took place after constable John Waldron ordered Christopher Lattimore to clear his tavern, where men were often found "drinking and sometimes fighting . . . both on Saturday and Lord's Day nights." Lattimore retorted that "he would keep them there as long as he pleased. . . . that the Constables were fooles to send the watch to clear any publique house for it is more than they could or should do."[15] Regularly reviled by their fellow townsmen, constables, tithingmen, and other local leaders probably resigned themselves to the disorder.

The departure of fishermen combined with the emergence of a group of pious town fathers steadily reduced the level of disruption in Gloucester over the latter decades of the seventeenth century. Meanwhile, Marblehead's maritime community continued to increase, and no stable leadership appeared to prevent local life from lurching along its chaotic course. The turnover among Marblehead selectmen was constant, and their average tenure in office short. Townspeople clearly lacked respect for and confidence in their elected local leaders. Three times during the 1660s, for example, Marbleheaders took their selectmen to court, charging that they had embezzled local taxes.[16] Men entrusted with public duties were not only suspected but actually shown to be lacking in the virtue that they attempted to impose upon

[15] *Essex Ct. Recs.,* IV, 275, 266–67; V, 90–92; VI, 101, 67.

[16] Between 1656 and 1683, thirty-nine different men served an average tenure of 3.5 terms on the board of selectmen. Twenty of these men served only one or two terms, while men serving six terms or more accounted for just over half of the total of 139 terms. This rate of continuity in office is quite low compared to Gloucester's during the 1670s and 1680s. For Marblehead officeholders in the seventeenth century, and for the tax embezzlement controversy, see William H. Bowden, comp., "The Marblehead Town Records, 1648–1683," *EIHC,* 69 (1933), 231, 253, and 256. After the 1680s, there is a gap in the town records until 1721. A typescript copy of the records for 1721 and after is at the Office of the Town Clerk, Abbot Hall, Marblehead, Mass. (Cited hereafter as MTR.)

their neighbors. Constable Waldron was so drunk that he "Reeled and was hardly able to stand" the night that he tried to close Lattimore's tavern. Convicted of assault, lying, and swearing, William Beale was also compromised as a leader of local society, as he discovered one evening. Beale came upon John Smith, who was staggering through the streets in a drunken rage, flailing a firebrand, shouting threats, and resisting the efforts of the constable to put him in the stocks. Beale solicited aid for the constable from a group of bystanders, all of them his neighbors. But instead of helping, they threatened Beale with a beating, "Called me dog rogue base fellow asked me what I did there and what I had to do to meddle told me I deserved to have my braines beat out for such absurd speeches."[17]

The record of misbehavior that discredited the authority of Waldron and Beale in the eyes of their neighbors was not unusual among Marblehead's leading men. Nearly half of the town's selectmen during the first forty years of its existence were at some time prosecuted for a breach of the peace, and some for several offenses. Fighting, cursing, drunkenness, and sexual misconduct were not crimes committed only by servants and poor fishermen, but were common offenses even among the town's more substantial residents and important officeholders. Their election to the board of selectmen notwithstanding, Beale and Waldron lacked credibility as communal moral leaders and their efforts to stem the disorder seemed hypocritical to inhabitants. Other locally prominent men dispensed with even the pretense of posing as civic patriarchs and openly repudiated the Puritan vision of good order. Selectman Christopher Lattimore neither obeyed the authority of the town constable nor relied upon local peace officers to protect his rights. When Faithful Bartlett and John Prest attempted to tie their boat to a stagehead owned by Lattimore, he threatened to cut their mooring; after the two men dared him to do it, he rushed down the rocks wielding an axe-heft that he applied to Bartlett's head. An equally prominent citizen, John Legg, Sr., whose career in town included prosecutions for "uncleanness," slander, and selling drink without a license, also depended upon

[17] Essex Ct. Recs., IV, 280–82; VI, 293; V, 90–92.

intimidation to maintain his dominant position. When his fellow townsman John Peach refused to invest with him in a fishing ketch, Legg threatened "that he would make him say that the crow was white before he had done with him and that he had not served seven years without learning some knavery."[18] Like most other leading local men, Lattimore and Legg, although more affluent than the average Marbleheader, lacked the attributes of a traditional elite. They had neither birth nor education nor a sense of responsibility to the community. They were simply the most successful members of the fishing community, men who had fought their way to the top of the local pecking order through shrewdness, ruthlessness, and luck.

If none of Marblehead's early local leaders could have been confused with a John Winthrop, neither were its ordinary inhabitants ideal material for a Puritan community. Seventeenth-century townspeople showed almost no interest in the traditions of consent and cooperation that constituted the basis of civic life in other New England communities. Early town records abound in references to fines levied on those who refused "to lend labor to the town's service" and threats to sue those who shirked paying taxes. Equally frequent were complaints over nonattendance at town meetings, "the backwardnesse of the Inhabitance of their comminge together." Participation in public affairs picked up briefly in the 1670s—only because the town meeting became a battleground between the proprietors of the commons and the nonproprietors, who were grazing their cattle there illegally. Not surprisingly, this flurry of popular involvement strained rather than strengthened Marblehead's civic institutions, and when townsmen proved incapable of resolving the dispute on their own, the quarrel ended up being waged in the county court.[19] But for the most of the seventeenth century, Marbleheaders had as little as possible to do with their local government.

[18] A comparison of town selectmen with the court records shows that 17 of the 39 were prosecuted for some breach of the peace. See also, *Essex Ct. Recs.*, III, 107–8, 334.

[19] "Marblehead Town Records, 1648–1683," *EIHC*, 69: 212, 214, 215, 218, 219, 221, and 234. For the controversy over the commons, see especially 277ff.

Townspeople displayed an equal lack of commitment to local church life. And Marblehead's spiritual leaders fared no better than civil officials in promoting order in town and claimed just as little deference from inhabitants. While the village's first minister, William Walton, complained of his "lawless, God-forsaken people among whom laboring seemed useless," some Marbleheaders were no more pleased with their preacher. Fisherman Henry Coombs charged that the parson preached "nothing but lies"; Andrew Moss refused to contribute to the maintenance of the ministry because "he had never heard the minister preach but once. . . . and he had a book which would do him more good." Nor was disaffection with Walton confined to profane fishermen. Twice the county court punished Madame Elizabeth Legg, the wife of John Sr., for traducing the pastor, calling him "a Catchpole," and saying that "we were all a company of fooles. . . . that if people followed Mr. Walton's preaching . . . they would all go to hell." Although no common doctrinal affinities unified Walton's detractors, the Jersey origins of some inhabitants inclined them to Anglicanism, while the West Country background of others bred both strong ties to the Church of England as well as some interest in Quakerism.[20] But adherence to heterodoxies of any kind among Marbleheaders derived less from any positive religious convictions than from their opposition to orthodoxy in New England. Joseph Gatchell, for example, joined the Quakers after discovering that they shared a common enemy in the "Parsecuting Dogs" of the Puritan establishment. But after a time he abandoned the Friends and decided that "when the Church of England shall be Satt up with the orgones than shall I come to religious services." Short of singing with the accompaniment of "orgones," Gatchell found little to commend Christianity of any kind for

> the Ministers preached Nothing but Damnation; and that which they Called the Scriptures was not the words of God but the

[20] Walton's remarks are cited in Stephen P. Hathaway, *The Second Congregational Church in Marblehead* (Marblehead, 1885), 3. On Elizabeth Legg, see *Essex Ct. Recs.*, I, 378; II, 190 and 221; III, 269 and 461; IV, 407—8. For the relationship between ethnicity and religious preference, see Konig, "A New Look at the Essex 'French'," *EIHC*, 110: 171, and Banks, *The Planters of the Commonwealth*, 16–17.

sayings of men, and that those that they called Preachers did only say that the Scriptures was the words of God to make simple People Believe so: to keepe them in Ignorance.

George Hardinge, Gatchell's fellow townsman, expressed a similar skepticism by vowing to have his dog christened.[21] Whether Marblehead held more village atheists than any other New England town is impossible to tell, but if the majority of inhabitants were not actually hostile to religion, they were indifferent to Congregationalist orthodoxy. While Gloucester's religious tensions eased after the mid-sixties and the church emerged as a cohesive force in communal life, the townspeople of Marblehead did not even gather a church until 1684, nearly half a century after the town's initial settlement. Nor did the belated formation of the church enhance religious enthusiasm among inhabitants. Less than ten percent of Marblehead's adult males comprised the founding membership of First Church, and that proportion did not appreciably increase over the next three decades. Walton's successor, the Reverend Samuel Cheever, proved less obnoxious to townspeople than his predecessor, but Cheever was a lackluster figure overwhelmed by the obstacles to imposing orthodox discipline upon his parishioners. Under his ministry, some years passed without anyone in town joining the church. During the last decades of the seventeenth century, the only aspect of church life that aroused widespread concern was the rearrangement of seats in the meetinghouse. This issue kept the town in contention over the allocation of status for most of 1672.[22]

The deficiencies of Marblehead's local leadership and the weakness of town institutions only reflected its inhabitants

---

[21] *Essex Ct. Recs.*, I, 170; II, 163, 190, 194, and 344; V, 121; VIII, 407–408. Gatchell was finally convicted of blasphemy in 1684 by the Massachusetts Court of Assistants, who sentenced him to having his tongue pierced with a hot iron. (*Records of the Court of Assistants of the Colony of Massachusetts Bay, 1630–1692*, I: 253–54.)

[22] Although Marblehead built a meetinghouse in 1638, the town had no ordained ministry or gathered church until 1684. Church members had to travel to Salem to receive the sacraments. When the First Church of Marblehead was gathered in 1684, it had only seventeen male members, although the adult male population of the town was in excess of two hundred. The

more general alienation from the dominant East Anglian Puritan culture of Massachusetts Bay. Not utopian communitarian commitment but interest in the fishery had drawn Marblehead's settlers to New England. This difference from the outset fostered an adversary relationship between the villagers and the colony government. Disgusted by the fisherfolk's contempt for colony laws, their remissness in forming a church, and their refusal to organize a militia, the General Court gave Salem a free hand in running Marblehead for some twenty years after its initial settlement in 1629. Salem's merchants made the most of their authority, often impressing Marblehead fishermen for unloading shipments of salt. Even after Marblehead became a distinct town in 1649, Salem magistrates and militia captains still oversaw the public order and military training in Marblehead for a number of years. And Marbleheaders had no formal means of protest or resistance, for the lack of qualified freemen deprived inhabitants of any representation in the General Court until 1684.[23]

The Indian wars of the late 1670s and the accompanying effort to effect a reformation of public morals throughout the Bay colony heightened the antagonism between Marblehead and the dread and sovereign Puritan lords of New England. Colony officials had never ceased to complain of widespread "iniquity" in the fishing village, but during the 1670s the incidence of crimes involving the defiance of authority rose sharply. Marblehead men like Thomas Baker "spoke reproachfully against the authority of the country, saying he did not care for all laws." The target of Baker's particular scorn was "that white hat, limping rogue," Major Hathorne, a commissioner from Salem appointed by the General Court to oversee order in Marblehead and to drill its trainband, or local militia.[24] These truculent responses

church records from 1684 to 1714 have evidently been lost or mislaid. A list of the founding members of First Church appears in *The Manual of the First Congregational Church, Marblehead, Mass.* (Marblehead, 1876). For Cheever's biography, see *SHG.* II, 38–39; on the seating controversy, see Roads, *History,* 26–27.

[23] Roads, *History,* 16–20, 23.

[24] *Essex Ct. Recs.,* IV, 275; VI, 101 and 234; VII, 41–42, 67, 331, and 407–8; VIII, 378.

confirmed Massachusetts Bay's godly leaders in the contempt bordering on racism that they harbored for Marbleheaders. Voicing the general view, the Reverend William Hubbard of Ipswich described Marblehead fishermen taken captive by the warring Eastern Indian tribes of Maine in 1677 as "a dull and heavy moulded sort of People, that had not either Skill or Courage to kill anything but Fish."[25]

It was this conflict with the Indians in 1677 that brought simmering local resentments against the central government to a full boil as the military crisis produced a brief but savage release of defensive passions among Marbleheaders. Unlike Gloucester, Marblehead was fairly secure from Indian attack, but fishing voyages to the Maine coast exposed local men to considerable danger. By July of 1677, the Eastern Indians had taken more than twenty vessels fishing off the northern New England coast, ketches owned in Salem but manned mainly by Marbleheaders. The "dull and heavy moulded" crew aboard one of these vessels managed to regain control of their ketch and made for Marblehead, taking along two of their former captors to turn over to the Bay government. But the Indian prisoners never reached authorities in Boston. Robert Roules, a member of the ketch's crew, described the events that followed the vessel's anchoring in Marblehead harbor:

> News had reached this place that we were all killed and many people flocked to the waterside to learn who we were and what other news they could. . . . when they saw the Indians, they demanded why we kept them alive and why we had not killed them. . . .
>
> Being on shore, the whole town flocked about them, beginning first to insult them, and soon after, the women surrounded them and drove us by force from them. . . . Then with stones, billets of wood, and what else they might, they made an end of these Indians. . . . we found them with their heads off and gone, and their flesh in a manner pulled from their bones. . . . They [the women] suffered neither constable nor mandrake, nor any

[25] William Hubbard, *The History of the Indian Wars in New England from the First Settlement to the Termination of the War with King Philip, in 1677*, ed. Samuel G. Drake (Roxbury, Mass., 1865), 236–37.

other person to come near them, until they had finished their bloody purpose.

Feelings of rage toward Boston officials, as much as racial hatred of the Indians, triggered these grisly murders. In defense of their bloody actions, according to Roules, the women "cried out . . . if the Indians had been carried to Boston, that would have been the end of it, and they would have been set at liberty." The widespread feeling that Marblehead could expect neither protection nor justice from the Bay government aroused local women to commit murder "though they should be hanged for it."[26]

The recurrence of military crisis ignited popular hostility against Boston again in 1690, touching off another violent confrontation. The renewal of war with the French in Canada raised fears among Marbleheaders of an imminent attack upon their coast. Oblivious to local anxieties, the Bay government dispatched Captain John Alden to Marblehead to impress two large guns mounted on a merchantman in the harbor, the town's sole effective defense. But the removal of the guns was thwarted by "sundry of the People being gathered together in a riotous and Tumultuous manner." This angry mob none of the local officials attempted to suppress, much to the dismay of the colony government.[27]

Underlying all of these local resentments of the Bay's political and religious establishment, and of the control emanating from Boston especially, was Marblehead's subordinate economic status. The merchants of Boston and Salem developed Marblehead in order to supply a single, marketable commodity, fish. In this sense, the village was a kind of colony within a colony. From the beginnings of Marblehead's settlement, Bay authorities had fostered the focus upon a single industry by permitting Salem to dole out only enough land for a house and a garden plot to village fishermen. This policy of limiting land allotments insured Marbleheaders' continuing dependence upon maritime pursuits for their

[26]Roules's deposition is reprinted in full in James Axtell, "The Vengeful Women of Marblehead: Robert Roules's Deposition of 1677," *WMQ*, 3rd ser., 21 (1974), 650–52. Axtell emphasizes the importance of this episode as an instance of military conflict intensifying racism against Indians.

[27]*MA*, 37: 162a, 163; 35: 303.

livelihoods and guaranteed Boston and Salem merchants sufficient labor to man the fishing fleet. The Bay's refusal to empower Marblehead to exclude seafaring strangers from town grew out of a similar concern. As a result, the exchange of cod for provisions and finished goods with Boston and Salem defined Marblehead's satellite commercial position for a century after settlement. But, while Marblehead developed an important fishing industry, outside capitalists continued to dominate the most remunerative end of the enterprise. It was the merchants of larger ports who actually marketed the highest quality of "merchantable cod" to southern Europe and the Wine Islands. Marbleheaders themselves neither exported directly to distant consumers nor imported directly from England. To them was left the less lucrative traffic in poorer quality fish bound for colonial markets. And compared with Salem, Marblehead's involvement even in this coastwise and Caribbean trade was limited.[28] The lion's share of the proceeds from Marbleheaders' labor went to the merchants of larger ports or to a few of their resident factors in Marblehead. The Boston and Salem traders who arranged for the marketing and transport of Marblehead catches amassed estates worth thousands of pounds. Captains Andrew Cratey and John Beale, Marblehead men who purchased consignments of fish for British firms, died with estates valued at 1388 and 857 pounds sterling, and a handful of local shoremen were worth a few hundred pounds. But the vast majority of inhabitants were not even worth a hundred pounds sterling, making seventeenth-century Marblehead a more economically unequal community than early Gloucester.[29]

[28] The large number of Boston and Salem creditors that appear in the estate administrations of the biggest Marblehead traders and shoremen illustrate their reliance upon these larger ports for finished goods, financial services and capital. See also, Bowden, "The Commerce of Marblehead," *EIHC*, 68: 124–25 and 132. Marblehead's limited participation in the actual marketing of fish is also indicated by the small number of its inhabitants who owned vessels between 1698 and 1714 and the town's lack of any significant shipbuilding industry. See Bailyn and Bailyn, *Massachusetts Shipping*, 90–91, 94–97, and 102–3.

[29] This generalization is based on two samples of inventories, the first, consisting of twenty-nine, was filed for the ten years between 1672 and 1681. The largest estate, John Legg's, was 316 pounds sterling, and only five of the twenty-nine inventories in this group were worth more than 100 pounds

Many seventeenth-century New England towns fell short of realizing their ideals of love, consensus, and perfect, godly order. Marbleheaders were spared the sting of this failure because they shared no broad commitment to the values and institutions that prevailed elsewhere in Puritan Massachusetts. Throughout most of New England during the seventeenth century, family groups of relatively homogeneous English backgrounds founded subsistence farming villages. These towns developed in isolation from other settlements and from a wider market economy, grew in population primarily because of natural increase among early settlers, and quickly established autonomous local institutions and an effective leadership. Contention was common enough, but it often bore the character of a "family quarrel" among townspeople who agreed upon fundamentals and established an essentially coherent social system. But in the fishing village of Marblehead, a diverse, mobile, male-dominated population, dependence upon distant consumers and nonlocal investors, and the slow and incomplete development of basic institutions fostered a different kind of existence. Deeper and more basic divisions and dislocations underlay much of the local strife.

But if Marblehead was not a representative seventeenth-century community, its pattern of development was not without parallels in early New England. During the first decades after its establishment, Gloucester exhibited many of the same social characteristics. Even closer counterparts

sterling. (*Essex Ct. Recs.*, vols. 5–8.) The second sample of thirty-two inventories, filed between 1690 and 1699, indicates the same low estate value for most Marblehead decedents, with only nine of the thirty-two worth more than 100 pounds sterling. (Essex Probate Files, Registry of Probate, County Courthouse, Salem, Mass.) By contrast, in Gloucester during the 1690s, half of the town's twenty-two inventoried decedents were worth over one hundred pounds sterling. By the late seventeenth century, Marblehead was also more unequal than Gloucester in its distribution of wealth. Marblehead's wealthiest decile of inventoried decedents between 1690 and 1699 owned approximately 40 percent of the total inventoried wealth, compared with 32.7 percent for Gloucester's richest decile. For the estates of Cratey and Beale, see EPF, #2192 and 6510. For a discussion of how the estates of fishermen compared to those of other occupational groups in seventeenth-century Essex County, see Vickers, "Maritime Labor in Colonial Massachusetts," 116–17 and 121.

to Marblehead were the settlements of the Isles of Shoals, centers of the fishing industry that stood in the same relationship to the burgeoning trading center of Portsmouth that Marblehead did to Salem and Boston. Founded like Marblehead as fishing camps for West Countrymen rather than as utopian experiments for devout East Anglians, the Shoals harbored the same transient, contentious, raucous, and intemperate male inhabitants, a smaller female contingent of notorious "fishwives," and a nest of illegal taverns frequented by both sexes. Common to both Marblehead and the Shoals settlements were strong objections to the magisterial authority of the Bay colony and indifference to Congregationalist orthodoxy. Given the choice in 1680 of coming under Massachusetts's jurisdiction as part of Maine or becoming part of New Hampshire, the population of the Shoals opted for royal government.[30] Nor were coastal fishing camps the only less-than-Puritan places in seventeenth-century New England. Another settlement where "conflict and not communalism was the rule" was Springfield, Massachusetts, in the Connecticut River Valley. This "company town" was founded by the merchant-entrepreneur John Pynchon for prosecuting the fur trade and dominated by his descendants, who during the seventeenth century developed their investment into a center for commercial agriculture. The monopolization of local resources by a single family and the dependence of almost everyone else in town upon the Pynchons for land, work, and credit produced high levels of economic inequality and chronic indebtedness, wage labor, and landlessness. Assaults, slander, family feuds, and allegations of fraud broke forth frequently among Springfield's assertive inhabitants, who subordinated neighborly cooperation to the goal of material security.[31]

By the end of the seventeenth century, however, fishing communities like Marblehead were harder to find in New England. As Gloucester turned to a self-sufficient, subsistence-oriented economy after the mid-1660s, local life there attained greater equilibrium. The Shoals settlements simply

[30] John S. Jenness, *The Isles of Shoals*, 2nd ed. (New York, 1875); Clark, *The Eastern Frontier*, 127–32.

[31] Innes, *To Labor in a New Land*, passim.

broke up as the island camps declined in importance as suppliers of fish by the end of the seventeenth century. Only
Marblehead, largely because of its proximity to Boston and
Salem, increased steadily in economic importance as a center
of the fishing industry. Yet even as the town became a critical link in New England's transatlantic commercial network, its incorporation into the colony of Massachusetts Bay
remained incomplete. Instead of facilitating its assimilation
into the mainstream of provincial Puritan culture, Marblehead's growing prosperity and industrial importance only
intensified the most divisive and disruptive dimensions of its
seventeenth-century beginnings. In particular, local economic underdevelopment and dependency kept alive the tradition of resentment and resistance to the domination and
authority of Boston and Salem. This animus emerged as the
most salient feature shaping local life by the early eighteenth
century. Throughout the later colonial era, the imagination
of Marblehead inhabitants continued to endow the capital
especially with a sort of sinister omnipotence, as is reflected
in the clearly focused fears of one John Gatchell. According
to Gatchell, as well as several of his fellow first-generation
townsmen, the malefic magic of Jane James, a local "fish-
wife," had spoiled all of the "fruits" that he had planted in
the small garden allotted to him by Salem. And many Marblehead fishermen while at sea had seen her in the shape of
a cat, sailing in a boat toward Boston.[32]

[32] *Essex Ct. Recs.*, I, 108, 199, and 229; III, 413.

7

Stirred Up by the Devil

THE WITCHCRAFT HYSTERIA that wracked other Essex County communities in 1692 had little effect on Marblehead. Although the town produced more than its share of defendants in other criminal cases during this period, the only Marblehead resident charged with witchcraft by Salem Village's "afflicted girls" was Wilmot Reed. Known to her neighbors as "Mammy Redd," she had succeeded Jane James as the village witch in Marblehead. If part of the purpose underlying the trials of 1692 was to discipline people whose social ties and sympathies with religious dissenters subtly subverted the orthodox order, it makes sense that the "afflicted girls" passed over Marbleheaders almost completely. That Marblehead had gone to the devil was too evident to require exposure, and charges to that effect would have created little sensation in Massachusetts. Its inhabitants were openly defiant in their departures from the New England way. But if, as one recent study of the Salem episode suggests, commercial capitalism was the devil that undermined communal stability in New England, the possession of Marblehead did not begin in earnest until the second decade of the eighteenth century.[1] The end of the second Anglo-French conflict, Queen

---

[1] Boyer and Nissenbaum, *Salem Possessed,* 209. On Wilmot Reed, see Roads, *History,* 33–36.

Anne's War, with the Treaty of Utrecht in 1713 inaugurated a period of peace, allowing for the rapid economic expansion that transformed Marblehead from an overgrown fishing camp into an undercivilized seaport.

The two decades of war before 1713 had brought hard times to the Marblehead fishery. The town's single-industry economy was always vulnerable to disruptions of all kinds. Storms, poor seasons, and leaking ships reduced the size and quality of the catch; the capture of men and vessels by pirates plagued the fishery well into the eighteenth century; small markets glutted easily and sent prices plummeting.[2] But the most serious economic setbacks for the fishery resulted from the intermittent military crises of the late seventeenth and early eighteenth centuries. While the second Anglo-Dutch War of the 1660s and King Philip's War during the next decade had briefly disrupted the infant New England fishery, the protracted warfare between England and France after 1690 plunged the industry into a trough of recession for some twenty years. Although these first Anglo-French wars benefited New England fishermen by reducing the involvement of West Country and French competitors in the north Atlantic, the hostilities also created conditions that limited Marblehead's ability to capitalize on this advantage. The prospect of a coastal invasion by the French threatened the security of Marblehead harbor, interrupting fishing and trade. Military expeditions launched against Canada enlisted or impressed local laborers, while the French and their Indian allies captured Marblehead boats and crews. Expenditures on harbor fortifications, ammunition, and ransoms of captives drained the resources of townspeople.[3] In the two decades of sporadic military conflict in the north Atlantic, Gloucester

[2] For example, see "Essex Notarial Records, 1697–1768," MS, Office of the County Clerk, Superior Courthouse, Salem, Mass., cited hereafter as ENR. On piracy, see John F. Jameson, *Privateering and Piracy in the Colonial Period: Illustrative Documents* (New York, 1933); and James G. Lydon, *Pirates, Privateers, and Profits* (Upper Saddle River, New Jersey, 1970).

[3] For the effects of King William's and Queen Anne's Wars on the Marblehead fishery, see MacFarland, *History of the New England Fisheries*, 73, 81, and 83–84; and *MA*, 35: 303; 70: 201, 356; 36: 422–422a; 63: 4, 5, 118; 71: 316, and 678–79. On the economic effects of the war against the Eastern Indians, see *MA*, 38: 44; 52: 222, 508; 63: 408, 410, and 415.

and Salem with their mixed economies of agriculture, lumbering, and shipbuilding were less seriously affected than Marblehead, where depression struck hardest because of the town's total dependence on the fishery.

It was only the restoration of peace in 1713 that wrought a reversal in Marblehead's fortunes. The most significant and sustained growth of the New England fishery began after the first decade of the eighteenth century, as the industry not only revived but expanded with the cessation of Anglo-French hostilities. As Britain extended its control over a larger stretch of the north Atlantic and secured for colonial vessels a wider expanse of more distant banks, fishing flourished as never before. The simultaneous rise in demand for fish in the West Indies and southern Europe stimulated commerce for the next quarter century. While these conditions encouraged the gradual growth of maritime economies in smaller, more remote coastal towns like Gloucester, they ushered in a more dramatic expansion in Marblehead. Its convenient location and established fishing industry made Marblehead the logical site for the most intense efforts to enlarge the production and shipment of cod. By 1727, Marbleheaders boasted that more than a hundred fishing boats and as many as twenty English trading vessels were anchored in their harbor at any given time.[4] Attracted by the opportunities for work and investment, a host of new merchants, mariners, and fishermen swarmed into town, some from Boston and Salem, some from smaller Massachusetts villages, and some from British ports in the Channel Islands, Scotland, Ireland, and the West Country counties.

But while Marblehead's economy not only recovered but expanded after 1713, the gains that came about after the peace caused the town deeper and more enduring difficulties than had the earlier losses of war. For, like all boom towns, postwar Marblehead yielded real rewards to only a few of its fortune-seekers. Many more inhabitants became the victims of increasingly harsh and unequal economic arrange-

[4] Petition of the Selectmen of Marblehead to the General Court, in "Documents relating to Marblehead, Mass.," comp. John H. Edmunds, *EIHC*, 56 (1920), 309–12; Innis, *The Codfisheries*, 160–66; MacFarland, *History of the New England Fisheries*, 85–86; and William H. Bowden, "The Commerce of Marblehead, 1665–1775," *EIHC*, 68 (1932), 121–26.

ments and a disrupted social life. The expansion of the fishery fostered intense competition for labor, but the demand for workers undermined rather than strengthened the bargaining position of fishermen. To recruit and retain laborers, major entrepreneurs relied on exploiting the growing poverty and indebtedness of many seafaring families, forcing some fishermen into a kind of indentured servitude. The new opportunities also encouraged aggressive, risk-taking behavior that kept many local entrepreneurs constantly on the brink of bankruptcy. At the same time, the great inequality among Marblehead's inhabitants and the mushrooming size and continuing diversity of its population contributed to a climate of violence and strife. Finally and perhaps most important, while Marblehead's fishing industry expanded over the second and third decades of the eighteenth century, other aspects of local commercial life failed to develop. Specifically, control over the financing of the fishery and over the shipment and marketing of cod to Europe, the Caribbean, and the southern colonies remained in the hands of outside capitalists, the merchants of Boston and Salem and their agents in Marblehead. As a result, the largest profits from the labor of Marblehead fishermen and the power to direct local development itself were lodged in the hands of men with only a limited connection to the town. This lack of autonomy was the underlying cause of many of Marblehead's other difficulties. Of course, the social tensions of the early eighteenth century had existed in Marblehead in some degree since the beginning of its settlement. But the postwar boom magnified them, creating serious and chronic social instability.

A significant increase in economic inequality among Marbleheaders was the first effect of the expansion produced by improved military security and strong market demand. While in Gloucester the growth of the fishing industry after 1713 benefited all inhabitants, in Marblehead the boom in cod set off a scramble for profits that made fortunes for a few but worsened the lot of the majority of townspeople. Reflecting the new prosperity of some, mean estate value rose steadily from its wartime level during the twenty-year period after 1715. In the same years, however, median estate value dropped from seventy to sixty pounds sterling, indicating that economic rewards were being unevenly shared. It was during this time that the distribution of wealth in Marble-head came to resemble that of Boston. Between 1715 and 1735, the proportion of the total wealth held by the richest decile of Marbleheaders jumped from one-third to over one-half, and a number of local merchants and shoremen acquired estates of over a thousand pounds sterling. But at the same time the poorest third of Marblehead's population, almost all fishermen, were leading hardscrabble, hand-to-mouth existences. The members of this group left estates under twenty pounds sterling in value that included no real property and barely covered the costs of funerals, legal charges, and outstanding debts. Marblehead's middling classes of smaller shoremen, more substantial fishermen, mariners, and artisans usually managed to acquire their own dwellings, but their share of the town's total wealth was also diminishing. Indebtedness is one index of their precarious economic position: forty percent of this middling group died insolvent or in debt for more than half the value of their total assets.[5]

The second consequence of Marblehead's economic expansion during the twenty-year postwar period was a sharp rise in debt litigation. During the seventeenth century, the total number of suits for debt involving Marblehead defendants had not exceeded ten annually. By the second decade of the eighteenth century, that figure had climbed to over one hundred per year, and during the 1720s, it grew to over two hundred. The rate at which debt litigation rose in Marblehead ran well ahead of the rate of population growth in town, and the total volume of civil actions exceeded even that of

[5] See appendix, tables I and II. Virtually all of the inventoried decedents who ranked among the poorest 30 percent of Marbleheaders were insolvent, their bankruptcy indicated either by a declaration of the judge of the probate court or by the bonding of major local shoremen or merchants, their principal creditors, as estate administrators. Of a total of sixty-one administrations of estates between 1716 and 1735 for the middle 60 percent of Marblehead decedents (decile groups 31–90), twenty-five administrations indicate that the deceased was either insolvent or owed more than half of his inventoried assets to creditors. In calculating the total debt against an estate, I attempted to exclude debts incurred by the estate after the death of the person inventoried, i.e., funeral charges, legal costs involved in settling the estate, etc. But the imprecision of some administrations does not always allow for this discrimination.

considerably larger seaports. In 1729, for example, Marblehead residents were involved in twice as many debt cases as Salem residents. While a growing number of cases involving nonlocal plaintiffs and Marblehead debtors contributed to the large volume of civil suits, a dramatic rise in intratown debt actions accounted for most of the increase. Prior to the postwar boom, creditors trying to recover debts from Marbleheaders divided almost evenly between locals and nonlocals. But by the 1720s, over seventy-five percent of all plaintiffs suing to recover obligations from Marbleheaders were fellow townspeople.[6]

Exchanges related directly to the operation of the fishery occasioned the largest amount of litigation among Marbleheaders. In 1719, over sixty percent of all defendants in intratown civil actions were fishermen, shoremen, or other mariners, and by 1729, nearly seventy percent. Merchants and shopkeepers hauled shoremen into court to collect on catches of fish promised in return for advances of goods and money, but not delivered; shoremen sued fishermen for the same reason, as well as for spoiling fish and damaging vessels. Innholders, physicians, butchers, and artisans of every description went to law against shoremen and fishermen to recover amounts due for liquor dispensed, illnesses treated, meat prepared, bread baked, shoes cobbled, clothing sewed, boats built, barrels made, sails mended, and anchors forged.

The swelling number of suits involving Marbleheaders was both a cause and a symptom of the inequality overtaking the town. Although a high level of debt litigation does not invariably correspond with growing economic hardship, the character of civil cases in Marblehead indicates that there it did, for intratown debt cases during the postwar boom typically pitted rich men against poorer ones. Fishermen comprised approximately half of all defendants in all civil actions—the largest single group. The debts of fishermen usually consisted of overdue book accounts for food, drink, clothing, and tobacco, provisions that they were advanced at the beginning of their voyages. Their principal creditors for these items were local merchants, shopkeepers, and shoremen, who together constituted the largest group of

6 See appendix, table III.

plaintiffs in intratown debt cases.[7] The high incidence of such suits between wealthier plaintiffs and fishermen defendants points up the severe strain that the expanding economy imposed on vertical social relationships.

The problem of indebtedness, like that of inequality, was not new to Marblehead. Fishermen defaulting on their debts had created difficulties in town ever since the seventeenth century. In 1678, for example, the town selectmen had called for more strictly regulating the proliferation of private tav-

[7] *Intratown Debt Litigation in Marblehead, 1719 and 1729*

Defendants	1719	1729	Plaintiffs	1719	1729
Fishermen	48	71	Merchant/Shpkpr	35	61
Shoremen	3	37	Inn/Butch/Phys	25	26
Artisans	16	28	Shoremen	7	21
Inn/Butch/Phys	8	9	Artisans	12	40
Mariners	5	4	Fishermen	7	11
Farmers	4	3	Mariners	1	3
Merchant/Shpkpr	1	8	Farmers	0	0
Other	2	5	Other	0	3
	87	165		87	165

In suits involving merchant, shopkeeper, and shoreman plaintiffs, twenty-nine of the forty-two actions in 1719 were against fisherman-defendants, and forty-six of the eighty-two in 1729. These figures are actually a conservative estimate of the number of suits in which major men in the fishing business took smaller ones to court, because of the ambiguity of the term "shoreman." Many of the shoremen who appeared as defendants in intratown actions, especially in 1729, were "boat shoremen," skilled fishermen who cured the catch, not "gentleman-shoremen," the owners of large fishing businesses who, like merchants and shopkeepers, were more likely to be plaintiffs in debt cases.

The other principal suppliers of goods and services to the fishing community—innholders, physicians, and butchers—were also fairly frequent litigants in cases against fishermen, relying on the courts to collect their bills for meat, liquor, lodging, and medicine. In suits involving these plaintiffs, twelve of the twenty-five actions in 1719 were against fisherman-defendants, and eight of the twenty-six in 1729. Artisans were less likely to take fishermen to court: in 1729, only eight of the forty actions initiated by tradesmen involved fisherman-defendants. Artisans' suits were more often lodged against shoremen (eleven of forty) or other artisans (eleven of forty).

The source for the table above and related data is writs to attach the person or property of defendants, pending a plea of the case, Files of the Essex County Court of Common Pleas, Superior Courthouse, Salem, Mass.

erns because it "Henders men of there Employment and Being Intrusted by other men for the gaining of a Livlihood what they should paye for To satisfie for their Clothing and Provisions It is Spent in these Private Houses. . . ." But during this earlier era, suits for debt against fishermen made up a smaller percentage of a much smaller total volume of civil prosecutions.[8] By the second decade of the eighteenth century, the indebtedness of the fishing community had become chronic, widespread, and a principal contributor to the rising level of litigation.

While fishermen generally appeared as defendants in debt cases, they occasionally came to court as plaintiffs. Their most common complaint was intentional fraud on the part of their shoremen-employers. Pressures upon shoremen to cover obligations to their own creditors among merchants and tradesmen encouraged these middlemen to put off paying their fishing crews. Long deferrals in the division of a voyage's profits among fishermen triggered a spate of suits generally brought by the master of the voyage, a fisherman with skill and seniority, on behalf of himself and his men. Hired by shoreman Ephraim Sandin, Joseph Doliber, Jr., captained a fishing schooner for two fares during the summer of 1726. At the end of the summer, Sandin was to cure and sell the fish and to pay Doliber and his men their share of the profits after deducting for wages and provisions advanced at the beginning of the summer. But by the winter of 1729, captain and crew had not seen any of their money, and Sandin was insisting that sadler Enoch Greenleaf, the vessel's owner, was responsible for paying out the fishermen's shares. Frustrated after waiting three years for payment, Doliber finally went to court claiming one hundred pounds New England money in damages. At about the same time, another Marblehead fisherman, James Trefry, lodged a similar complaint against shoreman Benjamin Stacey. Since 1726, Stacey had hired Trefry's services, crew, and shallop for six voyages, and at the end of each the shoreman had

[8] Petition of the Selectmen of Marblehead, June 25, 1678, *Essex Ct. Recs.*, VII, 70–71. Between 1670 and 1679, for example, there were fifty-six intertown suits in Marblehead, fifteen involving fisherman-defendants in debt cases; in the twenty intratown suits involving Marblehead defendants, five were suits for debt against fishermen. (Source: *Essex Ct. Recs.*)

cured and marked the catch. But Trefry had received no account of the sales nor any of the returns, an amount totalling two hundred and fifty pounds New England money. More infrequently fishermen of lesser stature than Doliber or Trefry brought suit on their own to recover returns due from a voyage. One such plaintiff, Bonnel Merryfield, who served as a crew member on a winter voyage under William Browne, went to court himself to claim his small share withheld by shoreman John Rockwood.[9]

Marblehead's mounting volume of litigation over debt confused the affairs and drained the resources of all participants in the fishing industry and trade. But the group that suffered most were the poorest fishermen, who defaulted on their debts and were taken to court by their creditors. The problem for these debtors was not that they served long sentences in jail, for compared to English law governing imprisonment for debt, New England practice was lenient, and creditors had far less legal coercive power. Under Massachusetts Bay's "Act for the Relief and Release of Poor Prisoners for Debt" of 1698, most defaulters imprisoned on a writ of execution could gain release from jail after a month by taking the "pauper's oath," a pledge that they were worth under ten pounds. Creditors who believed that defaulters were concealing property could keep convicted debtors in prison for three months. Yet few plaintiffs insisted on these longer terms of imprisonment, for a statute of 1672 made creditors liable for the costs of keeping their debtors in jail. Until 1737, the law also provided that creditors could compel the service of debtors without dependents, but such court-ordered indentures were infrequent in Essex County.[10]

Besides this legislation, continuing demand for labor in the fishing industry insured that most Marblehead debtors

[9] Doliber v. Sandin, 1729; Trefry v. Stacey, 1729; Merryfield v. Rockwood, 1729; and Rymer v. Calley, 1729 / 30, FCCP. The rise in prosecutions of shoremen and merchants for debt (see note 7 above) was primarily due to an increasing number of suits against shoreman-defendants who defaulted in their debts to larger merchants and to fishermen.

[10] Goodell, ed., *Acts and Resolves,* I, 330–33; II, 363, 656–58; see also, Robert A. Feer, "Imprisonment for Debt in Massachusetts before 1800," *Mississippi Valley Historical Review,* 48 (1960–61), 254–56; Peter J. Coleman, *Debtors and Creditors in America: Insolvency, Imprisonment for Debt and Bankruptcy, 1607–1900* (Madison, 1974), 3–5, 40–41.

neither spent long periods in jail nor submitted to terms of legally imposed servitude to make repayment. Merchants and shoremen short of hands for fishing voyages regularly arranged for the release of poor defaulters who had been committed to prison pending trial because they had no estate for the court to attach. In some instances, such indebted fishermen were employed by the same men who posted bond. John Clipsham, arrested on the complaint of a tailor over a four-pound debt, and Nicholas Twine, who owed his landlord eleven pounds, probably worked on board one of the fishing schooners of merchant Stephen Minot, Jr., who bailed out both men early in 1729. With the season about to begin, Minot could not afford a landlocked labor force. In other cases, a fisherman imprisoned by one employer was freed by another eager to acquire his labor. When shoreman William Mooney decided that the advantage of William Fettyplace's continued labor was offset by the fisherman's accumulated book debts, Stephen Minot secured the debtor's freedom. With many other merchants and shoremen following Minot's method of recruiting labor, the Salem jail doubled as a hiring hall. And just as few fishermen without property to attach were jailed for long periods prior to the trial of their cases, so also the imprisonment of convicted debtors following a finding for the plaintiff was rare. The small number of inmates in the Salem jail at any given time and the infrequent recourse to the pauper's oath among Marblehead debtors indicate that the imprisonment of convicted debtors was an uncommon occurrence. The same merchants and shoremen who posted bond for poor fishermen probably also satisfied the claims of creditors.[11]

[11] For examples, see the notations on the back of writs in Dennis v. Twine, 1729 / 30, Mooney v. Fettyplace, 1729 / 30, and Clarke v. Clipsham, 1729 / 30, FCCP. Feer's survey of commitment lists turned up few jailed debtors anywhere in eighteen-century Massachusetts. (See "Imprisonment for Debt," *MVHR*, 48: 257–58.) Lists of prisoners in Essex County jails confirm his findings: one list for the Salem jail dated July, 1734, showed five men imprisoned on writs of execution (two from Salem, two from Marblehead and one "stranger") and five others for theft. By September of 1734, only two of the original five debtors were still in jail, and two new debtors had been committed. These commitment lists are not arranged in any systematic order, but are interspersed throughout the files of the General Sessions of the Peace. For a court-ordered indenture, see MGSP, December, 1722.

Even if Massachusetts law kept Marblehead debtors from crowding the Salem jail and the scarcity of hands insured insolvent fishermen the freedom to keep working, the system still exploited a large segment of the labor force. For release from prison for poor debtors came at a cost: it meant mortgaging their labor for long periods in the future to whoever put up their bail or paid off their obligations—on whatever terms the bondsmen offered. This arrangement deepened the dependency of fishermen upon merchants and shoremen while obviating the need for imposing servitude by law. In the seventeenth century, the operators of fishing businesses had occasionally used the indebtedness of fishermen as a means of labor recruitment. But with the beginning of the postwar boom, a condition resembling debt peonage became common among Marblehead fishermen. This situation curtailed the freedom of many men to dispose of their own labor: a third of the fishermen arrested for debt in 1719 owed their release to merchants or shoremen.[12]

Though most Marblehead debt cases involved the richest men in the fishing industry prosecuting the poorest, all classes and occupational groups made liberal use of the law to sue one another with staggering frequency. The competition for profit and labor sanctioned the expression of assertive individualism in economic life even on the part of women, albeit only those of a certain social class. One of the most prominent participants in local commercial life was Madame Elizabeth Browne. A major merchant in the fish trade, her husband Captain John Browne had accumulated an estate worth nearly a thousand pounds sterling, making him one of the wealthiest men in Marblehead at his death in 1706. Modestly styling herself as "a shopkeeper," Madame Browne continued her husband's enterprises for the next twenty years, dispatching and provisioning fishing voyages and retailing goods to local customers. She was also Marblehead's most active litigant, bringing suit in a single year against fifteen of

[12] My figure of one-third is based upon a survey of writs for the year 1719. For an excellent discussion of a similar use of debt for the manipulation of labor in Springfield, Massachusetts, see Innes, *To Labor in a New Land,* chapter III. The best treatment of the role of credit in controlling labor in the seventeenth-century Essex fishery is Vickers, "Maritime Labor in Colonial Massachusetts," 110–16. See also, *Essex Ct. Recs.,* VII, 333.

her fellow townsmen, almost all fishermen in arrears for their purchases of provisions.[13]

Nor was Elizabeth Browne the only woman in town involved in business. Madame Miriam Gross invested in a fishing vessel after the death of her merchant-husband, and continued his local trade. More reluctant about personally managing her legal affairs than Madame Browne, Miriam appointed her relative, Captain John Stacey, to act as her attorney. But the widows of other wealthy Marblehead men were more like Madame Browne in their willingness to defend their interests in court. Widow Tabitha Woods took over her husband's tavern and, along with Captain John Stacey, John Edgcomb, and their Boston partner James Pitts, owned an interest in the *Dragon*, a merchant ship. When the schooner ran aground in 1714, she joined them in suing for damages. Mary Reed and Barbara Hayden, the wives of an innholder and a rich "victualler," brought a number of suits against debtors to the estates of their husbands and may have assumed the operation of their enterprises as well.[14] The active and aggressive role in economic life assumed by Marblehead women in the early eighteenth century contrasts strikingly with the behavior of their contemporaries in Gloucester. There the only woman running a local business was Widow Anna Judkins, who stayed off relief rolls by keeping the town's only tavern. The wives of Gloucester merchants and shop-keepers probably assisted their husbands, but once widowed, they appear to have retired from business. And the only Gloucester women who came into contact with the courts were local girls and young matrons charged with fornication.[15]

[13] In 1719, Elizabeth Browne initiated fifteen actions for debt, Nathaniel Norden five, Benjamin and John Stacey four, Mary Reed four, and two each, Azor Gale, Richard Skinner, and Richard Crafts. These plaintiffs accounted for thirty-four of the eighty-eight intratown debt cases in 1719, and 29 of the 34 involved fisherman-defendants.

[14] Savage v. Stacey, Edgcomb, Woods, and Pitts, MSCJ, May 21, 1717. Reed v. Luningen, 1719; Reed v. Coit and Sewall, 1719; Reed v. Turner, 1719; Hayden v. Trevett, 1729; Hayden v. Stacey, 1729; and Hayden v. How, 1729; all of the foregoing in FCCP.

[15] In Salem, there were several widows of merchants like Mary Lindall, Abigail Pickman, and Elizabeth Gerrish, who were active businesswomen, and like Elizabeth Browne, frequent litigants. But no Gloucester woman initi-

Perhaps the character of the fishing economy itself encouraged the litigiousness—extreme even by early eighteenth-century standards—manifested by Marbleheaders. The industry required a number of separate, independent merchants, shoremen, fishermen, vessel-owners, and investors to cooperate in a highly interdependent enterprise. But Gloucester's fishery was structured along the same lines and produced nothing like Marblehead's blizzard of litigation: suits between fellow townsmen in Gloucester were rare, and cases pitting rich against poor rarer still. Part of the explanation for the disproportionate number of Marblehead debt cases was the greater willingness of the town's middling and upper classes to succumb to the speculative fever of the post-war economic expansion. Middling Marbleheaders were in debt to major local merchants and shoremen who were in turn indebted to bigger men in Boston and Salem. And many members of both groups got in over their heads by borrowing against their expectations of greater gains in the fishery. A quarter of the Marblehead decedents worth more than eighty pounds sterling whose estates were administered between 1715 and 1735 died insolvent, in debt for more than they were worth. Another quarter were obligated for half or more of the value of their inventoried assets.[16]

At the top of the local credit structure were shoremen like Benjamin Stacey, who died in 1725 leaving inventoried assets and book debts that barely covered his outstanding obligations due to merchants in Boston and Salem. The expansion of the fishing economy also tempted Marbleheaders of middling means into overextension. Sadler Enoch Greenleaf's attempt to tap the fishery's profits by investing in a small boat with innholder James Perryman, another Marbleheader of average means, failed when Perryman could not meet his

ated any civil action suggesting business interests that I could discover. Nor do the inventories of wives of Gloucester merchants suggest that they continued to carry on the businesses of their deceased husbands.

[16] The wealthiest 40 percent of Marblehead's inventoried decedents between 1716 and 1735 were worth eighty pounds sterling and above, a group with some capital to invest. Out of forty available administrations for this group, ten indicated insolvency, and in eleven other cases, the total debt against the estate exceeded half of its inventoried value. (Source: Probate Files, Registry of Probate, Essex County Courthouse, Salem, Mass.)

portion of the costs for keeping the vessel in repair. Green-leaf ended up pursuing his erstwhile partner through the courts—and dying insolvent. But even for men without big ambitions, the fishery required economic risk. James Merrit, for example, was a modestly prosperous Marblehead fish-erman who owned his dwelling house and a boat. Yet Merrit still had to borrow considerable sums from other men sim-ply to underwrite the expenses of his small family fishing operation. After a storm at sea claimed the lives of Merrit and his young son in 1714, local merchant Nathaniel Nor-den took more than half of the fisherman's estate. This amount represented what Norden had advanced Merrit to outfit his vessel at the start of the season.[17]

Overextension on this scale—whether by necessity or choice—invited economic disaster for individuals and fami-lies. What made participation in the fishery even more pre-carious and unpredictable financially was that the ultimate control over the local economy and the flow of credit lay in the hands of merchants from larger ports. Even the biggest men in Marblehead still depended on these nonlocal traders for marketing, transport, stocks of provisions, and capital. As late as 1727, Marbleheaders petitioning for public funds from the province government to repair the harbor cited as one of its chief advantages being "nearly Scituated to the grand Merchandize of Boston."[18] In most cases, the credi-tors in the capital or the county seat had no reason to act with restraint in their business dealings with Marbleheaders, who were neither neighbors nor relatives. As a result, a sud-den determination to balance accounts with their Marble-head suppliers of fish could send shock waves throughout the credit structure. Larger men in Marblehead would attempt to extricate themselves from financial embarrassment by squeezing smaller ones.

The strife over debt in Marblehead had a social dimen-sion as well. While pressure exerted by creditors from out-side of town could set in motion a ripple of local prosecutions for debt, the essential estrangement of fellow Marbleheaders from each other also contributed to the high level of intra-

[17] Greenleaf v. Perryman, 1729, FCCP; EPF, #18346 and 26053.
[18] Petition of Marblehead Selectmen, *EIHC,* 56: 309.

town litigation. In Gloucester, the more cautious economic behavior of more conservative entrepreneurs occasioned fewer cases of overextension and made insolvency unknown. But the inhabitants of this smaller and more demographically stable port also harbored more scruples about suing fellow townsmen, most of whom they had known all their lives. Marbleheaders, on the other hand, treated their neighbors like strangers because so many of them were.

Some rough estimate of Marblehead's rapid rate of population growth is essential to understanding the social basis of its inhabitants' litigious behavior. In 1700, the town's population of approximately 1200 was just over one-third the size of Salem's. Within the next decade, Marblehead had become nearly half as large as Salem, and by the end of the 1720s, with its population at about 2000, it approached the size of the neighboring port. A sharp upsurge of in-migration was the critical factor effecting this expansion. In the three decades after 1680, some eighty new surnames appeared in church and town records. But in the twenty years following the first Anglo-French wars, the flow of newcomers turned into a flood, with upwards of two hundred and fifty additional family names recorded. Not only rapid growth but also continuing ethnic diversity characterized Marblehead's demographic development during this period. A steady trickle of Scots and Scots-Irish streamed into town, and the community continued to import bound labor from the Channel Islands at a brisk rate. Marblehead schoolmaster Josiah Cotton confessed that he spent less time teaching than "writing indentures for Jersey boys and girls." The bulk of the new arrivals entered town during the second decade of the eighteenth century, the period coterminous with the dramatic jump in intratown debt prosecutions.[19]

[19] The apportionment of the county rate among Essex County towns that appears annually in the MGSP is a good general index of their relative size. During the first three decades of the eighteenth century, Marblehead's population was slightly less than twice the size of Gloucester's, this proportion suggesting a population of about 1200 in 1704 when Gloucester held 700 inhabitants. In 1724, David Mossom estimated that there were 300 families in Marblehead, or between 1350 and 1500 inhabitants (based upon multipliers of 4.5 and 5, respectively). Mossom's estimate appears a bit conservative, because by 1735, Marblehead had 511 ratepayers, or between 2300 and 2555 total inhabitants. By 1748, with 620 ratepayers, local population

The correspondence between rapid demographic growth and rising legal strife is more than coincidence. The large percentage of nonnatives within the population contributed to the conviction of inhabitants that they owed nothing to each other that could not be proved in court. The sizeable proportion of Jersey immigrants in town may also have played a particularly important role in swelling the volume of intra-town litigation. Accustomed to the peculiarities of Jersey laws that encouraged promptness in bringing suits against debtors, immigrant-creditors took their defaulters to court as a matter of course. This practice fostered within the English community a prevailing stereotype of Jerseymen as "rapacious swindlers" and discouraged restraint on the part of those with claims against Jersey debtors.[20] The rate of persistence among new families settling in Marblehead also sheds light upon the correspondence between geographic mobility and civil litigation. Nearly two-thirds of these immigrants stayed in Marblehead for less than a generation, probably just a few years.[21] If new people appeared in town at a rapid rate to try their luck in the fishery, many were disappointed and departed just as quickly. This turnover in town membership suggests that recourse to the courts to collect debts reflected the limited engagement felt by people who had known each other for only a short time. It suggests too a belief among creditors that those owing them money might abscond without satisfying their obligations. The attach-

was between 2790 and 3100 inhabitants. (See Mossom to the Secretary of the S.P.G., April 28, 1724, in *Historical Collections Relating to the American Colonial Church. Massachusetts*, ed. William S. Perry, 3 vols. (Hartford, 1873). III, 149–50. The valuation list for 1735 appears in Tax and Valuation Lists for Massachusetts Towns Before 1776, Harvard University Microfilm Edition, Reel #12; see also "The Marblehead Tax list for 1748," *EICH*, 43 (1907), 209–22.)

My data on in-migration is based upon tracing surnames through the town records and the records of Marblehead's three churches. Eighty-one new surnames appeared between 1680 and 1709, and 276 during the decades between 1710 and 1730. For continuing Jersey migration, see Cotton's comment, cited in *SHG*, IV, 399–400. Newfoundlanders also remained a major immigrant group. (Innis, *The Codfisheries*, 147.)

[20] Konig, "A New Look at the Essex 'French'," *EIHC*, 110: 173–74.

[21] Only 111 of the 276 new surnames that appear in town and church records between 1710 and 1730 reappear on the Marblehead valuation list for 1735.

ment of property or the detention of persons was the simplest way to forestall such an eventuality, but not always the most successful. Local borrowers owed Benjamin Stacey considerable sums at the time of his death, and he had jailed several for debt. But the administrators of his estate had little hope of recovering these obligations for "a greate number of the Debtors are run away and Some Sworne out of Goale so that they can never be come at."[22]

The new economic opportunities created by increasing military security in the north Atlantic affected Gloucester and Marblehead in markedly different ways. While Gloucester's conversion to commerce did little to disrupt local society, the expansion of the fishing industry in Marblehead during the early eighteenth century was accompanied by the growth of economic inequality, labor exploitation, and social conflict. Everyone with a little capital to risk tried to tap the fishery for private profit, but the industry actually yielded large returns to only a few men and minimal subsistence for most others. Operations teetered on from one year to the next atop the fragile support of a complicated structure of credit. Smaller men were caught in an endless cycle of debt to bigger men in Marblehead, and bigger men were dangerously dependent upon the biggest dealers in Boston. Unscrupulous competition for labor reduced many fishermen to a kind of debt peonage. Aggressive litigiousness at the top of society poisoned vertical relationships, while geographic mobility, ethnic diversity, and the pressures imposed by financial dependence upon nonlocal creditors eroded reluctance about resorting to law.

As economic expansion exacerbated Marblehead's earlier difficulties involving inequality, debt, and labor, it also aggravated other problems that had plagued the town since the seventeenth century. Violence and disorder remained endemic to local life: all classes contended against each other, not only in the Court of Common Pleas, but also in the town's taverns and streets, in the harbor and aboard ship. While violations against persons and property were rare in eighteenth-century Gloucester, Marbleheaders were as well represented among criminal defendants as they were among

[22] See EPF, #26053.

debtors in Essex County. Between 1716 and 1738, the number of townspeople indicted for violent crime was more than double that of Salem and for crimes against property more than triple.[23] Whether the crime rate in Marblehead was higher in the early eighteenth century than it had been during the seventeenth century is impossible to tell. But what is clear is that breaches of the peace were far more common in Marblehead than in other provincial Essex County seaports, even Salem. It is apparent too, from the character of criminal activity, that Marblehead's rapid postwar expansion was largely responsible for sustaining disruption into the eighteenth century.

Trouble frequently began even before local fishermen and sailors came ashore, for the congestion of Marblehead harbor alone invited turbulent encounters. Court records suggest that brawls aboard ships moored in the harbor were a common occurrence, but probably only those cases involving serious personal injury or property damage reached the general sessions of the peace. In 1710, for example, Peter LeVallais was prosecuted for throwing a mooring buoy at Richard Rowland and injuring him critically. In 1719, John White, Jr. sued fellow fisherman Hugh Pedrick for damages, following a fracas in a sloop anchored offshore. Witnesses testified that Pedrick "twisted his hand in the plaintiff's hair and threw him over the Main Yard into the Carling and followed him and gott his Knee on his breast and bruised him so as he Voided much Blood at the Nose and Mouth. . . ." A few years earlier, a dispute over a vessel eventuated in the indictment and conviction of two Boston merchants for forcibly seizing a brig in the harbor.[24]

Controversies between fishermen and shoremen triggered a large share of disruptions as well. In July of 1723, fishermen James Trefry and James Maccolly came in from their second fare and fell out over the price of fish with shoreman

[23] Between 1716 and 1735, four Salem inhabitants were indicted for violent crime and fifteen Marblehead residents; there were four cases of theft / breaking and entering / receiving stolen goods in Salem and eleven in Marblehead. (Sources: MGSP and MSCJ, for 1716–1735.)

[24] MGSP, June 27, 1710; White v. Pedrick, 1719, FCCP; and MGSP, September 30, 1710.

Samuel Reed. The quarrel culminated when the two men and several companions surrounded Reed's house late one evening. Trefry swore that he would "drink a Glass of his [Reed's] blood before Morning," while Maccolly threatened to "kick him where the Divel should not find him."[25] Two years later, another member of the Reed family took his troubles to the justices of the peace. John Reed, the master of a fishing voyage for merchant John Calley, had put in at Canso harbor after Calley's vessel sprang a leak. At the complaint of Calley, who suspected his master of damaging the boat, Reed was detained in jail for a day while the merchant repossessed his schooner and removed all the fish from its hold. Following his release, Reed alleged, he received only a fraction of his rightful share in the voyage's profits from Calley. And to add insult to injury, Calley now demanded security for the future use of the vessel "by the threatening of Whiping and attendance of unchristianlike usages."[26] Violence also concluded a contretemps between shoreman Joseph Majory and his fisherman William Wendover, who forced his way onto Majory's boat, held a pistol to the shoreman's chest and swore "he would Shoot him through the Body." The only recorded murder in Marblehead during the first half of the eighteenth century involved two fishermen: John Royall clubbed Christopher Codner to death "with a stout cane" and fled town.[27]

Homecoming celebrations were another source of trouble. Long absences at sea accustomed fishermen to relative freedom from the constraints of individuals and institutions representing local authority. To make matters worse, many fishermen had no voice in the election of local officials, for even those who qualified to vote might be away at sea when March and May elections were held. A typical episode occurred in 1710 when John Yabsley and his shipmates returned from their summer fare and celebrated with an evening's drinking at one of Marblehead's many unlicensed taverns. The revels were ended by a brawl that brought Yabsley into court for assault, while five of his companions were

[25] MGSP, July 16, 1723.

[26] Protest of John Reed, September 7, 1725, ENR.

[27] MGSP, December 31, 1728; MSCJ, November 1, 1722.

charged with drinking at an illegal establishment, and their host with selling drink on the sly.[28] The onset of winter could also increase the incidence of disorder because the end of the fishing season left many Marblehead men with time on their hands. Town selectmen tried to minimize the mischief by outlawing "the Game Commonly Call'd Pitching-Penny or Coasting down the Hills in Sleads, or otherwise."[29] But sometimes the offseason spawned more serious breaches of the peace then gambling or illicit sledding. In November of 1723, four armed and intoxicated fishermen "terrorized" one Marblehead neighborhood, smashing windows in several houses and shops and finishing off the evening by breaking into a barn and demolishing a carriage. Property damage from the night's work amounted to sixty pounds New England money.[30]

While crimes of violence in Marblehead usually involved male defendants, local women occasionally joined the fray, just as they had during the seventeenth century. Their participation usually took the form of domestic disputes that escalated into street brawls and cursing competitions with offending spouses. Typical of these battling couples were John and Elizabeth Johnson, who faced charges of "profane swearing" and making "a public disturbance in the streets" of Marblehead in 1708. But occasionally women banded together, as they had earlier, to defend family interests. In 1706, for example, Lucy Codner, the wife of a poor fisherman, marshalled three other fishing wives in an assault upon the local constable who was trying to seize her husband's property for debt.[31]

The case of Lucy Codner suggests that the tensions generated by inequality and labor exploitation were responsible for some of Marblehead's violent crime. The hard lives led by the mass of townspeople contributed too to Marblehead's relatively high incidence of theft. Servants were the group most commonly charged with stealing goods or concealing loot, while the victims of theft, whenever named by

[28] MGSP, December 26, 1710.
[29] MTR, III, 122.
[30] MGSP, December 31, 1723.
[31] MGSP, July 9, 1706, and January 16, 1728.

the court records, invariably ranked at the top of society. Frequent prosecutions of runaway servants and apprentices were still another symptom of the friction between rich and poor, employer and employee, in Marblehead.[32] Also reflecting resentments rooted in economic grievances was the deliberate destruction of the carriage, a conveyance that only the wealthy could afford, that ended the rampage of the four fishermen in 1723.

While local inhabitants committed most of the crimes against persons and property in town, the seasonal influx of strangers contributed to the atmosphere of general disruption. With a month or more elapsing between the arrival of a British merchantman and its dispatch, crews had plenty of time to make mischief, and captains often could exercise little restraint. In 1719, Captain John Felmore complained to the justices of the peace that his four sailors refused to do any work, came and went as they pleased, beat the mate, and deserted for five days before one member of the crew ran away for good. Besides unruly English sailors, nonlocal servants hired out to the masters of fishing vessels for the season also swelled the number of transients in town during the spring and summer months. Often so poorly clothed and outfitted by their temporary employers that they could not perform their duties aboard ship, these servants provoked the resentment of native fishermen. The harbor assault involving Jerseyman Peter Le Vallais and native-born Richard Rowland was one instance of the way that rivalries between newcomers and local men could lead to trouble. The necessity of importing hired or indentured labor also exacerbated the problem of theft. During the summer season of 1731, three Boston "laborers," "being Instigated and Stirred up by the Devil in Marblehead," broke into merchant John Palmer's house and stole one hundred and fifty pounds worth of dry goods.[33]

Compared to Boston, the total volume of theft and violent crime in Marblehead does not seem staggering. Even after the first decade of the eighteenth century, when the

[32] MGSP, June 27, 1704, December 31, 1700, and February 8, 1715.

[33] Protest of Captain John Felmore, August 4, 1719, and Protest of Captain Jonas Mott, August 28, 1715, ENR; and MSCJ, October 26, 1731.

incidence of both increased sharply, years passed without a single assault or theft being reported in Marblehead. By contrast, in Boston during a single year one murder, one assault with a knife, one attempted rape, and four thefts took place.[34] On the other hand, Boston was six times as large as Marblehead, and within Essex County Marblehead offered far less security to persons and property than more populous Salem. Certainly, respectable Essex residents considered the extent of disruption in Marblehead extreme. Even at the end of the seventeenth century, Josiah Cotton, Marblehead's schoolmaster, observed the "extravagance, Intemperance, Negligence in Religion, and Disorderliness that is too rife in that place."[35] By 1718, the rising crime rate and Marblehead's distance from the nearest jail in Salem prompted John Calley, a local justice of the peace, to request county funds for constructing "a Cage" for holding nocturnal lawbreakers overnight. The town finally acquired a separate jail in 1731, after inhabitants complained to the Essex justices that Marblehead

> Continuously hath many Strangers and Seafaring men from other parts of the world coming and residing there who often prove Illminded disorderly persons and disturbers of the peace. So that by Reason of many Debts Contracted thefts and other offenses against the Laws . . . it falls out that there is occasion for near as many Commitments there as in all the County besides.[36]

The Essex County sheriff, Benjamin Marston, agreed with Marbleheaders on the need for a separate jail there. But like most observers outside of town, he ascribed Marblehead's troubles to the flawed character of its inhabitants and to the lawlessness of the fishing culture rather than to the evil influence of strangers. Marblehead's population, according to Marston, "consisting very much of fishermen and sailors occasions frequent Breaches of the Peace and great disorders

---

[34] The business of the General Sessions of the Peace for Suffolk County appears in the Minutebooks of the Superior Court of Judicature. For crime in Boston, see MSCJ, August 13, 1734.

[35] Cited in Roads, *History*, 40.

[36] Petition of the Inhabitants of Marblehead for a Jail, March 31, 1731, FGSP.

among the Inhabitants and by Reason of the prevalancy of an ungovernable Spirit 'tis rendered almost Impracticable to preserve peace and Good Order."[37]

Settled residents and strangers alike contributed to the chaos in Marblehead, but the most basic cause of communal disorder was rapid economic expansion engineered by non-local entrepreneurs. The postwar boom set off a scramble for profits that fostered social fragmentation in the form of economic polarization, friction among social classes, debt, and crime. After 1690, Gloucester too had increased in commercial importance and had relied initially on Boston for transport, marketing, and credit facilities as well as for finished goods. But the greater distance between Cape Ann and Massachusetts' major mercantile centers rendered less direct the influence of outsiders on local life. Gloucester was not subject to a seasonal influx of English mariners; the town did not draw a large, heterogeneous group of seafaring transients; and Boston and Salem merchants did not dominate the local economy to the extent that they did in Marblehead. More easily accessible to these larger ports than Cape Ann, Marblehead experienced with full force the postwar expansion and mushroomed from a straggling settlement of fisherfolk into a congested center of New England's most important industry. Economic development exaggerated the elements of instability endemic to the town since the beginning of its settlement in the seventeenth century. The poverty and indebtedness of fishermen, the competition for and exploitation of laborers by bigger men, and the fighting and drunkenness among all inhabitants were not novel phenomena in local life. These conditions had in some measure characterized social experience since the seventeenth century. What was new in early eighteenth-century Marblehead was the scale of the disruption, a level of inequality and exploitation, aggressiveness and antagonism, without parallel in the town's past or in the experience of neighboring secondary ports.

While runaway economic growth was responsible for much of the disorder that prevailed in Marblehead during the early eighteenth century, these distempers also reflected the basic

[37] Memorial of Benjamin Marston to the Justices of the Peace, March 31, 1731, FGSP.

weaknesses in local social organization. For it was the underdevelopment of town institutions and customs that allowed private enterprise to operate without restraint during the postwar period. Founded as a fishing camp for the benefit of Salem merchants, Marblehead embarked on its most rapid and sustained period of economic expansion after 1713 without having ever passed through a phase of utopian corporatism or even a period of stable, autonomous local development. From the outset, the fishing economy had undermined the strength of those institutions that in Gloucester and elsewhere in New England enhanced cohesion and stability in public and private life. Strong neighborhood and family ties, an acknowledged native elite, and an abiding commitment to Congregationalist orthodoxy and discipline were absent in seventeenth-century Marblehead. The expansion of the fishing industry at the beginning of the eighteenth century imposed an even greater strain on local social systems, magnifying their incapacity to maintain order. At the same time, the inability of these institutions to exert any countervailing influence against the centrifugal forces of commercial expansion maximized disruption and disunity. The persistence of weakness and division within families, the local elite, and the churches left townspeople without effective authorities or social organizations to offset the impact of rapid economic development.

Because of the town's continuing dependence on fishing, the weakness of family life remained a fundamental flaw in Marblehead's social organization throughout the later colonial period. And as the New England fishery evolved from an offshore, coastal operation to an enterprise encompassing more distant banks and requiring voyages of several weeks duration, local men spent longer and longer periods away from their homes.[38] While fishermen tried to get back to town in between fares, wind and weather often prevented their return, and at the end of the fishing season, some men sailed out again on coasting voyages in vessels that rarely returned from their destinations until the end of the winter. The risk and demands of the maritime economy caused basic discontinuities in the lives of Marblehead's seafaring families. Ship-

[38] Innis, *The Codfisheries*, 150.

wreck, storms, and disease made the sudden disappearance and premature deaths of male family members a more familiar occurrence among fisherfolk than among farmers. In addition, frequent and prolonged absences from town probably deprived Marblehead fathers of the strong authority wielded by the patriarchs of New England's rural villages.[39]

To some extent, the practice of family members shipping out on the same vessel mitigated the disruption of domestic life in seafaring households and afforded fathers some measure of control over and contact with their older sons. When Marblehead boys reached the age of ten or eleven, they began accompanying their fathers or other adult male relatives on fishing voyages and performing simple duties aboard the boats. After an apprenticeship at sea under paternal tutelage, some older boys and grown sons continued to work as crew members alongside their fathers, uncles, and other male family members and neighbors. But the speed with which seafaring apprentices mastered their craft conspired against the sustained exercise of patriarchial authority over male children. By their mid-to-late teens, young men could strike out on their own, sailing with any boat in the fishing fleet or shipping out on coasting vessels independent of paternal oversight. The economic circumstances of most Marblehead fishing families also restricted prolonged parental control over male children. An introduction to the skills of the fishing trade, a reputation for reliability with local shoremen and merchants, and in some cases, a small boat were the only material legacies that most Marblehead fathers could leave their sons. They had no land or livestock to transmit to their heirs

[39] For an example of the difficulties created by weather, see the Protest of Jethro Wheeler, September 3, 1724, ENR; for the time involved in coasting voyages, see *Abstracts of English Shipping Records*, vol. II, part 1. Daniel Vickers estimates that among Essex County fishermen, median age at death dropped from fifty-seven years of age for the period 1645 to 1675 to forty-eight for the period 1676 to 1775. He attributes this lower longevity to the greater rigors, hardships, and dangers of the bank fishery of the late seventeenth and early eighteenth centuries. ("Maritime Labor in Colonial Massachusetts," 122, and 202–3.) Douglas Jones's work on Beverly mariners corroborates Vickers's findings for fishermen. According to Jones, the mean age of death for mariners between 1750 and 1800 was fifty-one, compared with fifty-five for artisans, and sixty-six for gentlemen, farmers, and merchants. (*Village and Seaport*, 38.)

as a way of insuring that sons would stay in town and care for aged parents. In rural New England towns, fathers often worked farms together with their grown sons and used land legacies as leverage to encourage filial obedience to parental demands. The fishing economy deprived most Marblehead fathers of the same power over their mature male children.[40]

The seasonal demands of the postwar fishing economy took an even more serious toll upon the authority of Marblehead fathers over their wives and daughters. By the end of the seventeenth century, the numbers of men and women in the town's permanent population had evened out. But from February to September—the same months that English sea captains and sailors swarmed into Marblehead harbor—local households were comprised primarily of women, girls, and small children. Most of the town's adolescent and adult males were away at sea, usually for long stretches at the banks. This set of circumstances contributed to the increasing number of Marblehead women who were charged with sexual misconduct. In the twenty years after 1695, when the town's population was just under half the size of Salem's, proportionately more Marblehead women were indicted for fornication than inhabitants of its larger neighbor. And in the two decades following the expansion of the fishery, the problem became even more pronounced. Between 1715 and 1735, with its population now approaching that of Salem in size, Marblehead had nearly twice as many defendants charged with sexual misconduct.

Of course, Marblehead's outsized number of accused fornicators is not, by itself, proof that townspeople were unusually promiscuous. While a large number of presentments for sexual misconduct within a town could suggest a greater inclination and freedom among its inhabitants to

---

[40] The estate administrations of shoremen who died with their fishing fleet at sea often list crew members, and frequently administrations indicate members of the same family serving aboard a single vessel. See for example, EPF, #2820. Also see Roads, *History,* 68, and Jones, *Village and Seaport,* 87–88. On the family in rural communities, see especially Greven, *Four Generations,* 72–99, passim; Jedrey, *World of John Cleaveland,* 1–16 and 58–94; Daniel Scott Smith, "Parental Power and Marriage Patterns: An Analysis of Historical Trends in Hingham, Massachusetts," *Journal of Marriage and the Family,* 35 (1973), 419–28.

pursue illicit pleasure, it might also reflect the vigilance of neighbors in reporting such transgressions. Just such strict communal oversight seems to explain why a relatively large number of Gloucester's inhabitants were charged with fornication during the three decades after 1695. Although that town's population was only one-third the size of Salem's, the two ports had a nearly equal number of defendants presented for fornication over the same thirty-year period.[41] That communal "watchfulness" was responsible for Gloucester's high incidence of such indictments is suggested by the sharp drop in presentments for sexual misconduct during the period of difficulties within the First Parish, an episode that engaged the interest of the entire adult community. Local controversy presumably did not dampen the ardor of the young, but the unprecedented strife did provide their parents with more absorbing distractions than counting the months between banns and births. However, the same communal sensitivity to sexual misbehavior cannot account for the case of Marblehead, where a high rate of prosecutions for fornication reflected a very different social reality. While Gloucester's defendants were typically newlywed couples whose first child arrived too soon after the marriage, nearly half of Marblehead's defendants in fornication cases were single women or adulterous wives. And while almost all of Gloucester's transgressors were locals, both wife and husband, many of the men involved with Marblehead women were not settled inhabitants of town.[42]

[41] Prosecutions for Fornication in Essex County Ports:

	1696–1705	1706–1715	1716–1725	1726–1735
Salem	13 (5)	14 (6)	14 (5)	18 (7)
Marblehead	12 (6)	23 (9)	32 (15)	23 (11)
Gloucester	7 (3)	12 (5)	19 (7)	2 (1)
	(Numbers in parentheses represent defendants who were singlewomen.)			

SOURCE: Minutebooks, General Sessions of the Peace, 1696–1735, Office of the County Clerk, Superior Courthouse, Salem, Mass.

[42] The singlewomen arraigned for fornication generally named the father of their child and his hometown; none of the men charged by Gloucester singlewomen were nonlocal.

Sarah Hendley Westcott was a more habitual offender than most other Marblehead women, but her case indicates how the local fishing economy contributed to sexual misconduct. The daughter of a fisherman who had deserted the family or died at sea, Sarah first got into trouble in 1712 while she was a servant in Edward Brattle's household. John Hoyter, a fisherman employed for a season by Brattle, fathered her first child and then disappeared from town. A few years later she became pregnant again, this time by Thomas Westcott, a sailor who deserted the service of an English merchantman long enough to marry her. In 1719, Sarah was presented to the justices for giving birth to a third child, obviously another bastard, because Westcott had left Marblehead sixteen months earlier and thrown her upon the town for support. This record of misbehavior exhausted the patience of First Church members, who finally voted to excommunicate Sarah in September of 1720. They objected mainly to her "Gross repeated Whoredomes, even unto a Third Bastard Child born," but also rebuked Sarah's "long contempt of the Authority of Jesus Christ and his Church." After many "private admonishings" by other church members, Sarah had still refused to repent of her vile language, absences from public worship, "threatening carriage" toward her mother, and several suicide attempts. And when John Barnard, the minister of First Church, had paid her a pastoral visit, she defended her obstinacy by asserting that church discipline had been instituted by St. Paul, not Christ, and that the Scriptures contradicted themselves. As final proof of her degeneracy, Sarah stalked out of the First Church meetinghouse before Barnard had finished reading her sentence of excommunication.[43]

Sarah Westcott's case was extreme, but the conditions that continually disrupted her life were not atypical. In 1735, one-tenth of Marblehead's households were headed by women, mainly the widows of fishermen. Even under the best circumstances, the heads of families were separated from their wives and daughters for many months during the year, absences that accorded greater freedom to female family

---

[43] "Marblehead First Church Records," 1688–1800," MS, unpaginated, September 11, 1720, Old North Church, Marblehead, Mass. (Cited hereafter as MFCR.) See also MGSP, 1696–1719, 239.

members. And just as more local fishermen were leaving town
on the first fare of the spring, nonnative sailors and sea captains began streaming into Marblehead. Unmarried women
defendants in fornication cases usually named their male
partners in crime, and their lovers resemble Sarah's succession of mates. Mary Hooper charged Stephen Coffin of London; Martha Martin charged Andrew Anderson, "a sailor,
a stranger"; Elizabeth Blanch charged John Taylor, "a seafaring man"; Sarah Hinkes was caught in bed at a local inn
with Captain James Templer, commander of a British merchantman anchored in Marblehead harbor. The names of
local men cropped up in these confessions as well, but a
transient seafaring population of fishermen hired for a season and the sailors and ship captains of transatlantic merchantmen augmented significantly the illict sexual activity of
Marblehead's wives and daughters. The members of this
mobile, nonlocal maritime population figured in a few fornication cases involving women in Salem Town and in fewer
still with Gloucester women. But Marblehead harbor, as the
center of the Essex fish trade, drew the largest contingent of
strangers.[44] And with the growth of that trade after 1713,
the expansion of production and the intensification of commercial activity made family members even more estranged
and strangers even more familiar.

Besides contributing to the instability of family life, the
development of Marblehead's economy during the early
eighteenth century made even more tenuous the authority of
men at the top of the town's social structure. Although the
men who dominated Marblehead for most of the seventeenth century had failed to command much popular trust
or support, their successors were even more compromised as
an elite. For these new social leaders were mainly men who
had migrated to Marblehead from larger ports, along with a
few members of formerly obscure native families. Both groups
owed their prosperity and influence primarily to their partners and patrons in Boston and Salem, for whom they acted
as middlemen in the fishing industry and trade. The preponderance within the elite of these new families who lacked

[44]MGSP, 1696–1719, 291, 325, 239; MGSP, 1719–1727, 29, 30, and 134–
35.

any longstanding connection to local society or commitment to its welfare became another element compounding the volatility of local life.

By the end of the seventeenth century, merchants from bigger New England ports began to perceive the advantage of strengthening their interests in Marblehead by dispatching "to the spot" middlemen and agents who were trusted neighbors, friends, or family members. The first Anglo-French conflict, King William's War, reduced the involvement of both the West Country and the French in the north Atlantic fishery, opening up greater opportunities for enterprising New Englanders. As a result, an affluent and cosmopolitan class of immigrants moved into Marblehead. This group included English sea captains like John Browne and Andrew Cratey and the sons of Boston merchants and mariners like Edward Brattle, Richard Skinner, and Nathaniel Norden. After the Peace of Utrecht in 1713 secured New England's permanent advantage in the fishery, the attractions of Marblehead became even more manifest, and this steady flow of monied immigrants from larger towns turned into a flood. During the second and third decades of the eighteenth century, the influx from Boston brought into town the scions of several important merchant families, including Stephen Minot, Jr. and his brother George, Edmund Goffe, Jeremiah Allen, Jr., Samuel and John Bannister, and two lawyers, Richard Dana and Nathan Bowen. At the same time, Joseph Blaney, an affluent tanner, and several members of the prosperous Proctor family moved to Marblehead from Salem. The ranks of transplanted English sea captains and traders increased as well, with John Tasker, Abraham Howard, David LeGallais, and Joseph Smethurst numbering among the newcomers. These recent arrivals forged marital alliances, friendships, and business partnerships among themselves and with some native Marblehead families. A few of these favored native clans had been locally important since the beginnings of settlement, but most had risen to the top of society late in the seventeenth century through shrewd and successful competition in the fish trade.[45]

[45] For the backgrounds of the Minots, Allen, Bowen, Dana, Skinner and Blaney, see chapter IX, note 8; on Howard, Tasker, and LeGallais, see chapter XI, note 29. For Cratey, see Sidney Perley, "Marblehead in the Year 1700,"

The domination of Marblehead society by newcomers possessing capital and good connections, and by the aspiring sons of obscure fishermen, was already apparent at the end of the seventeenth century. Nearly half of the largest contributors to the building fund for the new First Church meetinghouse in 1698 had resided in town for less than twenty years. During the postwar period, the preeminence of new men became plainer still. Over one-third of the wealthiest decile of decedents inventoried between 1716 and 1735 represented the first generation of their families in Marblehead and another third, the first generation to acquire wealth. Politically, the gains of new men were even more impressive: in the 1720s, less than half of the men elected to the board of selectmen had been in town for more than a generation, and only ten percent of those serving came from families that had held the office during the seventeenth century.[46] Monied immigrants and newly rich native men eclipsed most descendants of the local leaders who had dominated Marblehead's affairs earlier in the seventeenth century. The second and third generations of families like the Peaches, Gales, Bartolls, Waldrons, and Devereux remained economically substantial traders, shoremen, blacksmiths, and farmers. But by the beginning of the eighteenth century, few could match

EIHC, 47 (1911), 67. Norden's Boston ties appear in his will, EPF, #19555. On Brattle, see *An Account of Some of the Descendants of Captain Thomas Brattle*, comp. E. D. Harris (Boston, 1867); for Smethurst and Browne, see *The Holyoke Diaries*, ed. George Francis Dow (Salem, 1911); for Goffe, see *SHG*, IV, 57–59. Samuel and John Bannister are identified as Boston merchants in several civil suits in MSCJ, 1715–1721.

[46] None of the twenty-two largest benefactors to the new meetinghouse built in Marblehead in 1698 were among local householders in 1674. (Meetinghouse contributors are listed on a loose sheet in MFCR.) Eight Marbleheaders who ranked within the wealthiest decile of decedents inventoried between 1716 and 1735 (seventeen total) represented the first generation of their families in Marblehead; another five of the seventeen men in the richest decile appear to have been the first members of their families to acquire substantial estates. Seventeen men served as selectmen between 1721 and 1729, but only eight of these men descended from Marblehead householders in 1674, and only two of these eight from seventeenth-century selectmen. A gap in the town records makes it impossible to trace officeholders for the first two decades of the eighteenth century. (Sources: Essex Probate Files, Registry of Probate, Essex County Courthouse, Salem, Mass.; MTR, III, 1721–1730.)

the wealth and political influence of Marblehead's new men, and many were failing to secure important political office.[47]

Behind the decaying influence of this old native ruling group was the advantage held by the ascendant elite in the form of connections with transatlantic fish exporters in larger commercial centers, principally Boston. The satellite status of Marblehead's commerce, the town's dependence upon outside sources for imported goods, credit, finance, marketing, and transport facilities, made close relations with the merchants in bigger ports of paramount importance for a man's economic success. Whether new to town or new to the top of society, Marblehead's rising men all shared a desire to extend or enhance their influence abroad. Their children regularly chose marital partners from other commercial centers, with the sons and daughters of Boston merchants making up the majority of these nonlocal mates. Three families also facilitated the forging of such alliances by sending sons to Harvard College. Wills provide other evidence of the importance of Boston ties. Captain John Browne named as guardians of his children two of the capital's merchants, John Mico and David Jeffries, while Edward Brattle left a large bequest to his business associate, kinsman, and "particular friend," Boston trader Jacob Wendall.[48]

A concomitant of the new elite's intense interest in cultivating connections with the capital was their disengagement from local society and, often, their adversary relationship to

[47] On this point, see the analysis of John Barnard's supporters in chapter VIII, note 5.

[48] The marriages of Col. John Legg's descendants illustrate the ascendant elite's interest in extending its influence through intermarriage. Legg's daughter Elizabeth married Captain John Browne, an English merchant who settled in Marblehead in 1686. Three of John and Elizabeth Browne's daughters married the sons of Boston merchants: the Reverend Edward Holyoke, Stephen Minot Jr., and John Legg, the nephew of Col. Legg of Marblehead. A fourth Browne daughter married John Oulton, a fish exporter from London who relocated in Boston and subsequently moved to Marblehead, and a fifth married Captain David Legallais, a Jersey sea captain. Col. John Legg's other daughter, Mary, married Edward Brattle, the scion of another Boston merchant family, in 1693, and their only surviving child married James Smith, a Boston merchant. (See also, Elizabeth Dana, "Richard Skinner and his Bible," *New England Historical and Genealogical Register*, 54 (1900), 412–13; SHG, VII, 441–42 and 592; IX, 106; and EPF, #3140 and 3619.)

many of their Marblehead neighbors. The political offices that they particularly coveted were posts like justice of the peace and deputy to the General Court, positions that would increase the frequency of their contacts with bigger ports. But purely local distinction meant little. For example, members of the new ruling group were even less likely than native townspeople to join the Congregational Church. The names of these men—and women—appeared far more often in the records of the Court of Common Pleas than in those of the church, for from their ranks came Marblehead's most active litigants. Their frequent recourse to the law to recover debts from their Marblehead neighbors was typified by Madame Elizabeth Browne's vigorous pursuit of her local defaulters. And other members of the new elite were just as aggressive about defending their interests in court. In a single year, 1729, Stephen and George Minot and Samuel and John Bannister, four merchants who moved from Boston to Marblehead, initiated a total of twenty prosecutions for debt against fellow townsmen, while Andrew Tucker and John Stacey, recently successful native men, sued twenty-two of their neighbors for debt.[49]

The contrasting situation in Gloucester during the same period illuminates both the cause and the consequences of the transformation overtaking the top of Marblehead society. The war years also initiated the movement of new families with commercial interests into Gloucester, and the postwar decades stepped up in-migration. But Gloucester was too remote to attract families from Boston and Salem: the sons and agents of big fish exporters from larger ports did not take up residence in town. Most of the town's new arrivals were not well-to-do, well-connected, well-educated cosmopolites, but young men from families of middling means in neighboring Essex County communities. While some of these new immigrants made money, they never crowded the old Gloucester elite out of the top of the economic hierarchy or displaced them as political and social leaders. An established, native-born circle of a few families continued to hold

[49] Out of twenty-three men who attended the Congregational Church in Marblehead who were either successful immigrants to town or the first generation of their families to enjoy wealth and political success, only seven were full church members by 1730. On civil litigation, see FCCP for 1729.

sway, their domination of local society spanning the transition from agriculture to commerce. Newcomers to Gloucester, however successful economically, held a subordinate status within local society. The retention of power by the town's traditional elite provided an atmosphere of continuity, a sense of the essential stability and integrity of social authority in the midst of changing material conditions.

To the south, Marblehead's more cosmopolitan immigrants, armed with the advantages of outside capital and connections, quickly overwhelmed the town's old native leaders. As the sons of major merchant families in Boston and Salem, some of these new men were more genteel than their rough-hewn predecessors. Yet the speed with which recent arrivals and native parvenus rose to elevated positions discouraged townspeople from perceiving as permanent the social order that had come to prevail by the early eighteenth century. Instead, the turnover at the top of society fostered an unsettling sense of the arbitrariness of social authority and eroded any impulse to defer. Because so many members of Marblehead's new ruling circle were unable to claim legitimacy by appealing to a long tradition of family dignity in town, their position as an elite was less secure, and vertical relationships were more strained.

That many members of the new Marblehead elite lacked longstanding connections to or inherited status within the local community might not have mattered so much if they had cultivated the respect of their lesser neighbors and assumed customary public obligations. Unfortunately, most of the new families lacked this attribute of a traditional elite as well. Mobile, deracinated, and identified with the interests and the culture of larger ports, the ascendant elite had bigger ambitions that limited their commitment to the welfare of Marblehead. Boston was their cynosure; Marblehead, only a way-station for making money. Unlike Gloucester's ruling group, for whom the preservation of local status was paramount and contact with the society of larger seaports intimidating, Marblehead's new elite focused all of their aspirations on the capital. Acquiring in-laws, business partners, and friends in Boston dominated their activities, while disengagement and detachment defined their attitude toward local society. The existence of a more deeply rooted and localistic, responsive and responsible ruling group in Marblehead might have counterbalanced the effects of economic expansion. But instead of lending to the social order an aura of stability and permanence, Marblehead's ascendant elite only added to the forces of fragmentation that pressed in upon the town. The character of the town's "governors" encouraged the prevalence of "an ungovernable spirit" among its inhabitants.

A final influence that intensified social conflict in Marblehead was the town's religious situation. After 1715, the First Congregational Church became more central to local life, but at the same time Marblehead's booming economy created conditions that made religion another source of sharp division. The growing fish traffic annually brought to town a large contingent of English sea captains and sailors, most of them members of the Church of England. In this group of Anglican seafarers, General Francis Nicholson saw his opportunity to encourage the growth of the Episcopal Church in Massachusetts. A former lieutenant governor of New York, Nicholson headquartered in Boston after 1711 when he was appointed governor of Nova Scotia. From there he combined service as a military commander in two expeditions against the French with work as a lay missionary for the Society for the Propagation of the Gospel in Foreign Parts, an organization for promoting Anglicanism in the American colonies. Nicholson's regular contact at Boston's Episcopal Church, King's Chapel, with sea captains routed to Marblehead, and his brief recruiting stints in the village convinced the general that sufficient support existed for an Anglican church. By 1714, he was overseeing the construction of St. Michael's Church in Marblehead. With the establishment of an Episcopal congregation, the townspeople split into two competing sectarian groups.[50]

In selecting Marblehead as the site for his missionary efforts, Nicholson had made a shrewd choice. A few years before the founding of St. Michael's, a handful of farming

---

[50] For Nicholson's role in founding St. Michael's, see Samuel Roads, "Historical Address," in *St. Michael's Church, Marblehead* (Marblehead, 1902). The list of British sea captains contributing to the church is in "St. Michael's Records," (transcript), 3, Diocesan Library, Boston, Mass.

families in Newbury, disaffected with a parish decision to relocate the meetinghouse, had formed Queen Anne's Chapel, the first Episcopal outpost in Essex County.[51] But while Newbury's small number of nominal and half-hearted Anglican converts wavered in their allegiance to the Church of England, Marblehead had a large contingent of families sympathetic to Episcopalianism. Perhaps one-fifth to one-quarter of Marblehead's inhabitants genuinely preferred Episcopal ceremony and "orgones" to Congregationalist austerity, and they joined St. Michael's. Even in the seventeenth century, some of the town's Jersey and West Country families had felt a greater affinity for Anglicanism than for Puritanism. Before the establishment of St. Michael's, these Marbleheaders had spent their Sabbaths at King's Chapel whenever business brought them to Boston. In addition, the surge of migration into Marblehead during the early eighteenth century, much of it from England and Jersey, swelled local Episcopal support. Nearly two-thirds of the subscribers to St. Michael's building fund in 1714 had arrived in Marblehead after 1700.[52] Besides its numerical strength, the Church of England in town also enjoyed the support of a number of affluent residents. Most of St. Michael's members were no better off than other Marbleheaders, but a number of families from the local elite of merchants and shoremen provided the church with financial backing and leadership in the vestry. This group include John and James Calley, important fish merchants and political leaders; Dr. George Jackson and his son Bartholomew, physicians and shoremen; Nicholas Andrews, a trader and innkeeper; and John

---

[51] James Morss, *A Sermon on the Nativity of Our Lord . . . to which is added a Succinct History of the Episcopal Church in this Town and Vicinity* (Newburyport, 1838), 15–28; Henry Wilder Foote, *Annals of King's Chapel*, 2 vols. (Boston, 1882), I, 241, 250–53, 259; and Joshua Coffin, *A Sketch of the History of Newbury*, 176–84.

[52] Marbleheaders who were early contributors to King's Chapel, Boston, included members of the Calley, Skinner, Codner, and Woods families. (Foote, *Anals of King's Chapel*, I, 229–30, 265.) On the Jersey preference for Episcopalianism, see Konig, "A New Look at the Essex French," *EIHC*, 110: 171 and 178. Of the thirty-two local families who were among the initial subscribers to St. Michael's building fund, only six had settled in Marblehead before 1675. Another seven came to town between 1675 and 1699, and the remaining nineteen after 1700.

Oulton, a fish exporter from London who had served on the vestry of King's Chapel before moving his business to Marblehead.[53]

The contrast between Marblehead and Gloucester again is important. With its more homogeneous population, its lack of regular contact with the Episcopal captains and crews of British merchantmen, and its entrenched Congregationalist establishment, Gloucester was a far less congenial environment for Anglicanism—or any kind of religious dissent. The town's Quaker community remained numerically insignificant and became leaderless after Jonathan Springer died a bankrupt in 1715. But while Gloucester was steadily pushing its few dissenters out of town, religious diversity was becoming yet another source of division in Marblehead. St. Michael's members schemed to turn controversies among the Congregationalists to Episcopal advantage; Congregationalists systematically harrassed St. Michael's members. And both groups squabbled over exempting dissenters from taxes that supported the established clergy. The Anglican outpost at Marblehead also created tensions that spilled over town boundaries, after Salem's substantial contingent of Jersey families decided to worship at St. Michael's. Their Sabbath boat pilgrimages across the harbor to Marblehead were conducted in an atmosphere of unseemly festivity that raised the hackles of Salem's orthodox residents.[54] Religious differ-

[53] John Oulton was a warden at King's Chapel, Boston, before he moved to Marblehead; he owned merchantmen with a number of other fish exporters in Britain and Boston, including the two largest vessels registered at Boston in 1711. (Anson Titus, "Mr. John Oulton, Merchant," *New England Historical and Genealogical Register*, 53 (1899), 391–92; *MA*, 8:417–18.) James and John Calley were major local shoremen and traders: they both served frequently as selectmen and deputy to the General Court, and both received commissions as justices of the peace. Their inventoried assets put them among the wealthiest decile of decedents whose estates were probated in the 1730s. (EPF, #4539, 4536) Nicholas Andrews, a substantial shoreman and Dr. George Jackson, a physician with interests in the fishery, also served as selectman and deputy. (EPF, #700, 14685; and MTR, III.)

[54] Salem's First Church complained that "a great many" people at the eastern end of the Neck "under pretense of being of the Church of England, went to Marblehead in boats, [so] that our harbor appeared more like a day of frolicking than anything else." Cited in James Flint, *Two Discourses Delivered on Taking Leave of the Old Church of the East Society* (Salem, 1846), 5.

ences and sectarian competition were superadded to the social, economic, and cultural divisions splintering Marblehead, compounding the occasions for conflict among people who already had more than enough to fight about.

From the end of the seventeenth century throughout the first three decades of the eighteenth century, the shocks of war and economic expansion produced progressively more severe social and cultural fragmentation in Marblehead. The growth of the fishing industry, especially after 1713, fostered a high rate of inward and outward migration and continuing ethnic diversity. Increasing inequality and exploitation of labor, a rising level of debt, and a high incidence of crimes against persons and property also accompanied economic growth. Magnifying the impact of economic expansion was the persistent weakness of local institutions. The disarray and discontinuity of family life, the ascendant elite's disengagement from local concerns, and the growth of religious diversity reflected and reinforced the splintering of the community by economic pressures. No social organizations or bonds exerted sufficient influence to offset the dominant force of the market in Marblehead. Unimpeded by local loyalties, established institutions, or traditional sanctions, individuals of both sexes competed ruthlessly for financial advantage and sought private advancement through assertive, risk-taking behavior.

Change was occurring in early eighteenth-century Marblehead, but the transformation entailed no transition from "Puritan" order to "Yankee" freedom. Marblehead's evolution instead exemplified the pattern of descent from underdevelopment into anarchy typical of all boom towns. Although the commercial expansion of most other New England ports was accompanied by a similar concentration of wealth and a heightening of social tensions, observers of Marblehead all agreed that the town's troubles were truly extreme. In the eyes of contemporaries, Marblehead was a disturbing aberration within the Bible Commonwealth, a sort of cultural barnacle attached to the New England coast. Yet, if a community like postwar Marblehead had sprung up several hundred miles to the south and a few decades earlier, it would have been less of an anomaly. For the closest analogues to the town in British North America were not other commercial communities in early eighteenth-century Essex County but the settlements of the seventeenth-century Chesapeake. Like Marblehead's fishermen and shoremen, Virginia and Maryland planters produced a single commodity in demand among distant consumers, but played no part in its transport and marketing. This control over the commerce in tobacco by outside merchants, combined with the lack of any significant economic diversification and the vulnerability of the economy to natural disasters, failures in production, and fluctuations in price and demand, contributed to the notorious indebtedness of Chesapeake growers. A similar set of factors in the fishing economy produced the same problems in Marblehead. And in fishing and tobacco plantations alike, the initial period of economic expansion was accompanied by gross social and economic inequalities and injustices. The concentration of resources in the hands of a few families made for a markedly uneven distribution of wealth. The drive for profit led to efforts on the part of elites to extract the labor and restrict the freedom of an ethnically diverse work force. And both economic inequality and the exploitation of labor fueled hostility between rich and poor and fostered lawlessness and disorder.[55]

Even closer counterparts to Marblehead were the British settlements at Newfoundland, small coastal fishing villages established by the end of the seventeenth century. In Newfoundland as in Marblehead, a variety of ethnic groups relied for their livelihoods upon fishing rather than upon farming infertile soil. By decreasing the participation of West Country operators and reducing the advantage of the French, the first Anglo-French wars increased the control of Newfoundland settlers over the fishery and enhanced the prosperity of a few inhabitants. Even so, Newfoundland fishermen and shoremen, like Marbleheaders, limited their participation in the fishery to production, and relied upon Boston and the ports of Britain for marketing, provisions, and financial services. Because of their dependence upon outsiders, one eigh-

[55] Edmund S. Morgan, *American Slavery, American Freedom: The Ordeal of Colonial Virginia* (New York, 1975), see especially 108–249; and T. H. Breen, *Puritans and Adventurers: Persistence and Change in Early America* (New York, 1980), 127–47.

teenth-century observer deemed Newfoundland's permanent residents to be "no better than slaves." St. John's and surrounding settlements suffered the same chronic high level of indebtedness and criminal disorders and the same seasonal influx of transient seafarers that kept Marblehead's social life in disarray. The magnitude of the disruption in Newfoundland was made even more severe by the lack of any agencies for keeping the peace, save for the admirals of the fishing fleet who occasionally dispensed justice during the spring and summer months. But the absence of regular courts to adjudicate civil claims led to the forcible collection of debts by the seizure of property and to the practice of defaulters indenturing themselves to creditors.[56]

Marblehead's flawed social organization, like its economic difficulties, was also characteristic of other raw, boom towns in the early Chesapeake and Newfoundland. All of these settlements experienced a significant volume of in-migration sustained over a long span of time, and all had to contend with a sizable transient population of young males. The large numbers of new immigrants and strangers made these towns far less cohesive than those communities comprised mainly of the native-born. The fragile and fragmented domestic life that characterized Marblehead also appeared in the early communities of the Chesapeake and Newfoundland. In the South, the early deaths of parents from epidemic disease created conditions similar to the situation prevailing in Marblehead and Newfoundland because of the recurrent absences of fathers from households and the frequent losses of men at sea. In all of these settlements, discontinuity in family life gave parents less control over their children and contributed to higher rates of premarital pregnancy.[57] The

---

[56] Innis, *The Codfisheries*, 103, 147–48, 153, and 155–59; R. H. Lounsbury, *The British Fishery at Newfoundland, 1634–1763* (New Haven, 1934), 228, 246, 253–55.

[57] In Newfoundland, a total population of between two to three thousand in 1710 contained only about six hundred women and children. (Innis, *The Codfisheries*, 147–148.) For other information on the demographic development of Newfoundland, see note 56 above. The effects of sustained in-migration and high levels of transiency on Chesapeake society are discussed in Morgan, *American Slavery, American Freedom*, 237–38, 158–59; and in James Horn, "Servant Migration to the Chesapeake in the Seventeenth

early colonial South and Newfoundland also replicated Marblehead's weak religious institutions. In both places, churches developed late, the clergy exerted limited influence, and religion played a negligible role in the lives of most people.[58]

Finally, the deficiencies in the local elite that contributed to the instability in Marblehead created tensions in other boom towns as well. While Newfoundland lacked a resident ruling group until the mid-eighteenth century, the experience of the early South conforms closely to that of Marblehead. For most of the seventeenth century, the largest Chesapeake planters failed to identify with their adopted communities, felt no responsibility to lesser men, and participated in public affairs only to advance their private interests. Drawn to the New World by the prospect of capitalizing on the tobacco boom, they desired above all to end their days back in England. An equally apt parallel appears in the commercially developing North Carolina backcountry of the mid-eighteenth century. Here a wealthy, well-connected clique of newly arrived merchants and lawyers from the eastern part of the colony shouldered aside the native planter leadership and exploited the economic and political advantages afforded by their connections with the powerful eastern seaboard establishment to dominate local society. The tenuous legitimacy of new elites in Marblehead, as in the settlements of the early Chesapeake and the towns of western Carolina, augmented unrest and instability.[59] The problem of estab-

Century," and David Jordan, "Political Stability and the Emergence of a Native Elite in Maryland," both in *The Chesapeake in the Seventeenth Century: Essays on Anglo-American Society,* eds., Thad Tate and David Ammerman (Chapel Hill, 1979), 51, and 246–47. On the family in the seventeenth-century Chesapeake, see Morgan, *American Slavery, American Freedom,* 164–70, and Lorena S. Walsh, " 'Till Death Us Do Part': Marriage and the Family in Seventeenth-Century Maryland," in *The Chesapeake in the Seventeenth Century,* eds. Tate and Ammerman, 126–52.

[58] Lounsbury, *The British Fishery at Newfoundland,* 207–8; and William H. Seiler, "The Anglican Parish in Virginia," in *Seventeenth-Century America,* ed. James M. Smith (Chapel Hill, 1959), 119–42.

[59] Bernard Bailyn, "Politics and Social Structure in Virginia," *In Seventeenth-Century America,* ed., Smith, 90–115; Carole Shammas, "English-Born and Creole Elites in Turn of the Century Virginia," in *The Chesapeake in the Seventeenth Century,* eds. Tate and Ammerman, 274–296.

lishing social authority exacerbated the problem of maintaining order: disaffection with unpopular elites and the direction of social development precipitated explosive protest. In Virginia, the resistance produced Bacon's Rebellion; in North Carolina, the reaction resulted in the Regulator movement. And in Marblehead, too, the events of the 1720s pressed toward a violent culmination, as the crisis of local society came to a head.

8

The Church Militant

FOR MOST of the first century of their town's existence, Marbleheaders displayed little commitment to each other or to the welfare of the town as a whole. Almost every aspect of Marblehead's development conspired against the formation of a strong sense of corporate loyalty and local solidarity. As a satellite seaport, its economy was shaped to supply the commercial demands of Britain, Boston, and Salem rather than to satisfy the desires of native inhabitants. The climate of aggressive individualism that pervaded the conduct of the fishing industry produced competition and chronic conflict among townspeople. Membership in the community also changed constantly as maritime laborers moved in and out of town, the crews of English merchantmen came and went, and local fishermen and sailors spent several months away at sea. Finally, linguistic and cultural differences created discord among Marblehead's diverse ethnic groups, while sectarian rivalries or sheer indifference to spiritual concerns made religion another source of disunity. All of these conditions limited the ability of Marbleheaders to regard themselves as members of the same community, and the recurrent strife that undermined social cohesion also overwhelmed the capacity of townspeople to create an ordered society. Throughout the seventeenth century and well into the eighteenth century, Marblehead inhabitants did nothing to curb the chaos of their daily lives, to create institutions that would promote public welfare, or to curtail their dependence upon Massachusetts's larger ports. The struggle of wringing a livelihood from the fishery, satisfying the demands of creditors and middlemen, and coping with disorder at home and intermittent eruptions of warfare in the Atlantic consumed the energies of most Marbleheaders.

Notwithstanding the many weaknesses of communal life in Marblehead, its inhabitants had at times recognized their common interests and unified to defend them. A few sparks of something like local solidarity flickered fitfully in occasional outbursts against external interference in town life, like the murder of the Indian captives in 1677 and the riot against the removal of the guns from Marblehead harbor in 1690. Communal feeling coalesced into collective protest at widely spaced intervals, whenever townspeople felt particularly threatened by the intrusion of outside influences. These sporadic manifestations of local identification and defensiveness in the late seventeenth century produced no longlasting results and did nothing to strengthen social stability. But such episodes are important because they point up the potential of antipathy toward "outsiders" to unify Marbleheaders. Moreover, this resentment of external control over local life deepened during the early decades of the eighteenth century, becoming a powerful force for conflict and change within the town.

What spurred local resistance to external domination in the early eighteenth century was the growing strength of outsiders in Marblehead. As the local fishery assumed a central position in New England commerce, strangers who during the seventeenth century had manipulated the destinies of Marbleheaders from a distance now worked from within the town itself. They did so through factors and agents like Edward Brattle, the Marblehead representative of a powerful Boston merchant family. The cessation of the first Anglo-French wars in 1713 inaugurated an increase in the ranks of this imported elite of nonnative traders and sea captains. During the postwar years, a second wave of these cosmopolitan immigrants from Boston, Salem, and the ports of Great Britain began pouring into town, tightening the grip of larger ports on local social and economic life. In the eyes of most Marbleheaders, such newcomers were as much "outsiders" as the bigger men with whom these immigrants did business, and they incurred the same suspicion and resentment. The deepening antagonism between natives and resident "strangers" intensified social conflict within town.

But while the growing prominence of outsiders in town compounded Marblehead's internal problems, it also stimulated the development of a stronger sense of local allegiance and solidarity among many families. The force of popular antipathy, once diffused among many distant enemies, now focused on nonnative leaders like Edward Brattle, men who personified outside control. Especially after 1713, townspeople contended directly against individuals who represented in Marblehead the interests and influence of larger ports. Confronting a common enemy at close range gave Marbleheaders a basis for unity. And as townspeople rallied to protest the domination of local society by the demands of outsiders, they also began to resist the molding of life in Marblehead by the impersonal forces of the market. The rising disorder and instability produced in town by the postwar boom led many inhabitants to reject a social order based on mobility, diversity, and assertive individualism. As a result, accompanying Marbleheaders' awakening sense of localism was their increasing attraction to conservative values. A growing number of residents came to prize the importance not only of local autonomy but also of a disciplined communal order, a "public-spirited" elite, and conformity to Congregationalist orthodoxy. These values, which had traditionally been the basis of social organization in other New England towns like Gloucester since early in the seventeenth century, began to take hold in Marblehead for the first time during the opening decades of the eighteenth century. At the center of this reaction against the direction of Marblehead's first century of development were the members of the First Congregational Church and their pastor, the Reverend John Barnard. What Marblehead gained in stability and autonomy by 1750 was due largely to the changes brought about in the town's life by this group. But in the wake of the initial stirrings of this militant localism and cultural conservatism among the First Church congregation came a rising tide of conflict and violence that enveloped Marblehead for fifteen years following Barnard's arrival in town.

The animosity building among Marblehead natives against Edward Brattle and other powerful outsiders in town first found an outlet in a controversy at the First Congregational Church over two ministerial candidates. This bitter dispute represented the first organized resistance to the growing domination of local life by Bostonians and their clients and connections within the Marblehead elite. The conflict among the Congregationalists began with the decision to find an assistant for the Reverend Samuel Cheever, the First Church's aging pastor. By December of 1714, three candidates, John Barnard, Edward Holyoke, and Ames Cheever had preached on probation. The church members were considering Ames Cheever, the undistinguished son of their present pastor, only as a courtesy. The real contest was between Barnard and Holyoke, and the strength of feeling for both candidates was such that on December 13th, the members of First Church resolved that, whichever candidate commanded a majority, "the rest of the Brethren should look upon themselves obliged to abide by it as the Church's act." In the balloting that followed, seventeen of the twenty-eight male church members voted for John Barnard.[1] By February of 1715, the town had concurred in the church's choice and sent a delegation to Boston to inform Barnard of his selection. The majority vote of the church and the town for John Barnard should have settled the matter of selecting Marblehead's next minister, but did not. Ignoring the church's resolution of December 13th, a number of influential men in the First Church congregation continued to lobby for Edward Holyoke.[2]

The quarrel over calling Marblehead's next minister did not involve significant differences between the two candidates themselves. For Edward Holyoke and John Barnard, at this stage of their careers, could easily have been confused with each other. Both were the Harvard-educated sons of substantial Bostonians; both had secular intellectual inter-

[1] MFCR, December 13, 1714.

[2] "Autobiography of John Barnard," 3 Collections of the Massachusetts Historical Society (Boston, 1836), V, 217, cited hereafter as "Autobiography of Barnard"; Hathaway, The Second Congregational Church, 4.

ests in the new science; and both had reputations for religious liberalism that had made it difficult for them to obtain permanent settlements. Samuel Sewall, the staunchly orthodox chief justice of Massachusetts Bay, detected a smattering of Arminianism in the sermons that Barnard had delivered at Boston's churches, while he censured almanacs compiled by Holyoke for their "Anglican bias," calendar references to Easter, Michaelmas, and Christmas. A certain cosmopolitan sensibility, an engagement with the wider Anglo-American world, characterized the two men as well. While a tutor at Harvard in math and astronomy, Holyoke corresponded with London scientists and imported the latest instruments from Europe for measuring solar eclipses. Meanwhile, Barnard was serving as chaplain in a military expedition against French Canada and later on a ship bound for London. During his stay in England, he became acquainted with Episcopal clergymen, whose polite manners and learning left a favorable impression. While abroad Barnard also socialized with several "considerable merchants," who solicited his services as a partner, possibly encouraged because he dressed more like "a small courtier than a dissenting preacher."[3]

Over these two seemingly interchangeable candidates, Marbleheaders divided bitterly. By the summer of 1715, Holyoke's supporters were openly collecting money to provide their preferred candidate with his own pulpit and themselves with a new parish. Undeterred by their opponents' threat of separation, Barnard's backers went ahead and urged their candidate to accept the position as Cheever's assistant. But Barnard now demurred, "knowing . . . some of the chief men in town were very fond of settling Mr. Holyoke."[4]

While many wealthy and prominent Marblehead Congregationalists did favor Holyoke's candidacy, the contest in the First Church was no simple alignment of a rich and powerful minority against a poorer and more obscure majority. The division reflected instead the way in which Marblehead's economic expansion had split the town's leading families into hostile camps of established natives and newcomers. Comprising the core of Barnard's support in the First Church

[3] *SHG*, V, 265–77; IV, 501–12; "Autobiography of Barnard," 191–209.
[4] "Autobiography of Barnard," 217; MFCR, February 10, 1715.

were members of the old elite, the more parochial and deeply rooted leaders of the local society who, lacking business and personal ties to larger ports, were declining in relative affluence and influence. The new families eclipsing this older ruling group were the leading supporters of Edward Holyoke.[5]

Nearly half of Edward Holyoke's adherents came from the ranks of relatively recent arrivals in Marblehead, the successful immigrants of the late seventeenth century like Edward Brattle, Richard Skinner, Richard Crafts, and Eleazur Ingalls. In addition to these newcomers, Holyoke also counted among his supporters prominent native families allied with the immigrant elite, those whose rise to the top of society began at the end of the seventeenth century. The ancestors of Holyoke-faction members like Richard Trevett, Captain Andrew Tucker, and Captain John Stacey had not been especially distinguished members of early Marblehead, but these three shoremen laid the foundations of family fortunes by success in the fishery, won political office, and ended their careers as merchants. Some of Holyoke's backing did come from a few native men whose local prominence dated from early in the seventeenth century, and one of them, Colonel John Legg,

---

[5] To analyze the alignment over ministerial candidates at the First Church, I reconstructed the Congregationalist leadership in Marblehead at the time of the controversy. No tax list for Marblehead survives from this period, so I based my reconstruction on inventories, including in that group of Congregationalist leaders any head of household worth over three hundred pounds sterling. This yields a total of twenty-seven men and women, fifteen of whom supported Holyoke and twelve, Barnard. As a group, Holyoke's supporters were twice as wealthy as Barnard's backers: the median estate value of Holyoke's supporters was 702 pounds sterling, and the average estate value 1010 pounds sterling, while for Barnard's faction the figures are 323 and 545 respectively. (Source: Essex Probate Files, Registry of Probate, Essex County Courthouse, Salem. Mass.) Holyoke's party also contained a larger number of people who were not well-established in town: six of the fifteen had not been among Marblehead's householders in 1674, but all except one of Barnard's leading supporters or their families were. An equally important point of contrast between the two groups is the disparity in former family prominence in town. While eight of Barnard's twelve leading supporters came from families whose members had held the office of selectman in the seventeenth century, serving altogether a total of fifty-one terms, only five members of Holyoke's faction descended from seventeenth-century selectmen, a group that served a net total of only thirteen terms. (For officeholding in the seventeenth century, see Bowden, comp., "Marblehead Town Records, 1648–1683," EIHC, 69: 207–329.)

was probably the town's most distinguished citizen. But this small segment of the established elite that supported Holyoke was closely linked with relative newcomers: Legg's two daughters were Madame Elizabeth Browne, the widow of English immigrant Captain John Browne, and Madame Mary Brattle, Edward's wife.

Most members of Marblehead's ascendant elite had not bothered to become full church members. As a result, they were barred from voting in the church election of December 13th and were unable to command majority support for their candidate. Neither were they the sort of men who felt bound to abide by the will of the rest of the town. They placed a greater premium on private preference than communal consensus, so they felt no compunction about seeking a separation from the First Church in the name of getting their own way. What made these families so set upon having Edward Holyoke in particular was the influence of a man who could distinguish between the Harvard tutor and John Barnard, namely Boston merchant Thomas Brattle, the treasurer of Harvard College. Thomas, through brother Edward Brattle in Marblehead, conveyed the message that there was all the difference in the world between the two candidates. And the "chief men" in Marblehead were not in the habit of ignoring directives from Boston.

The support of the Brattles and their circle for Edward Holyoke guaranteed John Barnard a staunch constituency among their rivals. Most members of the old native leadership and the majority of Marbleheaders had tired of the capital calling the shots, and they were determined not to allow Bostonians, their clients, and their connections among Marblehead's imported elite to name the town's next minister. To counter their opponents' threat to divide the parish and to deprive the First Church clergy of their financial support, Barnard's backers hit upon a most unexpected strategy. They struck a bargain with the vestrymen of St. Michael's to share local tax revenues for the support of the Congregationalist ministry with the Episcopal rector. According to the terms of their agreement in September of 1715, as long as only two ministers were in town, Cheever and Barnard, the First Parish would receive two-thirds of the rates and St. Michael's one-third; the establishment of a second Congregational

Church would automatically invalidate the agreement. The parties also pledged that "Both the Old Church and the Church of England shall Stand by One Another in Defending Each Others Rights and Priviledges . . . against any Party that shall make any Disturbance or Divisions in the Town for destroying of our Peace. . . ."[6]

To find Congregationalists offering to help maintain an Anglican clergy with a portion of local taxes is novel enough, for up to that time no group of Churchmen in New England had been exempted from paying for the support of the orthodox ministry. But even more remarkable is the way that the agreement of 1715 reversed previous social alignments in Marblehead. Many members of Marblehead's ascendant Congregationalist elite had strong kinship connections and marital ties to locally prominent families with Episcopal sympathies. The brothers and brothers-in-law of several members of Holyoke's faction were among the founders of St. Michael's. And in the years following the church's establishment, its communicants continued to intermarry with families like the Brownes and the Brattles, whose sons-in-law included St. Michael's members John Oulton and Captain David LeGallais and King's Chapel vestryman James Smith. With one out of every five of their children selecting an Episcopal partner, many families in the Holyoke faction had at least one marital connection to a St. Michael's member. The alliance was a natural one, for like their Congregationalist relatives and in-laws, Marblehead's Anglican elite included many recent immigrants and newly successful native men. These bonds of blood and marriage should have put St. Michael's vestry solidly on the side of Holyoke supporters. Instead, the agreement of 1715 allied local Anglicans with Barnard's faction at First Church, a group with few social ties to St. Michael's families. No blood relationships and only two marriages linked Barnard's supporters to a founding member of St. Michael's, and after the church's establishment intermarriage was equally infrequent.[7] In con-

---

[6] The original agreement of 1715 is at the Essex Institute. It appears in full in Thomas Barrow, "Church Politics in Marblehead, 1715," *EIHC*, 48 (1962), 122.

[7] This conclusion is based upon a correlation of genealogical reconstructions of the twenty-seven families with the church affiliation of the families

trast to Holyoke's party, Barnard's backers had kept—and were to maintain—their distance from Anglican families.

This social distance between the two parties to the agreement of 1715 indicates that their bargain owed nothing to any ecumenical acceptance of Episcopalianism on the part of Barnard's faction. Indeed, Holyoke's supporters seem to have been the more broadminded and "catholic" group within Marblehead's Congregationalist camp. But the agreement of 1715 owed everything to the intense desire of Barnard's backers to thwart the scheme for establishing a Second Church. The hostility among Barnard's advocates toward the likes of Edward Brattle exceeded even their prejudice against the Anglicans. Shrewdly exploiting the close familial and marital relationships between members of the Holyoke faction and local Anglicans, the agreement of 1715 confronted Edward Brattle and his circle with a distasteful choice. They could either accede to the selection of Barnard and remain within the First Parish, or they could insist on their own candidate and alienate Anglican in-laws and associates. By making the Episcopalians an offer of support that they could not refuse, Barnard's faction put their adversaries at First Church in a situation in which they could not win.[8] And from the vantage point of St. Michael's vestry, the agreement of 1715 was an offer too tempting to pass up. First, there was the attractive prospect of enhancing the Church of

with whom their children intermarried prior to 1715. Seven of the fifteen Holyoke supporters had at least one Anglican son or daughter-in-law, and three others had brothers or brothers-in-law who attended St. Michael's. By contrast, only two of Barnard's twelve supporters had marital or family ties to St. Michael's. (For identifying members of the local Anglican communion, I have relied upon "St. Michael's Records," including the minutes of meetings, and records of baptisms and marriages.)

[8] Thomas Barrow interprets the agreement of 1715 as a sign of the tolerant attitudes of Barnard and his supporters in "Church Politics in Marblehead, 1715," *EIHC*, 48:122–27. If Barrow had traced the social background of the participants in the contested ministerial candidacy or explored the subsequent history of intersectarian relations in town, he could not have reached this conclusion. Moreover, his evidence for Barnard's support for St. Michael's is based on misidentifying as the minister a "Mr. John Barnard" whose name appears on the list of subscribers to St. Michael's building fund. This donor was not the Reverend John Barnard, but a London merchant, who during trips to Boston also contributed to the support of King's Chapel. (See Foote, *Annals of King's Chapel*, I, 240.)

England's position in town by gaining tax support. And second, if the agreement succeeded in dissuading Holyoke's adherents from forming a second parish, the most disaffected might be drawn into St. Michael's communion. Eagerness to exploit this division within the Congregationalist camp made Episcopalians willing to abandon their family members, in-laws, and friends in the Holyoke faction. St. Michael's vestry instead threw themselves into the arms of Barnard's more parochial and less ecumenical backers, the First Parish majority. It was a politically astute if unlikely alliance. And it was not the last time in Marblehead that Anglicans would attempt to turn the rising tide of localistic loyalty and antipathy to outside domination to their own advantage. Nor was it the last time that strife caused by the private preferences of the cosmopolitan Congregationalist elite would bring together the town's Anglicans and John Barnard's supporters at First Church.

The conclusion of the contest between Marblehead's Congregationalists satisfied none of the parties involved in the controversy. St. Michael's did not benefit long from the agreement of 1715 because John Barnard's admiration for the Church of England did not extend to its outpost in Marblehead. Appalled by the prospect of pioneering a revenue-sharing plan with Episcopalians, he refused to accept the call from First Church unless his supporters abrogated their bargain with the Anglicans and agreed to Holyoke's installation as pastor of a new Second Church. Barnard's backers quickly acceded to their candidate's demands. By the beginning of 1716, Barnard was assisting Samuel Cheever at First, and the recently gathered Second Church of Marblehead had a new pastor and Madame Elizabeth Browne a new son-in-law, the Reverend Edward Holyoke. But local Anglicans were left only with lasting bitterness. Although many of the leading members of St. Michael's went on trading and intermarrying with Holyoke's prominent parishioners, the nullification of the agreement of 1715 rankled most Marblehead Churchmen. The support of both an orthodox ministry by compulsory taxes and an Episcopal rector by voluntary contributions strained the slim means of Anglican fishermen and laborers. Most communicants shared their rector's resentment of both Second Church, "Built in Damnable Spite and Malice against the Church of England," and John Barnard, for his role in breaking the agreement of 1715.[9] While the resolution of the contested ministerial candidacy strained relations between Marblehead's competing religious groups, it also failed to restore amity among the Congregationalists. Second Parish's leading men, chagrined at being first outvoted, then outmaneuvered, and finally made the objects of John Barnard's magnanimity, made a point of scheduling Holyoke's ordination well before Barnard's induction at First Church. This intentional violation of ecclesiastical protocol, a final display of contempt for the choice of the First Church and the majority of Marbleheaders, so infuriated Barnard's congregation that they refused to attend Holyoke's ordination.[10]

Although the events of 1715 and 1716 deepened divisions among townspeople, the campaign for the candidacy of John Barnard represented the first sustained assertion of local autonomy on the part of a majority of Marblehead's inhabitants. Barnard's backers did not enjoy a total triumph, for their strategy to keep Holyoke's supporters from forming a separate church failed. Still, native Congregationalist families succeeded in installing their choice as Cheever's assistant at First Church. And the contest over ministerial candidates was only the opening shot in a battle against the domination of Marblehead by outsiders that spanned the next three decades. It seems rather strange that Marblehead's most deeply rooted and parochial families chose as their minister an urbane Bostonian reputed for theological liberalism and enlightened ecumenicism. Still more unlikely is that Barnard's candidacy became the cause behind which townspeople rallied to express their distrust of cosmopolitan influences. The asset of being

[9] William Shaw to the Secretary of the S.P.G., January 13, 1716, in *Historical Collections*, ed. Perry, III, 116. On the economic standing of eighteenth-century Episcopalians in New England generally, see Bruce E. Steiner, "New England Anglicanism: A Genteel Faith?" *WMQ*, 3rd ser., 27 (1970), 129–35.

[10] "Autobiography of Barnard," 217; "Records of the Second Church of Marblehead," MS, April, 1716, repr. in *Memorial History of the Unitarian Church of Marblehead, Massachusetts, Commemorating the 250th Anniversary* (Marblehead, 1966). Minutes of the Second Church's meetings have been lost, but a copy of membership during the eighteenth century still exists at the Unitarian Church of Marblehead.

unknown to the Brattles undoubtedly gave Barnard an initial advantage. But his real appeal to native Marbleheaders
became more apparent once, after his installation as Cheever's assistant, the First Church's new minister began living
down his reputation.

John Barnard shared with other early eighteenth-century
observers of Marblehead a low opinion of the town's moral
tone. His impression of townspeople upon his arrival was
that "they were as rude, drunken, swearing, and fighting a
crew as they were poor." But Barnard was unique in assign-
ing the source of local troubles to something other than the
moral deficiencies of its maritime population. According to
Barnard, the critical weakness of the community was economic: Marbleheaders were "in debt to the merchants [of
larger ports]. . . . more than they were worth." Underlying
this dependency of townspeople was a larger liability, their
failure to market their own fish. Marbleheaders would never
gain control over their lives as long as they "contented themselves to be the slaves that digged the mines, and left the
merchants of Boston, Salem, and Europe to carry away the
gains." To realize the greatest returns on the town's principal resource and to extricate themselves from the web of
indebtedness, Marbleheaders had to break into the transatlantic trade circuit monopolized by Boston, Salem, and the
ports of Britain. Townsmen needed to develop a fleet of locally
owned merchantmen that could transport the catch from town
wharves to Europe and the West Indies.

Convinced that the "town had a price in its hand," if only
"I could stir up my people to send the fish to market themselves," John Barnard started spending time down at the
docks, talking to the "English masters of vessels . . . that I
might be let into the mysteries of the fishing trade." Once he
had acquired "a pretty thorough understanding of the business," the parson began disseminating his ideas about local
economic development, especially among the younger men
of his congregation. With Barnard's encouragement, some
of these townsmen, like Joseph Swett, Jr., were undertaking
their first coastwise trading ventures by the 1720s. This program for curtailing the control of Marblehead's commerce
by nonlocal merchants and their resident middlemen ultimately figured as a fundamental part of the campaign against

external domination of the town. But decades of dependency on outsiders made culling disciples from the ranks of First Church shoremen, fishermen, and artisans a slow process. Barnard confessed that at first "I could inspire no man with courage and resolution enough to engage in it [the fish trade]." [11]

Perhaps because he recognized the obstacles to any rapid expansion of Marblehead's direct trade, John Barnard implemented other strategies for bringing order to town that promised more immediate results. Despite his thoroughly secular diagnosis of Marblehead's social ills in its economic difficulties and his interest in the intricacies of the fishing trade, Barnard was deeply engaged in his pastoral duties and in the religious concerns of his day. To increase lay involvement in local ecclesiastical life, he urged his congregation to avail themselves of membership under the more inclusive halfway covenant, a measure that brought more Marbleheaders under church discipline. He also instituted a variety of other practices designed to increase his parishioners' participation in the church. Shortly after his installation, the First Church chose two additional deacons, raising the number of these officers from one to three. Barnard also included a number of the church's most prominent lay members in delegations to ordination councils held in neighboring parishes. And although the First Church instituted no ruling eldership, Barnard frequently asked the brethren to admonish backsliding members privately before the entire church heard cases calling for discipline. [12]

As the strengthening of discipline at First Church suggests, Barnard's campaign to curb disorder in town coupled measures for enhancing lay engagement in religious life with a concern for improving the personal morality of church members. The kinds of discipline cases that came before the church in the 1720s and 1730s point to a particular concern with problems of sexual promiscuity and domestic disruption. In May of 1727, for example, First Church members considered the case of Mary Graham, a woman suspected of marrying a second husband while her first, a fisherman, was

[11] "Autobiography of Bernard," 239–40.
[12] MFCR, March 12, 1716, November 4, 1716, August 24, 1720.

still alive. But the most notorious of these disciplinary actions was the excommunication of Sarah Hendley Westcott in 1720. Barnard included in the church records a detailed account of lay members' private endeavors to encourage her repentance as well as a verbatim dialogue between Sarah and himself before the entire congregation.[13] Barnard appreciated the influence that he could exert among male parishioners by establishing himself as a credible guardian of female virtue, and this public confrontation with so egregious an offender as Sarah provided an ideal opportunity. It also afforded Barnard a chance to dramatize for his parishioners the benefits of a strong church discipline.

The First Church's concern for stricter oversight of sexual mores was not, however, restricted to female members. In 1727, Marblehead's saints heard the case of David Parker, an affluent shoreman and selectman accused of fathering an illegitimate child. Nor were the cases of male members charged with sexual misconduct confined to their alleged indiscretions with women. In 1732, four male church members claimed to have witnessed Ebenezer Knight engaged in "impure and sinful practices" and "a long series of Uncleanness with Mankind," probably references to homosexual activities. Knight confessed and declared his repentance, but the church still suspended him from communion. He was not restored to membership until he returned to town after a sojourn of six years in Boston. Efforts to extend the church's disciplinary function cut across the lines of class as well as those of gender. The case of David Parker indicates that at First Marblehead, as at First Gloucester, wealth and social position granted no one immunity from the surveillance of the saints. While members cleared Parker of the charge of sexual misconduct, they admonished him for "a vain, Impure and Scornful way of talk both relating to himself and others."[14]

At the same time that Barnard was invigorating discipline at First Church, he was also trying to strengthen Congregationalist orthodoxy in Marblehead by one other means—

[13] *Ibid.*, September 11, 1720.
[14] *Ibid.*, May 18, 1727, May 25, 1727, February 4, 1732.

exploiting the prejudice against its competition, the Church of England. Despite his earlier friendships with Episcopal clergymen in London, Barnard came to share the increasing alarm of his Congregationalist colleagues over aggressive Anglican proselytizing in settled New England communities. Initial efforts on the part of some liberal Massachusetts ministers to cooperate with the missionary aims of the Society for the Propagation of the Gospel at the beginning of the eighteenth century had quickly given way to suspicion of Episcopal objectives. And in the 1720s several developments produced near-panic in New England Puritan ranks over Episcopal encroachments. First, there was the "Yale Apostasy" of 1722, the defection of Timothy Cutler, the head of the college, two Yale tutors, and the minister of a New Haven Congregational church, to the Church of England. Shortly thereafter, Connecticut residents received word that an Anglican church, the first in that colony, was to be built at Stratford. Meanwhile, in Massachusetts, the attacks of John Checkley were arousing a furor among the orthodox clergy and laity of Boston. A member of King's Chapel in Boston, Checkley held the most extreme opinions of the High Church party, and for a time his views commanded considerable support among other local Anglican leaders. In a pamphlet published in 1720, he defended the apostolic origins of the episcopacy and charged that all Congregationalist ordinances, including baptism and ordination, were invalid. The General Court finally silenced Checkley in 1724 by fining him for printing and selling libel against the orthodox clergy, but the Anglican assault on other fronts was sustained by his fellow churchmen: Timothy Cutler, now the rector of Christ Church, Boston's second Anglican chapel; Samuel Johnson, missionary to the church at Stratford; and George Pigot of Marblehead. Throughout the 1720s, these three S.P.G. missionaries pressed London for the appointment of an American bishop. During the same years, Cutler lobbied for Anglican representation on the Harvard College board of overseers and for the founding of a separate Episcopal college. While Anglican leaders succeeded neither in instituting an American episcopate, nor in establishing a college, nor in storming the citadel of Harvard, their efforts persuaded most ortho-

dox New Englanders that the Church of England was implementing a master plan to destroy the Congregationalist
establishment.[15]

These Anglican challenges to orthodoxy intensified religious tensions throughout New England during the early
eighteenth century. Clergymen from the two competing
churches waged a war of words in pamphlets and newspa-
pers and from their pulpits. But while the agitation was general, sectarian antagonism had the greatest potential for
generating severe social disruption in towns like Marblehead, where Episcopalians were encamped a few yards from
the First Church meetinghouse. The problem in Marblehead
was not only the proximity of the Anglican community but
also the power that they exerted within town. With Anglican
families comprising perhaps a quarter of the population,
religious heterodoxy was not the bar to political and economic success in Marblehead that it was in Gloucester. St.
Michael's vestry included a number of the town's wealthiest
merchants and shoremen, who ranked among Marblehead's
most important officeholders. Anglicans were numerous
enough to place one of their brethren on the board of selectmen every year during the 1720s. Divisions among the Congregationalists also allowed St. Michael's members several
terms as Marblehead's representative to the General Court
during the same decade. Good connections with Bostonians
and the Second Church elite even garnered Churchmen
appointments as justices of the peace in Essex County. Possessed of considerable influence, Marblehead's leading Episcopalians did not shrink from efforts to advance their sectarian
interests. They promoted the proposals for instituting an
American episcopate and petitioned the governor to put an
Anglican clergyman on the Harvard board of overseers.[16]

[15] Carl Bridenbaugh, *Mitre and Sceptre: Transatlantic Faiths, Ideas, Person-
alities, and Politics, 1689–1775* (New York, 1962), 59 and 78–80; Foote,
Annals of King's Chapel, II, chapters I, VII, and VIII; Miller, *The New
England Mind: From Colony to Province,* 468–75; Middlekauff, *The
Mathers,* 221–22, 359–60.

[16] David Mossom estimated that Episcopalians comprised seventy to eighty
of the town's three hundred families in 1724, a figure probably inflated
somewhat to impress the S.P.G. (Mossom to S.P.G. Sec'y, April 18, 1724,
in Historical Collections, ed., Perry, III, 149–50. Besides their strength on

And since the founding of their church in 1714, St. Michael's members had been aggressively agitating for relief from the taxes that supported the Congregationalist clergy in town.

Appraising the difficulties of his own situation as coolly as he did the troubles of Marblehead, John Barnard realized that St. Michael's was a force to be reckoned with. So, while Edward Holyoke at Second Church was socializing with the leading members of St. Michael's and making solicitous notes in his diary of the departure and arrival of their vessels, over at First, Barnard was launching a vigorous counter-offensive against the Church of England.[17] Barnard's first published attack on Anglicanism appeared in 1725, in a sermon appended to *Ashton's Memorial,* his popular account of the adventures of a local fisherman. Taken captive by pirates in the north Atlantic, Philip Ashton survived every conceivable hardship and catastrophe before making his way back to Marblehead and relating his exploits to parson Barnard. In his homily, Barnard compared Ashton's doughty resistance to the seductions of piracy to the Biblical story of three young Jews who refused to accept the "idolatrous worship" of King Nebuchadnezzar's golden image. Their steadfastness in the true faith enraged the king of the "bigotted Chaldeans," who dispatched to the royal furnace anyone "that Dared Dissent from his Established Religion." Divine intervention delivered the three Jews from this punishment, which, according to Barnard, demonstrated the Lord's special care for those believers who were governed "more by the Dictates of their own Minds, informed by the Law of God . . . than by Royal Will and Pleasure." Such faith, Barnard promised, was proof

the board of selectmen, between 1715 and 1730 Episcopalians John and James Calley and John Oulton received appointments as justices of the peace, and nine of the twenty terms of deputy to the General Court were also served by Anglicans. In addition, ten of the forty-two Marblehead decedents inventoried who ranked among the wealthiest quartile between 1716 and 1735 were Anglicans. (Sources: Essex Probate Files, Registry of Probate, Essex County Courthouse, Salem, Mass.; MTR, III, 1721–1729; Whittemore, *Massachusetts Civil List,* 132–33.) For Marbleheaders' support of Cutler's efforts to gain Episcopal representation on the Harvard board of overseers, see "Memorial of Sundry Ministers and Others of the Church of England in New England," December, 1727, *MA,* 11: 431.

[17] *The Holyoke Diaries,* 3–4.

against the "best laid schemes" and "craftiest plots" of one's adversaries.[18]

Barnard's homily may seem a straightforward retelling of a story from the Old Testament, but eighteenth-century Marbleheaders recognized in his language a more ambitious agenda. If Sarah Westcott, a housemaid, had enough sophistication to claim that the Scriptures were internally contradictory and that St. Paul, not Christ, had instituted church discipline, most Marblehead fishermen knew that when idolatry, bigotry, crafty schemes, persecution, and arbitrary royal authority turned up in the same plot, the story was not about Chaldeans but about Churchmen. Nor could they have missed the implication of Barnard's allegorical assertion that membership in the Episcopal communion entailed unquestioning conformity to the dictates of bishops and kings back in England. In the parson's view, this allegiance to a distant, hierarchical authority was dangerous because it limited the strength of all other loyalties and compromised any capacity for real autonomy in thought or action. "I would turn Churchman tomorrow," Barnard declared, if given "any clear proof and tolerable satisfaction that the great Head of the Church had empowered any man or number of men, civil or ecclesiastical, upon earth, to give law to his church, to appoint the regimen, modes of worship, and what ceremonies they pleased." But since the Church of England could not produce such a demonstration, "I refuse coming under the yoke of bondage to any merely human authority."[19] This sort of talk must have impressed independent-minded Marbleheaders, who had themselves experienced the effects of subjection to distant powers. And after sitting under the parson's

[18] John Barnard, God's Ability to Save His People, appended to Ashton's Memorial (Boston, 1725), 45–46. Ashton's Memorial is less strenuously edifying and much more exciting than other clerical publications aimed at reclaiming members of the fishing community. Besides relating Ashton's adventures, the Memorial also provides a vivid picture of his pirate captors, especially their captain, "the infamous Ned Low," who is portrayed with considerable sympathy. Cf. Thomas Cheever, The Mariner's Divine Mate, or Spiritual Navigation (Boston, 1715), and Cotton Mather, The Fisherman's Calling (Boston, 1716).

[19] "Autobiography of Barnard," 207. For Sarah Westcott's religious views, see MFCR, September 11, 1720.

preaching, they could eye only with suspicion anyone who would submit willingly to such external influences.

Barnard's account of Philip Ashton's adventures probably attracted a wide audience among the fisherfolk of Marblehead. The pastor's ability to relate orthodox religion to the lives of ordinary people, combined with his popular attack upon Episcopalianism and his revitalization of ecclesiastical institutions that promoted order, gave John Barnard the largest congregation in Marblehead. Increased church membership was the measure of his success: nearly 200 people became full members of First Church and over 300 owned its covenant between 1715 and 1730, the first fifteen years of Barnard's ministry.[20] This was double the number of admissions during the fifteen years prior to Barnard's arrival in Marblehead. Of course, his predecessor, Samuel Cheever, had worked among a smaller total population, but unlike Barnard, he had not contended with competition from the Anglicans and a second Congregational church in town. Barnard's achievement was impressive.

Perhaps it was this success that tempted Barnard into abandoning allegory in favor of overt ridicule in his next published attack on Anglicanism. This was a sermon condemning the Episcopal custom of celebrating Christmas that he delivered at First Church in December of 1729, a performance that even St. Michael's rector conceded was "long expected and much applauded." According to Barnard, commemorating Christmas was not only superstitious, since not even the most learned theologians had been able to determine the true date of the Nativity, but downright foolish. He explained to his congregation that during those cold winters in Judea, no sensible shepherds would have been watching on a hillside and hearkening unto the herald angels. ("Could any of you stay out in One of our Severe Frosts?") Nor were stupidity and superstition the worst of it, he continued, for Christmas was never a custom practiced among primitive Christians. The feast was instead a "Romish inno-

[20] Under Samuel Cheever, 98 new full members were admitted to the First Church between 1700 and 1715; under Barnard, between 1716 and 1730, 183 new full members were admitted and 332 halfway members. No record of halfway admissions under Cheever survives. (Source: MFCR.)

vation," a Christianizing of the pagan festival of the Saturnalia calculated to attract converts from the ranks of the heathen. And Anglican fesitivities in commemoration of the day still smacked of these dark origins:

> 'Tis indeed a common appendage to vain Superstition, to be mightily concerned for the outside, and regard the shew only while the Inward and Vital Part of Religion, pretended to be promoted thereby, is greatly Neglected. This we have a sad Instance of, in those that are so Strongly Set to keep a Day in Commemoration of the Birth of Christ (any day rather than none) that instead of observing it in an Holy and Religious Manner . . . it is more generally a day separate to Vanity and Folly, to Sin and Debauchery, to Revelling and Drunkenness.

Not simply misguided ceremonialism, the Anglican Christmas was for Barnard a violation of order and civility, an invitation for men to backslide into vice and "to sacrifice to Devils."[21]

Nothing in Barnard's attack upon Anglicanism was particularly novel. His criticisms of ecclesiastical hierarchy and his strictures against superstition and ceremonialism were staples of stock anti-Anglican polemics produced a few years earlier by Cotton and Increase Mather. But Barnard presented these familiar themes in popular, accessible forms. *Ashton's Memorial* vividly recreates the exploits of a local hero and a shipload of colorfully depraved buccaneers, purportedly in Philip Ashton's own words. And the Christmas sermon, delivered during the winter season when everyone was in town to hear, was couched in such simple language that St. Michael's rector sneered that the parson stooped to persuade through "Homely Arguments." Barnard was a the-

[21] John Barnard, *The Certainty, Time and End of the Birth of Our Lord and Saviour, Jesus Christ* (Boston, 1731), 28 and 31–33. For a similar argument against the celebration of Christmas, see Cotton Mather, *Advice from the Watchtower* (Boston, 1713). Barnard's rejection of the Christmas celebration on the grounds that it was a "pagan survival" that encouraged licentiousness is characteristic not only of contemporary Puritan attacks upon this Anglican custom but also of the broader criticism of traditional popular culture by reformers of the early modern period. See Peter Burke, *Popular Culture in Early Modern Europe* (repr. New York, 1978), 209–13.

ological liberal, but the refined, high-flown rhetorical style
typically associated with that school, its fondness for classi-
cal allusions, ornate vocabulary, and a polite, rarefied manner of expression, did not characterize his mode of discourse.[22]

In his opponent, George Pigot of St. Michael's, Barnard
was also greatly favored, for the rector's response to the
Christmas sermon played right into the parson's hands.
Bombarded by "divers and hourly complaints" from his vestry after Barnard's performance, Pigot had no choice but to
respond from his church's pulpit a few days later. He immediately got off on the wrong foot by warning that his opponents should "Stop their mouths from Spitting in the Faces
of their Superiors and order themselves more lowly and reverently toward their Betters." What followed only made
matters worse, especially when he took aim at Barnard's
"Homely Argument" against a winter Nativity. "Poor Souls!"
the rector lamented, "who have no Idea of the World's Situation, and were Induced to believe it as difficult to keep
watch in Judea in December as in their New England." In
the same condescending tone, he proceeded to discourse upon
Middle Eastern climate, geography, and the seasonal habits
of sheep predators, a display of erudition that must have
mystified most members of the congregation.

Pigot's superciliousness and pomposity were bad enough,
but he buried himself completely by using sarcasm to refute
Barnard's assertion about the "pagan origins" of Christmas.
"Why did not this Man [Barnard] tell his Credulous Fisherman," he asked, "that the Saturnalia were Feasts naturally
resembling the Churchman's Christmas, and that every Master
put his Man drunk to Bed twelve nights successively?"[23] Now,
few men in Marblehead cherished firm convictions concerning grazing practices, but a judgment upon the mental capacity
of fishermen was another matter entirely. And in December,
most of them were in town to take exception to being called

[22] On the rhetorical style of liberal clergymen, see Miller, *The New England
Mind: From Colony to Province*, 269–73, and Alan Heimert, *Religion and
the American Mind: From the Great Awakening to the American Revolution* (Cambridge, Mass., 1966), 166, 214 and 215.

[23] George Pigot, *A Vindication of the Practices of the Ancient Christians . . .
in the Observation of Christmas Day* (Boston, 1731), 10, 19, and 20–23.

"Credulous." By Pigot's own admission, such "great Offense" was taken at his description that a delegation of Barnard's parishioners visited the rectory, demanding to know "the Difference between *my* Fishermen and his." The vicar told his outraged visitors that he had meant only "that Fishermen were plain and honest Men, as easily induced to believe any Thing conveyed to them in an Authoritative Way." But the damage had been done, and Pigot defeated, as much by his own lack of tact as by his opponent's shrewder rhetorical strategy. Even he conceded that Barnard's parishioners took their parson's "Homely Arguments" as "unanswerable against the Church of England in particular."

John Barnard's cleverly calculated assaults upon Anglicanism and the inadvertent assistance supplied by George Pigot strengthened the local perception of St. Michael's members as an alien and dangerous element in Marblehead society. After Barnard's attack on the Anglican celebration of Christmas, tense confrontations between the members of First Church and St. Michael's occurred not only in the rectory but on the streets of Marblehead as well. According to Pigot,

> some of his [Barnard's] greatest Admirers did frequently and loudly upbraid the Members of my Church, even in the very Streets, with such Taunting as these:—What is become of your Christmas Day now; for Mr. B——d has proved it to be nothing else but a Heathenish Rioting?—Will you never have done with your Popish Ceremonies that you have four or five days running, to observe what Mr. B——d has made out to be no such thing as you Pretend?[24]

The response among Congregationalists to the Christmas controversy of 1729 demonstrates Barnard's success during this decade in associating Anglicans with the larger threats of domination by outsiders and the sorts of volatile behavior that augmented social disorder. His strategy effectively enlisted localism in the service of orthodoxy. Over the 1720s, local Congregationalists increasingly came to regard Episcopal communicants as people estranged from the rule of reason, discipline, and self-control and identified with authorities and

[24] *Ibid.*, preface, 6 and 23.

interests an ocean away. But Barnard's campaign against the
Church of England did not introduce religious intolerance
to Marblehead: his attacks on Anglicanism only capitalized
upon religious prejudices already rooted among his parishioners. And the hostile encounters that took place between
local Congregationalists and Anglicans in the winter of 1729
were not the first manifestations of strained intersectarian
relations in Marblehead.

From the time of Barnard's installation at First Church
and the abrogation of the agreement of 1715, a whole range
of problems plaguing St. Michael's reflected the growing
strength of sentiment against Churchmen in town. One index
of the intensifying hostility toward Episcopalians was the
running political battle over the issue of exempting religious
dissenters from taxation. In a community as poor as Marblehead, insuring the maintenance of the clergy was a particular problem, especially after 1715, when the town had two
ministers to support. Local Congregationalist leaders feared
that any general exemption of Anglicans from ministerial
rates might produce a flood of "converts" to Episcopalianism among the hard-pressed families of the fishing community. As a result, Barnard, and even the "catholic" Edward
Holyoke, lobbied against granting tax relief to dissenters.
According to St. Michael's first rector, William Shaw, both
orthodox clergymen reported to local officials that "my People should be Tributary to their Ministers, my flock being
very poor are mighty uneasie at it." Governor Joseph Dudley offered the struggling Anglican church some relief in 1717,
when he exempted St. Michael's members from paying the
ministers' rates. But the Marblehead town meeting got around
this order in subsequent years by discounting the taxes of
only those Anglicans whose names had appeared on the
original list of 1717. The complaints of Shaw's successor,
David Mossom, to Governor Shute in 1722 produced another
executive directive to the town to exempt Churchmen from
rates. Confident of their advantage, St. Michael's vestry voted
to pay the legal charges of any member prosecuted for non-
payment, posting their promise on the church gate for "the
satisfaction of all persons concerned." But the Anglican victory again obtained only on paper. When Mossom protested
to the county court in 1723 that the town of Marblehead

persisted in taxing some Churchmen, the justices of the peace refused to consider his petition and left local officials to hammer out a compromise. St. Michael's members could take little satisfaction from the eventual settlement of the exemption dispute. The town ordered local constables to present annually a list of those claiming membership in St. Michael's to the selectmen who, "at their discretion" decided each individual case. This decade of maneuvering to evade granting exemptions to Episcopal dissenters diminished considerably any financial incentive for defecting from the orthodox fold. It also may have offset the significance of a concession won by New England Anglicans in 1727. In that year, both Connecticut and Massachusetts succumbed to pressure from England and began to relax the colony laws that had obliged Episcopalians to contribute to the support of the Congregationalist establishment. The new, more liberal legislation relieved Anglicans from paying for the construction of Congregational meetinghouses and also awarded the ministerial rates of all Churchmen living within five miles of an Anglican chapel to the incumbent S.P.G. missionary. Nevertheless, with the determination of an individual's dissenting status left up to the discretion of local authorities, it was still possible for communities like Marblehead to circumvent the spirit of the law.[25]

While a series of rectors struggled for freedom from ministerial rates for their parishioners with uneven success, the inconstancy of some wealthy patrons also imperiled the financial survival of St. Michael's. By the 1720s, a few prominent Marbleheaders who had been among the church's earliest supporters began to waver in their allegiance to Anglicanism, and some even embraced Congregationalism. George Pigot complained particularly of "the fluctuating of two peevish men, who now as in Mr. Mossom's time bandied from Church to Meeting." The objects of his irritation

[25] "St. Michael's Records," 2 and 26; William Shaw to S.P.G. Sec'y, January 13, 1716, Church Wardens and Vestry to S.P.G. Sec'y, May 10, 1717, David Mossom to S.P.G. Sec'y, June 11, 1722, Petition to Governor Shute, June 27, 1722, David Mossom to S.P.G. Sec'y, April 28, 1724, David Mossom to S.P.G. Sec'y, August 25, 1724, in *Historical Collections*, ed. Perry, III, 117, 126–27, 136–37, 139, 149–50, and 165; MTR, III, 25, 31, and 37; MGSP, 1719–1727, 95.

were two of Marblehead's richest merchants and justices of the peace, John Oulton and James Calley, both of whom were drawing closer to the Second Church, where their in-laws worshipped.[26] More surprising than the Episcopal elite's attraction to Holyoke's meetings was the ability of the First Church to recruit permanent converts of all social classes from the Anglican communion. As Barnard admitted trader George Finch, sea captain Giles Russell, and fishermen Nathaniel Evans and John Eletrop, Jr., to membership, he had the satisfaction of noting next to their names, "from the Church of England."[27] Only a small number of families moved from St. Michael's to Marblehead's Congregational churches. But flirtations with Second Church on the part of men like Oulton and Calley and the outright defections to First by Finch and Russell heightened the vestry's concern over the fiscal future of St. Michael's. The situation was especially alarming because the Church of England was drawing no defectors from the ranks of Marblehead's orthodox elite during the 1720s.

Difficulties in gaining relief from ministerial rates might explain why ordinary Episcopal fishermen would be drawn into Congregational meetinghouses, for poorer men could not support an Anglican rector by voluntary contributions if they were also compelled to pay taxes for maintaining the orthodox clergy. But why did more prominent Marblehead inhabitants desert St. Michael's? Men of means like Giles Russell and George Finch could have afforded both public taxes and private donations, and their influence in town would probably have earned them exemptions in any case. And there

[26] George Pigot to S.P.G. Sec'y, August 1, 1730 in *Historical Collections,* ed. Perry, III, 262. A comparison of "St. Michael's Records" against "The Record Book of the Second Church of Marblehead," a list of church members, indicates that five members of St. Michael's defected to the Second Church between 1714 and 1738, and another eleven members of St. Michael's had wives who joined Second as full or half-way members over the same period.

[27] See membership entries for 1727, 1729, 1734, 1736 in MFCR; Finch's estate was inventoried at 902 pounds sterling in 1742; Russell's was valued at 500 pounds sterling in 1753; Eletrop's estate was inventoried at 79 pounds sterling in 1751. No probate file exists for Nathaniel Evans. (See EPR, #9475, 24384, 8686.)

is no evidence of discrimination against Anglican dissenters in local business or politics in the 1720s, so embracing orthodoxy could not have been a way of escaping ostracism. The most probable source of elite disenchantment with Episcopalianism was the unsavory reputation that St. Michael's was acquiring, not only in Marblehead but throughout Essex County. Between 1715 and 1735, its congregation claimed the dubious distinction of contributing to the quarterly sessions of the peace more criminal defendants than First and Second Churches combined. This was a considerable achievement for a church that could not have included more than a quarter of the families in Marblehead.[28] Anglicans of all classes found themselves facing prosecutions for every conceivable infraction. Phoebe Severy, a servant, and Deborah Tasker, a merchant's wife were brought up before the court for fornication; fishermen Andrew Trimblett and Philip Thrasher for stealing a cow; Dr. Aaron Bourne for keeping a poor man without posting security; militia captain Joseph Majory for selling liquor illegally; and trader Abraham Howard for absence from public worship. Even John Calley, Esquire was arraigned by his fellow justices for an outburst of profanity and, along with his brother James, appeared before the Admiralty Court to answer charges of smuggling French brandy.

Especially embarrassing to the local Episcopal community was the frequency with which their members were indicted for crimes of actual or threatened physical violence. Most of the defendants in these cases of assault were not battling couples, drunken servants or fishermen on a spree,

---

[28] Between 1726 and 1735, Marblehead defendants were prosecuted for twenty-three cases of fornication and for thirty-six cases involving other criminal charges. I could identify the church affiliation of defendants in twenty-two of the fornication cases, and ten involved Anglicans. I could ascertain the church affiliation of thirty-three defendants in the thirty-six other criminal cases, and seventeen were Anglican. In the preceding ten-year period (1716–1725), the number of Anglican defendants was less outsized but still larger than their representation in the population at large: they comparised one-third of all criminal defendants in cases other than fornication, and just over one-quarter of all defendants in fornication cases. This data on criminal activity is compiled from the Minutebooks of the General Sessions of the Peace for Essex County and of the Superior Court of Judicature for the province.

but came from among St. Michael's most substantial vestry-men. And their victims were mainly other Episcopalians, not the members of the Congregational churches. In 1723, for example, Anglican Richard Hayden, an immigrant butcher who had amassed a large estate by provisioning fishing voyages, was convicted of threatening his coreligionist Captain James Smith with a club and vowing to "knock his brains low." Three years later, Hayden turned up in court again, this time as the victim of an attack by fellow Churchman David LeGallais, a prominent Jersey sea captain. In the summer of 1729, John Tasker, an Anglican merchant who had already appeared in court, charged with selling drink without a license, confessed to beating Episcopal fisherman Thomas Ceward "so that his life was greatly despair'd of." Fisherman William Wendover, presented earlier for attacking Joseph Majory with a pistol, was also a Churchman, as was Majory. More occasionally, members of the orthodox community were the victims of Episcopal violence. Thaddeus Riddan, a Lynn Congregationalist, complained to the court in 1729 that vestryman Bartholomew Jackson, a wealthy doctor and innkeeper, had menaced him with a stout cane and "swore by God he would be revenged."[29]

The high incidence of Episcopal prosecutions for criminal activity is intriguing, especially the alleged involvement of so many of St. Michael's most prominent members in violent episodes. While the Church of England styled itself as a bastion of order and rationality, this image is at odds with the image of Churchmen that emerges from the records of the quarterly sessions of the peace. One influence contributing to the disproportionately large number of Anglican criminal defendants was the ethnic diversity of Episcopalians. A substantial portion of St. Michael's members were Jersey men and women, a group whose incomplete integration into provincial New England society made clashes with the law more common. Even by the third decade of the eighteenth century,

---

[29] MGSP, January 17, 1722 (Calley); December 27, 1726 (Bourne); January 22, 1723 (Hayden); January 18, 1727 (Thrasher and Trimblett); July 11, 1727 (Severy, Howard); August 1, 1727 (Majory); December 31, 1728 (Wendover); January 21, 1729 (Jackson); April 14, 1730 (Tasker, D.); and July 19, 1730 (Tasker, J.). MSCJ, May 1722 and May 1724 (Calleys).

mutual hostility and suspicion still characterized relations between Jersey families and other Essex residents. Magistrates were more prone to take legal action against such outsiders, while the immigrants resented any intervention in their affairs by officials whose authority they did not fully accept.[30] Another possible reason for the larger volume of law-breaking among its communicants was the Episcopal church's lack of a mechanism for disciplining members and resolving grievances among coreligionists. Nothing like Barnard's mobilization of pious laymen and assertion of pastoral authority to censure wayward saints appears in St. Michael's records. Besides the absence of a lay organization for overseeing morality and arbitrating disputes, St. Michael's lack of continuity in clerical leadership also weakened ecclesiastical control over members' behavior. Three different rectors passed through Marblehead in the twenty years after the church's founding. This high rate of turnover, a product of low salaries, could hardly have enhanced the exercise of discipline within the church, nor could penury have made for priestly authority.

The ethnic diversity of Marblehead Anglicans and the institutional weaknesses of St. Michael's explain, in part, Episcopal prominence among criminal defendants. But the high incidence of Anglican presentments also reflected the mounting religious antagonism in Marblehead. The orthodox perception of Episcopalians as a particularly disorderly and dangerous group became a self-fulfilling prophecy in an outsized number of Anglican defendants. Repeated public emphasis from the pulpit of First Church upon Anglican aggressiveness, volatility, and irrationality encouraged among Congregationalists a particular sensitivity to violent outbursts on the part of St. Michael's members. The large number of Episcopalians indicted for assault and disruption of the peace that resulted in turn reinforced orthodox expectations. The high crime rate among Anglicans reflected not only the self-confirming tendency of stereotyping but also the discovery on the part of the orthodox that reporting Episcopal transgressions was an ideal way to harrass and embarrass the Church of England. Criminal prosecutions insured that

[30] Konig, "A New Look at the Essex 'French'," *EIHC,* 110: 167–80.

what individual Churchmen gained in tax exemptions, they
lost in fines and court costs.[31] To some of St. Michael's early,
eminent supporters, association with a church receiving this
sort of adverse publicity became a blot on their own respectability. Their solution was to seek out the company of the
Congregationalists.

During the 1720s, John Barnard fostered among his congregation an attitude toward the Anglicans that approxi-
mated what Gloucester's Congregationalists intuited about
the Quakers. Like the orthodox of Cape Ann, Barnard's
parishioners came to believe that the commitment of religious dissenters to the local community would always be
incomplete because heterodox affiliations necessarily weakened civic attachments. While the Quakers cleaved to a religious fellowship that extended beyond the borders of the
town, so too did Anglicans. Barnard impressed on his
parishioners that Churchmen constituted a "counter-community" in which translocal sectarian solidarity and allegiance to the English episcopacy subverted localistic loyalties.
That was the message of *Ashton's Memorial*. But in addition, Barnard encouraged his parishioners to perceive Episcopalianism as a kind of "counterculture," one sanctioning
beliefs, values, and standards of conduct at variance with the
end of communal stability. That was the point of his Christmas sermon. To insure that similar charges could not be leveled against the Society of Friends, eighteenth-century Quaker
leaders had instituted "the Discipline" and local visitation
committes to enforce it. But New England Anglicans were a
good deal more lax about chastising transgressing Churchmen. And instead of adapting church customs to accommodate the ascetic ethos of Congregationalism, S.P.G.

---

[31] For a discussion of the frequency with which Massachusetts residents
made use of the law "as an instrument of defamation," see Hendrik Hartog,
"The Public Law of a County Court: Judicial Government in Eighteenth-
Century Massachusetts," *American Journal of Legal History*, 20 (1976),
318–19. Hartog also notes that, during the first half of the eighteenth century, defendants were routinely charged with the costs of prosecution, whether
or not they were convicted. These expenses were "hardly nominal," often
in excess of five pounds. As a result, Hartog concludes, "to make a formal
charge against a person was a way of insuring that that person would be
put to cost." (320–21)

missionaries like George Pigot made a point of defending celebrations like Christmas. This Episcopal miscalculation provided the Puritans with what they thrived upon striving against even more than a wilderness—a maypole. In fact, no great gulf separated the lawlessness and violence that Barnard ascribed to Churchmen from the realities of daily life in Marblehead among both Congregationalists and Anglicans during the 1720s. But by identifying these disorders with the Episcopalians, Barnard was able to draw religious prejudice into the service of disseminating greater discipline and self-control among the orthodox inhabitants of town.

By creating a Congregational church that offered something to every order of local society, John Barnard managed to dispel the religious indifference of many Marbleheaders. The pastor's promotion of local economic development and a church government that accorded greater responsibility to the best men among the brethren attracted the more substantial members of Marblehead society. On the other hand, his lionization of Philip Ashton, his lingering around the wharves, and his evenhanded discipline of both poor transgressors like Sarah Westcott and wealthier ones like David Parker also made Barnard popular among ordinary fisherfolk. And all Marbleheaders appreciated Barnard's commitment to the town and his flair for the fray, whether against the "Papist" French or local Anglicans. The parson was a Boston-bred, Harvard-educated gentleman, and more a man of the world than most other New England clergymen. Even so, he possessed to perfection the virtue of local loyalty.

The rallying of the First Church behind Barnard's candidacy in 1715, and afterwards his campaign for commercial independence, stronger, more coherent ecclesiastical organization, and resistance to the Anglican challenge, set in motion the forces of localism and intolerance that would reshape Marblehead by the middle of the eighteenth century. But the pastor's ability to heighten religious engagement effected no significant alteration in the overall character of local life prior to the 1730s. On the contrary, the increasingly fervent commitment of Barnard's parishioners to Congregationalist orthodoxy amounted to an added threat to social stability, for their antagonism toward outsiders was only one of several stresses that were stretching tensions in town to the breaking point during the fifteen years after 1715. Coinciding with the burgeoning resistance to the domination of the local economy by larger seaports and the rising tide of religious prejudice were the severely disruptive demographic and economic developments of the postwar era. The peaking of in-migration, the arrival of a second wave of monied newcomers, the period of most pronounced economic inequality, and the high-water mark of suits for debt and crimes against persons and property accompanied the growth of localistic and religious restiveness. Temporary dislocations produced by short-term crises also punctuated this period, adding to the general sense of disorientation. A smallpox epidemic struck the town in 1721; the depredations of the Maine Indians interrupted the fishery between 1723 and 1725; a dispute over enclosing the commons divided the town throughout the 1720s; and a violent storm and high tides damaged Marblehead harbor in 1727, the same year that a series of strong earthquakes shook the entire New England coast.[32] All of these pressures, and the added catalyst of a second smallpox epidemic, brought the crisis of local society to a climax on the night of December 10th in 1730. On that evening, a popular uprising erupted in Marblehead, an outbreak of "heathenish rioting" with consequences far more portentous for local life than anything foreseen a year earlier at Christmas by the Reverend John Barnard.

[32] On the war with the Maine Indians, see Chapter VII, n. 5. On the epidemic of the 1720s, and the debate over the commons, see MTR, III, 13, 14, 19–20, 22–23, and 36.

9

A Heathenish Rioting

THE RIOTING that took place at Marblehead in December of 1730 is one of those "dramatic clashes that suddenly illuminates the plot of people's lives."[1] Like the Salem witchcraft hysteria and the Gloucester First Parish controversy, this popular uprising, a protest against the new practice of smallpox inoculation, was a key crisis in local life. From several eyewitness accounts of the Marblehead crowd's actions, there emerges an unusually detailed portrait of the social relationships, the patterns of deference and defiance, and the dominant values of this early eighteenth-century seaport. In addition, the anti-inoculation riot pinpoints the major source of social strain within Marblehead in 1730. Postwar economic development had deepened the town's complex array of class divisions, social and cultural cleavages, and competing religious and ethnic allegiances, making it difficult to discern which among these multiple tensions was most basic to generating conflict and defining the direction of change. But through firsthand descriptions of the Marblehead mob's behavior, it is possible to delineate the most fundamental

---

[1] The phrase is from Margaret Mead, who uses it to describe the kinds of events, confrontations, or rituals that anthropologists hope to discover in their fieldwork in order to enhance their understanding of another culture. (*Blackberry Winter* [New York, 1972], 247.)

division that determined social alighments, attitudes, and actions in this economically expanding society.

The smallpox epidemic that struck Marblehead in 1730 originated, like many of the town's problems, in Boston. It was not Marblehead's first experience with the disease: late in 1721, when a smallpox contagion spread from Boston to Marblehead, the community had closed itself to strangers and isolated the infected. The town meeting had also expressly forbidden any inhabitant from receiving inoculation against the smallpox, a practice being pioneered in Boston by Dr. Zabdiel Boylston. No physician favoring the treatment or anyone who had been inoculated was allowed into town. In August of 1730, at the first signs of a recurring infection, Marblehead again posted constables at its gates and quarantined anyone exhibiting dangerous symptoms. But the town meeting did not immediately interdict inoculation of inhabitants. Boston's experience during the earlier epidemic had vindicated Boylston's discovery and silenced even the most stringent critic of inoculation, Dr. William Douglass. Boylston's publication of his success in Boston led many literate New Englanders to approve the new method, and in Marblehead inoculation found its staunchest evangel in the Reverend Edward Holyoke. He had gone to Boston for treatment in 1721 and stayed at the home of the Reverend Cotton Mather until he was allowed to return to Marblehead. New England's most vigorous proponent of inoculation, Mather noted in his diary that until Holyoke had fled to Boston he was "Likely to be murdered by an Abominable People, that will not Lett him Save his Life in the way of Innoculation." But despite his awareness of strong local opposition to inoculation, Holyoke took up his public advocacy of the new treatment again when the epidemic struck in 1730. Throughout the summer and early fall of that year, he encouraged the congregation of Second Church to avail themselves of Boylston's discovery.[2]

---

[2] MTR, III, 23. On the Boston smallpox epidemic and the work of Boylston, see Ola Winslow, A Destroying Angel: The Conquest of Smallpox in Colonial Boston (Boston, 1974); John Blake, "The Inoculation Controversy in Boston, 1721–1722," New England Quarterly, 25 (1952), 489–506; John Duffy, Epidemics in Colonial America (Baton Rouge, 1953), 32–42. Yellow fever and smallpox were the diseases most feared by colonials: with

For a time, the Marblehead town meeting countenanced the inoculation of inhabitants. But as the death toll in town mounted during September, most Marbleheaders grew more alarmed and more certain that the preventive was deadlier than the disease. On October 12th, some inhabitants petitioned for a special town meeting at which a majority voted to prohibit inoculation, "which is judg'd to be a means for the spreading of the maligority [malignity]."[3] This action by the town did not represent an atavistic recoiling from the clear light of scientific progress by a panic-stricken population. The town meeting did not deny that inoculation reduced the risk of dying from smallpox among those who had been treated. Their fear instead was that the introduction of a milder, nonfatal form of the disease by the inoculation of some inhabitants was increasing the incidence of virulent cases of smallpox among townspeople who had not received treatment. This concern was not peculiar to Marbleheaders but was widely shared by Boston's medical practitioners and even by proponents of inoculation like Mather and Boylston. It was in fact possible for those who had been inoculated to infect others who had not been vaccinated, and physicians administering the treatment were not always careful to isolate their patients. During the Boston epidemic of 1721–22, Boylston had allowed his sick patients to receive visitors and even to go outdoors with their sores still running. And when the smallpox struck Boston again in 1730, town selectmen ordered local doctors to record the number of persons vaccinated, hoping in this way to watch the course of the epidemic and to interdict inoculation if it appeared to contribute to the spread of the disease.[4]

smallpox, the mortality per cases untreated was about 15 percent, and 1 to 2 percent per cases inoculated. (Richard Shyrock, *Medicine and Society in America, 1660–1860* [Ithaca, New York, 1972], 57 and 94.) On Holyoke, see Cotton Mather, *Diary*, 7 *Collections of the Massachusetts Historical Society*, VIII, 670; SHG, V, 269.

[3] MTR, III, 95–96. The petition for and minutes of the Marblehead town meeting of October 12, 1730 are in the files of the Essex County General Sessions of the Peace.

[4] Middlekauff, *The Mathers*, 354–56; Patricia Cline Cohen, *A Calculating People: The Spread of Numeracy in Early America* (Chicago, 1982), chapter three. I am indebted to Professor Cohen for allowing me to read her study when it was still in manuscript.

While Boston continued to allow inoculation throughout the epidemic of 1730, by the time of the town meeting on October 12th, a majority of Marblehead voters were unwilling to take the same risk. They judged that anything short of a general inoculation of all inhabitants would be a means of spreading the disease throughout their densely populated community. And the treatment of all inhabitants was impracticable. Some townspeople were still suspicious of the new medical technique, and many could not afford treatment. Nor could the town have covered the expense of inoculating its entire population. As late as 1768, when Norfolk, Virginia, was faced with a similar crisis, residents there claimed that a general inoculation would cost "more money than is circulating in Norfolk."[5] The only alternative left to Marblehead for arresting the progress of the disease and for protecting townspeople from this latest invasion from Boston was prohibiting inoculation.

But not everyone in Marblehead accepted the will of the town meeting's majority. Some quietly slipped into Boston for treatment; others voiced their dissent openly. On December 7th of 1730, with the disease still raging, shopkeeper Elias Waters overheard Stephen Minot, Jr., one of Marblehead's justices of the peace, talking with another townsman. Minot declared that if his wife were not pregnant, "he would inoculate all his family in half an hours time and would do it himself."[6] Early in the evening of December 10th, three days later, Justice Minot was at the Marblehead tavern of William Man, socializing with two of his merchant friends, Jeremiah Allen, Jr., and John Tasker, when Richard Dana, the local schoolmaster, burst in upon the company. Dana had just confronted a company of twenty armed men who had called him to the window of his lodging and asked if he intended to be inoculated. In 1721, Dana had gone to Boston for just that reason, and everybody in town remembered it. Dana assured the men that "They was no body a going to be inoculated here," but this response dissuaded the crowd

[5] Shyrock, *Medicine and Society,* 99; Patrick Henderson, "Smallpox and Patriotism: The Norfolk Riots, 1768–1769," *Virginia Magazine of History and Biography,* 73 (1965), 413–24.
[6] Depositions of Andrew Stacey and David Furneux, January 1, 1731, FGSP.

gathering below his window only temporarily. Shortly thereafter, his neighbor, William Goodwin, warned Dana that over fifty armed men were coming up the street to pull down his house. This news sent Dana scurrying off to William Man's tavern in search of the law. But just after Dana had finished telling his tale to Justice Minot and his friends, Nathan Bowen, a lawyer in town, brought word to the tavern that the schoolmaster was out of danger. The crowd had changed its mind and decided to pull down Minot's home instead. As Bowen spoke, the mob was regrouping around the justice's dwelling.

Minot, along with Allen, Tasker, Bowen, and Dana, rushed to the scene of the disturbance. There they found over two hundred people milling about Minot's gate, most of them wielding clubs and staffs. The din made by the crowd was deafening, some sounding off horns, others shouting, cursing, and swearing "in an Horrible Manner." Minot pushed into the center of the crowd and commanded some of the rioters to seize one member of their company. Momentarily stunned by the justice's self-possession, they actually started to obey, but then regained their resolve and released the culprit. By this time, Joseph Blaney, a Marblehead tanner who also served as the county sheriff, had arrived at the scene to assist Minot. When Blaney asked the crowd what they wanted, several shouted, "Damne you, its none of your business!" Despite Blaney's protests that as "A King's Officer" this breach of the peace was his concern, the rioters refused either to disperse or to help in apprehending one of their number, Richard Searle, Jr. Searle, a fisherman, was egging the crowd on, shouting that he would "knock the Sheriff's brains out" and swearing that "he valued not Justice Minot nor Sheriff Blaney nor anybody else, nor would he lay down a club for them." With the aid of Ebenezer Lowell, a local merchant, Blaney finally managed to bring Searle and another mob member, fisherman Jacob Ball, into Minot's home. Elsewhere in the crowd, Minot was writing down the names of the rioters. But since several members of the mob were shaking their clubs over his head, urging the crowd to "fall on," and shouting "Damne Justice Minot do not Care for him," Minot finally decided that he would be safer inside his house. Before retreating, he apprehended two other rioters, Nicholas Bezoone and Richard Meek, both fishermen, and took them into his home. Posted as guard at the gate, Sheriff Blaney continued to urge the crowd against attacking Minot's house, but only when he too began to take down names did most of them withdraw to the townhouse, a few yards down the street. As Ebenezer Lowell left the scene of the fray, he was assaulted by several members of the mob, including fisherman Thomas Horton who swore "that he would be the death of me."

Just as the main body of rioters was receding from Minot's gate, Sheriff Blaney was "surprized" to see another group of about fifty men approaching him, headed by Dr. Bartholomew Jackson, a local shoreman and physician and one of Marblehead's militia captains. "Damne you," the doctor demanded of Blaney, "what Business have you to take downe our Names; Cannot we pass in the Street without having Our Names taken downe?" Relieved, the sheriff apologized for mistaking Jackson's intentions and thanked him for bringing reinforcements to help suppress the riot. But Blaney had been right the first time, for Jackson declared himself the leader of the crowd. The mob had risen, he told the sheriff, because Blaney and others had "medled in what was none of their business." Shortly after this confrontation, Captain Joseph Majory, another shoreman and militia leader, appeared at Minot's gate and gained an audience with the justice. Once satisfied that his brother William was not one of the men in custody, Captain Majory began behaving himself "after an isolent manner." He coolly related how he had engineered the riot by entertaining the men at his tavern with "a Dram apiece" and ordering them not to curse but "to sing until nine o'clock," after which time "he had Cables and Cordage enough . . . to pull down any House in Town." Meanwhile, the object of Captain Majory's fraternal concern was outside at Minot's gate, boasting to Blaney that if he had gotten there earlier, he would have led the mob. Local shoreman and militia captain Ebenezer Hawkes, Jr., stopped by too, assuring the sheriff of "bloody work" in Marblehead if the prisoners were not released.

Convinced by now that the situation mandated drastic measures, Minot decided to raise the militia to restore order. This was not the most promising course of action, since three of the five militia captains were Jackson, Majory, and Hawkes. Nevertheless, Jeremiah Allen, Jr., acting as Minot's emissary, sought out Captain Hawkes and ordered him to muster his men. Hawkes offered instead to "give a thousand pounds toward pulling down any house" and then suggested that Minot could find something better to do than suppressing the riot, "or some other such words tending to the loosening of the Justice's Character and Authority." Hawkes's insolence prepared Allen for his reception at Captain Jackson's inn. Here a servant maid slyly responded to Allen's request to see the doctor by asking who was sick. Allen departed without delivering his message but noticed that the "great chamber" of Jackson's home was brightly lit and filled with people who were presumably not patients.

Marblehead's militia captains had no intention of complying with the orders to quell the mob. Nevertheless, after they had savored the satisfaction of insulting Minot, Allen, and Blaney, the insubordinate officers could not pass up another opportunity to observe firsthand the distress of their adversaries. So later in the evening, they called at the justice's home and asked "what he wanted." Minot, who still did not completely comprehend the futility of summoning the militia, earnestly replied that "there was a considerable riot" and that he was in "no small danger." Captain Majory allowed that public cursing was deplorable and that he personally preferred singing to swearing; then he offered to post bail for the four imprisoned crowd members. Captain Hawkes repeated his prediction of "bloody work." A fourth militia captain, Richard Reith, a trader, declared that he would rather lead the mob than disperse it. At these responses, Justice Minot began to suspect an intentional affront to his authority. Captain Jackson, however, seemed more accommodating: he "made great offers of assistance" and left to muster his company. He returned with his ensign, David Furneux, reporting that "he had his Men in Arms, and . . . that if they had sent to him before he could have dispersed them [the crowd] and that it was his business to do it." All that Captain Jackson expected for his services was the release of the prisoners on bail. Outraged by Jackson's demand but unwilling to keep the prisoners in his custody, Minot ordered them transferred for the rest of the evening to a makeshift prison, the home of Richard James, one of Marblehead's constables. As a parting gesture of defiance, Ensign Furneux rebuffed the request of Thomas Elkins, another constable, for assistance in transporting the prisoners. Furneux explained that he took orders only from his "superior officer." Captain Jackson told his ensign that such loyalties were quire correct, and then all of the militia captains left.

For the rest of the night the town was quiet, and the constables somehow managed to move the accused rioters to James's home. But on the following day, popular unrest again flared up into violence. Jonathan Boden, a local fisherman, accosted Jeremiah Allen, Jr., on the way to his warehouse and warned, "Damne you, you shall not come off tonight as you did last night." As it happened, the suspense was shortened, for this time, the crowd did not wait until dark to act. Around noon, a group of between fifty and one hundred men led by Joseph Majory, Ebenezer Hawkes, Jr., and fishermen Bonnel Merryfield, Peter Pollo, Elias Bezoone, Benjamin Codner, John Sasser, William Majory, Thomas Main, and John Chappell, Jr., attacked Richard James's house, entered by the windows, and liberated the four prisoners. In the fracas that ensued, Merryfield knocked James senseless, and Pollo threatened to finish off constables Elkins and Stephen Chapman with "a great stone . . . about thirty pounds weight." Alerted to the trouble by Jeremiah Allen, Joseph Blaney and a fifth militia captain, John Stacey, a merchant, mounted their horses and rode to Dr. Jackson's house, where the mob had gathered after freeing the prisoners. Their appearance in the midst of the crowd triggered the familiar objection to such interference as "none of their business." Blaney's telling the mob that he was the king's officer and ordering them to disperse still had no effect; they cursed, "demanding his power," and "advanced toward Me Flourishing their Clubs." On that cliffhanger, the testimony concerning the Marblehead crowd ends and, after the release of the prisoners, so too did the mob's activities.

If Stephen Minot and his friends hoped to settle the score in the courts, they were disappointed, for popular sympathy was with the rioters. In the legal proceedings that followed, an Essex County jury convicted only one man, Richard Meek, of participating in the December 10th riot; they acquitted three others, Bartholomew Jackson, Joseph Majory, and Ebenezer Hawkes, Jr., who were indicted on the same charge. And only two members of the mob of that stormed the James home on the afternoon following were found guilty of that breach of the peace. There is evidence that a few of the eight other men who were indicted for the attack of December 11th left town to avoid prosecution, but the legal peril that they would have faced was apparently not great. Juries were in no mood to convict, and in the few instances where they did, the penalties imposed were light.[7]

In every respect, Marblehead's anti-inoculation riot conforms to a pattern characteristic of other crowd actions that took place during the eighteenth century throughout the American colonies and in Europe as well. Like other popular uprisings elsewhere, the Marblehead riot was not a formless melée or an outburst of indiscriminate violence and vandalism: activity was focused and well-organized, first around Minot's home and later around the makeshift jail. The crowd carefully selected the targets that reflected their grievances most clearly, as their decision to pull down Minot's home instead of Dana's indicates. Several times the rioters articulated a collective protest: "It's none of your Business." Local

[7] My account of the riot is based on the depositions of Joseph Blaney, December 29, 1730 and February 21, 1731; Ebenezer Lowell, December 22, 1730; Richard Dana, December 22, 1730; John Tasker, December 22, 1730; Thomas Elkins, February 2, 1731; Jeremiah Allen, Jr., December 22, 1730; Nathan Bowen, December 22 and 29, 1730; Stephen Chapman, February 21, 1731; and John Stacey (undated). All of these depositions are in the FGSP. In a joint deposition, officers of the peace Minot, Blaney, Elkins, and James alleged that Jackson, Majory, and Hawkes were the "encouragers and promoters of the mob." On December 29, 1730, these three men, along with Richard Meek, were indicted by an Essex County grand jury and tried for their role in the December 10th riot. On February 11, 1731, the ten men involved in the December 11th riot were indicted and tried; only Peter Pollo and Benjamin Codner were convicted, and they were immediately released on bonds posted by Jackson, Majory, Hawkes, and one Samuel Bridges. In the end, the three convicted rioters were penalized only by paying court costs. Stephen Minot was one of the presiding justices at both of the trials. (MGSP, 1727–1744, 182ff.) A third member of the December 11th mob, Elias Bezoone, was presented for trial in August of 1731 and later acquitted. (MGSP, 1727–1744, 213, 230.) He may have been one of the rioters who fled town temporarily to avoid prosecution. On the back of a few of the warrants that survive in the FGSP, officers serving the summonses noted that the accused men had left Marblehead.

authorities in town were unable to control the disorder because the only agency available for suppressing the mob, the militia, was itself part of the crowd. Members of the mob also exhibited considerable solidarity among themselves, something shown both by Captain Jackson's efforts to blackmail Minot into releasing the imprisoned rioters and by the subsequent assault on the makeshift jail. Any number of other colonial crowd actions featured this configuration of elements—the Boston market riot of 1737, the Knowles anti-impressment protests ten years later, the land actions in the Middle Colonies, the Carolina Regulator movements, and the Norfolk anti-inoculation agitation. In all of these cases, well-disciplined crowds pursued clearly defined objectives and were protected by widespread communal support for their extralegal activities as well as by the concern among protesters to shield comrades from prosecution. Because it typifies much of colonial crowd activity, the Marblehead riot sheds some light on the causes and the significance of popular uprisings generally. It also allows for a reassessment of what mob violence reveals about social alignments and attitudes in the commercially developing areas of the eighteenth-century American colonies.[8]

Historians have recently come to appreciate the extent to which provincial seaports, especially Boston, suffered from periodic economic dislocations produced by either military crisis or the vicissitudes of colonial commerce. This recognition has heightened awareness of the role played by economic antagonisms in precipitating popular uprisings in urban centers. Boston's market riot of 1737, for example, took place after the town had weathered several years of severe economic difficulties. Hoping to restore prosperity, a group of younger merchants allied to the royal governor attempted to introduce strictly regulated public markets in 1734 as part of a broader program for enhancing the efficiency of the town's political and economic institutions. When the markets failed to arrest Boston's economic decline, their merchant-sponsors became the focus of popular antipathy.

[8] Pauline Maier, "Popular Uprisings and Civil Authority," *WMQ*, 3rd ser., 27 (1970), 3–35; Gordon Wood, "A Note on Mobs in the American Revolution," *WMQ*, 3rd ser., 23 (1966), 635–42.

Already a dead letter by 1736, the city's experiment with public markets came to a permanent end one night in the spring of 1737. On that evening, a mob, with many of its members disguised as clergymen, leveled one public market-house and sawed through the supports of another. In the following days, the saboteurs advertised their readiness to resort to more violent tactics if regulated markets were reintroduced.[9]

Although Marblehead's commerce was expanding rather than contracting, the smaller port was experiencing many of the same tensions that contributed to the market riot in commercially decaying Boston. If anything, inequality, aggressive economic behavior, and the systematic exploitation of labor in Marblehead strained relations between rich and poor even more severely than the situation that prevailed in the capital. This feature of local life lends significance to the difference in economic status between those resisting the Marblehead mob and the men who made up the majority of crowd members. Minot, Allen, Tasker, Bowen, Lowell, Stacey, and Blaney were all wealthy men, major figures in Marblehead's economy and in Essex County politics. In fact, many were allied by blood, business, marriage, and friendship to the merchant proponents of the public markets in Boston. Arrayed against these rich traders, lawyers, and master craftsmen were the fishermen who comprised the rank and file of the mob. Merryfield, Pollo, the Bezoones, Codner, Sasser, Main, Chappell, Boden, Horton, Ball, Meek, Searle, and William Majory were all ordinary laboring men in the Marblehead fishing community.[10]

[9] G. B. Warden, *Boston, 1689–1776*, 121–23; Nash, *Urban Crucible*, 130–36.

[10] As Minot's commission as justice of the peace indicates, he was an important man in town, the son of Boston merchant Stephen Minot, Sr., whose estate he inherited in 1732. (See Suffolk Probate Files, #6310, Suffolk County Courthouse, Boston, Mass.) Jeremiah Allen, Jr. was also the son and namesake of a wealthy Boston merchant, and, upon his father's death in 1736, Allen followed Minot back to Boston and received his patrimony. (See Suffolk Probate Files, #7702.) Tasker, Bowen, and Blaney all ranked in the top decile of Marblehead ratepayers in 1748. ("Marblehead Tax List for 1748," *EIHC*, 43 (1907), 209–222.) Richard Dana was a Harvard graduate born in Cambridge, a lawyer, and the town schoolmaster at the time of the riot. (*SHG*, VI, 236.) Ebenezer Lowell, originally of Boston, was the

Most of the members of the Marblehead mob probably occupied a status in local society similar to that of Jacob Ball, one of the rioters jailed for threatening Justice Minot. Like many of his companions in the crowd, Ball was an immigrant from Jersey who had crossed the Atlantic as an indentured servant. At the time of his death seven years after the riot, Ball was a free man but extremely poor. The inventoried value of his estate, which included only clothing and a few household goods but no real property, placed him at the very bottom of the town's economic hierarchy. No administration of his estate survives, but the bonding of two major Marblehead shoremen as sureties, probably his principal creditors, suggests that Ball died bankrupt. The equally meager estate of "mariner" Lawrence Ball, most likely Jacob's brother, reveals more about the family's circumstances. Lawrence shipped out on a coasting vessel owned by Justice Stephen Minot and died on the return voyage from Honduras Bay in about 1738. At his death, Lawrence owed seventy pounds to Simon Proctor, a substantial shoreman and the Marblehead representative of a wealthy Salem family. Proctor was determined to recover whatever he could from Lawrence's estate by superseding the deceased sailor's mother as administrator. "Her Carrecter is so mean," the shoreman advised the Essex County judge of probate, that

> if she had Ever so much Money She wold Soon Destroy it in Strong liquor as is well known to the Neighbors. . . . I believe there is not many Debts but what is justly due to me for the pore

local factor of Peter Faneuil, one of the biggest Boston fish exporters. Like Minot, Allen, and Dana, Lowell also returned to Boston in the 1730s. (*SHG*, XIII, 3 3 2; Faneuil V. Reed, Faneuil v. Tucker, and Faneuil v. Proctor, all October 28, 1735, MSCJ.) John Stacey was probably the son of Captain John Stacey, who died in 1722 with an estate worth over seven hundred pounds sterling. (EPF, #26080)

Precise information concerning the economic standing of the fourteen rank and file mob members is more difficult to find, which in itself suggests their poverty. Aside from Ball's inventory, only one other exists: Richard Meek died in 1739 worth four pounds sterling. (EPF, #18179) Four other mob members appear in the province tax list of 1748, all ranking in the bottom half of the ratepayers. Nine of the mob members are identified by court or probate records as "fishermen" and two as "shoremen." But the two "shoremen," Sasser and Codner, were probably "boat shoremen" rather than "gentlemen-shoremen."

man has Lived with me for almost this six years since he had bin out of his Time and I have kept him out of jayle Several Times. . . .[11]

At least a third of the families in Marblehead in 1730 shared the portion of Jacob Ball and his family. Poverty, dependency, crippling indebtedness, the constant risk of sudden, premature death, and the contempt of men who profited from their labor were their common lot. It would be surprising if they had not welcomed a chance to strike back at the likes of Stephen Minot and Simon Proctor. The furor over inoculation afforded the laboring classes an opportunity to vent hostilities generated by the hardships of their daily existences. Widespread public opposition to members of the elite who advocated inoculation allowed ordinary fishermen license to revile and threaten their social superiors. Moreover, the issue of inoculation itself bore directly on the problem of inequality. While inoculation improved the chances of surviving smallpox epidemics for the privileged segment of Marblehead society that could pay for preventive medicine, it increased the hazard for those who could afford neither inoculation, nor medical care in the event of contracting the disease, nor the loss of income produced by the illness of family members and the shutdown of commerce. Smallpox snuffed out the lives of Marblehead-ers from all social classes. But in any society where medical care is not equally available to everyone, disease discrimi-nates against the poor. This held true in early Marblehead, but here, in the case of the smallpox epidemic, the poor were at the greatest risk not only from the contagion but also from unequal access to the cure.

Class divisions and antagonisms were an element in the anti-inoculation riot because they were part of life in Mar-blehead. Nevertheless, the riot was not primarily a protest against inequality; nor did tensions between classes define the basic character of the uprising. For although all of the known proponents of inoculation were wealthy and influ-ential men, not all of the rioters and their supporters were poor fishermen like Jacob Ball. In fact, three of the men

[11] EPF, #1582, 1584.

indicted for leading the Marblehead mob came from the top of local society. Dr. Bartholomew Jackson, the self-proclaimed head of the crowd, had built up a large estate between his inheritance from his father, a former selectman and deputy to the General Court, and his medical practice, fishing business, and tavern. Jackson's associates, militia captains Joseph Majory and Ebenezer Hawkes, were also substantial and prominent men. Hawkes was the eldest son and namesake of Ebenezer, Sr., a blacksmith who was one of the richest men in Marblehead. Majory had served as selectman and as the commander of a man-of-war guarding the fishing fleet during the most recent campaign against the Maine Indians. Richard Reith, another militia captain who had offered support to the mob but escaped indictment, was also wealthy and a frequent member of the board of selectmen. The conspicuous absence of Marblehead's other justices of the peace from the scene of the riot also suggests upper class opposition to inoculation and tacit elite endorsement of the crowd's objectives.[12]

The animosity that fishermen who formed the rank and file of the crowd felt toward Stephen Minot and other major merchants and shoremen who advocated inoculation did not prevent them from accepting the leadership of rich and prominent men like Jackson, Majory, and Hawkes. And despite their wealth and standing, these three men allied with their less affluent neighbors on the issue of inoculation and served as the riot's ringleaders. Nor was class antipathy intense enough to dissuade one faction of the elite from mobilizing their inferiors as a mob, and the other faction, led by Minot, from plunging into a crowd of armed men in the middle of the night. The confidence of both sets of leaders was borne out by the behavior of the crowd itself. Even fortified with rum and strength of numbers, members of the mob impulsively obeyed Minot's first command to apprehend one of their number. And Jackson, Majory, and Hawkes appear to have kept the crowd firmly under their control throughout

[12] Jackson and Majory ranked among the top quartile of Marblehead ratepayers in 1748, as did Ensign David Furneux. Reith ranked in the top decile, along with blacksmith Ebenezer Hawkes, Sr., the father of the rioter. On Majory's military career, see *MA*, 38: 44; 63: 410–15.

the two days of disruption. Even the liberation of the jailed
rioters, a rescue undertaken mainly by ordinary fishermen,
was orchestrated from Captain Jackson's inn and joined by
Majory and Hawkes. The habit of deference also limited the
expression of popular resentment against big men like Minot
to curses and threatening gestures: the crowd actually
assaulted only the lowly constables, Elkins, James, and
Chapman.

The composition of the two opposing sides in Marblehead's anti-inoculation riot was characteristic of popular
uprisings in other provincial seaports. These conflicts often
pitted one faction of the elite against another group of leaders who commanded mass support from an economic cross
section of local society. In Boston, for example, the advocates of the regulated public markets in the 1730s were all
wealthy merchants, but leading resistance to this reform was
Elisha Cooke, Jr., one of the richest men in Boston. Like the
opponents of inoculation in Marblehead, Cooke's "popular
party" cut across class lines, taking in other merchants, as
well as shopkeepers, artisans, and urban laborers. That some
members of the mob which vandalized the markethouses in
1737 appeared in disguise to protect their anonymity suggests that Cooke's prominent allies not only participated in
but probably also led the crowd's activities. The same kinds
of cross-class alignments appeared in other colonial crowd
actions as well—the Norfolk anti-inoculation riot in 1768
and the Regulator uprisings in the commercially developing
North Carolina backcountry, to name just a few. This recurrent pattern suggests that in such places, despite the growth
of inequality, opposition to wealth was not the most salient
aspect of social protest.[13]

But if the Marblehead riot was not essentially a protest
against economic inequality, neither was it simply an attack
of individuals who were unpopular solely because of their
support of inoculation. The Marblehead crowd repudiated
the authority of men like Justice Minot and Sheriff Blaney in

[13]Nash, *Urban Crucible,* 136; Maier, "Popular Uprisings and Civil Authority," *WMQ,* 27:13; James P. Whittenberg, "Planters, Merchants, and Lawyers: Social Change and the Origins of the North Carolina Regulation,"
WMQ, 3rd ser., 34 (1974), 215–38.

no uncertain terms and disregarded their demands for obedience and deference. Although this behavior on the part of
the mob could be seen simply as diffuse antiauthoritarian-
ism, more commonly this kind of conduct has been construed as indicating something more significant, namely, a
serious weakening of the deferential order of traditional
society. Of course, the consciousness of the Marblehead crowd
can never be known with complete certainty. Even so, the
mob's challenge to Stephen Minot and his circle seems to
have been more than a mere outburst of ritualized insolence,
if rather less than a fundamental protest against social sub-
ordination. The crowd's motivation was neither lawlessness
nor levelling, but instead, an issue of longstanding concern
to local society.

What distinguished Stephen Minot and the other men who
opposed the rioters from other Marbleheaders was less their
wealth and power than their shared social background. They
were all members of the small, privileged clique comprised
principally of transplanted Bostonians who profited from
connections with larger seaports. All of the five men who
first moved to quell the riot had impeccable cosmopolitan
credentials. Stephen Minot, Jr., and Jeremiah Allen, Jr., were
the sons of major Boston merchants. Nathan Bowen had come
to Marblehead from the Boston countinghouse of James
Bowdoin, one of the capital's major fish exporters. Cam-
bridge-born Richard Dana, a lawyer like Bowen as well as
Marblehead's schoolmaster, had enjoyed a gentleman's education at Harvard College. John Tasker, a recently arrived
English merchant, had just married the daughter of another
former Bostonian turned Marblehead trader, Richard Skinner. Among the men who lent their support to Minot, Ebenezer Lowell was the local agent for Boston's Peter Faneuil,
a major fish dealer, and Joseph Blaney was a wealthy tanner
who had emigrated from Salem. Even William Man, the owner
of the tavern where Minot first received news of the riot, was
a brazier from Boston turned innkeeper. Of the entire group
of men named as opponents of the riot, only John Stacey,
the militia captain whom the mob routed at Jackson's inn,
was a native of Marblehead. And even he was connected to
Minot's cosmopolitan circle by his marriage to another
daughter of Richard Skinner. Besides their cosmopolitan

connections, what all these men had in common was that they attended Second Church. The only exception was John Tasker, an Anglican; but his father-in-law Skinner was the Second Church deacon.

Stephen Minot and his fellow members of the Second Church elite had never paid much attention to the desires of the majority of other Marbleheaders. Their disregard of the town's opposition to inoculation in 1730 recalled their determination fifteen years earlier to override local preference in the matter of ministerial candidates. Nor were Second Church leaders concerned with the welfare of local inhabitants or of the town as a whole. On the contrary, they made their money by encouraging dependency on bigger ports and indebtedness at home. Their advocacy of inoculation and disdain for the town meeting's interdiction of the practice epitomized their essential disengagement from local life and lack of concern for the common good. To the minds of most Marbleheaders, this was the real problem with the Second Church circle. What galled townspeople was less the wealth and power of this ruling group than their ability to acquire these badges of status while lacking the attributes of a traditional elite: identification with the local community and commitment to the public welfare. The Marblehead crowd's actions constituted a protest against this aspect of the basic structure of local society in 1730. The mob repudiated the dominance of men whose loyalties lay outside of town and who secured their livelihoods—and their lives—at the expense of the rest of the community. Marbleheaders did not rise up in the hope of recalling an elite whose legitimacy they acknowledged to fulfill its customary responsibilities. The crowd rather rejected the claims to authority and deference advanced by men like Stephen Minot, who exercised no restraint in the pursuit of private will and interest. In the view of most local inhabitants, the Second Church circle had cut themselves loose from the communal matrix of mutual obligations that validated hierarchical relationships.[14]

[14] On Minot, Allen, Dana, and Lowell, see note 8 above. For Blaney's background, see *The Essex Antiquarian*, 9 (1905), 32–36; on Tasker, see Elizabeth Dana, "Richard Skinner of Marblehead and his Bible," *New England Historical and Genealogical Register*, 54 (1900), 412–13. William Man is

The alienation of most Marbleheaders from likes of Stephen Minot was summed up by Dr. Bartholomew Jackson's
response to Sheriff Blaney's request for assistance in suppressing the mob. According to Blaney, "He [Jackson]
answered Me what Mobb that I was one of them and that it
was I and some others that medled in what was none of their
Business that occasioned it."[15] What happened in Marblehead was "none of the business" of men like Blaney and
Minot because they had forfeited their right to exercise legitimate leadership within the community. Lacking any connection to local society, the Second Church circle could claim
no authority in town. In the eyes of Jackson and his supporters, Minot and his friends *were* the "mob," the lawless,
disruptive element in Marblehead.[16] Deeper than the divisions of class, status, and power was the difference between
"insiders" and "outsiders," the distinction between those who
were committed to the town and those who were not.

This shared sense of the importance of local identity and
loyalty unified all classes in Marblehead against a deracinated, privileged faction within the town's elite in 1730. And
the influence of localistic sentiment in determining political
alignments was not peculiar only to conflicts in Marblehead.
Several years later in Boston, the same animus of "insiders"
against "outsiders" shaped the controversy over public regulated markets. What was distinctive about the younger
merchants who were the markets' proponents was not their
wealth but their connections to the royal governor's circle of
patronage. Like Marblehead's Second Church leaders, these
traders formed a privileged clique within local society, and
their outlook generally reflected a greater affinity for and
awareness of the culture of the wider Anglo-American world
than was characteristic of most other Bostonians. Their
political program included not only the introduction of regulated markets but a set of other reforms that would have
remodelled the town's political and economic institutions

identified as a Boston brazier in several civil cases appealed to the Supreme
Court of Judicature. (MSCJ, 1715–1721.)

[15] Deposition of Joseph Blaney, December 29, 1730, FGSP.

[16] Maier, "Popular Uprisings and Civil Authority," *WMQ*, 27: 12.

along the lines of English boroughs. Arrayed against this group were the majority of Bostonians, who preferred their old way of life and "antiquated" civic institutions and who responded to their cosmopolitan opponents with the market riot of 1737. The force of localistic attachments played an equally important role in the North Carolina Regulation of the 1760s and 1770s. Here the counterparts of Marblehead's Second Church elite were a group of wealthy, sophisticated, and well-educated lawyers and merchants closely associated with the colony's eastern seaboard establishment. These traders and professional men parlayed their connections with powerful eastern interests into political and economic influence in the western part of the colony. To resist the encroachment of this elite of eastern-sponsored newcomers, backcountry farmers of all classes rallied behind their old local leaders, a long-settled group of larger planters. The result was the Regulator movement, a series of uprisings in the backcountry that culminated with the defeat of the agrarian insurgents at the Battle of Alamance in 1771. In this instance too, the basis of the conflict was culture rather than class, the opposition of all planters, both rich and poor, to the increasing control of local society by a socially polished, politically privileged commercial clique.[17]

In Marblehead, as in Boston and the Carolina backcountry, a crowd claiming the traditional rights of local autonomy and self-determination contended against cosmopolitan adversaries. By asserting local solidarity and by refusing to

[17] Warden, *Boston,* 123; Whittenberg, "Planters, Lawyers, and Merchants," *WMQ,* 27: 12. The Marblehead riot also bears some resemblances to other forms of collective action in eighteenth-century English coastal towns. See especially, Cal Winslow, "Sussex Smugglers," and John G. Rule, "Wrecking and Coastal Plunder," in E. P. Thompson, et al., *Albion's Fatal Tree: Crime and Society in Eighteenth Century England* (New York, 1975), 119–88. Winslow and Rule emphasize that activities like smuggling and wrecking were ways that the Enlgish poor resisted the advance of capitalism and the market economy, but they also note that the presence of substantial men in the smuggling and wrecking gangs suggests the significance of local traditions and attitudes in shaping collective activity. English coastal mobs, Winslow concludes, were thus "a mixture of social forms of resistance" that involved not only elements of class antagonism but also "a regional and traditional response" by an economic cross section of local society to the centralization of wealth and power in larger commercial centers. (158–59)

recognize the authority of men who had abandoned the customary obligations of an elite, the Marblehead rioters affirmed an older set of cultural values. But unlike Bostonians and Carolina farmers, Marbleheaders had had very little direct experience of a social life shaped by those ideals. It was not the strength of their shared past but the pressures of the present that enhanced the attraction of townspeople to communal social arrangements and ideals. The anti-inoculation riot thus represented not an effort to protect the traditional order of society but a protest against Marblehead's failure to establish this kind of social organization in the first place, particularly a legitimate hierarchy. The members of the Marblehead crowd were not rejecting a deferential order. Rather, they were repudiating the Second Church elite, men who claimed to be leaders but refused to share in the common peril and put private preference over their responsibility to the rest of the community in matters of business, religion, and in 1730, life and death.

In many respects the anti-inoculation riot of 1730 reenacted the struggle against the domination of local life by outsiders that had taken place fifteen years earlier in the controversy among Marblehead Congregationalists over rival ministerial candidates. But there was one difference. In 1715, it was the adherents of John Barnard at First Church who had spearheaded local resistance to the transplanted Bostonians who backed the candidacy of Edward Holyoke and subsequently formed the Second Church. In 1730, it was Marblehead Episcopalians who led local society against the same Second Church circle. To find the Anglicans in this position is unexpected, to say the least. Episcopalians were often the targets of "traditionalist" crowd attacks in colonial New England, but the Marblehead uprising presents Churchmen in a less familiar role as organizers of the mob. The known participants in the anti-inoculation riot, almost to a man, were members of St. Michael's. Among the crowd's ringleaders, Dr. Bartholomew Jackson and Captain Joseph Majory were both members of St. Michael's vestry and, within the rank and file of the mob, Churchmen also predominated. William Majory, Jacob Ball, Peter Pollo, Richard Searle, Jr., John Chappell, Benjamin Codner, John Sasser, Thomas Main, and Nicholas Bezoone were all among Pigot's parishioners.

Ebenezer Lowell's assailant, Thomas Horton, was an Episcopalian; so was Elias Waters, the shopkeeper who overheard Minot profess his support for inoculation and perhaps spread the story to other townspeople. Other Anglican abettors of the riot included Ensign David Furneux, who refused to assist the constables, and Jonathan Boden, who threatened Jeremiah Allen. Finally there was Captain Ebenezer Hawkes, Jr., another prominent promoter of the disruption, who was also a dissenter although not an Anglican. As a member of Marblehead's only Quaker family, Captain Hawkes had struck an odd alliance theologically but one that made sense politically.[18]

Participation in the riot was not limited to St. Michael's members, nor was opposition to inoculation in Marblehead restricted to Episcopalians. A majority of the Marblehead town meeting had voted to renew the earlier interdiction of the treatment. And not all of Marblehead's Anglicans supported the rioters. The fundamental issue of local identification divided leading Episcopalians just as it cleaved their Congregationalist counterparts. Members of the Anglican elite like John Oulton and James Calley, who had intermarried with Second Church families, either stayed away from the action in the streets or, like John Tasker, aided in attempts to quell the mob. On the other hand, Anglican leaders like Jackson and Majory, who lacked cosmopolitan connections and close ties to Second Church, figured prominently in the crowd's activities. Yet notwithstanding the lack of universal support for the mob within the Episcopal elite and the widespread opposition to inoculation among Marbleheaders generally, it was mainly St. Michael's members who escalated the controversy into a violent confrontation. And it was the Anglicans who played the most active role in the riot itself. Perhaps there was even a precedent for the lead taken by Marblehead Episcopalians in the anti-inoculation protest. During the earlier Boston epidemic of 1721, Cotton Mather

[18] Fourteen of the nineteen men who were either indicated or named in the depositions as supporting the riot were Episcopalians who appear in the "Records of St. Michael's Church, 1716–1784." Among the remaining five, one was a Quaker, two were at Second Church but with family ties to St. Michael's members, and two attended First Church. On Quakerism in the Hawkes family, see EPF, #12913.

had charged that Churchmen used the issue of inoculation to attract popular support and to whip up resentment against the Congregationalist clergy.[19] Though Perry Miller dismissed these allegations as evidence of Mather's paranoia, the Marblehead riot of 1730 shows that religious tensions could decisively shape the politics of popular uprisings. After all, even paranoics have enemies.

For most Marblehead Episcopalians, the anti-inoculation riot was a means to two ends. First, it was a way of settling old scores with the Congregationalists, who had insisted on building Second Church "in Damnable Spite and Malice against the Church of England." Second and more important, Episcopal prominence in this popular cause advanced their claim to full membership in the local community and countered the insinuations of John Barnard. By leading the anti-inoculation forces, Anglicans publicly displayed the authenticity of their antagonism to outsiders, their commitment to local autonomy, and their conformity to the entire constellation of communal values. The success of this strategy in enhancing the public acceptance and political strength of Episcopalians in town was immediate. In a special election called for January of 1731, Dr. Bartholomew Jackson and his fellow vestryman Abraham Howard replaced two Congregationalists on the board of selectmen, with Churchman James Calley ousting Stephen Minot as Marblehead's representative to the General Court. In the regular March elections two months later, Episcopalians took an unprecedented three of the five selectmen's slots.[20]

The public acclaim and popularity accorded Anglican leaders in the wake of the riot set back John Barnard's strategy of tapping the power of localism to undercut the Episcopal position in town. Throughout the 1720s, Barnard had been striving to identify orthodoxy with the cause of local autonomy and Anglicanism with extralocal power and authority. In 1730, by exploiting the opposition to inoculation, St. Michael's members had turned the tables. It was bad enough that both of Marblehead's orthodox ministers had joined with their clerical colleagues in Boston in support

[19] Perry Miller, *The New England Mind: From Colony to Province*, 355.
[20] MTR, III, 97, 100, 102.

of inoculation. Ministerial solidarity and enthusiasm for scientific innovation induced both Holyoke and Barnard to
endorse Boylston's discovery, the former fervently, the latter
more circumspectly. By their advocacy of inoculation, Marblehead's clergymen were pitting themselves against the
majority of townspeople. But to make matters even worse,
after the riot Holyoke again fled Marblehead for Boston,
just as he had during the earlier smallpox outbreak.[21] His
abrupt departure left Barnard alone to stem the tide of
antiministerial sentiment that rose in the wake of the 1730
epidemic, as it had after the initial inoculation controversy
in Boston nine years earlier. To Barnard fell the task of prov-
ing that, in supporting inoculation, he and Holyoke had at
heart Marblehead's best interest and that in opposing Boylston's discovery, local Anglicans had betrayed the town.

Barnard took up the challenge a few weeks after the riot
in the winter of 1731, as he preached a series of sermons on
salvation. Using the recent epidemic to arouse his congregation's concerns about the afterlife, Barnard also attempted
to associate the opposition to inoculation with superstition,
disorder, and the Episcopacy's master plan to dominate New
England. Without ever mentioning inoculation, he drew an
analogy between spiritual and physical perils, arguing that
only "stupid men" faced "with a threatening danger" failed
to use "the most probable and likely means . . . to divert the
stroke." And without ever naming Dr. Bartholomew Jackson, Barnard related the Biblical story of a bad character at
Philippi who employed a female fortuneteller possessed by
"a Foul Spirit" and enriched himself by playing upon popular superstitions. When the apostles Paul and Silas cast out
the fortuneteller's demon and ended her profitable "divina-
tions," this fellow "stirred up the Rabble to join with him in
a Tumult," and the apostles landed in prison. But that evening, an earthquake freed Paul and Silas from their fetters, a
providential deliverance that so impressed their jailer that he
began treating them "with civility and respect." The jailer
even asked for religious instruction, "tho' he had once
regarded them as the troublers of their City, by their teaching of Customs which it was not lawful (they tho't) to

[21] *Holyoke Diaries,* 3.

observe."[22] No earthquake vindicated the apostles of inoculation in Marblehead, but by April of 1731, tempers in town
had cooled enough for Holyoke to return to Second Church.

As Barnard's retreat into allegory indicates, the anti-inoculation riot had put the parson on the defensive in his crusade against the Church of England in Marblehead. Although
the Anglican role in the riot only confirmed Barnard in his
conviction that Churchmen constituted an aggressive, volatile, and irrational element in Marblehead society, there was
widespread support for the crowd's objectives, especially at
First Church. Despite the unpopularity of his position on
inoculation, Barnard was able to remain in town throughout
the crisis, and his influence with his congregation kept most
of them on the sidelines during the uprising itself. Only one
member of Barnard's church, Bonnel Merryfield, was indicted
for being a participant in the riot, while another, Richard
Reith, had refused to assist Minot in suppressing the mob.
But most of Barnard's parishioners probably opposed inoculation, and although they were reticent about rallying behind
Anglicans in the streets, they could not resist rewarding them
at the polls. This was reflected in the immediate gains made
by St. Michael's members in the elections of 1731 and in
their continuing political success throughout the 1730s.
During that decade, Churchmen doubled their representation on the board of selectmen, filling over one-third of all
terms.[23] Disproportionate to the percentage of Episcopalians within the total population, this new electoral strength
had to come from somewhere, and the voters in the First
Parish are the most probable source. The Marblehead elec-
torate rewarded even Quaker riot leader Ebenezer Hawkes,
Jr., with a term in office. The popular trust and credibility as
communal leaders acquired by Churchmen through their
participation in the anti-inoculation riot precluded overt
attacks upon religious dissenters from the pulpit of First
Church for the future.

The collusion of First Church Congregationalists in Epis-

---

[22] John Barnard, *Janua Coelestis* (Boston, 1750), 9–10, 115–16.
[23] Episcopalians held sixteen of the fifty selectmen's terms between 1730
and 1739, or about one-third of all terms. In the decade prior, they had
held ten of the fifty, or twenty percent. (See MTR, III, 1720–1739.)

copal political successes during the 1730s indicates that widespread support for the most basic objectives of the Marblehead crowd overrode even religious differences in town, sectarian animosities that had peaked only a year before. In this respect, the alliance between Congregationalists and Churchmen that emerged during the epidemic of 1730–31 recalls the agreement of 1715, when First Church members also made common cause with local Episcopalians against the families that came to comprise the Second Church. The division between orthodoxy and heterodoxy, like the gulf between the affluence of Dr. Bartholomew Jackson and the desperation of Jacob Ball, could be bridged in the winter of 1730–31 because of the values and goals that the majority of Marblehead inhabitants had come to hold in common. Resentment of external control over and interference in local life, represented by Stephen Minot and other cosmopolitan members of Marblehead's elite, abetted internal unity. A shared commitment to communal autonomy submerged the significance of cleavages based upon class position and sectarian affiliation.

The strong resurgence of localistic identification and the accompanying assertion of older values pertaining to social organization were at the center of the riot's significance. The crowd's actions dramatized that even in a community as disrupted as Marblehead, cravings for particularism and traditional expectations of the elite still persisted. Despite—or perhaps because of—economic expansion, many townspeople yearned for a society structured to accord with communitarian ideals. This traditionalism was not peculiar only to the laboring people of Marblehead, but was spread throughout local society, an outlook shared even by wealthy entrepreneurs like Dr. Bartholomew Jackson and Richard Reith.

Though opposition to inoculation mobilized Marbleheaders against men like Stephen Minot, townspeople did not find their quest for order fulfilled in the riot. The protest was a short-lived uprising against outside domination of local life, an outburst reminiscent in some ways of the earlier Indian murders or the riot sparked by the removal of guns from Marblehead harbor. The crowd's actions brought about no changes in the social and economic order and did nothing to reduce the town's dependency on nonlocal merchants. On the other hand, the anti-inoculation riot, together with the calling of John Barnard in 1715 and the popular response to his ministry throughout the 1720s, reveals the intense desire for order and autonomy fermenting from within local society. It was these communal and localistic affinities that sustained the deep and enduring transformation that began to take place in Marblehead during the 1730s. What prompted the emergence of a new order in Marblehead at this time was the development of a locally controlled direct trade, a commerce initiated principally by the parishioners of John Barnard.

10

The Making of the "Marblehead Gentry"

MARBLEHEAD'S EMERGENCE as an independent commercial center was part of the wider change overtaking the organization of maritime activity in Massachusetts by the beginning of the 1730s. For one hundred years after the first settlement of New England, Boston and Salem had monopolized the marketing of both fish and lumber supplied by smaller coastal towns and the agricultural surplus produced by the surrounding countryside. These two larger ports had also served as the sole conduits for the distribution of finished goods imported from England. But starting in the 1720s, coastal settlements like Gloucester and Marblehead began to develop a locally controlled direct trade, packing, transporting, and marketing their own catches. By the middle of the eighteenth century, the evolution of these former fishing villages into autonomous commercial centers was virtually complete. Native merchants had taken over the traffic in cod to the Caribbean and the Mediterranean, and they had started importing manufactures directly from Europe. The structure of credit in these smaller seaports was also becoming almost entirely local, as Gloucester and Marblehead men financed with their own capital fishing and trading voyages. By claiming a larger share of the shipbuilding trade, Salem's economy sustained this increased commercial competition from secondary ports without suffering any serious setback. Boston did not fare as well. Weakened by high taxes, declining population and productivity, and rising prices, the capital stagnated while its former satellites surged ahead.[1]

The evolution of an independent commerce in Marblehead began with its inhabitants' increasing participation in the coastwide trade. The success of a few native entrepreneurs who opened a direct trade with the southern colonies and the Caribbean in the 1720s encouraged a growing number of townsmen to follow their example during the next decade. This early, locally controlled commerce in fish was of limited scope: vessels of small tunnage were dispatched only to colonial markets in the Chesapeake, the Carolinas, and the West Indies. Nevertheless, the rising price of fish and the continuing expansion of demand, especially in the Caribbean, made such undertakings profitable and yielded the capital necessary to enlarge the town's trading circuit. By the end of the 1730s, several of the most successful coastal traders were pooling their resources for investment in the transatlantic trade to the Wine Islands and southern Europe. To keep pace with the growth of the direct trade, the local fishery expanded its operations as well. By the early 1740s, Marblehead had over 150 fishing schooners and again as many ketches and shallops, about one-third of the total tunnage of the Massachusetts fishing fleet. The returns of the coastwide trade alone underwrote the costs of operating the fishing industry, leaving as clear profit the proceeds of sales to European markets.[2]

By the middle of the eighteenth century, Marblehead's transatlantic traffic had become considerable. Between the fall of 1752 and the summer of 1753, the first year for which shipping manifests are available, over half of the thirty-seven locally owned merchantmen that cleared the port of Salem-Marblehead were bound for southern Europe. Forty years earlier, only a handful of vessels owned in Marblehead had been involved in the fish trade to the Caribbean and none to

[1] See chapter II, notes 1 and 19.

[2] Innis, *The Codfisheries*, 159–61; MacFarland, *History of the New England Fisheries*, 88; Bowden, "Commerce of Marblehead," *EIHC*, 68: 132–34. The price of fish declined after 1749, but the decrease was offset somewhat by increasing production.

the Mediterranean. In terms of distances traveled and the tunnage of vessels involved, the scale of Marblehead's commerce by the 1740s outstripped even that of Salem, its nearest competitor in Essex County. Salem traders claimed the largest number of ships clearing port in 1752–53, but their craft were generally smaller than Marblehead-owned vessels, and only one in five was destined for a Mediterranean port with a load of fish. During the middle of the eighteenth century, Salem maintained a small, coastal trade in agricultural produce, refuse fish, and odd lots of crude home manufactures. Meanwhile, Marblehead emerged as the center of foreign commerce in the county and began diversifying into ropemaking and distilling as well.[3]

Though the maturation of a locally controlled direct trade during the years after 1730 freed Marblehead from the domination of larger ports, the period was not one of even, unbroken, economic progress. Fishing and commerce sustained intermittent setbacks after military conflict between England the other European powers flared up again in 1739. The war with Spain between 1739 and 1742 increased privateering in the Caribbean, disrupting Marblehead's West Indian trade and reducing the purchasing power of sugar planters. New Englanders continued their lucrative commerce with Spain itself by using neutral vessels to transport cargoes from reshipment stations in England, Jersey, and Holland. But the cost and complexity of these arrangements afforded French fish exporters a decided edge in the Iberian

---

[3] Bowden, "Commerce of Marblehead," *EIHC*, 68: 132–34; *MA*, 117: 56, 57, and 66. The table below illustrates local vessel-ownership in major Essex County ports and the destinations of these ships:

CLEARINGS FROM THE PORT OF SALEM-MARBLEHEAD, FALL, 1752
THROUGH SUMMER, 1753

Vessels owned	To Southern Europe/Wine Islands	To Southern Colonies/Caribbean
Salem, 56	10	46
Marblehead, 37	20	17
Gloucester, 28	2	26

SOURCE: *Abstracts of English Shipping Records*, volume 3, Essex Institute.

market.[4] The entry of France into the war in the spring of 1744 plunged the fishing industry and trade into even deeper difficulties. French privateers patroling the Atlantic kept Marblehead fishing vessels "hawled up" in the harbor until August of 1744 when, under the protection of government convoys, they ventured out to the grounds again. Adding to Marbleheaders' disappointment at the short season and the fleet's small catch was their discovery that the hostilities had made a shambles of the trade to Europe. The French threat in the Atlantic disrupted Marblehead merchants' correspondence with their foreign factors, inflated the price of maritime insurance, interfered with the arrival of imports from England, and brought to a standstill the shipping of fish. The Caribbean also continued to prove an inhospitable environment to colonial shipping, as enemy privateers seized several Marblehead coasting vessels.[5]

At the beginning of January in 1745, the town's prospects worsened when Spain interdicted commerce with New England completely. At the same time, the Massachusetts provincial government imposed an embargo on all maritime traffic that extended until the first of April, a measure that cut nearly two months out of the fishing season. And after the embargo was lifted and fishing boats began embarking on their first fares in the late spring, the organization of the expedition against Louisbourg siphoned off Marblehead's men and vessels into government military service. The campaign against the French fortress on Cape Breton Island was a popular cause among Marbleheaders, who had always wanted to expel the French entirely from the north Atlantic fishery. But the town paid dearly for its involvement in the conquest of Louisbourg. Although the actual fighting at Cape Breton

[4] MacFarland, *History of the New England Fisheries*, 88; and Innis, *The Codfisheries*, 161 and 173. Robert Hooper to Samuel Storke, September 2, 1741, to Storke, February 15, 1742, and to Gedney Clarke, August 22, 1741, in "The Letterbook of Robert Hooper and Joseph Swett, 1740–1747," MS, Essex Institute, Salem, Mass. (Cited hereafter as HSL.)

[5] Hooper to Storke, May 2, 1744, June 1, 1744, August 1, 1744, and May 29, 1745; to Clarke, August 13, 1744; to Mme. Ferrand Whaley, September 10, 1744, and November 13, 1744; to Steers and Barons, November 1, 1744, HSL; and Protest of John Jones, June 28, 1746, ENR.

claimed few casualties, a "raging distemper" that swept through the army camp after the victory and the loss at sea of a government sloop manned mainly by Marbleheaders cost a large number of local men their lives. Military campaigns also undermined the town's economy by reducing the catch of the fishery and interrupting the flow of commerce throughout 1745 and 1746.[6]

Compounding the economic setbacks produced by the Spanish and French wars between 1739 and 1746 were the calamities dealt Marblehead by natural disasters. In 1741, a storm at sea took the lives of so many local fishermen that the town asked for an abatement of their share of the province tax. Five years later in 1746, another maritime disaster prompted Marblehead selectmen to make a similar request. In that year, one-quarter of Marblehead's fishing fleet went down in a strong gale, a loss that the recent casualties of the Louisbourg campaign made even more staggering. After the peace of Aix-la-Chappelle in 1748, the Marblehead fishery revived and commerce resumed, just as the economy had recovered following the peace of Utrecht in 1713 and would again after the Treaty of Paris ended the Seven Years' War in 1763.[7] But the fighting of the 1740s and of the following decades interrupted local economic development for long periods.

War and natural disaster also took their toll upon the welfare of Marblehead families, particularly those occupying the lower echelons of the fishing community. While the share of the town's total wealth held by the bottom half of Marblehead society between 1736 and 1755 did not diminish appreciably, median estate value plummeted from sixty pounds sterling during the 1730s to forty-five pounds sterling during the 1740s and 1750s. More than offsetting the economic advantages that the military crisis afforded ordinary members of the maritime community—a rising price for their fish and high wages for sailors—were the loss of

[6] Hooper to Joseph Gardoqui, January 7, 1745, and June 25, 1745; to Storke, February 25, 1745, and July 20, 1745; to Clarke, January 20, 1746, and May 17, 1746; and to Steers and Barons, April 25, 1745, HSL.

[7] Petition of James Skinner to the General Court, January 7, 1742, MA, 115: 6–7; MTR, III, 266; Hooper to Steers and Barons, April, 1746; to Clarke, April 22, 1746, HSL; and Innis, The Codfisheries, 161.

heads of household to storms and disease and the inflated
prices for necessities such as bread and firewood. The numbers of dependent women and children in Marblehead multiplied in the wake of natural and man-made catastrophes,
and their claims upon public support augmented the burden
upon local taxpayers.[8]

The disruptions of war, the sufferings from losses at sea,
and the straitened economic circumstances of many Marble-

[8] For information on wealth distribution and median estate value, see
appendix, table I. The drop in median estate value and the declining range
of real and personal wealth (table II) among all decile groups except the
richest ten percent of inventoried decedents may be related to changes in
the composition of the fishing industry's labor force during the eighteenth
century as well as to the disruptions of war. Daniel Vickers believes that
the greater rigors of the offshore banks fishery, coupled with the growing
availability of maritime labor, increasingly made fishing "a young man's
profession." Fishermen over the age of thirty found that their declining
productivity made them less attractive to employers, forcing their retirement from the sea. (Vickers, "Maritime Labor in Colonial Massachusetts,"
221–26.) Unless these former fishermen had acquired either land or a trade
suited to life in town, they probably faced a future of low-paid casual labor
or dependence on their seafaring sons. As a result, a retired fisherman's
estate may have been considerably smaller at the end of his life than during
his years at sea. Unlike many heads of farming households, whose inventoried wealth at death often represents the summit of their economic attainments, the inventories of retired fishermen may distort downwards. In
addition, the preference for and availability of young fishermen would have
deprived Marblehead's older artisans and laborers of the opportunity to
supplement their incomes by hiring out on occasional fishing voyages.
Gloucester does not exhibit a similar decline in median estate value over
the eighteenth century, possibly because the more sustained growth of that
town's fishery, coupled with the continuing scarcity of labor, kept older
men in the industry.

On the hardships of the Marblehead maritime community during the
war years, see Hooper to Clarke, May 11, 1741 and May 17, 1746, HSL;
and MTR, III, 26. Town taxes fluctuated during the 1740s in response to
needs created by military conflict and natural disasters. In 1745, the year of
the embargo and the Louisbourg expedition, the town voted a total tax of
ninety-eight pounds sterling; in 1746, the town tax decreased to seventy-
two pounds sterling, but losses at sea that summer pushed the tax burden
back up to ninety pounds sterling in 1747. Marbleheaders were still paying
less in taxes than Bostonians, who in the late forties paid an average of fifty
shillings in total taxes. In 1748, when the town tax had again dipped to
seventy-two pounds sterling, the average Marbleheader paid about twenty
shillings in total taxes. (For the town tax, see MTR, III, 1745–48; for the
province rate, see "The Marblehead Tax List for 1748," *EIHC*, 43: 209–
22. On taxation in Boston for the 1740s, see Nash, *Urban Crucible*, 173.)

headers might have ushered in yet another stormy period in the town's troubled history. But that did not happen. Instead, despite the hardships endured by inhabitants, local social life exhibited greater stability during the decades after 1730 than it had at any time in the past. Not only was Marblehead free from the severe internal turmoil that had typified the town earlier in the eighteenth century, but it also showed signs of becoming a more settled and cohesive community. By mid-century, Marbleheaders were fighting over fundamental issues far less frequently and finding that they shared more in common.

Part of the basis of this new order was a change in the pattern of local demographic development that altered both the composition and mobility of Marblehead's population. After peaking in the two decades after 1710, migration into Marblehead began to taper off throughout the 1730s and 1740s. By the middle of the eighteenth century, over eighty percent of all Marblehead's adult male inhabitants came from families that had resided in town for at least thirty years. Despite this decline in in-migration and the loss of men in military campaigns and maritime disasters, local population continued to expand over the middle decades of the eighteenth century. But according to the Reverend Alexander Malcolm, the rector of St. Michael's during the 1740s, "The place [Marblehead] grows in Number of Inhabitants not by Strangers Settling here, But by their own Natural Encrease."[9] The expansion of the native-born population in town reduced the necessity of importing large numbers of indentured servants from the Channel Islands to supplement the labor force of the fishery. In addition, local development of a direct trade to Europe greatly diminished the number of transient English mariners in town during the spring and summer months. The largest single contingent of new arrivals in Marblehead after

[9] Alexander Malcolm to S.P.G. Sec'y, April 16, 1744, in *Historical Collections,* ed. Perry, III, 379. In the 1730s and 1740s, 159 new surnames appear in town and church records, yielding a figure of about eighty newcomers per decade, approximately half the size of the in-migration between 1710 and 1730. More important, families who had been settled in town for a long period were now predominant in the local population. Of the 620 ratepayers on the tax list of 1748, the families of 495 had been in town since 1720.

1730 were neither culturally and linguistically distinct Jersey families nor seafaring "strangers" but migrants from neighboring Essex County coastal towns.[10]

The decline of migration into Marblehead and the predominance of native-born or long-established residents within its population markedly reduced the strain on local society. The greater social harmony and integration that resulted from these changing demographic patterns was reflected in the decreasing incidence of both intratown civil litigation and criminal prosecutions involving townspeople. During the 1730s and 1740s, Marbleheaders became far more reluctant to sue each other in court, and the total number of intratown suits for debt declined dramatically. In 1739, for example, Marblehead plaintiffs and defendants were involved in a total of 67 suits, about one-third the number of intratown civil actions initiated ten years before; and in 1749, only twenty-nine actions for debt involved fellow townsmen.[11] At the same time, Marblehead inhabitants were also making less frequent appearances before the justices of the peace for crimes against persons and property. The number of cases involving violent crime in Marblehead between 1736 and 1755 was

[10] Tracing the places of origin of families who migrated to Marblehead is a difficult undertaking, but conservatively estimated, over one-third of the new arrivals in the thirties and forties (57 of 159) came from the neighboring North Shore ports of Salem, Lynn, Charlestown, Beverly, Gloucester, and Newbury. This count is based on tracing surnames in the indices to the Essex County probate records for the seventeenth and eighteenth centuries and in the local histories cited in Chapter II, note 6. The majority of other newcomers probably came from inland country towns in Essex County and elsewhere in Massachusetts or from Boston, where continuing economic troubles encouraged out-migration. The occasional appearance of new French and Scot-Irish surnames in the records for the thirties and forties indicates that some of the newcomers to Marblehead were not New England–born. Their numbers, however, are much smaller by the middle of the eighteenth century than earlier in the period. Daniel Vickers's study of maritime laboring populations in Essex County reveals a similarly sharp decline in the proportion of immigrants into the 1760s and 1770s. He estimates that 89 percent of the fishermen sailing out of Marblehead between 1766 and 1775 were native-born, while even in Gloucester, where a smaller total population necessitated the importation of more nonlocal labor, fully 70 percent of the fishermen were native-born. ("Maritime Labor in Colonial Massachusetts," 205, 207–211, and 220.)

[11] See appendix, table III.

one-quarter of the total for the preceding two decades; cases of theft, breaking and entering, and receiving stolen goods also decreased by better than half. An equally striking decline occurred in indictments for sexual misbehavior. While the courts stopped prosecuting prematurely blessed parents in the general sessions of the peace at the beginning of the 1740s, grand juries continued to arraign singlewomen (and the men that they charged as fathers) for fornication. In Marblehead, the number of such single parents prosecuted between 1736 and 1755 was half of that for the twenty years earlier.[12]

The significance of Marblehead's declining number of civil suits and criminal prosecutions becomes more apparent when compared to the situation in Salem. Here, over the same period, the incidences of assault, theft, fornication, and debt litigation either rose or remained constant. The contrast suggests that Marblehead's decreasing number of civil and criminal defendants did not represent a wider trend within Essex County but reflected instead the improvement of relations among townspeople and the greater security of persons and property. Earlier in the eighteenth century, the volume of prosecutions for debt and crime in Marblehead had been, in comparison with Salem, disproportionately high. But during the two decades after 1735, the level of civil litigation among Marbleheaders was receding rapidly, while the incidence of criminal activity within the town was actually smaller than that in Salem.[13]

[12] In Marblehead between 1736 and 1755, there were four cases involving violent crime, four cases involving crimes against property and sixteen indictments for fornication that came before either the Essex County General Sessions or the Massachusetts Supreme Court. (Sources: MGSP, MSCJ.) Cf. chapter VII, note 23.

[13] For debt litigation involving Salem residents, see appendix, table III. In Salem between 1736 and 1755, there were nine cases involving violent crime, four theft-related cases, and thirty-eight indictments for fornication that came before either the Essex County General Sessions or the Massachusetts Supreme Court. (Sources: MGSP, MSCJ.) The contrast with Salem's relatively constant level of intratown debt litigation and rising crime rate and the evidence of other stabilizing trends within Marblehead make it most plausible to construe Marblehead's declining number of intratown suits and criminal prosecutions as reflecting a real decrease in the level of local conflict. The wartime disruption of the fishing business may have contributed to the decrease of both inter- and intratown litigation in Marblehead as well as in other ports during the 1740s. But the decline in Marblehead's

Demographic changes account in part for the easing of social tensions in Marblehead during the middle decades of the eighteenth century. As the flow of people into and out of town slowed and membership within the community became more permanent, Marbleheaders developed closer personal ties and a trust that precluded quick legal recourse to collect debts. The smaller population of transients and imported servants was also influential in reducing the volume of theft, violent crime, and sexual misconduct. The fighting against the Spanish and French may also have afforded Marblehead's men an outlet for the aggression that they had earlier vented in street brawls, domestic quarrels, and "riotous assemblies." In the opinion of contemporaries, however, there was another explanation of what had transformed Marblehead. As John Barnard reflected on the changes that had taken place in town between the time of his ordination in 1716 and the close of his pastorate in the 1760s, he made the following observations:

> When I first came, there were two companies of poor, smoke-dried, rude, ill-clothed men, trained to no military discipline . . . whereas now, and for years past, we are a distinct regiment, consisting of seven full companies, well clad, of bright countenances, vigorous and active men, well trained in the use of their arms. . . . When I first came there was not so much as one proper carpenter, nor mason, nor tailor, nor butcher in town, nor anything of a market worth naming; but they had their houses built by country workmen, and their clothes made out of town, and supplied themselves with beef and pork from Boston, which drained the town of its money. But now we abound in artificers, and some of the best, and our markets are large, even to a full supply. And what above all I would remark, there was not so much as one foreign trading vessel belonging to the town, nor for several years after I came into it; though no town really had greater advantage in their hands. . . . From so small a beginning the town has risen into its present flourishing circumstances,

intratown debt actions was particularly sharp and started in the 1730s. It is possible too that individual justices of the peace were handling out of sessions more local debt cases and criminal prosecutions by the mid-eighteenth century. But there is no way of ascertaining whether this change in jurisdiction took place, and if it had, one would expect to see a similar decline in the volume of civil suits and criminal indictments in Salem as well as in Marblehead.

and we need no foreigner to transport our fish, but are able ourselves to send it all to the market. . . . Whereas, not only are the public ways vastly mended, but the manners of the people greatly cultivated; and we have many gentlemanlike and polite families, and the very fishermen scorn the rudeness of the former generation. . . . Let God have the praise, who has redeemed the town from bondage into a state of liberty and freedom.[14]

It was the growth of Marblehead's independent and direct involvement in the market economy that had, in Barnard's eyes, fostered not only prosperity but also moral discipline and good order in town. Far from being at odds with the ends of community, commercial development was, in his view, conducive to social stability and cohesion.

Commerce had not created in Marblehead quite the idyllic community depicted by the pastor of the First Church. The fishermen of Barnard's congregation in the middle of the eighteenth century may have been better behaved than their forebears, but most remained poor. And the welfare of the town as a whole and of most of its families was still vulnerable to the vagaries of war, weather, and the demands of distant consumers. The comfortable community of morally upright and self-reliant fishermen and tradesmen evoked by Barnard was an image cast by his own desire. And that image owed as much to the influence of Montesquieu's writings on commercial republicanism as it did to the pastor's observations of Marblehead.[15] Still, Barnard's portrayal of the town in 1760 was more than merely wishful thinking: Marblehead was, by the middle of the eighteenth century, a far more stable society than it had been a generation earlier. This new order in town arose not only from changes in the composition and mobility of Marblehead's population but

[14] "Autobiography of Barnard," 239–41.

[15] Montesquieu, *The Spirit of the Laws*, ed. David W. Carrithers (Berkeley, 1977), XX, 1, 2, 7, 8. Montesquieu is the most likely influence upon Barnard, but several other eighteenth-century political economists and philosophers also emphasized the salutary consequences of commercial development. For a full discussion of commercial republicanism, see Drew R. McCoy, *The Elusive Republic: Political Economy in Jeffersonian America* (Chapel Hill, 1980), 25–40; and Ralph J. Lerner, "Commerce and Character: The Anglo-American as New Model Man," *WMQ*, 3rd ser., 36 (1979), 3–26.

also, as Barnard noted, from the town's increasing independence from larger ports and greater control over its own
economy. The commercial autonomy attained by Marblehead after 1730 diminished conflict in town by reducing the
influence of outside capitalists. And equally important, the
growth of the direct trade was accompanied by the emergence of a strong, native-born merchant elite, a ruling group
whose claims to leadership the rest of the community recognized as legitimate. Most of these "gentlemanlike and polite
families" created by commercial development after 1730 were,
not coincidentally, the parishioners of John Barnard.

As Marblehead's economy started to change in the 1730s,
so too did its social structure. In fact, a nearly total reconsti-
tution of the town's leadership took place within little more
than a decade, an overturning at the top of society without
parallel in the history of other Essex County ports. Economic and political power gravitated slowly toward the First
Church until, by the 1740s, the old Second Church circle
had been eclipsed almost entirely by the successful families
of John Barnard's parish. As the First Parish dispute in
Gloucester illustrates, more subtle reshufflings of the social
order elsewhere in Essex County occasioned the most intense
controversy and disruption. But in Marblehead, the dis-
placement of Second Church leaders from their dominant
position by the new men at First placed social authority in
town on a sounder footing and established a more deferential communal order.

The first sign that a major shift at the top of Marblehead's
society was underway appeared within a few years after the
anti-inoculation riot, as many of the most prominent members of the Second Church circle left town permanently. Stephen Minot, Jr., Jeremiah Allen, Jr., Ebenezer Lowell, Richard
Dana, Samuel and John Bannister, and Edmund Goffe all
returned to Boston during the 1730s. In the same decade,
the heads of the Browne, Legg, and Brattle families died out
in Marblehead, and most of their descendants also moved to
the capital. Even the pastoral leader of Second Church,
Edward Holyoke, left Marblehead to take the presidency of
Harvard College in 1737. Another symptom of change was
the diminishing influence of those Second Church leaders who
remained in Marblehead. Joseph Blaney, an important mem-

ber of Minot's clique, was one of many others who never held elective office in town after the 1730s. Overall, Second Church members served only twenty percent of all terms on the board of selectmen during that decade, half of their representation over the 1720s. Other Second Church leaders not only faded from politics but failed in business as well. John Oulton, originally an Anglican but drawn through marital ties into the Second Church orbit, left town after his fishing business went bankrupt in 1735. Several other once successful Holyoke parishioners died insolvent or with debts so large that the administrators of their estates were forced to sell off large parcels of real property. By 1748, only a quarter of the wealthiest decile of Marblehead ratepayers were members of the Second Church congregation.[16]

A number of circumstances contributed to the departure from Marblehead of so many members of the Second Church circle and the loss of wealth and office suffered by others who remained. For most of those who went to Boston, leaving Marblehead represented the fulfillment of long-cherished aspirations. Inheriting paternal estates or marrying into one of the capital's merchant families made their moves possible. But what hastened the exodus of these fortunate families and caused the decay of others, who were less lucky, was the altered character of Marblehead's economy. The develop-

---

[16] See chapter IX, note 8 for the return of the Minots, Allen, Dana, and Lowell to Boston during the 1730s. Civil suits in the 1730s identify the Bannisters as residents of Boston and Goffe as a resident of Cambridge. None of these men, nor any members of the Browne, Legg, and Brattle families, appear on the "Marblehead Tax List of 1748." On the collapse of Oulton's business, see Titus, "Mr. John Oulton," *NEHGR*, 53: 391–92. See also note 20 below.

Between 1730 and 1755, administrators of the estates of fourteen principal Marblehead traders petitioned the Superior Court to allow the sale of part or all of the decedents' real estate to cover outstanding debts. Seven of these estates were those of Second Church members; another five were the estates of older traders and shoremen at First Church who had also relied on bigger Boston merchants for shipping and capital. (For the estates of Second Church members, see MSCJ, October 26, 1731 (Roads), May 13, 1735 (Calley), May 10, 1737 (Skinner), November 16, 1742 (Tucker), October 15, 1754 (Stacey), June 2, 1752 (Palmer), and October 15, 1751 (Smethurst). Debt on this scale was uncommon elsewhere in maritime Essex County among major merchants: in Salem over the same period, only four merchants left debts large enough to necessitate the sale of real property.

ment of the direct trade made men like Stephen Minot economic dinosaurs. As Marbleheaders took control over the
commerce in fish, Boston's representatives became ciphers in
the local economy. Moreover, most of the factors who stayed
in town failed to make the transition from middleman to
independent merchant. Second Church leaders were unable
to strike out on their own, for they were too entangled by
their obligations to the Boston credit network. As a result,
their interest in the Marblehead fish trade declined along with
that of their clients and creditors in the capital.

By the end of the 1730s, it was already apparent that
Marblehead's entry into the direct trade was cutting into the
profits of Bostonians and their agents at Second Church. A
rash of insolvencies and forced sales of property among the
ranks of Second Church's gentleman-traders and shoremen
was one symptom of their difficulties. Other evidence of the
changing balance of economic power can be seen in the troubles of Peter Faneuil, one of the capital's major fish exporters. For example, in 1737, Faneuil initiated a spate of suits
for debt against several Second Church shoremen, charging
that they had failed to keep him supplied with fish. At the
same time, Faneuil wrote to his agent who purchased catches
at Canso, Nova Scotia to keep a close watch on the cod
being cured by shoremen there. "Our Marblehead Gentry,"
he warned, "wants much to hear of their Spoiling . . . were
it in their power, they would gladly Imbrace any Opertunity
of destroying it."[17] But these measures were not enough to
keep Faneuil competitive, and he was already reducing his
involvement in the fish trade. Earlier that season, when an
English factor operating in the Mediterranean requested a
cargo of fish for a ship captained by Charles Wheldan, Faneuil
flatly refused, conceding that

> the best advice with fish is what I will meddle with Upon no
> Pretense whatever for I will not Accept any more commercial
> business as I have wrote you heretofore   recommend no more
> to me for I will not do any   [I do] not doubt but your good

[17] Faneuil v. Reed, v. Tucker, v. Proctor, October 28, 1735, MSCJ; Faneuil
to Thomas Kilby, July 5, 1737, "Peter Faneuil's Letterbook," MS, Thomas
Hancock Papers, New England Historical and Genealogical Society, Boston, Massachusetts.

friends Messrs. Swett and Hooper will load Wheldan for by your writing you reckon them to be very great men.[18]

The targets of Faneuil's sarcasm were Joseph Swett, Jr., and his son-in-law, Robert Hooper, Jr., partners in the Marblehead fishing trade. By the early forties their firm was annually exporting more fish in larger vessels to Portugal, Spain, Barbados, and Holland than any other firm in Marblehead.[19] Swett and Hooper were among the most eminent members of the new Marblehead gentry, merchants in the coastwise and foreign trade and successful shoremen. The majority of these men belonged to John Barnard's congregation, and most were church members. Half of the richest quintile and over half of the top ten per cent of the town's ratepayers in 1748 attended the First Church, and in local politics they were equally preeminent. Beginning in the 1730s and for several decades thereafter, they dominated Marblehead's most important elective and appointive offices. For some of these new traders, the link with First Church was even more intimate. Four were related to John Barnard through marriage, and most, as young men in the 1720s and 1730s, had taken his advice and channelled their energies into developing an independent commerce.[20]

[18] Faneuil to William Limberry, June 20, 1737, Letterbook.

[19] Hooper to Storke, October 7, 1742, HSL.

[20] The sixty-two ratepayers who ranked in the richest decile in the tax list of 1748 included thirty-three that attended First Church. Among this group of thirty-three were two sons of Joseph Swett who died in 1745, so I substituted him in place of the two adolescent sons in the analysis below and used a figure of thirty-two instead of thirty-three. Of these thirty-two heads of household at First Church, two-thirds were church members before the revival of 1738–1742; twelve were full members, and eleven, halfway members. After the revival, eighteen of the thirty-two were full members and ten were halfway members.

CHURCH AFFILIATION AMONG THE WEALTHIEST QUINTILE AND
DECILE OF MARBLEHEAD RATEPAYERS, 1748

	91–95	96–100
First Church	17	15
Second Church	8	7
St. Michael's	3	7

The new Marblehead gentry's manner of doing business reveals a great deal about the ways in which the conduct of the direct trade shaped and was shaped by social relationships in town after 1730. First of all, Marblehead traders, like other merchants of the early modern era in both America and Europe, relied heavily in the operation of their enterprises on personal contacts and the ties of family and friendship. Individual merchants did not finance and carry out their trade independently but received investment capital and other forms of assistance from fellow entrepreneurs, usually other members of First Church related by blood or marriage. Merchantmen were not owned by a single investor but by four or five partners who each held shares of varying size in the same vessel.[21] The close coordination of commercial activity for mutual benefit also typified relations within the new Marblehead merchant community. Local traders helped each other in the often complicated system of com-

Quaker	0	1
Non-Resident	1	1
Unidentified	1	0

CHURCH AFFILIATION AMONG MARBLEHEAD SELECTMEN, 1730–1755

	1730–39	1740–49	1750–55
First Church	24	28	15
Second Church	10	16	11
St. Michael's	15	4	4
Quaker	1	0	0

CHURCH AFFILIATION AMONG MARBLEHEAD DEPUTIES, 1730–1755

First Church	2	1	4
Second Church	10	8	0
St. Michael's	3	1	2

First Church members received eight of the commissions of the peace between 1730 and 1755; Second Church members, three; and St. Michael's members, five. (Sources: "Marblehead Tax List for 1748," *EIHC*, 43: 209–22; MTR, III, 1730–1755; Whittemore, Civil List, 132–35; MFCR, "Records of the Second Church," and "St. Michael's Records.") On Barnard's family connections, see *SHG*, V, 265–77.

[21] For example, Robert Hooper mentioned seven vessels in his business correspondence, and all were owned with several other local traders. For a more detailed discussion of these partnerships, see Bailyn and Bailyn, *Massachusetts Shipping*, 27–40.

municating with agents in distant ports, who supplied Marbleheaders with information on market conditions, maritime insurance, and a variety of other services. In the winter of 1742, for example, Swett and Hooper asked their Lisbon correspondent to obtain the release from a Spanish prison of two Marblehead sailors. The men in jail had been crew members aboard a vessel belonging to another First Church merchant, Joshua Orne. A few months later, the partners approached their London contact, Samuel Storke, to arrange for insurance on Orne's behalf. At the same time, another merchant-member of First Church, Thomas Peach, extended Swett and Hooper the courtesy of transmitting in his coasting vessel letters to Gedney Clark, the partners' factor in Barbados.[22] Quarrels within this local mercantile community were infrequent, but the few that did arise created considerable consternation because of the importance of maintaining networks of interdependence. On one occasion, Samuel Storke commissioned Swett and Hooper to collect a long overdue debt owed him by Deacon Benjamin Hendley of the First Church. After months of prevailing privately upon Hendley, the partners finally prosecuted, their recourse to the law producing "a Vast Deal of Ill Will," Hooper complained.[23] Going to court to collect obligations from a fellow trader—and a coreligionist at that—was clearly the exception rather than the rule among the new Marblehead merchant community.

But the good will that generally existed within the Marblehead mercantile network did not carry over into their relations with traders in other New England ports. This animosity toward the traders of Boston and Salem distinguished the Marblehead gentry from the middlemen and factors of Second Church, who had dominated the local economy earlier in the eighteenth century and had identified with the interests of these larger commercial centers. As Peter Faneuil's complaints about Swett and Hooper indicate, Marblehead's new merchants defined their "neighbors" as narrowly as did their counterparts in Gloucester: everyone

[22] Hooper to Gardoqui, February 2, 1742; to Storke, May 5, 1742; and to Clarke, December 27, 1744, HSL.

[23] On the suit against Hendley, see Hopper to Storke, October 7, 1742, HSL.

outside of town was fair game. With Boston, the competition for cargoes of the best quality cod, the quickest dispatch to market, and the consignment trade of English fish exporters was especially intense. Even with nearby Salem, relations were cool and commercial involvements infrequent. Marblehead merchants rarely offered Salem traders an opportunity to invest in their vessels, and Salem's grandees returned the slight. Robert Hooper complained that Salem merchants jealous of his success even refused to carry his correspondence on their vessels bound out to foreign ports, "tho' such a Conduct would be [thought] below a person in trade."[24] Marblehead's sudden prosperity and the competitive spirit of its new merchants strained relations with larger ports, but the town's commercial autonomy had hardly invented this antagonism. Before the beginning of Marblehead's direct trade, only the Second Church elite had established harmonious relations with Boston and Salem; for most townspeople, dealings with these larger ports had always been far from amicable.

If the Marblehead gentry's success in the fishing trade demanded a willingness to engage in a cut-throat competition with "strangers," it required an entirely different kind of conduct at home, and not only among fellow members of the merchant community. Cultivating the loyalties of men at all levels of the industry was critical in the fishing business, for the close coordination of production and trade was essential. Only the good will of sea captains and sailors who manned merchantmen, dockworkers who loaded ships, and shoremen and fishermen who cured and caught the cod could guarantee merchants a prime cargo available for quick shipment to market at a reasonable price. Behind the confidence of Swett and Hooper that they could command "¾ of the Isle Sable fish that is Caught in this town" were scores of small accommodations and understandings between the firm

---

[24] Swett and Hooper's correspondence makes mention of only two ventures involving Salem traders. On one occasion, Swett and Hooper chartered a vessel belonging to Benjamin Lynd of Salem. They offered another Salem merchant, Joshua Ward, a share of their vessels after his marriage to a Marblehead woman. On the tension between Salem and Marblehead traders, see Hooper to Steers and Barons, November 1, 1744 and to Whaley, September 10, 1744, HSL.

and the local maritime community. Despite their affluence and local importance, Swett and Hooper were not divorced from the actual operations of the fishery. On the contrary, the partners spent most of their time in Marblehead, personally involved in the mundane details of production and transport, in the concerns of ordinary fishermen, and in the daily lives of the masters and sailors who manned their merchantmen.

Outside of their own circle of kin and marital connections, the Marblehead gentry's closest personal relationships were with the masters of their vessels. These sea captains were charged with keeping up morale and discipline among other crew members, piloting the ships along a safe course, and disposing of their cargo to the greatest advantage. Swett and Hooper maintained cordial friendships with all of their captains, kept them informed about their families when they were at sea, and praised their skills to their correspondents in distant ports. All of the masters of merchantmen in which Swett and Hooper held an interest were Marblehead men, except for one Captain Dunn, an Englishman who commanded a vessel owned principally by Samuel Storke of London. Dunn's employment was a sticking-point in the partners' relations with Storke, and they repeatedly urged replacing this "stranger" with one of their own masters. Marblehead sailors did not ship out with nonlocal captains whenever they could avoid it, and Swett and Hooper, who themselves invested total trust only in their neighbors, knew that it was good business to respect the preferences of local mariners. According to Hooper, "as he [Dunn] is a stranger it is more difficult for him to get men here than it is for one of this place. . . . last year . . . he lay here a month after he was loaded."[25] A delay of this length could mean lower prices and poorer markets, a loss that the partners were anxious to avoid.

Marblehead's new merchants cultivated with equal care the good opinion of local shoremen, the fishing business operators. Extending liberal credit on easy terms for the supplies needed by shoremen for fitting out fishing vessels was

[25] Hooper to Steers and Barons, January 26, 1745; to Ambrose James, August 10, 1742; and to Storke, April 23, 1742, HSL.

one means for traders to "command the catch." At the beginning of 1743, Swett and Hooper reported being "larger in advance in the Fishery this year than ever we were yet Oblig'd . . . to Grease the Wheeles." Paying close attention to local taste and requirements in the matter of rigging materials, salt, and other items in demand among shoremen was also important to the partners' successful trade. Their instructions to the European suppliers of these goods indicate a precise knowledge of the fishing industry's operations on the banks. Writing to Madame Ferrand Whaley, the head of a Dutch mercantile house that supplied their sailcloth, Hooper advised that

> we would not have any midling or Ordinary duck on any Account as it does not Suit this Markitt. . . . the Fishing vessels Who are Vastly Exposed in the winter season on the Banks . . . have need of Canvis made of Iron if possible for they often Catch their Fish lying by as the Seamen call it with their sailes hoisted day and night stalling in the Wind.

The partners were just as knowledgeable and particular about the salt used for curing Marblehead catches: they instructed Samuel Storke to ship them only "Lisbon salt," for "French salt . . . our People Esteem but little better than Sand." Failure on the part of European suppliers to meet Marblehead specifications aroused considerable resentment. After receiving a shipment of inferior cordage from Storke, Hooper bristled in reply:

> Do let the ropemakers know we are not quite Indians altho' born in an Indian country they know in their own Soul they often send bad stuff here and really it will not do for these sort of Vessels Ride in the Ocean on the fishing banks and that in part of the Winter Season and they must have good Goods.[26]

The contacts and concerns of the Marblehead gentry were not restricted to a circle of sea captains and shoremen at the top of the maritime community but encompassed common sailors and fishermen as well. Marblehead's new merchant

[26] Hooper to Storke, April 15, 1743, November 15, 1743, June 15, 1743; and to Whaley, February 28, 1744, HSL.

elite sought to establish personal ties with members of the lowest echelons of seaport society as carefully as they curried the favor of its more important men. One way in which traders nurtured the loyalty of maritime laborers was by deferring to the customary rights and practices of the fishing community. Rather than insisting upon a work discipline designed to maximize efficiency and profit, Marblehead merchants conformed the conduct of industry and commerce to accord with these traditional claims and allowed popular preference to shape the rhythms of production and trade. Swett and Hooper, for example, honored the superstition against Friday sailings among fishermen and mariners, and observed the traditional obligation of purchasing lots of fish unsorted by size. And as their objections to employing Captain Dunn indicate, the partners took into account the prejudice of Marblehead crews against nonlocal masters.[27] Swett and Hooper also capitalized upon every opportunity to increase local employment by using only Marblehead crews aboard all of their merchantmen, hiring local mariners as masters, and insisting that all vessels in which they held a share were built at home.[28]

The sense of obligation among Marblehead entrepreneurs to their maritime labor force involved not only a concern for supplying reliable goods and steady employment and catering to local custom but also influenced their treatment of debtors. The kind of civil prosecution that underwent the most dramatic reduction during the 1730s and 1740s were those debt cases that earlier in the eighteenth century had clogged the Court of Common Pleas, suits against Marblehead fishermen by local merchants and shoremen. In the year 1739, for example, only eleven intratown actions for debt involved merchant or shoremen plaintiffs and defendants who were fishermen or sailors, and in 1749 there were just six cases of this kind. Marblehead's major entrepreneurs were no longer resorting to legal action to compel the labor of maritime workers or to press for the repayment of book

---

[27] Hooper to Storke, May 29, 1745, HSL: ". . . it is a very difficult thing to prevail upon our people to pick their fish the small from the great . . . unless we engage to take them both."

[28] Hooper to Storke, April 23, 1742, HSL.

debts.[29] Even Swett and Hooper, Marblehead's largest creditors, initiated only a few suits annually to recover debts
against anyone in town. This restraint is remarkable when
compared to the litigiousness of the old Second Church circle, each of whom had averaged several prosecutions
annually.[30] In view of the declining level of median estate
value in Marblehead, it seems unlikely that local fishermen
in the 1730s and 1740s were more prompt in paying their
obligations than the preceding generation of maritime workers had been, and the fishery itself was still financed by
advances of credit from merchants to shoremen and from
shoremen to fishermen. The scarcity of labor created by the
Spanish and French wars probably contributed somewhat to
the extremely low level of litigation against fishermen and
sailors at the end of the 1740s. But the incidence of prosecutions for debt had started to decline even before the renewal
of war reduced the ranks of the labor force. Most likely,
Marblehead's big men had found that forebearance in financial dealings "Greased the Wheels" of their relations with
the fishing community.

The military crisis of the 1740s was particularly influential in strengthening the bonds between the Marblehead gentry and the rest of the maritime community, ties upon which
local commerce depended. Although the Spanish and French
conflicts imposed new hardships on ordinary fishermen and
their families, efforts on the part of Marblehead entrepreneurs to mitigate deprivation and danger and to share in the
community peril offset the potential for internal social disruption. In response to the wartime crisis, Congregationalist
merchants, shoremen, and sea captains became local military leaders. First Church merchant Thomas Gerry captained the fort in Marblehead harbor, while the local militia
units that manned that fortress were headed by other officers
who ranked among Marblehead's most prominent orthodox

---

[29] See Chapter VII, note 7. Data on the declining number of cases involving
merchant- or shoreman-plaintiffs and fisherman-defendants is drawn from
the writs in the FCCP for 1739 and 1749.

[30] In 1749, for example, the major merchants and shoremen of First Church
initiated a total of only six prosecutions of other townspeople. Twenty years
earlier in 1729, the members of the Second Church elite had initiated fifty-
six debt prosecutions of fellow townsmen.

traders. Even the Reverend John Barnard asked his congregation to release him for temporary service as a chaplain to the Louisbourg expedition, a request denied by the First Church because the parson was in his sixties.

During the same period that the Congregationalist elite took the lead in local mobilization, its members also implemented measures to insure that the need for military preparedness did not rob fishermen serving in the militia companies of their livelihoods. Thomas Gerry requested permission from the General Court to hire men for keeping watch at the fort by day, "It being a Season of the year that the Families of Men belonging to the Fort would Suffer (as they had no pay) to be Oblig'd to watch both day and night." Local orthodox leaders also tried to reduce the burden that relieving larger numbers of dependent widows and orphans imposed upon Marblehead taxpayers. In 1746, Marblehead merchants initiated a fund for the families of men aboard a government sloop lost at sea and another for the dependents of soldiers from town who had died of disease at Louisbourg. And at the close of the campaign against the French, Robert Hooper singlehandedly underwrote the establishment of Marblehead's first free school and the costs of the town's first fire engine.[31]

Marblehead's new elite's sense of having a particular obligation to the community during the years of military crisis was also expressed in their providing protection for ordinary seafaring men. War increased the hazards facing local sailors. Spanish and French privateers preyed upon New England vessels, imprisoning the men aboard their prizes, while Britain naval press gangs swept through the English ports in the West Indies, forcing the crews of colonial merchantmen into the King's service. Robert Hooper regularly instructed his Barbadian factor, Gedney Clarke, to "get clear" any sailors from Marblehead pressed into the royal navy, and on several occasions, Hooper interceded personally on behalf of individual seamen whose plight had come to his attention. His descriptions of the impressed men point up

[31] Thomas Gerry Papers, MS, Massachusetts Historical Society, Boston, Massachusetts; "Autobiography of Barnard," 231, MFCR, February 10, 1745; Hooper to Clarke, January 20, 1746, May 17, 1746, HSL; MTR, III, 273; and Roads, *History*, 69.

again the mingling of economic and personal considerations
that motivated Hooper's concern for the local labor force:
"Our friend James Wiggins . . . a married man, has a wife
and children," and one "Thomas Ebden, a sailor . . . a young
fellow for whom I have a great Value and indeed some
dependence on for Business as well as Pity to his aged Parents and Friends." Earlier in the eighteenth century, Marblehead traders had also tried to ransom employees who had
been imprisoned by the French, captured by the Indians, or
impressed into the British navy. But while one such early
merchant, Nathaniel Norden, had solicited the release of a
local fisherman from the French "Provided it doth not cost
more than sixty pond monys," in 1746, Robert Hooper sought
Thomas Ebden's freedom, "let it cost what it will."[32]

It served the interests of Marblehead's new elite to support the wars with Spain and France while striving to preserve social harmony and solidarity at home, but these
objectives also dovetailed with the welfare of the wider community. All Marbleheaders stood to benefit by restoring
security to the Caribbean and by excluding the French from
the north Atlantic fishery. Moreover, major merchants shared
with ordinary townspeople the conviction that Britain's
imperial wars, especially the conflicts against France, were
religious crusades that advanced the Protestant cause. Robert Hooper's interpretation of New England's successful siege
of Louisbourg—which appeared not in a public address but
in his private business correspondence—echoed the significance assigned to that episode throughout local society:

> . . . its plain and obvious to the meanest and most shallow capacity
> that the very Heavens have fought for us, God has been on our
> side and who then can be against us. . . . 'tis the right hand and
> Holy arm of almighty God that has given us the Important Vic-
> tory—and New England—say the province of Massachusetts
> Bay—(under God) has the greatest share in the glory and I am
> in hopes will reap the fruit of their Labour, as to the Strength
> and Importance of the place. . . .[33]

[32] Hooper to Clarke, May 11, 1741, April 10, 1742, and April 8, 1746;
Hooper to Gardoqui, February 2, 1742, HSL; and Nathaniel Norden to
Andrew Belcher, April 10, 1706, *MA*, 63: 5.
[33] Hooper to Clarke, July 3, 1745 and August 13, 1745, HSL. Cf. Jedrey,
World of John Cleaveland, 123–26.

Hooper's enthusiasm for the Louisbourg campaign was not unrelated to his interest in protecting his investment in the fishery or to his concern for enhancing his standing as a public-spirited town leader. But his support for the war also reflected his commitment to the local community and his orthodox religious principles and prejudices. These ideals Hooper refused to subordinate to his private aims: he did not capitalize on the war with France to gain personal economic advantage. When Gedney Clarke proposed a privateering venture to Swett and Hooper, the partners flatly refused because "we think there is little Honest Money gott that way." Other Marblehead merchants also resisted the lure of lucrative opportunities that the hostilities offered shipowners inclined to prey on enemy vessels for profit.[34] This unwillingness to exploit the conflict for private gain, coupled with the patriotic commitment to share in the common danger and to minimize the risks of their neighbors, enhanced the standing of the Marblehead gentry within the local community.

The ease with which members of the Marblehead gentry moved within the personalized economic world of the fishing community reflected their corporate, paternalistic conception of the social order. They expected that local custom and traditional obligations to their fellow townsmen would shape the scope and character of their operations, and they accepted that definition as proper. Identifying their interests with the welfare of Marblehead as a whole, they felt responsible to the wider community and cultivated reputations for integrity, reliability, and benevolence. Except for the introduction of the direct trade, the organization of the economy under this new elite was not dissimilar from the one that Madame Elizabeth Browne, Edward Brattle, and Stephen Minot had dominated earlier. The difference was that the old Second Church leaders had existed uncomfortably within the fishery's web of loyalties and interdependencies. Their cosmopolitan preferences and origins had undercut the

[34] Hooper to Clarke, June 2, 1742. See also, Howard Chapin, *Privateering in King George's War, 1739–1748* (Providence, 1927). Chapin lists only one Marbleheader, Joseph Smethurst, as commander of a vessel in the service of the province. This ship was a government-owned patrol boat, not a privateer. (71–73)

strength of local customs and rights in shaping their dealings with the maritime community of Marblehead. Their obligations to advance the interests of merchants in larger ports had militated against their full integration into local networks of cooperation and had diminished their identification with local interests. Like Marblehead's seventeenth-century elite, they had relied on ruthlessness, intimidation, and the exploitation of smaller men to attain their ends. Instead of providing townspeople with civic improvements, military leadership, and personal and financial security, they had pursued profit and advancement for themselves and commercial advantage for outside capitalists, often at the expense of local welfare. The contrast between the social style of Second Church leaders and that of their successors, the Marblehead gentry, was complete.

The members of the Marblehead gentry were also more cautious in their economic behavior than the town's earlier elites, possibly because these new men had a very old-fashioned view of commerce, conceiving of it as an activity imbedded in a moral and communal matrix. The same values that put wartime profiteering beyond the pale of honesty for merchants like Swett and Hooper lent a conservative cast to their general approach to commercial development. While the old Second Church circle had favored a speculative, risk-oriented entrepreneurial style, John Barnard's successful parishioners were too careful to die insolvent, or even heavily in debt. Despite their daring in undertaking a direct trade, even major local merchants conducted a carefully limited commerce with a few trusted associates. They also resisted opportunities to expand their investments beyond the familiar traffic in fish. "The trade of this town is very different from other places in New England, as the chief of it lies in the fishery," Swett and Hooper explained to Samuel Storke, "and we do not Incline to be Concerned in but Little Else as we can Improve our small Stock in that Trade with a Small Matter of our Friends. . . ." Storke's offer to supply the partners with a wider variety of imported goods, not just supplies restricted to the fishery, provoked a chilly reproof from Marblehead. "We shall readily Come into Such a Small Trade as we can Comfortably manage so as to do you Justice," Hooper replied, "but should not Incline to be Concerned very Largely nor no further than we should order, as we are determined not to out trade ourselves." And although they were acutely attuned to the operation of supply and demand in the fish market, the partners still perceived providence rather than impersonal economic mechanisms as the original cause of all profit or loss. Writing to John Tallamy, a West Country fish merchant, Hooper commented characteristically that "As to our own Circumstances [in the Marblehead fishery]we have reason to Bless God as much Better than we deserve and thro' Divine Goodness much better than when we saw you last." This prosperity Hooper perceived as the reward of ascetic virtue, for "we think there is but Little to be Gott unless People are Industrious and Frugal."[35]

With its emphasis upon local loyalty, communal order, moral obligation, and the avoidance of risk, the outlook of Marblehead's new entrepreneurs conformed more closely to that of Gloucester's ruling circle than to that of earlier Marblehead elites. This world-view reflected the origins of both Gloucester's maritime elite and Marblehead's gentry outside of the larger, more cosmopolitan centers of trade. Although the commerce carried on by new Marblehead merchants like Swett and Hooper was more ambitious and extensive than the businesses of middlemen like Edward Brattle and Stephen Minot, the new direct trade was conducted by men who had fewer close connections to the world outside of town. Three-quarters of the major merchants and shoremen of First Church in the middle of the eighteenth century were native-born Marbleheaders, and two-thirds could trace their families' tenure in town back to the seventeenth century. Among those men who represented the first or second generation of their families in Marblehead, the most common points of origin were the neighboring North Shore ports of Charlestown, Beverly, Manchester, and Newbury. Only one member of the new commercial elite at First Church was a recent immigrant from England; a few had moved to town from Salem, but they were not the sons of important mer-

---

[35] Hooper to Storke, April 23, 1742, May 5, 1742, and June 23, 1742; to Edward Winslow, February 1, 1746; and to Captain John Tallamy, January 27, 1742.

chant families; and former Bostonians were conspicuous by their absence.[36]

While most members of the First Church merchant elite came from Marblehead or from adjacent seacoast towns only a few miles away, the distance that they had traversed to enter the top of local society was equally short. The fathers of most men in this new ruling circle belonged to a skilled, substantial, entrepreneurial class. In this respect, the fathers of the Marblehead gentry were not unlike the founders of Gloucester's leading families, men of ability and some means who had, because of the absence of cosmopolitan competitors, been able to dominate Cape Ann. Their counterparts in Marblehead had been overshadowed by Bostonians like Stephen Minot, but they still had enjoyed a comfortable standard of living and occasional success in local politics. For example, Robert Hooper, Jr., a fourth generation Marbleheader, was the son of a prosperous chandler who had served a single term as town selectman. The ancestors of Deacon Benjamin Hendley, another successful merchant, included several generations of local shoremen. Joseph Swett and Joshua Orne, both cordwainers turned traders, came from families of artisans in Newbury and Salem. Merchant Jacob Fowle was born in Marblehead shortly after his father, a sailmaker, had migrated from Charlestown. A few First Church leaders, both new and native, had longstanding claims to elite status. Richard Reith and the Devereux brothers, for example, represented families whose wealth and standing in

[36] I relied upon a range of town, church, and probate records as well as published genealogies and biographies to reconstruct the backgrounds and careers of the leading families at First Church. Among the thirty-two heads of First Church families who ranked among the top 10 percent of Marblehead ratepayers in 1748, twenty-four were natives of the town. Of the remaining eight, Jeremiah Lee was from Manchester (Thomas A. Lee, "The Lee family of Marblehead," *EIHC*, 52 (1916), 329–44; 53 (1917), 153–68); Joshua Orne, Sr. and John Felton were sons of Salem artisans (Sidney Perley, *History of Salem*, I, 153 and 241–44; Joseph Lemmon was the son of a Charlestown merchant (*SHG*, IX, 549); John Brooks was from Lynn (Lewis and Newhall, *History of Lynn*, I, 576); and Thomas Gerry was from England (George A. Billias, *Elbridge Gerry* (New York, 1976), 3–5. I could not identify the towns of origin for two others, Giles Ivemay and Nehemiah Skillions.

Marblehead dated back to the seventeenth century, while Samuel Lee simply transferred the interests and influence of his family from Manchester to Marblehead when he moved to town with his son Jeremiah in 1743. Another small contingent of families within the new First Church commercial elite was comprised of families who had dramatically improved the position of the preceding generation. The merchant Peter Homan and his three brothers, all wealthy shoremen, were sons of an ordinary fisherman, while Christopher Bubier, at mid-century the owner of a large fishing business, came from a Jersey family who had probably immigrated to town as indentured servants. But for most new First Church leaders, a position at the top of local society represented neither a sudden ascent nor a perpetuation of former family prominence. The typical pattern was progression from the respectable ranks of prosperous shoremen and artisans into the vacancies at the summit of the social order created by the departure or decline of members of the old Second Church circle.[37]

In other words, the members of the Marblehead gentry, like their counterparts in Gloucester, were either native-born or, in some cases, brought up in adjacent country towns and fishing villages. And in all cases, their origins lay outside the established merchant elite of major ports like Boston or Salem. No great gulf separated these men from the ordinary people of Marblehead, and their peculiar world-view derived from

[37] Charles H. Pope, *Hooper Genealogy* (Boston, 1908) and EPF, #13834 are the best sources for Hooper's background. For Swett, see Everett Stackpole, *Swett Genealogy* (Lewiston, Maine, 1913); Barnard described him as "a young man of small fortune" ("Autobiography of Barnard," 240). For the father of the Homan brothers, see EPF, #13745; for Hendley's family, see EPF, #13060; on Bubier and Fowle, see EPF, #3910 and 3917, and #10025. For Orne and Lee, see note 26 above. Both the Reiths and the Devereux held important local office in the seventeenth century and in 1698 ranked among the largest benefactors to the new meetinghouse. (See EPF, #7614, 23463; MFCR, loose sheet, dated 1698; Bowden, comp., "Marblehead Town Records, 1648 to 1683," *EIHC,* 69: 207–329.) Information on all of these families is also available in the genealogies on file at the Marblehead Historical Society. The list of meetinghouse benefactors in 1698 confirms my characterization of the status of the fathers of the mid-century elite, for no families except the Reiths and the Devereux ranked among the largest contributors of ten pounds; the others were instead among the middle group contributing six to three pounds.

that position. They were comfortable within the local community but also concerned to prove themselves worthy of their social position by behaving in a manner consonant with their conception of a responsible elite. This imperative produced the blend of deference to local preference and paternalistic concern for employees that is evident in their words and actions. Judged strictly in terms of former "family dignity," Edward Brattle and Stephen Minot, both scions of distinguished Boston families, had better claims to high status than did Joseph Swett or Robert Hooper. But because of their origins in Marblehead or neighboring communities, the Marblehead gentry of First Church possessed something that Brattle and Minot lacked, an identification with local interests and a commitment to local society. These qualities compensated for the comparative inferiority of their social origins and conferred credibility on their claims to deference in the eyes of ordinary townspeople.

Something of the character of this communal regard is conveyed by the nicknames that townsmen awarded to members of the Marblehead gentry, honorific titles of purely local significance. Both Joseph Swett, Jr., and Robert Hooper, Sr., were known in town as "Doctor," although neither had even an informal medical practice or any professional training. Swett's partner, Robert Hooper, Jr., inhabitants referred to as "King" Hooper, and in this case the origin of the distinction is clear. Hooper had begun his career as a shoreman, and in Newfoundland, some of the most successful of these operators were known as "fishing kings." Marbleheaders borrowed the title from Newfoundlanders, who used it to connote admiration for the entrepreneurial ability of men perceived as permanently connected to local society and capable of maintaining order.[38]

The new Marblehead elite sought to extend their claims to local status to their families, another characteristic that they shared with Gloucester's ruling group. By exposing few of their sons to the sort of influences that might draw them out of town, merchant fathers in Marblehead insured that their children took up trade as a way of life and that local businesses passed from one generation to another. Only a

[38] Lounsbury, *The British Fishery at Newfoundland*, 261.

handful of the wealthiest First Church families sent sons to Harvard College, and then that privilege was usually accorded to only one boy. Even the exceptional case of Robert Hooper, Jr., who sent three of his four sons to Harvard, is nonetheless demonstrative: two of the Hooper boys interrupted their studies and returned to town because their father required assistance in his business. In a time of expanding trade, practical Marblehead merchants believed that the training of sons in countinghouses or aboard vessels promised a more secure future for family fortunes than a liberal arts education. Perhaps a second strike against sending sons to Cambridge was Edward Holyoke's long tenure there as president of the college. Robert Hooper peppered the president with letters protesting "discrimination" against his sons in class placement and caused a scene at one commencement by charging that Holyoke had deliberately slighted his boy in the ceremony. In any case, a Harvard education rarely kept Marblehead graduates from returning to town and taking their place in the family business. Of the eleven graduates among the sons of First Church leaders, one died at college, one on the Louisbourg expedition, two took up trade in other Essex County ports, and all of the rest except for Elbridge Gerry became merchants in Marblehead.[39]

Marriage to a nonlocal mate, another influence that might have taken children out of town, was also infrequent among the First Church's leading families. Less than fifteen percent of the marriages of the children of prominent First Church families involved a partner from outside of Marblehead. And in over half of these marriages to nonlocal mates, the partner from out of town moved to Marblehead after the wedding. Moreover, the marriages contracted by just two Marblehead families, the Hoopers and the Lees, account for over half of the unions with nonlocal spouses, their mates coming mainly

[39] Among the men attending the First Church who ranked among the top decile of ratepayers in 1748, Samuel and Jeremiah Lee, Robert Hooper, Joshua Orne, Jacob Fowle, Thomas Gerry, and Humphrey Devereux sent sons to Harvard. So did Joseph Swett, who died in 1745, and Benjamin Marston, who had moved to his farm in Manchester by 1748. Except for Hooper, these fathers gave only one of their sons a college education. See *SHG*, XI, 310; XII, 280 and 439–52; XV, 53, 239 and 404; XVI, 75–76 and 455, 158 and 172–73; XVII, 183.

from Newbury. Newbury alliances attracted Marbleheaders, not only because of that port's complementary shipbuilding economy but also because of the Swett family
connections there. No other North Shore port besides Newbury was especially favored by First Church leaders. Like
Gloucester's major merchant families, they preferred to consolidate claims to local prominence by marrying among
themselves. Not surprisingly, only three alliances were made
with Boston families, and in every case, the Boston-born
partner moved to Marblehead.[40]

The aspirations of First Church traders are reflected not
only in the lives that they wanted for their children but also
in the careers that they created for themselves. With their
fortunes made and their families established, few waited for
death to claim them at their countinghouses and none moved
to Boston or Salem, let alone London, to savor more cosmopolitan splendors. Most instead retired to comfortable
farms in the rural communities surrounding Marblehead.
Lynn, Topsfield, Danvers, Beverly, Middleton, and the outlying precincts of Newbury became the retreats of aging
Marblehead magnates turned country gentlemen. And at least
one, Samuel Lee, sent to England for a parchment pedigree
certifying his family's descent from English nobility.[41] For
the Marblehead First Church elite, as for many other Massachusetts entrepreneurs, the summit of social attainment
remained a sort of gentry status—or the closest approxima-
tion to that condition that New England could afford, a farm
in the country. The object of their successful competition in
the world of trade was not unlimited accumulation, ever-
widening and diversifying economic expansion, or a cosmopolitan life-style. The members of Marblehead's new

[40] This data on marriage is based reconstructions of the families of the thirty-
two First Parish ratepayers who ranked in the wealthiest decile on the list
of 1748. I relied upon published *Vital Records* and published and unpublished genealogies at the American Antiquarian Society and the Marblehead
Historical Society for compiling a sample of ninety-five marriages between
1738 and 1775. Only twelve of these marriages were to nonlocal mates,
with the unions of the Lee and Hooper families accounting for nine of the
twelve.

[41] EPF, #26963, 10025, 16718, 14659, 7612, 13746. See also, Lee, "The
Lee Family of Marblehead," *EIHC,* 58: 149–68.

merchant elite wanted instead to make enough money to live like landed gentlemen and to leave business behind.

The commercial elites of provincial seaports are typically depicted as having been more disengaged from the local community and from traditional culture than were other classes. Involvement in the wider, Anglo-American trading world supposedly fostered among merchants a more cosmopolitan outlook, a sense of themselves as members of a business community that crossed town and colony borders. It is also said that commercial activity encouraged traders to adopt more liberal attitudes toward social and economic life, values at variance with those held by the rest of local society. Imbued with the impersonal, individualistic mores of the marketplace, merchants became narrowly profit-oriented and paid little heed to their responsibilities to the public welfare or the customary imperatives of "the moral economy." Both their competing values and their business connections outside of town weakened the ties of traders to their own communities.[42] But in fact, the character of New England's commercial classes was more varied and complex than this depiction suggests. Some members of the colonial merchant elite seem to fit the familiar stereotype—Edward Brattle, Stephen Minot, and other members of the old Second Church circle, for example. But those like Robert Hooper and Joseph Swett may have been even more numerous.

The members of the new Marblehead gentry were major merchants, but their attitudes and values bore little resemblance to the cosmopolitan and liberal outlook commonly attributed to colonial traders. The men conducting Marblehead's commerce by the middle of the eighteenth century were closely involved in the wider market economy, but instead of being divorced from the community by their business interests, they appear to have been drawn by these enterprises more deeply into the web of local social relations and concerns. And while they were outside the counting-house and away from the wharves, the world beyond Marblehead mattered little in their lives. The careers that they

[42] Bailyn, *New England Merchants in the Seventeenth Century,* 134–42, 192–94; Nash, *The Urban Crucible,* 78–79 and 164; Nelson, *Dispute and Conflict Resolution in Plymouth County,* 140–42.

carved out for themselves and those that they planned for their children reflect, more than anything else, the persistence of parochial attitudes and affinities. Added confirmation that major traders were in no sense alienated from local society appears in the response of other townspeople to the Marblehead gentry. No outraged mob ever protested that what happened in Marblehead was "none of the business" of Robert Hooper and his fellows at First Church. Indeed, the reelection year after year of the same commercial leaders to important positions of public trust and the honorific titles bestowed on them suggest that townspeople were of the opposite opinion.

The close integration of the Marblehead gentry into the local community goes a long way toward explaining why it is also difficult to detect in their attitudes any burgeoning liberal values. Both their behavior and their business correspondence express a conception of commerce as a highly personalized and interdependent enterprise that served the ends of the community as well as creating wealth for individual families. These traders were interested in turning a profit from their undertakings, but their sense of loyalty to local society was not subordinated to the goal of acquisition. The members of the Marblehead gentry themselves seem to have perceived a difference between their outlook and that of their predecessors at Second Church or of Boston's "codfish aristocracy." "That Gentleman is full of this World," Robert Hooper wrote of Charles Apthorp, a major merchant in the capital. It was not a description that Hooper would have applied to himself.[43]

Elites cast in the mold of the Marblehead gentry—localistic, wary of outside influences, conservative in outlook and aspiration—existed everywhere in New England, both in other seaports like Gloucester and in inland market towns. What probably made Marblehead atypical among commercially expanding New England communities was the length of time that it took for such a stable and credible leadership to emerge, a process shaped by the peculiarities of its geographic location and early economic development. In Gloucester, for example, the transition from farming to trade was accom-

[43] Hooper to Steers and Barons, June 13, 1746, HSL.

panied by an essential continuity in local leadership. Most of that port's social and political leaders in 1750 had simply inherited their status from their ancestors among the old agrarian elite of the seventeenth century. Because of the town's comparative isolation and more self-contained economic development, Gloucester's local elite had at no time confronted a challenge to its domination of the community from cosmopolitan newcomers. By contrast, the process of elite formation in Marblehead was more similar to the evolution of a stable leadership in another maturing plantation society, the colonial Chesapeake. In Virginia during the late seventeenth century, as in Marblehead a few decades later, a permanent elite patterned on the English gentry displaced a more ruthless, assertive set of leaders after a period of violent social disruption. Like Marblehead's new commercial elite, the great planters of provincial Virginia came not from the ranks of an established ruling class but from families of means and respectability near enough to the top of society to nurture ambitions for genteel status. And like Marblehead's new elite, the eighteenth-century Chesapeake's leaders owed their social attainments to a combination of family capital, identification with the local community, and the proper mixture of paternalism and respect in their dealings with social inferiors. Parvenu status prodded both the Marblehead gentry and their southern counterparts to cultivate the respect of lesser men, and such behavior in both instances enhanced social stability despite the continuing existence of extreme economic inequality.[44]

But if the gentlemen-planters of the Chesapeake and the

[44] The parallels between the situation in Marblehead and that in the Chesapeake are not exact, but the comparison is suggestive nonetheless. Many members of the old Second Church circle in Marblehead had more genteel backgrounds than the rough-hewn and low-born elite of early seventeenth-century Virginia planters could claim, although both groups were equally aggressive and indifferent to local welfare. Similarly, the great planters of the provincial South were descended from English families of higher status than those of the Marblehead gentry, and they gained an advantage from their connections to these transatlantic mercantile and landowning interests. Nevertheless, both elites were intensely localistic. See especially, *Morgan, American Slavery, American Freedom*, 250–70 and 338–87; Bailyn, "Politics and Social Structure in Virginia," in *Seventeenth Century America*, ed. Smith, 100 and 106.

gentlemen-merchants of Marblehead were similar in many ways, their fates diverged in at least one important respect. In Virginia, and perhaps elsewhere in the South, an upsurge of evangelical religious enthusiasm started in the 1740s, driving a wedge between the gentry and the lesser planter class. The revival drew most of its converts from the lower strata of Chesapeake society and created an ascetic, egalitarian "counterculture." By implicitly challenging the materialistic, hierarchical values of the old gentry-dominated culture, the evangelical movement alienated its adherents from the mores and authority of their social superiors.[45] Evangelical enthusiasm made a profound impression on Marblehead society as well. But in this New England community, the resurgence of religious zeal in the late 1730s and 1740s consolidated and confirmed the power and legitimacy of the new Marblehead gentry and lent greater stability to local life.

[45] Isaac, "Evangelical Revolt," *WMQ*, 31: 345–68.

11

The Church Triumphant

FOUR YEARS before the Awakening began in Gloucester, it came to Marblehead in the person of Simon Bradstreet. Chosen by the Second Church to succeed Edward Holyoke as pastor, Bradstreet was the son of the minister of Charlestown, a man known throughout Massachusetts for his theological liberalism. Indeed, when they agreed to settle the younger Bradstreet, the members of Second Marblehead may have assumed that the son shared his father's liberal religious leanings, an orientation similar to that of Edward Holyoke. If so, the congregation was in for more than one kind of "awakening," for their new pastor had repudiated the position of his father and cast his lot with the colony's rising generation of evangelically minded preachers and their older counterparts like the Reverend John White. Bradstreet's ministry thus introduced at Second Marblehead the strict Calvinist theology and adherence to pristine Congregationalist orthodoxy that had always characterized Gloucester's religious life.

The difference between Simon Bradstreet's inclinations and Second Church's expectations might have resulted in a disastrous mismatch of clergyman with congregation. Instead, almost immediately after the installation of the twenty-eight-year-old minister in 1737, his parishioners started to show signs of unusual religious engagement. Although Edward

Holyoke had been well-liked by the elite families of his flock, his genial, rationalistic theology had not produced many conversions. Between Holyoke's ordination in 1716 and his elevation to the Harvard presidency in 1737, a total of ninety-three new members, an average of less than five annually, had joined Second Church. And Holyoke's last seven years in Marblehead, those following the anti-inoculation riot, were almost biblically lean: from 1731 to 1737, he added only fourteen new communicants. Bradstreet's ministry altered the church's fortunes entirely. Perhaps it was his youthful appeal or the novelty of a new preaching style that engaged the interest of the congregation. Or perhaps those attending Second Marblehead were adopting a new attitude toward church membership. Whatever the reason, between 1738 and 1742, the peak years of Marblehead's revival, Second Church acquired seventy-nine new communicants, nearly doubling its total membership at the time of Holyoke's departure.

Religious excitement spread simultaneously through John Barnard's congregation, although the revival at First Church represented less a novel development than a recovery of the congregation's former spiritual fervor. By "improving" natural disasters and military crises and by playing on popular religious prejudice, Barnard had drawn nearly two hundred new members into the First Church during the fifteen years following his ordination, an average of thirteen communicants annually. But at First Church as at Second, admissions had declined in the years after the anti-inoculation riot: only thirty-nine members of Barnard's congregation became full communicants between 1731 and 1737. With the coming of the revival, however, membership rebounded; fifteen men and women joined the First Church in 1738 and another fifty-two in the four years that followed.[1] In pastoral matters, Barnard was a pragmatist, and although he was nearly sixty at the time of Bradstreet's arrival in town, the senior minister quickly appropriated the successful evangelical techniques of his young colleague.

The popularity of the revival in Marblehead and Gloucester alike points up the strength of the first Great Awakening

---

[1] For Bradstreet's biography, see *SHG*, VIII, 108–9. Computations of the membership in Bradstreet's Church are based on entries in "Records of the

in New England's coastal ports and market towns. Although social histories of the revival have focused mainly on rural villages, many commercial centers were just as receptive to the New Light. Not only in Gloucester and Marblehead, but also in Boston and the trading towns of eastern Connecticut, the Awakening was a central event in local life. In fact, the revival fervor in New England began at Jonathan Edwards's church in Northamptom, Massachusetts, an important market town on the Connecticut River. Additional study of the Awakening in port towns is needed before the sources of its appeal, its social base, and its significance can be generalized about with any certainty, but the religious excitement in Marblehead conforms to the enthusiasm in Gloucester and other trading towns in two important ways. First, the Marblehead revival received strong support from families that belonged to the local elite. Second, in Marblehead, as in other port towns, relatively powerless groups also responded warmly to the New Light. But while it was the young people of communities like Gloucester and Northampton who were especially receptive to the Awakening, in Marblehead, it was

Second Church of Marblehead," MS, Unitarian Church of Marblehead. The data for Barnard's congregation are drawn from MFCR.

FULL MEMBERS ADDED TO SECOND CHURCH,
1738 TO 1742

	Men	Women	Total
1738	7	7	14
1739	2	5	7
1740	1	3	4
1741	7	15	22
1742	5	28	33

FULL MEMBERS ADDED TO FIRST CHURCH,
1738 TO 1742

	Men	Women	Total
1738	4	11	15
1739	3	13	16
1740	0	6	6
1741	1	10	11
1742	6	14	20

women from lower- and middle-class families who played a particularly prominent role at one critical stage of the local revival. Like the adolescents and young adults of some other towns, these ordinary Marblehead women were particularly vulnerable to the unsettling events of the 1740s. There was, however, an important contrast between the characters of the revivals that were initiated by these two different groups. While the young people of Gloucester and Northampton led their elders into local revivals characterized by moderation and restraint, Marblehead's female converts precipitated an outburst of evangelical extremism and emotionalism toward the end of that town's awakening in 1742. This final, "radical" phase of revivalism bypassed some places like Gloucester, but it struck hard at Marblehead, as well as other towns like Boston, Salem, and Charlestown, temporarily upsetting patterns of worship and social behavior. Crowds of the pious and the curious flocked to outdoor meetings to hear dramatic sermons delivered extemporaneously by itinerant preachers and lay exhorters of both sexes.

Because such religious gatherings attracted a popular audience and took place outside of the churches, and often over the opposition of the settled clergy, it is tempting to see in these events portents of a major cultural change. The mass support for evangelists could be read as an expression of mounting discontent with the deferential social order and an early stirring of social and political egalitarianism.[2] But Marblehead's religious upheaval lends little support to this way of interpreting the revival. While the "radical" phase of the Awakening in town reflected certain social tensions, this period of evangelical extremism was short-lived and produced no serious disruption in or permanent alteration of local life. In the long run, the revitalization of religious piety begun by Simon Bradstreet and John Barnard buttressed the strength of both the established Congregational churches and the social arrangements that had taken root in town after

---

[2] Nash, *Urban Crucible,* 204–19; Harry Stout, "Religion, Communications, and the Ideological Origins of the American Revolution, *WMQ,* 3rd ser., 34 (1977), 519–42. For a critique of these studies linking the First Great Awakening with the growth of democratic and egalitarian views, see Jon Butler, "Enthusiasm Described and Decried: The Great Awakening as Interpretive Fiction," *Journal of American History,* 69 (1982), 314–22.

1730; the Awakening enhanced the authority of the orthodox clergy and the new Marblehead gentry alike. In addition, the revival in Marblehead—and even the phase of "radical" enthusiasm in 1742—spent itself without shattering the unity of the orthodox churches or enhancing the position of local Anglicans. In some other towns marked by similar excesses of evangelical zeal, the most extreme New Light enthusiasts broke with the orthodox establishment to form "Separate" or Baptist churches, while some conservative and moderate Congregationalists entered the Episcopal communion. But Marblehead's Awakening was a triumph for orthodoxy, and instead of undermining Congregationalist cohesion and hegemony, the evangelical fervor among First and Second Church members renewed their mistrust of dissenters, especially the Episcopalians at St. Michael's. In Marblehead, as in Gloucester, the consequences of the revival were basically conservative.

Although the religious enthusiasm that began in Marblehead in 1738 caught up both of the town's Congregational churches, the character of the revival within each congregation was distinctive. First Church's awakening was "general," the new spiritual fervor cutting across class lines and touching both the wealthiest families and those at the lowest levels of the maritime community. By contrast, Bradstreet's converts were a remarkably genteel group that included a disproportionate number of people whose families ranked— or had ranked—among the town's elite. By the end of September in 1741, Bradstreet had added forty-four full members to his church: one-quarter of these new communicants came from households headed by men who ranked among the wealthiest decile of Marblehead's ratepayers in 1748, and fully sixty percent belonged to families who had bought or inherited the choice pews on the first floor of the Second Parish meetinghouse. The young pastor was particularly successful at arousing religious commitment among the male leaders of Second Church, a group that his predecessor's tepid rationalism had failed to touch. During the final years of Holyoke's ministry in the 1730s, only twelve of the seventy-eight male heads of household who owned pews on the floor of the meetinghouse were full church members.

Bradstreet doubled that number in the space of four years.[3]

What motivated the sudden interest in joining the church among Bradstreet's leading parishioners may be illustrated by the career of one convert who was in many ways a representative recruit of the Second Church revival, James Skinner. He was the son of Richard Skinner, Sr., a former Boston merchant who had moved to Marblehead and led the separation that formed the Second Church in 1715. Like many members of this group, Richard cultivated his connections back in the capital: he married two of his children into prominent commercial families in Boston and sent his son James to Harvard College. James stayed on in Cambridge for fifteen years after taking his degree. He held no position at the college, but he resisted returning to Marblehead and apparently shared his family's cosmopolitan preferences. It was probably financial difficulties that dictated James's reluctant resettlement in his home town in 1735. For although his father had been one of Marblehead's richest merchant-middlemen, the Skinner fortunes were slipping during the 1730s as the direct trade developed. In 1737, the administrators of the estate of James's brother, Richard Jr., who had inherited his father's business in Marblehead, were forced to sell off some of the family's real estate to satisfy creditors. Many of Bradstreet's other converts between 1738 and September of 1741 had histories like that of James Skinner, and some were his relatives and in-laws. There was James's

[3] My generalization about the social composition of new converts at First Church is based on a comparison of their names with the "Marblehead Tax List of 1748" (*EIHC*, 43: 209–22). This comparison indicates that twenty-one of Barnard's forty-eight new converts between 1738 and September of 1741, or about 44 percent, came from the upper half of the families who were rated. My characterization of the new converts at Second Church is based in part on the same method of matching the names of converts to the tax list of 1748. However, the tax list indicates only which Second Church families had been able to maintain—or perhaps recoup—their economic position during the late forties. It gives no information concerning former family prominence in town. The best source for this point is the floor plan of the Second Church meetinghouse that designates family pews, for such seating was usually retained despite reversals in family fortunes. This plan is in the files of the Marblehead Historical Society at Abbot Hall, Marblehead, Mass.

nephew, William Nick, whose father had also been an affluent merchant in Marblehead and helped to found Second Church. But William failed to follow his father into commerce, took up the trade of a joiner, and never prospered as his family had earlier. There was James's brother-in-law, Captain Joseph Smethurst, a mariner from London and a former Anglican drawn into the Second Church and Stephen Minot's circle by marriage into the Skinner family. But despite his influential in-laws, Smethurst never held an important public office in Marblehead. And there were James's cousins, Edward Stacey, a physician, and Samuel Stacey, the town schoolmaster. Both men were Harvard graduates, but they lacked the political influence and economic standing of their wealthy merchant fathers, members of the original Second Church establishment.[4]

The similar backgrounds of many of Bradstreet's new church members suggest that their conversions were a way of acknowledging their identification with the community, something that joining a church had traditionally validated. The remaining members of Stephen Minot's circle and their grown sons had discovered during the 1730s that the disengagement of their families from local life translated as a tangible liability in Marblehead's business and politics. Perhaps not all of Bradstreet's new converts had fallen as far and as

---

[4] For James Skinner, see SHG, VII, 441–42; Elizabeth Dana, "Richard Skinner of Marblehead and his Bible," New England Historical and Genealogical Register, 54: 413–22; Petition to sell the real estate of Richard Skinner, Jr., MSCJ, May 10, 1737. Shoreman William Nick, Sr. left an estate worth over one thousand pounds sterling in 1723, but his son William Jr. ranked below the richest quartile of ratepayers on the tax list of 1748. Another son, Richard Nick, died in 1745, with an estate inventoried at only 270 pounds sterling. (See EPF, #19540, 19546.) Like William and Richard Nick, Joseph Smethurst never held important public office in town, nor did he enjoy conspicuous financial success. Some of his real property was sold after his death in 1751 to cover debts owed by the estate. (See MSCJ, October 15, 1751.) The fathers of Dr. Edward Stacey and Samuel Stacey, William Stacey and Captain John Stacey, were major middlemen in the early eighteenth century who served regularly as selectmen and deputies to the General Court. No inventory survives for William, but Captain John Stacey was worth 702 pounds sterling at his death in 1722. (EPF, #26080.) By contrast, their sons Edward and Samuel never held important offices, and in 1748 both ranked below the top decile of ratepayers on the tax list, in the top quartile and the top half respectively. See also, SHG, VII, 106 and 592.

fast as the Skinners, Smethursts, and Staceys. But as a group, the best families of Bradstreet's congregation had been lagging behind economically and losing ground politically during the decade that had begun with the anti-inoculation riot and witnessed the development of the direct trade. The Awakening now afforded them an opportunity to establish their membership within the community by forging stronger ties to the church. For some, the reconciliation produced immediate results.

James Skinner did not seem the likely candidate to retrieve his family's fortunes until his conversion in 1738. But in that same year, he was elected Marblehead's representative to the General Court, although he had never held an important public office before, and he served as the town's deputy for most years thereafter until his death in 1747. After he became a full church member, economic opportunities in town also opened up for Skinner. By the early 1740s, Joseph Swett and Robert Hooper were offering him shares of their merchantment—despite their belief that Skinner had no head for business and despite his lack of marital connections to either of the partners. Of course, not all of Simon Bradstreet's new communicants succeeded so handsomely. There is no indication that the fortunes of William Nick, or those of Dr. Edward Stacey and his cousin Samuel, were similarly enhanced after their conversions. In any case, scarcity of evidence makes positing a positive correlation between conversion and business success problematic. On the other hand, a close correspondence did exist between involvement in the revival and the political prominence attained by some other Second Church members. Five of Bradstreet's parishioners won important elective offices in Marblehead for the first time after the revival began, and all of them came from families who had figured prominently as participants in the Awakening. Three of the new officeholders were converts of the revival; two others had not themselves joined the church, but most of the members of their households had, including their black servants. Besides the greater political influence attained by awakened Second Church members, their role in the wars against Spain and France in the 1740s also suggests both their success at winning local recognition and their heightened interest in Marblehead's welfare. Like the leading men of First Church, Bradstreet's parishioners were prominent in local defense and poor-relief efforts of this period. James Skinner, for example, led the town's attempt to secure an abatement from province taxes in 1742. Another new Second Church convert, Joseph Smethurst, commanded a Marblehead crew aboard a government sloop that patrolled the seacoast. Smethurst died before he could translate his military service into political prominence in town, but his career and those of Bradstreet's other revival converts suggest that the Awakening effectively integrated Second Church's leaders into local society.[5]

While there was an important social dimension to the Second Church's susceptibility to the revival, the extent to which the sustained efforts of settled clergymen like Simon Bradstreet fostered religious enthusiasm cannot be overlooked. Church membership in Marblehead actually fell off during 1740, the year of George Whitefield's arrival in Boston and his triumphal tour of Essex County and the coastal towns of New Hampshire and Maine. By all accounts, Marblehead accorded "the Grand Itinerant" a warm reception. Whitefield reported preaching at eleven o'clock on Monday, September 29th, "to thousands in a broad place in the middle of town" and dining afterwards with John Barnard before proceeding to Salem. A week later, Whitefield addressed Marbleheaders again on his return trip to Boston. During this visit, he enjoyed the hospitality of a local First Church merchant and collected seventy pounds from Bradstreet and Barnard for his orphanage in Georgia. On both occasions the Whitefieldian spectacle drew considerable crowds that

[5] James Skinner owned shares in three of Swett and Hooper's vessels, and his brother John owned part of several others. James's lack of talent or interest in business tried the patience of Hooper, who complained to one of his European correspondents that a ship "shod sail this day . . . but Mr. Skinner according to custim is gone out of town." (Hooper to Steers and Barons, February 1, 1746, HSL.) The Second Church members who won important local office after their conversions were James Skinner, Dr. Robert Hooper, Sr., and Isaac Mansfield. Ebenezer Stacey and Benjamin Boden, Jr., who also won election to the board of selectmen after 1738, came from families with a large number of revival converts. For Skinner and Smethurst's roles in the military crisis of the 1740s, see Petition of James Skinner, January, 1742, *MA*, 115: 6–7, and Howard M. Chapin, *Privateering in King George's War, 1739–1748* (Providence, 1927), 71–73.

responded favorably to the New Light. The evangelist noted with characteristic modesty after his second trip to Marblehead that "the Lord attended his Word with such mighty power, that I trust it will be a day much to be remembered by many souls."[6] But Whitefield's ministry had an insignificant impact upon church membership: a total of only ten new members joined Marblehead's Congregational churches in 1740. The number of new converts did not rise substantially until 1741, months after Whitefield's last appearance in town.

Through September of 1741, the Awakening retained its original character at each of Marblehead's churches. Barnard's converts continued to come from a cross-section of Marblehead society, while Bradstreet still drew disproportionately upon the best families in his flock. But by the beginning of 1742, a decisive shift had occurred in the character of the revival at Second Church. Francis Salter and Joseph Roads, two middle-class, middle-aged shoremen, set up as lay exhorters and began holding evening meetings that drew large crowds of women. By the end of January, some of the female members of Second Church had organized a separate "women's meeting" for devotions, and several were speaking publicly to large assemblies of both sexes. The altered ratio between male and female converts joining Second Church in 1742 also reflects the disproportionately greater enthusiasm that this phase of the Awakening aroused among the women of Bradstreet's congregation. In that year, twenty-eight women became full members of Second Church, but only five men. And at least two of these males may have entered the church because of the influence of pious women: one new male communicant was a black slave belonging to a family that included three recent female converts and another was the young son of a woman church member who was admitted along with his sister. The new women communicants of 1742 represented a distinctive strata in Marblehead's social order as well. None of the twenty-eight female

---

[6] William V. Davis, ed., *George Whitefield's Journals* (Gainesville, Florida, 1969), 466 and 470. J. William T. Youngs also emphasizes the extent to which the revival was the work of the settled clergy. (*God's Messengers,* 109–19.)

converts came from local elite families; they were instead wives, daughters, and widows belonging to middling and lower-class households. And as ordinary women became more actively engaged in religious life at Second Church, the enthusiasm of that congregation's elite males cooled: not a single one entered the church in 1742.[7]

The turn taken by the revival at Second Church was unpalatable to many of Marblehead's leading men. Foremost among these critics was Nathan Bowen, one of the members of the old Minot circle who had remained in town after the 1730s. As soon as young Bradstreet's evangelical inclinations had become manifest, the ultra-rationalist and arch-conservative Bowen had defected to St. Michael's, and the enthusiasm of 1742 only deepened his alienation from Congregationalist orthodoxy. Like many other opponents of the Awakening throughout New England, Bowen objected to the emotionalism of itinerants and lay exhorters who behaved "as if the only way to Heaven was thro' Bedlam." He also ridiculed shoremen-turned-preachers like Salter and Roads for pretending to "extraordinary Gifts" and presuming upon the prerogatives of educated elites. But it was the effect of this irregular preaching upon women that violated most deeply Bowen's sense of order and decorum. Most of the occurrences of 1742 that struck Bowen as especially obnoxious involved female participants. He made disapproving note of the news that the evangelism of Salter and Roads had "set a women's meeting on foot," and scornfully observed the spectacle of "silly women in Great Multitudes

---

[7] Nathan Bowen, "Extracts from Interleaved Almanacs, 1742–1799," *EIHC*, 91 (1955), 164. (Cited hereafter as Bowen, "Almanacs.") During the first four years of the revival, nearly 40 percent of the converts at Second Church were men; in 1742, men accounted for only 15 percent of all converts, a proportion even smaller than that obtaining in the period between 1716 and 1737, when men comprised about 20 percent of all converts. One could argue that in 1742, the proportion of male to female converts was just returning to its prerevival ratio. But in absolute terms, the number of women entering the Second Church in 1742 was significantly larger than it had been in any of the preceding years of the revival or for any year of Holyoke's pastorate. I determined the economic standing of the families of female converts in this later phase of the revival by tracing their husbands or fathers in the Marblehead tax list of 1748. All of these men ranked below the wealthiest quartile of Marblehead ratepayers in that year.

. . . thrown into Swounds" by the performances of lay exhorters. Equally irksome to Bowen was word that Bradstreet had actually forbidden "One Man Communion upon an idle suggestion of his wife." But worst of all, "women and even Common Negroes take upon them to extort (sic) their Betters even in the pulpit before large assemblies."[8] Bowen's private almanac, in which he recorded the course of the Second Church revival, reads as a long and increasingly irritable indictment of the active role being taken by Marblehead women in religious life.

The radical New Light message spread throughout New England by itinerants and exhorters during 1741 and 1742 appears to have held particular appeal for the poorer and more powerless segments of society in many colonial seaports. But as the unfolding of the revival at Marblehead's Second Church suggests, gender may be as important as class as a category for analyzing religious engagement during this later phase of the Awakening. Significantly, lower-class men in Marblehead played only a small part in the enthusiasm of 1742. Male exhorters like Salter and Roads were solid, middle-class shoremen, not dispossessed seamen, unskilled laborers, or apprentices.[9] And the audiences that they attracted, as well as the new converts of 1742, did not come chiefly from Marblehead's laboring-class males. According to Bowen, there were instances of blacks setting up as lay exhorters at Second Church, but his reference to "Common Negroes" does not specify the gender of the popular preachers. What was distinctive about the latter phase of the Second Church revival was the prominence of women participants. A flood of new female converts in early 1742,

[8] Bowen, "Almanacs," 164, 165, 167, and 169. On female exhorters, see Ebenezer Turrell, *Mr. Turrell's Directions* (Boston, 1742); Andrew Croswell, *A Letter . . . to Mr. Turrell* (Boston, 1742). See also *Diary of William Bentley, 1803–1810* 3 vols. (Gloucester, 1962), III, 477–78. On Bowen's theological views, see *Journals of Ashley Bowen*, ed. Smith, *Publ. C.S.M.*, 44: 8.

[9] Gary Nash emphasizes the role of class in his account of the radical phase of the Awakening in Boston. (*Urban Crucible*, 204–18.) Marblehead's exhorters, Salter and Roads, were both in their forties. Salter, who had been converted in 1741, ranked among the upper 40 percent of Marblehead ratepayers in 1748; Roads, a church member since 1724, ranked in the upper half of ratepayers.

nearly twice the number of women entering communion between 1738 and 1741, became full members of Second Church. In addition, women formed an independent religious association, predominated at the gatherings of lay preachers, and even served as exhorters themselves.

While the Awakening in Gloucester did not pass through a similar, female-dominated phase, impressionistic evidence concerning the later stage of the revival in some other seaports also points to a preponderance of women participants. In Salem, for example, the prominence of women in public religious activity recalled for some contemporaries an earlier outbreak of hysteria in which women had also played a principal role, the witchcraft controversy of 1692. Nathan Bowen observed that when one young itinerant preached at Salem in February of 1742, his performance

> affrighted . . . the old women . . . into Fits of Screeching; and the utmost confusion, Many Actions of the persons affected have put some of the more Thinking in that Town in Mind of the worm wood and the Gall of 1692.[10]

In Boston, too, women appear to have experienced the final phase of the Awakening with particular intensity, as the publication of a poem by a "female friend" of the revival there suggests. Attributed to one Sarah Parsons Moorhead, the poem reflects the anxieties aroused among evangelical moderates by the Reverend James Davenport, one of New England's most extreme New Light evangelists. Of particular concern to the author were Davenport's attacks upon the spiritual credentials of some of Boston's pastors: "I love the Zeal that fires good Davenport's Breast / But his hard Cen-

---

[10] Bowen, "Almanacs," 165. The extent to which women dominated the final phase of the Awakening in other port towns is difficult to trace in church records for a number of reasons. Records for Salem's East Parish are no longer extant, and the First Church of Salem was too badly disrupted by the Fiske controversy to become deeply involved in the enthusiasm. Cedric Cowing's study of Boston church membership during the Awakening shows little change in the ratio between males and females entering the churches during 1741 and 1742: women continued to outnumber men by about 2 to 1. ("Sex and Preaching in the Great Awakening," *American Quarterly*, 20 (1968), 624–44. However, church membership is not the only index of involvement in the revival.

sures give my Soul no rest." In the following stanzas, Moor-head recounts a "dream" in which Davenport repents of his uncharitable criticisms of his colleagues and joins a unified clergy in carrying forward the work of the revival. A post-script to the poem also chides Andrew Croswell, another controversial itinerant, for his strictures against the settled clergy: "I cannot bear a Mortal should reflect / Or treat our Precious Guides with cold Neglect." The publication of works by women was not unheard of in New England, but it was far from a common occurrence, and Sarah Moorhead's muse was not the stuff of which exceptions are made. Clearly the appearance of her work in print was calculated to serve ends other than literary enrichment: it points to the recognition on the part of male critics of Davenport and Croswell that women comprised a significant segment of the constituency of New Light extremists.[11]

Why did women in many Massachusetts port towns take a leading role in this final outburst of religious enthusiasm? The rekindling of military conflict after 1739 is one likely source of their greater engagement. For men in Marblehead, Salem, and Boston, the fighting posed dangers, but the con-stant recurrence of military crisis since the middle of the sev-enteenth century had inured sailors and fishermen to wartime risks. Unlike Gloucester men, who were unaccustomed to such disruptions, the maritime laborers of larger ports had experienced such dislocations many times in the past. And for men the conflict was not without its compensations. War promised high prices for fish in a market cornered by New Englanders once the French were routed, opportunities for a share of the spoils of enemy vessels seized by privateers, full employment at high wages for crew members on merchant-men, and a taste of military adventure and glory.[12] Finally, men could alleviate their anxieties through direct action—enlistment aboard privateers and government coasting ves-sels, training with the militia band, and assisting in the repair of harbor fortifications.

For the wives and daughters of ordinary seaport families,

---

[11] Sarah Parsons Moorhead, *To the Reverend James Davenport On His Departure from Boston* (Boston, 1742).

[12] Nash, *Urban Crucible,* 165, 167, 170, and 173.

on the other hand, the risks attending the renewal of warfare seemed more real than the rewards. Female members of middling and lower-class households were both more likely and less able to withstand the loss of men than were women from wealthier families. With Marblehead, Salem, and Boston serving as key recruiting stations, these poorer women faced the prospects of widowhood, spinsterhood, a life of marginal subsistence, and dependence on public relief or relatives. Even families whose male members did not enlist or who escaped impressment still confronted the threat of French privateers in the north Atlantic attacking the fishing fleet or Spanish ships seizing local crews aboard coasting vessels in the Caribbean. As a result, the anxieties of local women in Marblehead were aroused with the outbreak of war with Spain in 1739 and continued to mount as fears grew that the French would enter the conflict. And adding to their apprehensions over the military situation was the blow dealt to seafaring families in the fall of 1741, when a storm killed so many fishermen that the town asked for a tax abatement. Almost immediately after this maritime disaster, as ordinary Marblehead women experienced directly what the loss of a large number of men could mean, the religious excitement at Second Church started to swell.

Confronted with conditions that portended a complete loss of control over their lives, ordinary Marblehead women found in the revival of 1742 a release for their fears in religious catharsis. They took solace in the solidarity of spiritual fellowship at women's meetings; they sublimated their anxieties in assurances of eternal salvation and in the claims of "extraordinary power" advanced by shoremen like Salter and Roads, the traditional leaders of the fishing community. Conversion carried with it purely practical advantage as well, for churches were more disposed to distribute private charity among poor members than to the needy outside the fellowship of believers. Claims on the charity of the churches and the special consideration of the saints became critical to many local women as the events of the 1740s bore out their apprehensions. In 1735, 57 widows were among Marblehead's 511 ratepayers, but by 1748, only 11 women appeared among the 620 inhabitants paying town and province taxes in that year. The intervening years of military crisis and disaster at sea could only have increased rather than reduced the total number of widows in Marblehead. But the loss of breadwinners among sons and other male relatives, coupled with the toll taken by wartime inflation on the income of widows, had reduced the number of women in town with taxable property. These women now probably ranked among the fifty-three Marbleheaders who were not rated at all in 1749.[13]

On one level, the revival of 1742 was a reaction on the part of women to fears and hardships created by a crisis of relatively short gestation caused by the renewal of warfare. But female participation in the final phase of the Awakening also represented a response to more subtle and long-term changes taking place within the culture of colonial seaports. The appearance of Second Church women in assertive public, religious roles is especially striking because in the decade preceding the revival of 1742 and throughout the period after, the female members of Marblehead society recede from view— save for this single episode. No comparable instances exist of the aggressive behavior that earlier had made merchants' widows major figures in local commerce and active litigants in the Court of Common Pleas. By the middle of the eighteenth century, a few local widows supported themselves as petty shopkeepers, but no counterparts of businesswomen like Madame Elizabeth Browne remained. Now the relics of Marblehead's major traders did not assume control of

[13] Petition of James Skinner to the General Court, January 7, 1742, *MA*, 115:6–7; Marblehead Valuation Lists for 1735, 1749, Tax and Valuation Lists of Massachusetts Towns before 1776, Harvard University Microfilm Edition, Reel #12; "Marblehead Tax List of 1748," *EIHC*, 43: 209–22. Throughout eastern Massachusetts, the number of widows was increasing over the first half of the eighteenth century, a result of the combined effects of declining longevity among men, the preponderance of males migrating to the frontier, and the casualties of war. In seaports, widows were even more numerous than in country towns. If the figure of 1200 for Boston in 1742 is correct, about 8 percent of the capital's population consisted of widows. In Marblehead, widows paying rates accounted for 3 percent of my estimate of the 1735 population and for 10 percent of all ratepayers in that year. By contrast, in rural Woburn, widows accounted for fewer than 8 percent of all ratepayers by 1750. See Alex Keyssar, "Widowhood in Eighteenth-Century Massachusetts: A Problem in the History of the Family," *Perspectives in American History*, 8 (1974), 96 and 98; Nash, *Urban Crucible*, 172.

their husband's affairs, but instead subsided into genteel retirement or quickly remarried. Also absent from local annals are the equals of vivid, defiant females like Lucy Codner and Sarah Westcott, women from the laboring classes who had earlier in Marblehead's history challenged the authority of clergymen, county sheriffs, and the Bay colony government itself.[14]

This receding of women from public view may indicate an increasing circumscription of acceptable female social roles within the wider culture, the spread of sanctions against women running businesses and aggressively defending their interests. Whether women welcomed or resented this reduction of their autonomy and responsibility is uncertain. But it is clear that by the third decade of the eighteenth century,

---

[14] My research in the probate and civil court records turned up no Marblehead women after the mid-1730s who were actively involved in commercial life on the scale of Madame Browne and her contemporaries, although a few local widows kept small stores or grog shops. And except for cases of fornication involving singlewomen, female Marbleheaders disappear from the criminal court records as well until the 1750s, when a few of the widows that supported themselves by shopkeeping were fined for failing to pay an excise tax. (MSCJ, March 31, 1752.) C. Dallett Hemphill has found a similar change in the lives of Salem women beginning even earlier, the late 1670s and 1680s. See "Women in Court: Sex-Role Differentiation in Salem, Massachusetts, 1636–1683," *WMQ*, 3rd ser., 39 (1982), 172–75. The differing rates of commercial development in Salem and Marblehead may account for the earlier disappearance of Salem women from an active role in business.

The reduction in the economic power and authority within the family allotted to Marblehead women may also be reflected in the diminishing number of women ratepayers. Possibly fewer women had rateable estates by the 1740s because widows were receiving smaller shares of their deceased spouses's estates. In the case of intestate estates, province law provided for a widow to receive one-third of her husband's personal property forever and one-third of his real property as a life estate or dower, property that she had the right to improve but not to sell. A husband could, however, bequeathe control of a larger share of his estate to his widow or his entire estate, as Captain John Browne did in 1708. (EPF, #3619) Since most men died intestate, the number of wills available within any single community for tracing changes in the size of widows' legacies over time is too small to be statistically significant. But a study of wills drawn from several communities would constitute a sample large enough to determine shifts in the willingness of husbands to entrust property to their wives. (See George Lee Haskins, *Law and Authority in Early Massachusetts* (New York, 1960), 180–82.

women were occupying a less prominent place in Marblehead society than they had previously. The crises of the early
1740s temporarily reversed this direction of social development. By imperiling a substantial portion of the adult male
population, military disruptions and maritime disasters
renewed the need for Marblehead women to assume more
assertive roles, especially poorer women whose position was
particularly vulnerable. The revival of 1742 offered such
ordinary women one avenue for reentering public life by
taking on the role of spiritual leaders.

Another aspect of female religious fervor suggests an
additional way in which the lives of women and the culture
of provincial seaports were changing during the middle
decades of the eighteenth century. The swooning and
screaming of women at revival gatherings that led Nathan
Bowen to characterize the enthusiasm as an "infatuation"
points to a sublimation of suppressed physical passion in
religious ecstasy. The strong sexual undercurrent of religious
excitement is also captured by the language of Sarah Moorhead's poem, particularly in her frequent use of words carrying both a spiritual and a sexual connotation. For example,
responding to James Davenport's charges that many of Boston's clergymen were unconverted, she wrote: "Our worthy
Guides whom God had much inflam'd / As inexperienc'd
Souls, alas he [Davenport] nam'd / Hence giddy Youth a woful
License take. . . ." And Moorhead's description of Andrew
Croswell's preaching skills could easily be confused with the
charms of a lover: "You have the Art to Win with melting
Words. . . ." Certainly she was smitten: "My Bosom warms,
all my Affections melt." Even more revealing is the author's
dream of Davenport's recantation of his errors, a fantasy
which situates the "fainting hero" in his bed as the poet
secretly looks on. No ascetic cell, Davenport's bedchamber
resembles a romantic retreat, a "bower" replete with flow-
ers, singing birds and "gentle Zephyrs." [15]

The channelling of sexual impulses into spiritual intensity
on the part of Sarah Moorhead and other female participants in the revival corresponds with an increasing reticence
within the wider culture about acknowledging the capacity

[15] Moorhead, *To the Reverend James Davenport*, 1–8.

of women for physical passion. The repression of female sexuality from open view is evident in the changing character of prosecutions for fornication in Essex County ports over the first half of the eighteenth century. During the first four decades following 1700, grand juries routinely indicted newlywed couples who produced a child too soon after marrying. But it became increasingly common for husbands only to appear in court, offer excuses for the absences of their wives, and to confess on behalf of both offending parties. Presiding justices accepted these excuses for the nonappearance of offending female spouses as a matter of course. And by the opening years of the 1740s, prosecutions for fornication before marriage begin to disappear from the records of the General Sessions of the Peace altogether. The legal system had not relinquished its oversight of sexual conduct nor had society at large abandoned its proscription of premarital sex: the courts still tried single women for fornication and their partners were sued for bastardy. But criminal cases involving couples who produced a child too soon after marriage were now handled by the justices out of sessions.[16] Perhaps this change in the treatment of married defendants was designed to cope with an increasing caseload: the rate of premarital pregnancy was rising steadily during the middle of the eighteenth century in Massachusetts. But the removal of jurisdiction from the sessions could also have reflected an antipathy on the part of justices, jurors, and defendants alike to publicize in open court the physical passions of young matrons.

Set against the context of this change in attitudes toward the expression of female sexuality, the revival of 1742 may

[16] I am indebted to John Murrin for my information on the changing jurisdiction of fornication cases. On this point, see also, Hartog, "The Public Law of a County Court," *American Journal of Legal History,* 20 (1976), 300–302. The change in the character of fornication prosecutions can be traced in the Minutebooks of the General Sessions of the Peace. The 1730s marked the last decade that a substantial number of defendants in fornication cases were newly married couples. In the 1740s, only one husband and wife from Marblehead were presented. The last married defendants from Marblehead were indicted in 1744; from Salem, in 1743. For the general rise in premarital pregnancy in eighteenth-century Massachusetts, see Daniel Scott Smith and Michael Hindus, "Premarital Pregnancy in America," *Journal of Interdisciplinary History,* 5 (1975), 553–54.

have figured for women participants as an opportunity to communicate in religious form feelings that their society increasingly—if unsuccessfully—sought to suppress. The retreat of women from public life and the repression of feminine sexuality are generally considered the themes of nineteenth-century American history rather than those of the prerevolutionary period.[17] But in seaports like Marblehead, both developments were underway by the mid-eighteenth century and seem to have been closely connected to the participation of women in the final phase of the Awakening. The response to these long-term cultural trends combined with the fears and anxieties generated by the renewal of military crisis brought women to the foreground of public religious life for a brief period at the end of the Awakening.

Despite—or because of—its intensity, the female-dominated phase of the Second Church revival did not even outlast the year 1742. While evangelical extremism alarmed conservatives like Nathan Bowen, who had opposed the Awakening from the outset, it also alienated moderates like John Barnard, who generally supported the revival. As soon as the enthusiasm at Second Church took a more radical turn, Barnard began appealing privately to Simon Bradstreet, who sanctioned both lay exhorting and the women's meeting, to moderate the fervor.[18] For Barnard, the need to rein in the excesses at Second Church derived in part from his concern that an inexperienced, young minister like Bradstreet might not be able to preclude a challenge to his spiritual leadership on the part of charismatic lay preachers. But more than perceiving lay exhorters and their female followers as a potential threat to pastoral authority, Barnard feared that these irregularities would discredit the revival itself. Of particular importance was securing for Marblehead's Congregational churches the continuing support of those "respectable families" who had entered full communion in increasing numbers since 1738.

What had emerged in Marblehead as a result of the revival

---

[17] The literature on this subject, is considerable, but see especially Nancy Cott, *The Bonds of Womanhood: "Women's Sphere" in New England, 1780–1835* (New Haven, 1977).

[18] "Autobiography of Barnard," 229–30.

was the town's first coherent, staunchly orthodox elite, a set of families whose close connection to the Congregational churches underwrote their larger social commitment to a godly communal order based upon piety, discipline, and restraint. Prior to 1738, less than half of the male heads of Marblehead's leading Congregationalist families had any formal connection to First or Second church. But by 1743, over seventy percent of these men were either joined to the orthodox churches in full communion or had owned the covenant. The number of full church members within local elite ranks had nearly doubled over the years of the revival. To Barnard's mind, the danger of the enthusiastic excesses at Second Church—where the greatest gains among the elite had been made—lay in their potential to alienate this newly committed constituency.[19]

Throughout his ministry, Barnard had aimed to identify Congregationalist orthodoxy with communal order and to strengthen the church as an institution for stabilizing the rest of society. Bringing the local elite into the church was essential to this end, for it would endow the emerging social order with a spiritual sanction. But the disruptions in Bradstreet's congregation during 1742 threatened the continuing integration of social and religious authority. Unlike Nathan Bowen, most of Marblehead's major merchants and shoremen had responded warmly to the New Light of evangelical preaching, but they most likely shared his chagrin at its sudden heat—the spectacle of shrieking women, female preachers, and lay exhorters invading the very institution that had

[19] My reconstruction of Marblehead's Congregationalist elite at the time of the revival (1738–1742) is based upon the tax list of 1748 and the Essex Probate Files. I included in the elite all adult males resident in town at the time of the Awakening who ranked among the wealthiest decile of Marblehead ratepayers in 1748, as well as all adult males who died between 1738 and 1747 and ranked among the top 10 percent of inventoried decedents—a total of fifty-two persons. Of these fifty-two, twenty-five had some affiliation with First or Second Church prior to the revival, but only thirteen of the twenty-five were full members. By 1743, three of the original fifty-two were dead, and thirty-three of the surviving forty-nine persons were either full or half-way church members. Between 1738 and 1743, eight men with no previous church connection became full members, one owned the covenant, and another who had been a half-way member became a full communicant. (Sources: MFCR, "Records of the Second Church of Marblehead.")

promised to promote social order. It all conjured up bad memories of the prophetic period of early Quakerism. What was worse, those disaffected with the disorder in the Congregationalist camp would have someplace else to go: they could follow Bowen into St. Michael's communion. In 1730, Barnard had learned not to underestimate the Anglicans; in 1742, he was not about to allow the Second Church excesses to become an issue that Episcopalians could exploit as successfully as they had the sentiment against inoculation.

The initial years of the revival in Marblehead had been a godsend to Barnard in his competition with a reinvigorated St. Michael's. Throughout the 1730s, George Pigot had capitalized on the favorable climate following the anti-inoculation riot to extend the Church of England's influence in Essex County. In 1731, he started gathering contributions to build St. Peter's Church in neighboring Salem. By 1734, the rector was holding regular Sabbath services there and claiming a congregation two to three hundred strong. This expansion of Episcopal influence in Essex County so alarmed Benjamin Colman, one of Boston's leading Congregationalist ministers, that he advised the Bishop of London that the place for S.P.G. missionaries was not "the great seaports of trade," but New England's hinterland.[20] The early years of the revival in Marblehead retarded this Anglican resurgence, not only by strengthening religious commitment among Congregationalists but also by attracting local Churchmen into the orthodox fold. Thirteen of the new communicants added to First and Second Churches between 1738 and 1742 had previously attended St. Michael's and included members of several substantial Episcopal families.[21] The early years of the

[20] George Pigot to S.P.G. Sec'y, December 27, 1734, in *Historical Collections*, ed. Perry, III, 303; Benjamin Colman to the Bishop of London, September 13, 1734, Colman Papers, Massachusetts Historical Society; Harriet S. Tapley, *St. Peter's Church, Salem Before the Revolution* (Salem, 1944), 5.

[21] This data on Anglican conversions to Congregationalism is based upon a comparison of the names of people who became full members of First or Second Church between 1738 and 1742 with the names of persons listed in the "Records of St. Michael's." The wife of Alexander Watts, an Episcopal merchant, who was one of Marblehead's wealthiest men, and several adult children of John Roundey, an Anglican shoreman who ranked in the richest decile of ratepayers in 1748, were among the defectors to orthodoxy.

Marblehead Awakening also wrought a reversal in the political fortunes of local Churchmen. The year 1738 marked the end of Dr. Bartholomew Jackson's long tenure on the board of selectmen, and until 1742 no other Episcopalian won election as either selectman or representative. Instead, dominating all of these offices in the years between 1738 and 1742 were Congregationalists, many of whose families were caught up in the revival.[22]

But with the beginning of the radical phase of the revival at Second Church, Episcopalians started to recoup their losses. One St. Michael's member was elected selectman in 1742 and again in 1743. And as Nathan Bowen surveyed the scene at Second Church, he projected even more grandiose gains:

> I expect the Dissenting Clergy will ferment these practices, til they end in the Destruction of their Kingdom and a more general and happy Introduction of our Mother Church of England which (happy for the people) admits of no such Confusion.[23]

Bowen was not the only Churchman who hoped that the turbulence of the times would promote the Episcopal cause in New England, and in some towns Old Lights and alarmed moderates embraced Anglicanism as an escape from radical enthusiasts.

The beginnings of an Episcopal political recovery after the outbreak of enthusiasm at Second Church in 1742 indicate that the zeal of some Congregationalists could have presented St. Michael's with a prime opportunity. Instead, events defeated the expectations of Nathan Bowen. Barnard's influence began to tell in Bradstreet's behavior, and even by the end of March in 1742 the younger man seemed somewhat chastened. In a wry comparison of the revival to the course

[22] Dr. Bartholomew Jackson and his coreligionist William Bartlett had been regularly elected to the board of selectmen throughout the 1730s. One of the men replacing them in the late 1730s and 1740s was George Finch, a former Episcopalian whom Barnard had drawn away from St. Michael's and into the First Church. The Awakening struck directly at Anglicanism through the ministry of preachers like George Whitefield, who despite his ordination in the Episcopal Church was sharply critical of the Church of England and of S.P.G. missionaries. (Nash, *Urban Crucible*, 207.)

[23] Bowen, "Almanacs," 164; Gaustad, *The Great Awakening in New England*, 119; and Goen, *Revivalism and Separatism in New England*, 111–13.

of a comet, Bowen observed that "the Hot Spirit of Enthu-
seasm . . . is now on the Decline. . . . Our Priest Bradstreet
who has been Retrograde sometime is now Stationary and I
expect he will soon be Direct again." Admissions to Second
Church bear out Bowen's impression that the force of popular enthusiasm was spent: after the flock of new communicants who joined the church in March of 1742, the number
of converts tapered off steadily through the subsequent
months. Even the sensation created by the preaching of radical New Light itinerants James Davenport and Andrew
Croswell in Boston and Charlestown during the late spring
and summer of that year made no impression upon Marblehead. By early in 1743, the social composition of new converts also reverted to its earlier character as several prominent
men entered Second Church. In the same year, Bradstreet
publicly repudiated evangelical extremism by joining with
Barnard and other moderate ministers in signing the *Testimony* against the revival's recent excesses. The young parson also took steps to assert his authority over the Second
Church congregation, an about-face sarcastically noted by
Nathan Bowen. He recounted how, at one Sabbath lecture,
Bradstreet stopped his sermon to reprimand a parishioner
for reading a psalmbook instead of attending to "the divine
Oracles."[24]

For the restoration of peace to Second Church, Barnard
claimed full credit, reporting that his influence had prevented "the other church in town, and their minister, from
being thrown into . . . disorders and confusions." Even Nathan
Bowen, normally no admirer of orthodox "Priests," gave the
devil his due. "We have been happy in this Town, under the
protection of Mr. Barnard!" he exclaimed after witnessing
the itinerant "Impostures and their Cursed train of Followers" in Charlestown and Boston during the summer of 1742.
Within his own congregation, Barnard had also maintained

---

[24] Bowen, "Almanacs," 166; and Bentley, *Diary*, III, 477. The decline of the
enthusiasm appears clearly in entries of new members in "Records of the
Second Church." Seventeen new members were added to Second in March,
five in April, but then only one or two for each remaining month in 1742.
Samuel Parker, the son of a wealthy shoreman and selectman, and Isaac
Mansfield, a Harvard graduate and the town's schoolmaster, joined Second
Church in 1743.

"peace and quiet," and had controlled the entire course run by the revival. Although religious zeal remained intense at First Church throughout 1742, no exhorters or women's meetings materialized, and the Awakening there retained a "general" character. Twenty new converts came into the church, six men and fourteen women, and as in the previous four years the new communicants came from every level in Marblehead society, ranging from the poorest fishermen to the wife of Robert Hooper, Jr.[25]

Barnard's shrewdness in staking out a position that avoided both the extremes of radical New Light revivalism and a thoroughgoing rejection of evangelicalism is reflected in a sermon that he delivered in March of 1742 entitled *Zeal for Good Works*. Out of diplomatic deference to his younger colleague, Barnard did not deliver this indictment of the revival's recent excesses in Marblehead but in Boston at the Thursday lecture. The instances of misguided zeal that Barnard scored in his sermon, however, were drawn from his familiarity with the disruptions at Bradstreet's church. Citing St. Paul's reproof of the Corinthians for "what was disorderly in their Church Assemblies," Barnard condemned "Speaking with Tongues, and one singing, another teaching, a Third uttering a Revelation, and Their Women speaking in the Church and taking upon them to Teach. . . ." He was careful not to attack the evangelical emphasis upon religious zeal but insisted upon the importance of tempering pious commitment with "knowledge," "prudence," "charity," and above all, good works. The last point he explained with particular care, aligning his position with the orthodox theological formulation that in New England dated back to Thomas Hooker:

> Let no man now be so vain as to imagine that this is such a Preaching of Morality, as is inconsistent with the Tenor of the Gospel Dispensation; for though we do not preach up good Works as meritorious of Salvation, yet we do, and must preach them as necessary to Salvation.

[25] "Autobiography of Barnard," 229–30; and Bowen, "Almanacs," 171. Among Barnard's twenty new converts in 1742, two came from families that ranked in the richest decile of 1748 ratepayers and four from families that ranked among the upper half of ratepayers.

"Evangelical perfection" was Barnard's happy phrase for the Christian convert's duty to conform his behavior to the will of God.[26]

Because Barnard was not an "opposer" of the Awakening but an evangelical moderate, he prevented the revival in Marblehead from polarizing the Congregationalists. In this way, he preserved the gains of orthodoxy while quelling religious radicalism and eliminating the threat of defections to the Church of England. In many surrounding towns the Awakening undermined the unity of the orthodox establishment, ruptured relations between clergymen and their congregations, and strengthened the numbers and influence of religious dissenters. But the revival in Marblehead permanently enhanced the vitality of the Congregational churches and left undiminished the authority of the settled clergy. Most important, the resurgence of piety offset the advantages enjoyed by Anglicans for several years after 1730. In the wake of the revival, Episcopal influence receded in nearly every sphere of Marblehead's life, reducing the Anglicans to an isolated minority of incidental significance to local society.

The increasing exclusion of Churchmen from the mainstream of Marblehead society is the dominant theme of the correspondence with the Secretary of the S.P.G. by Alexander Malcolm, who replaced George Pigot as the rector of St. Michael's in 1740. Malcolm voiced the opposition to the Awakening characteristic of colonial Episcopalians in his report of 1745 that "Our People are Sober and Orderly.... And have been very Steady in the Midst of the Confusion occasioned here lately by the Enthusiasts." But aside from his congregation's cool reception of the revival, Malcolm had little cause for comfort. With two large congregations, the "Dissenters," he admitted, were "Vastly Superior" in numbers to the Anglicans. As for the prospect of winning converts from within the Congregationalist camp, he continued:

> It would be a great Pleasure to me To be able to inform you of any persons or families brought over to the Church lately; But

[26] John Barnard, *Zeal for Good Works* (Boston, 1742), 12 and 14–15. Cf. Thomas Hooker, *The Saints Dignitie, and Dutie* (London, 1651), especially Sermon V, 155–87.

> . . . [Marblehead Congregationalists] being Sufficiently Bigotted in their Way We can expect few proselites.

Except for Nathan Bowen, St. Michael's acquired no defectors from orthodox ranks as a result of the revival. Membership in the Episcopal church was restricted to relatively recent immigrants from England and Jersey and to "Young families rising up from our Stock," the children of St. Michael's original founders.[27]

The peculiar position in town occupied by local Episcopalians after the revival is exemplified by the histories of the leading families of St. Michael's during this period. The "bigotry" of Marblehead's Congregationalist community was not "sufficient" to deprive some skilled and well-connected Episcopalians of a profitable share in Marblehead's thriving trade. At the middle of the eighteenth century, ten Anglicans ranked among the top decile of Marblehead's ratepayers and seven of those ten in the top quintile, a representation within the local economic elite roughly proportional to their numbers within the total population.[28] The similar backgrounds of many of these wealthy Episcopalians indicate the basis of their business success: all of them had specialized skills and most of them, influential connections crucial to the development of Marblehead's direct coastal and transatlantic trade. Joseph Howard and John Tasker were merchants who had emigrated from Barbados and Wales; traders Alexander Watts and William Hylegher were recent arrivals from Scotland and the West Indies respectively; Nathan Bowen was a lawyer from Boston, where he had served as clerk to James Bowdoin, one of New England's biggest fish dealers; David LeGallais and Robert Parimore were sea captains from the ports of Jersey. Only three members of the Episcopal economic elite, Captain Moses Calley and shoremen Samuel Chambliss and John Roundey, were Marblehead natives. Major Congregationalist merchants had no scruples about

---

[27] Alexander Malcolm to S.P.G.Sec'y, April 16, 1744, July 30, 1745, in *Historical Collections,* ed. Perry, III, 379 and 390.

[28] Episcopalians comprised 16 percent of the richest decile of Marblehead ratepayers in 1748. My estimate is that Anglicans comprised about 20 percent of Marblehead's population in the mid-eighteenth century.

investing in voyages and vessels with their counterparts at St. Michael's or about relying on the skills and prudence of Episcopal shoremen and mariners.[29] The ongoing competition with Boston for the fishing trade submerged the sectarian differences that divided Marbleheaders and encouraged cooperation among local orthodox and Episcopal entrepreneurs.

Yet while religious dissenters in Marblehead incurred no economic penalties, their integration into the upper echelons of local society and their ability to acquire political influence commensurate with their wealth remained restricted. Even by the middle of the eighteenth century, full acceptance of local churchmen obtained only at the countinghouse and on the wharves. Only three of the ten leading Anglican entrepreneurs in town won election to the board of selectmen in the fifteen years after 1740, and only one served more than a single term. And between 1740 and 1755, Episcopalians held only ten percent of all selectmen's terms, a share smaller than their representation on the board during the 1720s and a sharp reduction of their influence during the 1730s. This erosion of Episcopal political strength is particularly surprising because some of the fathers and fathers-in-law of these ten men had been major officeholders in town earlier.[30] Abraham Howard, for example, emigrated to Marblehead

---

[29] On Joseph Howard, see Joseph Howard, *Abraham Howard of Marblehead* (New York, 1897); on Tasker, see Dana, "Richard Skinner and his Bible," *NEHGR,* 54:413–22; on Watts and Bowen, see *Journals of Ashley Bowen,* ed. Smith, *Publ. C.S.M.,* 2 and 31. Robert Parimore, whose name is sometimes spelled Paramour, was presumably, as was David LeGallais whose will names his relatives still living on Jersey. (See EPF, #16684.) William Hylegher is referred to as a merchant from St. Eustacius in "Extracts from Francis Goelet's Journal." *NEHGR,* 24: 50–63. For Anglican business dealings with Congregationalists, see citations above and Hooper to Storke, December 21, 1741, HSL.

[30] David LeGallais and Nathan Bowen each served a single term as selectman during the 1740s and 1750s; Robert Parimore served four terms. John Tasker was Marblehead's only Anglican justice of the peace over the same period. Captain John Browne, Richard Skinner, Sr., and William Bartlett were the politically prominent fathers-in-law of Le Gallais, Tasker, and Hylegher, respectively. The fathers of Moses Calley and Joseph Howard, who held no important political office, were among Marblehead's selectmen, deputies, and justices of the peace during the 1720s and 1730s. (Sources: MTR, 1740–1760; Whittemore, *Civil List,* 132–35.)

from London in the 1720s and established himself as a merchant in the fish trade. His political star ascended after the anti-inoculation riot, and during the 1730s he served several terms as selectman and representative, besides receiving an appointment as justice of the peace. But Abraham's son, Joseph, who followed his father to town after serving an apprenticeship as a clerk in a Barbados mercantile house, enjoyed no political success, despite the considerable estate that he amassed through his trade to the Mediterranean.[31]

Marblehead's Episcopal elite was interested in local politics: they served regularly on town committees and in lesser offices that carried out the most burdensome tasks involved in local administration. Marblehead voters nevertheless were reluctant to reward Anglican civic service with the distinction of high political office, and that reticence corresponded closely with the progress of the revival. Voters in the elections of 1739, 1740, and 1741 excluded Episcopalians from high political office entirely. The elections of 1742 and 1743, years when the revival was endangered by extremism, brought one Anglican onto the board of selectmen. But with the restoration of order to the revived churches, Congregationalist candidates swept elections to the board of selectmen and the General Court again, maintaining their monopoly of political office to the total exclusion of Episcopalians until 1748. During the late forties and through the fifties, Anglicans began to regain some of their former political influence but did not enjoy anything approaching their electoral success in the period prior to the Awakening.[32]

Related to the decline in the political power of Anglican leaders was their virtual exclusion from opportunities to marry into local Congregationalist clans of equal prominence. The best orthodox families of mid-eighteenth century Marblehead preferred to marry among their coreligionists, a reversal of the practice current among the old Second Church circle, who earlier in the eighteenth century had not hesitated to ally themselves to the merchant families of St. Michael's. In the decades following the revival, prominent

[31] Howard, *Abraham Howard of Marblehead.*

[32] See notes 22 and 30 above. During the 1720s, Anglicans held 20 percent of all selectmen's terms, and 32 percent during the 1730s.

Episcopalians seeking to consolidate and perpetuate family wealth and influence either had to find suitable mates within their own small communion or to seek eligible partners out of town. The effects of endogamy among the orthodox are exemplified in the genealogies of Churchmen David LeGallais and John Tasker, both of whom ranked just below the grandees of the Lee, Hooper, and Swett families on the tax list of 1748. During the 1720s, Tasker and LeGallais found their membership at St. Michael's no bar to marrying the daughters of two of Second Church's wealthiest merchants, Captain John Browne and Richard Skinner. But when the Tasker and LeGallais children married in the 1750s, their mates came from Barnstable, Massachusetts; Newport, Rhode Island; and the Anglican Calley family of Marblehead. The Congregationalist elite had no shortage of marriageable sons and daughters or eligible widows and widowers, but few found mates among their counterparts at St. Michael's. And infrequent intermarriages almost invariably resulted in the Anglican partner's entering the orthodox fold. Reverend Alexander Malcolm observed in 1744 that "as to what we might expect [in Anglican converts] by Intermarriages, we rather Lose than Gain."[33]

The inability of many leading Churchmen to complement their economic success with political power and marital ties to powerful orthodox families owed in part to the origins of many members of the Episcopal elite outside of New England. Marblehead's Anglican community at mid-century drew many of its members, and especially its leadership, from the ranks of recent emigrants from England, Scotland, the Channel Islands, and British possessions in the Caribbean. These new

[33] From the published *Vital Records* and a number of published and unpublished genealogies at the American Antiquarian Society and the Marblehead Historical Society, I derived a sample of 113 marriages to local partners between 1738 and 1775 in Congregationalist families whose head of household ranked in the richest decile of ratepayers in 1748. In only 10 of the 113 marriages was the partner an Episcopalian. Of the 16 marriages in Anglican families whose head of household ranked in the richest decile of the 1748 list, 11 involved other St. Michael's members, two were to nonlocal mates, and in three of the four marriages to Congregationalists, the Anglican partner entered the Congregational church. This confirms Malcolm's observation to the S.P.G. Secretary in *Historical Collections*, ed. Perry, III, 379.

Anglican arrivals had not lived in town long enough to develop strong kinship networks or to establish a firm basis of trust and understanding with their neighbors. St. Michael's vestry acknowledged the liabilities of immigrant status when they requested a replacement for Alexander Malcolm, who resigned his Marblehead post in 1749 and moved to Annapolis, Maryland. "From too long experience," the vestrymen advised the Secretary of the S.P.G.,

> we find that the good Intentions of the Society are often frustrated by some of their Missionaries who, not being born among us, are not so well acquainted with the spirit and temper of those committed to their care, and the way to promote their Happiness, which gives great Advantage to those of a different persuasion.[34]

The nonnative origins that limited the effectiveness of English-born S.P.G. missionaries also circumscribed the ability of many leading lay members of St. Michael's to win full acceptance from Marblehead's orthodox community. Churchmen were excluded from high public office and marital alliances with powerful Congregationalist families, avenues for institutionalizing and consolidating Anglican authority and influence in town. By contrast, in Connecticut during the same period, the political strength of Episcopalians increased steadily. But in that colony, Churchmen came chiefly from established local families: they were native-born converts to the Anglican communion. Their New England origins made it easier for Connecticut Anglicans to win positions of trust in their hometowns.[35]

[34] St. Michael's Vestry to the S.P.G. Sec'y, December 5, 1749, in *Historical Collections*, ed. Perry, III, 436.

[35] Bruce Steiner found that in Connecticut towns where the Episcopal population was comprised principally of native defectors from orthodoxy, the ties of kinship and community quickly overcame sectarian differences. ("Anglican Officeholding in Pre-Revolutionary Connecticut: The Parameters of a New England Community," *WMQ*, 3rd ser., 31 (1974), 369–406.) The opposite view is Michael Zuckerman's, who stresses continuing intolerance and argues that dissenters were entirely excluded from anything aproaching full membership in the community. (*Peaceable Kingdoms*, 253–58.) The situation obtaining in Marblehead at mid-century seems to lie in between Connecticut's quick acceptance and the sustained hostility that Zuckerman posits.

Yet, important as immigrant status was, it could not have been the only influence that inhibited the full integration of Episcopalians into Marblehead society. During the 1730s, orthodox voters favorably impressed by the Anglican role in the anti-inoculation riot had helped to elect Churchman Abraham Howard, then a recent arrival from England, to the board of selectmen. But just a decade later, even native-born Episcopalians like Captain Moses Calley, men commended both wealth and former "family dignity," were passed over as political leaders and as potential marriage partners by local Congregationalists. On the other hand, Thomas Gerry, a newcomer from England who was a paragon of Puritan piety and a pillar of the First Church, enjoyed considerable political success in the 1740s. Despite his origins outside of New England, Gerry inspired so much public confidence that he was appointed captain of the Marblehead fort in 1744 when the war with France began.[36]

What the contrasting careers of Moses Calley and Thomas Gerry suggest is that another reason for the incomplete incorporation of Anglicans into local society was the resurgence of religious prejudice among Marblehead's orthodox families in the wake of the revival. The concurrence of the Awakening with the stagnation of St. Michael's growth, the collapse of Anglican political power in town, and the exclusion of important Episcopal families from marital connections to the Congregationalist elite was not mere coincidence. By reasserting the religious dimension of the distinction between "insiders" and "outsiders," the revival promoted among the Congregationalists a propensity to divide local society into evangelicals and and nonevangelicals, and to allocate trust, political advancement, and social honor accordingly. In the climate of renewed religious fervor, sectarian intolerance reappeared as a significant element shaping social relations.

Orthodox perceptions of local Episcopalians at the time of the Awakening and its aftermath were complex. On the one hand, there was no denying the right of Churchmen to membership in the community: the anti-inoculation riot had established where Anglican loyalties lay. But if the leading

[36] Thomas Gerry Papers, MHS; Billias, *Elbridge Gerry,* 3–5.

role taken by St. Michael's members in the 1730 uprising had affirmed their allegiance to Marblehead, it had also confirmed the prevailing stereotype of Episcopalians as a volatile and violent group. The cultural distinctiveness of the Anglican community was thrown into even sharper relief by their response to the revival and by the accompanying transformation of Marblehead society during the late 1730s and the 1740s. The open opposition to the Awakening among Anglicans made them appear to devout Congregationalists deficient in the "amiable passions" of religious piety and fervor, aliens in an evangelical culture. In addition, Marblehead Churchmen still seemed dangerously prone to "irrational passions" that did not usually serve the end of godly local order, strangers to the "zeal" for ascetic self-control of emotional impulses stressed by John Barnard.

The basis of the persistent orthodox perception of Episcopalians as a volatile element in local society is suggested by court cases involving violent crime in Marblehead during the twenty years after 1735. The total number of these cases was quite small, but the defendants arraigned were invariably Episcopalians, and all of them ranked high in Marblehead's social order. In June of 1735, for example, First Church shoreman and peace officer David Parker went to the assistance of Anglican "scrivener" William Crabb, whom Captain Moses Calley was beating "in a very barbarous Manner." Parker commanded Calley to desist, but "he was the more Violent," and threatened that "if he [Calley] ever Catch'd him [Crabb] alone he would lick him heartily and Twist or wring his nose out of his face." In 1748, carter and First Church member Nehemiah Skillions sued Samuel Webber, Jr., the son of an affluent Anglican farmer and former selectman, for deliberately trampling his wife with a horse. A few years later, Episcopal convert Nathan Bowen complained to the justices of the peace about Captain Robert Parimore, one of Marblehead's wealthiest Anglicans, alleging that Parimore had already attempted to assault him once and that he was "still Afraid of Some injury from the said Robert in Person or Estate." Even toward members of their own families, some Anglican leaders behaved with little self-restraint: in June of 1754, Abraham Roundey, a rich shoreman, was arraigned for beating his brother Joseph. But perhaps the most notorious instances of Episcopal violence involved the Reverend George Pigot. In the fall of 1735, Jeremiah Allen, Jr., caught the rector trespassing on his land and trying to steal some corn. After exchanging harsh words, Pigot went after Allen with a cartwhip and beat him on the head until Deputy Sheriff Thomas Chewte interposed. A year later, Pigot became embroiled in another altercation after First Church member Knott Martin called the clergyman "a long black Coated Rascally Dog" and declared that the rector was "not fit for the place he was in." Pigot's response to these insults was not recorded, but his adversary's side of the fracas suggests a considerable scuffle: Martin threatened to "cause a fire to be Seen a long way" and to break the rector's neck, before he attacked Pigot wielding a pair of iron tongs.[37]

These outbursts of violence occurred at widely spaced intervals from the late 1730s through the mid-1750s, an infrequency indicating that the orthodox were not reporting Episcopal breaches of the peace to the authorities to harass St. Michael's members as they had during the 1720s. Probably Episcopalians remained more prone to private "resolutions" of their differences because St. Michael's still lacked effective institutions and leaders for disciplining individuals and adjudicating disputes among coreligionists. And there existed no mechanism besides the courts for the arbitration of their quarrels with local Congregationalists. Whatever their cause, these violent episodes confirmed the orthodox community in their suspicions concerning the dark side of dissenting culture. Although Anglican implication in violent crime during the middle of the eighteenth century was not as common as it had been earlier in Marblehead's history, assaults and threats of bodily injury involving Episcopalians after 1730 took place during a period when disorder in Marblehead

---

[37] Between 1736 and 1755, for example, there were only five cases of actual or threatened physical violence involving Marbleheaders, but four of the five defendants in these cases were Anglican. See Deposition of David Parker to John Oulton, J. P., June 25, 1735, FGSP; MGSP, December 31, 1751 (Parimore), June 30, 1754 (Roundey); Skillions v. Webber, October 18, 1748, MSCJ; Deposition of George Pigot, November 17, 1735, of Thomas Chewte, December, 1735, of Jeremiah Allen, December, 1735, of Jonathan Phillips, January 20, 1736, FGSP; and Deposition of Richard Mobbs and Benjamin Codner, September, 1736, FGSP.

was decreasing. This reduction in the total volume of violence made even occasional acts of aggression on the part of Anglicans more conspicuous, especially since they involved particularly prominent members of St. Michael's, including rector Pigot. In contrast to the pious, disciplined grandees of First and Second Churches, known to their neighbors as revival converts, church officers, and presiding justices of the county courts, leading Churchmen lingered on in the long, collective memory of local society as a group liable to passionate, impulsive, and disorderly behavior. The penchant among Anglicans like Nathan Bowen for depicting the Church of England as a bastion of order and rationality continued to strike local Congregationalists as an ironic claim on the part of defensive dissenters who protested too much.

While the Anglican community remained effectively segregated from Marblehead's orthodox majority, the fervor of revival religiosity did not renew the overt sectarian antagonism of the 1720s. Intolerance in Marblehead after 1740 was of a different character from the virulent anti-Anglican animus of the earlier eighteenth century. The surface of interdenominational dealings throughout the 1740s and 1750s was all smoothness and civility, and for the first time in St. Michael's history, its rector described to the S.P.G. relations with the orthodox as something better than swords' points. Although dismayed by the spiritual darkness that dimmed the understanding of the orthodox majority, Alexander Malcolm reported that his congregation lived in "Civil and peaceable Neighborliness" with the local Congregationalists, which, he added uncertainly, "I hope will give no offense." Both orthodox pastors occasionally accorded Malcolm the courtesy of attending his services, and John Barnard characterized his Episcopal colleague as "a Scotch gentleman, of great learning . . . far from a bigot."[38]

Accompanying the "Civil and peaceable Neighborliness" that supplanted open intersectarian hostility in Marblehead during the 1740s was the public acclamation of religious toleration as a central cultural value. Barnard began promoting this liberal outlook as early as the 1730s when, a few weeks

[38] Alexander Malcolm to S.P.G. Sec'y, July 30, 1745, in *Historical Collections*, ed. Perry, III, 390; "Autobiography of Barnard," 234.

after the anti-inoculation riot—little more than a year after
he had denounced the Anglican celebration of Christmas—
he declared to his congregation that

> 'Tis an amazing Guilt to take away the Liberty and Lives of
> Men, that are otherwise honest and good Subjects as though
> they had forfeited the Common Rights of Mankind, and their
> very Being, merely because they differ from others in their Faith,
> or differ from them in the Circumstantials of Religion, while yet
> they may Agree with them in the Essentials.

The Awakening afforded Barnard another occasion and
inducement for announcing his adherence to the principle of
toleration and for censuring "professed Christians that have
persecuted one another . . . and all for the Sake of Some Differences in Sentiments or Modalities in Religion, wherein real
Holiness has been little or nothing concerned."[39]
It seems paradoxical that the subsiding of intersectarian
strife and the affirmation of religious toleration coincided
with the de facto exclusion of Episcopalians from the mainstream of Marblehead society. But the logic of this correspondence is illuminated by the larger context of Barnard's
strictures against religious bigotry. Before making his first
plea for toleration in the winter of 1731, Barnard recounted
for his congregation the early career of the apostle Paul,
known before his conversion on the road to Damascus as
Saul, "an hot-headed, furious, bigotted Jewish zealot" who
persecuted the early Christians. "Madly set upon cutting all
Men to his own size," Saul toadied to the Jewish "episcopate" and "meanly craved Power and Authority from the
Chief Priest." Backed by that corrupt hierarchy, he plotted
to "lord it over the Estates and Persons and Lives and Consciences of his honest Neighbors, who could not go his Lengths
and Conform to his Rites and Ceremonies."[40] Barnard proceeded to argue for religious toleration as a protection against
violent schemers like Saul, whose character bore an uncanny
resemblance to the orthodox stereotype of S.P.G. missionaries. Ten years later, at the time of the Awakening, Barnard
again invoked liberty of conscience to counter "censorious"

[39] Barnard, *Zeal for Good Works*, 14; "Autobiography of Barnard," 230.
[40] Barnard, *Janua Coelestis*, 116.

radical enthusiasts who "persecuted" evangelical moderates, and "all for the sake of Some Differences in Sentiments or Modalities in Religion."[41] In both cases, Barnard's intention in asserting the importance of toleration was not to protect the rights of dissenting religious minorities but to shore up the defenses of orthodoxy against challenges from groups occupying either extreme of New England's religious spectrum. More than anything, Barnard's advocacy of religious libertarianism was a measure of his alarm at both radicals and conservatives who, in his view, threatened the liberty of New England's Congregational churches.

The influence of Barnard's ideas on intersectarian relations in Marblehead points up the complex, dialectical interplay between toleration and prejudice in eighteenth-century Massachusetts. On one level, Barnard's emphasis upon the common ground shared by Protestant denominations that agreed in "the Essentials" of religion conduced toward an outward ecumenical harmony and an end to overt expressions of antipathy against Anglicans. But in a curious way, his underlying rationale for overlooking differences of religious "Circumstantials" and for publicly promoting toleration subtly sustained orthodox suspicion of dissenters. By Barnard's lights, what made toleration imperative was less an enlightened acceptance of religious diversity than a firm belief in the diabolical designs of his sectarian adversaries. His defense of religious liberty was predicated upon his conviction that a conspiracy was being hatched among the heterodox, a secret master plan for subverting Congregationalist orthodoxy.[42] This image of a dissident cabal plotting the overthrow of the establishment and a renewal of religious persecution implicitly reinforced sectarian prejudice among Marblehead's orthodox community.

By the middle of the eighteenth century, Marblehead Congregationalists had become broadminded enough to

[41] Barnard, *Zeal for Good Works*, 14.

[42] A similar fear of Anglican intentions influenced another advocate of religious toleration in New England, the Reverend Ezra Stiles. It was at Stiles's suggestion, in fact, that Barnard wrote his autobiography. See Edmund S. Morgan, *The Gentle Puritan: A Life of Ezra Stiles, 1727–1795* (Chapel Hill, 1962), 210–25.

coexist with the local Episcopal community and even to cooperate with Anglicans in economic enterprises. Yet being still "Sufficiently Bigotted in their Way," the members of Marblehead's orthodox congregations remained resistant to the complete assimilation and full incorporation of Churchmen into local society. They stopped short of according dissenters permanent positions of trust as family members or as important officeholders. The climate of diffuse mistrust that characterized Marblehead's religious life by the middle of the eighteenth century fostered the separation of the orthodox and dissenting communities just as effectively as the intense religious prejudice of the 1720s had formerly. But the elevation of formal religious toleration to the status of a public value now minimized the chances for sectarian hostility to erupt again into social conflict.

By the middle of the eighteenth century, Marblehead was a "pluralistic society," in that the members of its competing religious sects no longer clashed openly nor regarded such behavior as proper. And compared to Gloucester, Marblehead was a more hospitable environment for dissenters. The sheer numerical strength of the Episcopal population in Marblehead made impossible the total purge of dissidents that took place in Gloucester. Nevertheless, the orthodox community's misgivings about Episcopalians insured that in Marblehead, as in Gloucester, the Congregationalists held sway. It was not until two decades before the War for Independence that the Episcopalians of Marblehead began to regain any significant political strength, and not until the 1760s that the orthodox started intermarrying more frequently with local dissenters. These changes came about after the old pastor of the First Church and his parishioners passed from the scene and a new generation of Marblehead's young people came of age, a group whose experiences had not included the founding of St. Michael's, the anti-inoculation riot, and the revival. And this prerevolutionary generation encountered in town not a church of immigrants and English missionaries but one presided over by a rector who had graduated from Harvard College and led by a vestry of native-born Churchmen. Only then did the behavior of Marblehead townspeople begin to approximate the libertarian ideals that John Barnard had preached to their parents.[43]

MOST STUDIES of New England's port towns posit that commercial expansion propelled provincial society in a single direction. The trajectory of change that they trace from involvement in the market economy is plotted by the points of mounting economic inequality, deepening social and political conflict, and increasing individualism and diversity. At the end of this line is the collapse of "community," the inception of a "liberal" society, and the acceptance of more "modern" values. But the history of early Marblehead raises even more pointedly than the case of Gloucester the difficulties with this view of development. For the emergence of a communal order in Marblehead involved no repudiation of the market. On the contrary, the groups and individuals in town who adhered to conservative values and sought to strengthen traditional institutions also took the leading role in promoting commercial expansion. And the town's development of stronger and more direct links to the Atlantic economy after 1730 accompanied the transformation of Marblehead into a more stable society than it had been at any time in its history. By the middle of the eighteenth century, Marblehead was untroubled by any significant volume of crime, debt, or internal strife. Many townspeople remained poor, but inequality was not a novel element in local life, and relations among social classes were far less strained than they had been a generation earlier. Engagement in military campaigns and religious revivals channeled popular hostilities against French fishermen and local Anglicans while enhancing deference to the local orthodox elite. The members of this new Marblehead gentry, men who figured prominently as public-spirited leaders, zealous patriots, and pious Christians, commanded widespread acceptance as a local ruling group. By the middle of the century, Marblehead society was also more uniformly characterized by an antipathy

---

[43] *SHG*, XII, 110–112; William McGilchrist to S.P.G. Sec'y. June 27, 1769; Peter Bours to S.P.G. Sec'y, July 20, 1760 and August 21, 1761; and Joshua Wingate Weeks to S.P.G. Sec'y. August 13, 1764 and June 21, 1768, in *Historical Collections,* ed. Perry, III, 547, 456, 467, 515, and 539.

to cosmopolitan influences, a widespread suspicion of dissenters, and a conservative, communally-oriented ethos in economic life. Most members of the elite now shared with other social classes a common commitment to local solidarity and prosperity and to evangelical Calvinism.

That such an order emerged in Marblehead, where the strength of Puritan ideals and communitarian institutions had been most attenuated and where the force of commercial expansion had operated with the fewest restraints, underscores the power and persistence of conservative patterns and values in shaping social development. To discover that a town like Gloucester made the transition from farming village to major seaport without undergoing any significant social and cultural transformation is less surprising. Gloucester's strong communal past, its well-developed local institutions, its traditions of autonomy, religious conservatism, and corporatism all acted as countervailing influences that guaranteed a glacial pace of change. But in Marblehead, matters were much different. Destabilized by rapid demographic growth, cleaved by disparities in wealth, ethnic differences, and religious divisions, and dominated by outsiders for the first century of its existence, the town should have succumbed to a future shaped solely by market forces. Instead, localistic and communitarian impulses exhibited a totally unexpected resilience among all classes and groups in town. Commercial expansion after 1730 deepened rather than diminished their influence on local life and redefined the entire character of the community in the years that followed.

Epilogue

DYNAMIC DEVELOPMENT took place throughout the late seventeenth and eighteenth centuries in parts of provincial New England, especially its coastal centers like Gloucester and Marblehead. Population grew rapidly; trading networks expanded; society became more stratified and political authority more centralized; dissenting congregations multiplied. But these shifts in demographic, economic, and political scale and structure are not in themselves sufficient evidence that a major transformation was also taking place in the way that New Englanders looked on the world and one another. For innovation in material and institutional life does not necessitate change in social character, attitudes, and values. People who lived in towns that relied on trade did not always subordinate all other goals to the pursuit of profit. People who lived in places where the possibility of social mobility existed or where economic inequality increased did not always reject the ideals of hierarchy and deference. People who lived in communities that included religious dissidents did not always embrace toleration. People who lived in ports that had frequent contact with the wider world did not always become less insular and localistic. As the histories of Gloucester and Marblehead indicate, the relationship between commerce and culture was considerably more complex.

The notion that commercial development dramatically transformed the society of colonial port towns rests in part on the assumption that social strain invariably increased in proportion to economic inequality. But in fact, the growth of relatively steeper gradations of wealth that apparently characterized all provincial trading towns did not in every instance mean that ordinary people faced greater economic difficulties. Although most members of Marblehead's maritime labor force failed to share in that town's commercial prosperity, in Gloucester the opportunities for employment and investment created by the conversion to a maritime economy actually produced a steady rise in median estate value over the eighteenth century. Gloucester's development also suggests that the maritime industries and trade provided an economic base that contributed in many ways to the stability of coastal communities. The expansion of the fishing industry prevented towns like Gloucester, places with little good farming land, from suffering severe economic stagnation. And by providing employment for an increasing number of young men who could expect to inherit no portion of their parents' farms, trade mitigated the potential for conflict within families and between landed and landless men, established settlers and newcomers.

More important, whether the lot of most seaport dwellers improved over time or deteriorated, shifts in the distribution of wealth over the first half of the eighteenth century were of a magnitude insufficient to bring about a decisive change in class relations. This is not to say that port towns were free from tensions between social classes: Marblehead's history provides numerous instances of such antagonisms. But as the experience of Marblehead also confirms, no direct relationship existed between the growth of economic inequality and mounting unrest among the lower orders of provincial port society. Hard times did not always translate into social protest on the part of the poor, nor did conflicts between classes and interest groups inevitably intensify as commercial expansion proceeded apace. In both Gloucester and Marblehead, the periods of most severe social disruption, the times with the highest incidence of debt and crime, did not correspond to the attainment of commercial maturity in the mid-eighteenth century, but occurred when these communities were in an earlier stage of development. It was during the first decades of settlement in Gloucester and, in Marblehead, the boom years of the 1710s and 1720s, that social tensions ran highest. As maritime development peaked in both ports during the 1730s and 1740s—and even as inequality became most pronounced—Gloucester's stability was undiminished and the level of conflict in Marblehead was actually receding.

Similarly, the notion that the growth of trade introduced greater impersonality and ruthlessness into the conduct of economic life needs, at the very least, substantial qualification. What determined the climate of business dealings within a community was the closeness or distance of relationships between debtors and creditors, employers and employees. In a town like Gloucester, a relatively settled and homogeneous community, litigation involving fellow townsmen was minimal. Neither is there any evidence that merchants or shoremen used the indebtedness of fishermen to compel their labor on unfair terms. The growth of Gloucester's commerce created no conflict in transactions among its inhabitants but only in their dealings with outsiders. It was the incidence of litigation between Gloucester residents and nonlocal plaintiffs and defendants that climbed after 1690. The number of these intertown debt cases rose dramatically throughout New England over this period, as colonials extended their trading networks across town borders but not their definition of "neighbors." What the contrasting patterns of inter- and intratown litigation in Gloucester reveal is that the mistrust of strangers was as deeply ingrained among eighteenth-century New Englanders as it was among their ancestors and that the bonds between settled inhabitants of the same community were just as strong. In Marblehead, a somewhat different pattern appeared but for similar reasons. The highwater mark of intratown litigation and the hardest time for indebted fishermen was the twenty-year period after 1710, when Marblehead's population contained the highest proportion of new inhabitants and the fishing industry was under the control of nonnative entrepreneurs. After 1730, as migration into town slowed and local men took over the conduct of the fishing industry and trade, both debt, litigation and the exploitation of labor diminished. In other words, the critical variables influencing levels of civil litigation and the treatment of workers were the balance between natives and newcomers within a population and the extent to which those deemed "outsiders" dominated local economic development. In neither Gloucester nor Marblehead did the conduct of business within the community become harsher and more depersonalized because of economic expansion alone. On the contrary, when the native-born came to predominate in the populations of both towns, cooperative effort and investment typified commercial ventures undertaken by inhabitants.

If economic antagonism among port dwellers did not mount incrementally with commercialization, their conception of the proper social order came to conform still more closely to the traditional ideal, even as maritime development wrought changes in social structure. Economic expansion within both communities made the fortunes of some families but diminished the standing of others. In Gloucester, the old elite faction of Annisquam harbor lost ground to their rivals in the southern part of town as a result of the growth of commerce. In the same way, the leaders of early Marblehead were displaced by the agents of merchants in bigger ports who engineered the postwar expansion of the fishery, and this Second Church circle was in turn supplanted by the Marblehead gentry after the development of the direct trade. Yet despite this fluidity at the top of society, older notions concerning the allocation of prestige and the responsibilities of an elite persisted, and the major merchants of Gloucester, and ultimately, even of Marblehead, shared in and conformed to these expectations. Neither town's inhabitants came to regard social honor purely as the prize of successful competition. In fact, major conflicts occurred in both places precisely because of the popular mistrust of monied newcomers and the strength of the traditional ideal of the social order. And in neither community were men who based their claims to local distinction on material achievement alone able to secure or retain acknowledgment as social leaders.

Religion was another aspect of provincial seaport culture that failed to register the changes usually associated with the conversion to a trading economy. It has been said that the

inhabitants of trading towns, particularly prosperous merchant families, were more worldly and less pious than their
ancestors. Drawn to rationalistic religious doctrines like
Arminianism and repelled by strict Calvinist orthodoxy, they
supposedly grew less engaged with ecclesiastical institutions
and spiritual concerns. Some groups in port towns answered
this description—Edward Holyoke's prominent parishioners
at Second Marblehead, for example, and their friends and
relatives at Anglican St. Michael's and Boston's Brattle Square
Church. Even so, the overall direction of religious development in Gloucester and Marblehead was not toward greater
liberalization of orthodox belief and practice. Neither did
the growing affluence of the commercial classes nurture the
spread of skepticism, rationalism, and formalism within their
ranks. In Gloucester and Marblehead alike, adherence to
Congregationalist orthodoxy and formal church affiliation
were actually weakest during the first decades of settlement,
not at the point of their commercial maturity. Gloucester's
early ecclesiastical disorganization and spiritual apathy gave
way to conformity to strict Calvinism and a conservative
Congregationalist polity by the middle of the seventeenth
century, and the coming of commerce did nothing to alter
the character of local religious belief and practice. Marblehead was much longer in coming to this kind of commitment
to orthodoxy, but by the opening decades of the eighteenth
century, John Barnard's church, the largest congregation in
town, was instituting a stricter ecclesiastical discipline and
enlarging its membership. And in the 1740s, both First and
Second Marblehead and the churches of Gloucester's maritime neighborhoods participated enthusiastically in the Great
Awakening. Equally important, it was the major merchant
families of these ports that played a leading role in the outpouring of religious piety and the reaffirmation of traditional Calvinist theology. In other words, what was happening
to Gloucester and Marblehead over the colonial period was
not secularization but something like its opposite.

A consequence of the intense religious commitment of many
orthodox port dwellers was their continuing dislike and suspicion of dissenters. The notion that provincial New Englanders became increasingly receptive to sectarian diversity
as groups like the Quakers and the Anglicans grew in num-

bers finds little confirmation from their experiences in Gloucester or even Marblehead. Though the flourishing economies of these coastal communities attracted settlers from dissenting sects, their presence in these two towns did not promote progressively greater tolerance among the Congregationalists. In fact, the Puritans of both Gloucester and Marblehead were probably less hostile to deviations from orthodoxy during the seventeenth century than they became thereafter as dissenters multiplied. The first and second generation of settlers in Gloucester and Marblehead were relatively tolerant of the heterodox views of Quakers and Anglicans as well as the anticlericalism, doctrinal idiosyncrasies, or indifference of many nominal Congregationalists. It was only after about 1690 that orthodox resistance to religious dissent coalesced and rigidified, precipitating conflicts that took the form of social or economic ostracism, public ridicule, legal harassment, and occasionally, outright violence. As a result, the Quaker community in Gloucester virtually disappeared after 1730, forcing that town's Puritan zealots to pursue their defense of orthodoxy abroad. Marblehead's beleaguered Anglicans at last achieved an uneasy accommodation with the dominant Congregationalists after both their brief popularity following the anti-inoculation riot and the divisions among the orthodox over revivalism failed to secure the sect more substantial gains. Neither town assimilated religious outsiders into the mainstream of local life. In Gloucester, the sustained hostility of the Congregationalists insured that the Friends were never able to gain a foothold in local commerce. Even in Marblehead, where dissidents were more numerous and as a bloc more influential, orthodox mistrust of Anglican outsiders barred their full integration into Congregationalist families and local political life. And the religious prejudice that was so pronounced in both communities was not peculiar only to the lower orders: sectarian bias permeated the attitudes and shaped the behavior of leading orthodox merchants, shoremen, and tradesmen as well.

An important influence sustaining the suspicion of dissenters among the orthodox majorities of Gloucester and Marblehead was another inherited habit of mind that commercial development did nothing to modify—loyalty to the local community. Although awareness of the outside world is assumed to have made colonial port dwellers broader in their sympathies, more catholic in their outlook, and more divided in their allegiances, the reverse appears to have been the case among the inhabitants of these two trading towns, even their principal merchant families. Indeed, localism is the main thread running through the fabric of life in Gloucester and Marblehead. Not only did the inveterate mistrust of strangers shape the perception and treatment of religious dissenters, but it is also the recurrent theme of almost all other instances of significant conflict. In Gloucester, it was the wariness of that town's newly successful emigrant entrepreneurs among the southern harbor's established elite that motivated the changes in church placement practices and triggered the First Parish controversy. A similar animus against outsiders underlay the conservative view of Gloucester inhabitants on church doctrine and polity: their obsessive fear of liberal Arminian theology, which Cape Ann's strict Calvinists associated with cosmopolitanism and moral laxity; their long-standing suspicion that other churches and ministers might infringe on the autonomy of individual congregations and the power of the laity. These issues bearing upon local independence and identity were the ones over which Gloucester inhabitants fought—not among themselves but against erring Congregationalists in other towns. In Marblehead the same localistic cast of mind was manifested in disputes at every phase of its history, from the popular uprisings against the Bay government's authority in the seventeenth century to the controversy over John Barnard's candidacy and the anti-inoculation riot of the eighteenth century.

Although in many ways Gloucester and Marblehead were among the most dynamic societies in eighteenth-century New England, they were hardly in the vanguard of a cultural change that would bridge the distance between the communitarian order of the Puritan past and the secular, individualistic society of the future. Not only localism and insularity but also intense engagement in religious concerns, intolerance of dissent, and acceptance of a deferential social order were prominent patterns of continuity with traditional culture in these provincial seaports. And, in a sense, that these ideals and values came to prevail, persisted, and shaped behavior and daily life in colonial port towns is not really remarkable. Dramatic changes in the economic and political institutions of traditional societies, as one historian recently observed, "can actually reinforce a people's commitment to a particular world-view."[1] For this reason, instead of imploding the framework of colonial society, commercial expansion was contained within and molded by an older structure of relationships and beliefs.

Throughout New England, whether in trading towns or in farming villages, men and women clung to the past, relinquished their hold on it reluctantly, tried to recapture it, and gave no thanks to those who would wrest it from them. This was particularly true of maritime towns like Gloucester and Marblehead, where unsettling changes in many of the basic conditions of life quickened the impulse of inhabitants to take refuge in the familiar. In these commercial communities, the order of the past drew its power to endure from the dimensions of change itself.

[1] Timothy Breen, *Puritans and Adventurers,* xvi.

Appendix

TABLE I. DISTRIBUTION OF REAL AND PERSONAL WEALTH AMONG
GLOUCESTER AND MARBLEHEAD DECEDENTS, 1690–1770

GLOUCESTER	1690– 1715	1716– 1735	1736– 1755	1756– 1770
Decile Group	Percentage of Wealth			
Richest 91–100	29.3	42.2	55.7	51.6
61–90	49.0	40.9	31.9	33.6
31–60	18.0	13.0	9.9	11.1
Poorest 0–30	3.7	3.9	2.5	3.7
No. of Inventories	44	59	136	131
Median Estate Value*	81	95	101	104
Mean Estate Value	122	188	260	248

MARBLEHEAD	1690– 1715	1716– 1725	1726– 1735	1736– 1755	1756– 1770
Decile Group	Percentage of Wealth				
Richest 91–100	46.4	54.0	59.3	63.0	61.8
61–90	37.4	35.1	31.3	31.0	29.4
31–60	13.2	9.1	8.4	5.5	6.9
Poorest 0–30	3.0	1.8	1.0	0.5	1.9
No. of Inventories	110	76	93	140	136
Median Estate Value	69	70	60	43	41
Mean Estate Value	132	180	165	192	162

* All estate values are in pounds sterling. For the multipliers to convert Massachusetts currency into pounds sterling, I have relied on the table in Nash, *Urban Crucible,* Appendix, 405.
SOURCE: Essex Probate Files, Registry of Probate, Essex County Courthouse, Salem, Massachusetts.

TABLE II. RANGE OF REAL AND PERSONAL WEALTH AMONG GLOUCESTER
AND MARBLEHEAD DECEDENTS, 1690–1770

GLOUCESTER	1690–1715	1716–1735	1736–1755	1756–1770
Decile Group	*Range of Real and Personal Wealth in Pounds Sterling*			
Richest				
91–100	339–447	584–1014	607–3755	531–2479
61–90	120–312	137–439	143–539	137–520
31–60	38–108	47–132	50–137	63–126
Poorest				
0–30	4–30	10–44	1–45	2–62

MARBLEHEAD	1690–1715	1716–1725	1726–1735	1736–1755	1756–1770
Richest					
91–100	344–1388	506–1594	354–2822	408–4907	399–2264
61–90	90–327	102–395	81–334	76–404	75–350
31–60	33–87	22–91	15–79	13–75	18–73
Poorest					
0–30	2–32	3–22	2–13	2–12	3–17

SOURCE: Essex Probate Files, Registry of Probate, Essex County Courthouse, Salem, Massachusetts.

TABLE III. CIVIL LITIGATION IN GLOUCESTER,
MARBLEHEAD, AND SALEM

	1709	*1719*	*1729*	*1739*	*1749*
GLOUCESTER					
Intratown Suits	1	8*	2	6	3
Intertown Suits	7	8	16	14	3
Gloucester Pltf.	0	3	1	8	1
Gloucester Dfdt.	7	5	15	6	2
MARBLEHEAD					
Intratown Suits	8	87	165	67	29
Intertown Suits	15	33	53	88	37
Marblehead Pltf.	7	15	17	34	15
Marblehead Dfdt.	8	18	36	54	22
SALEM					
Intratown Suits	33	23	35	44	30
Intertown Suits	34	45	56	94	51
Salem Pltf.	31	35	47	67	40
Salem Dfdt.	3	10	9	27	11

* Jonathan Springer was one of the parties in five of these eight actions.
SOURCE: Writs to attach the defendant's person or estate, Files of the Essex County Court of Common Pleas, Superior Courthouse, Salem, Massachusetts.

INDEX